Jack Lawrence

FANFARE

FANFARE

The Confessions of a Press Agent

by

RICHARD MANEY

ILLUSTRATED

HARPER & BROTHERS PUBLISHERS NEW YORK

To Betty,
my fair lady

Contents

Contents

A section of illustrations will be found following p. 118

FANFARE

1

Overture

SCOFFERS have called my profession the second oldest in the world. Other hostiles have been more vindictive. Some likened press agents to snake-oil salesmen. Some charged we were thimbleriggers, out to dupe the innocent. Some branded us paid perjurers and menaces to the public weal.

The rancor of these hooligans echoed ancient prejudices. The theatre long was regarded as a disreputable activity. Those who practiced in it were considered riffraff. In early Rome actors were recruited from the slave class. Trollops were the only women permitted to act in the open and even this license was refused the doxies of Athens. With the advent of Christianity things got worse. All performers save acrobats and jugglers were proscribed. Shakespeare had been in his grave for forty years before a woman could play in England.

Cromwell rated actors no better than Irishmen and hunted down both with equal fury. Molière, high in the favor of Louis XIV, on his death was denied burial in consecrated ground because of his odious trade. The prospect of the player brightened when, enchanted by her performance in Dryden's *Secret Love*, Charles II made Nell Gwyn his mistress. It flamed when David Garrick was buried in Westminster Abbey, the first actor ever to profane that shrine.

Today only the Social Register discriminates against performers. Hillbilly singers have become governors. Banjo players have crashed the Senate. A grateful king knighted Laurence Olivier and a queen did as much for John Gielgud. Robert Montgomery was just short of cabinet stature as he supervised Dwight Eisenhower's make-up, and counseled him in camera decorum. Tallulah Bankhead was a front-page heroine when she excoriated Thomas Dewey to a radio audience of millions. That was in '48 when the Albany baritone was bushwhacked by Harry Truman and the pollsters.

In lesser degree, and in snail-like fashion, theatrical press agents have approached legitimacy. The Frank McCarthy named Assistant Secretary of State to George Catlett Marshall earlier had been press agent for *Brother Rat* and other George Abbott farces. With fellow press agents I rejoiced at McCarthy's choice. It made recognition of our craft official. Confabs with Molotov and border incidents in Trieste would be no problem to a man who had been exposed to the vapors of ingenues and the ennui of editors. Tact, resource and coolness under fire are musts for the press agent who would retain his sanity.

Since failures in the theatre outnumber successes in the ratio of seven to one, "under fire" tends to become the chronic status of the press agent. If the play he exploits boasts a line at the box office, he lives in an opium world, his reveries interrupted only by requests for house seats, by editors pleading to photograph his star, to interview his author and to eulogize his employer. But if the play fizzles, if the critics call it a lesser *East Lynne* he's in trouble. When mice start to romp in the ticket racks the press agent stands naked and alone. All hands fix him with an accusing stare. The dud might be redeemed, cry the condemned, if the press agent would pull himself together and dream up a sensation to inflame page 1. Any hack can sell a hit, they chant. It takes a man of character, perhaps a magician, to palm off a stinker.

Woe betide the press agent who advises the fledgling producer, or the ersatz star, to adjourn lest they be charged with compounding a nuisance. At best this suggestion will be looked upon as an unfriendly act, at worst as outright treason. So conspicuous a lady as Sarah Churchill charged me with treachery when I recommended a quick and merciful end to *Gramercy Ghost,* the mishmash in which she was floundering. The backer of *Blood Stream,* a primitive from Harlem, had a blunter technique. When I suggested it would be wise to fold up on Saturday, he snarled, "Yellow, eh?" I didn't press the point. Gin was coming out of his ears and a holster bulged under his armpit. Before he could underwrite another fiasco his wife plugged him right between the eyes with her .44. Had her mate heeded me, her inheritance would have been $15,000 larger, the sum this diehard lost in his attempt to confound the critics.

There is another reason press agents are no longer among the untouchables. For years we were regarded as harmless Munchausens, an evil peculiar to the theatre. All that's been changed. Today press agents are employed by the doughnut industry, the Republican party, kings in exile, Park Avenue debutantes, channel swimmers, trade unions, hamburger havens, sponsors of Mother's Day and Father's Day, evangelists, the Stork Club, the Air Force, and the Waldorf-Astoria.

On a summer night in '43 I arbitrated a barroom dispute between Hickman Powell and Lem Jones. Each swore he would be sheltered by the White House in November of '44. Powell was the press agent for Thomas E. Dewey, Jones for Wendell Willkie.

Thanks to the insistence and diligence of Paul E. Stewart, the Waldorf's man, General of the Army MacArthur witnessed every attraction with a roof over it within six months of his return from Japan. Seeking to salvage something from this give-away derby, press agents for the shows honored by the General, by his aides and immediate relatives, hinted he might like to call on the cast after the performance. When the General picked up his cue, the press agents alerted editors, suggesting the backstage meeting be photographed for posterity or next day's edition. Mr. Hearst's *Journal-American* was fascinated by the proposal. Framed by the flower of Equity, the

General's likeness appeared day after day on its drama page. It was a poor actor who couldn't boast he had been photographed with the hero of Anacostia Flats and Corregidor.

Although New York swarms with press agents for institutions, rackets and cartels, with press agents for climbers seeking applause or whitewash, few of these conspirators are readily identifiable because of their disguises. Propagandists who operate from Park Avenue salons scorn "press agent" when queried about their calling. It's a label associated with deception, they say, hence stigmatizes their lofty missions. They find "public relations counselor," "research consultant," "opinion builder" and "communications advisor" satisfactory masks for their plots. "Institute of public opinion" is another popular, if baffling, façade. But in dodging one tag these sorcerers have been noosed with another. Those who think their devices meretricious dub them "hucksters."

Since a client is the first need of any press agent, regardless of his standing, high-pressure operators in the commercial field lay great stress on front. An impressive address, rich furnishings, gaudy testimonials, a feverish show of industry, name dropping and hints at intimacy with the mighty—all tend to impress the prospect. Familiarity with headwaiters, with the management of caste-crazed saloons and the ability to summon sultry wenches to solace the lonely render the prey more susceptible.

Compared to these sybarites, the theatrical press agent practices in squalor. A dingy cell in the Times Square area is his conventional base. It is serviced by a wheezy elevator and is littered with files, typewriters, posters, photographs and other ocupational debris. Contesting with the foreman for elbow room in this menagerie may be two associates, obligatory by union edict when the press agent has as many as four attractions. If prosperous the press agent may have an apprentice, even a stenographer, luxuries which add to the clutter. The hutch which I occupied for fifteen years in the Empire Theatre was described by Tex O'Reilly, *Herald Tribune* ace, as "a steam-heated sty."

The press agent worth his salt will concentrate on eligibles whose personalities, performances, and off-stage didos excite the public, hence have impact on the box office. There's no point to raising a din over a drab. Most stage folk, no matter how lowly or colorless, dissent from this dictum. If by-passed, they scream discrimination. By their code the press agent is either a sycophant or a clod insensitive to merit. Thus incensed an acrobat or an ingénue may engage a personal press agent, in this fashion seek to circumvent the management.

This practice leads to confusion and hostility. The show's press agent has but one concern, boosting business and prolonging the run. The only concern of the personal press agent is the inflation of the aggrieved. Musical shows, their personnel largely made up of fugitives from vaudeville, night clubs, the screen and television, boil with personal press agents. These gnomes vie with night-club flacks for occupancy of the publicity pit. (*Flack* is a word coined by *Variety*, bible of the amusement world, to identify all Broadway press agents.) Both tribes are suspect since they lack official status. Both are short on scruples. As often as not these braves operate from their bedrooms. Their term of office depends upon the frequency with which they insinuate their clients into the columns of Walter Winchell, Ed Sullivan, Danton Walker, Louis Sobol and other oracles who feed on the famous and the infamous.

Traffic between columnists and night-club and personal press agents is based on barter. In return for juicy items about non-clients, the commentator will cite an escapade of his informant's client. This arrangement tests the ingenuity of the flack. He may seethe with tidbits about the ecdysiast to whom he is pledged, but lack compensating gossip about other showoffs. But this deficit doesn't throw him. In such extremities he whips up a few fictions and passes them on as gospel. Crafty as a Cherokee, he's aware that the columnist cannot check all the rumors and suspicions which funnel to his desk. He's aware, too, that column mention in many quarters is looked upon as a certificate of distinction. Many of those cited would rather be libeled than ignored.

Night-club operators value the approval of columnists above the blessings of their bishops. I learned this from Lou Walters in '43. Mr. Walters was the proprietor of the Latin Quarter. Addled by its success, he decided to invade the song-and-dance field. He dubbed this mistake *Artists and Models.* A Latin Quarter audience gassed up on Old Grandpaw would have loved it. Before a sober theatre audience, it was the catastrophe of the season. The day after this debacle I tried to solace Walters for the ill temper of the reviewers on the *Times, Herald Tribune* and *News.* I could have spared him my condolences. He hadn't read any of them. He'd rest his case on the judgment of Winchell, Sullivan, et al. *Artists and Models* was overtaken by the coroner after three weeks. Mr. Walters retreated to his Forty-eighth Street cellar, ever since has resisted the urge to emulate Ziegfeld, George White and Earl Carroll.

The incidence of ulcers is almost as high among the moles who grub in night-club caves as it is among the yogis who counsel industrial giants. Of all the press agents who practice in New York, those in the theatre enjoy the most satisfying hours and the greatest freedom. Their employment may be haphazard. They do not command wages of their opposites in commerce. But they sleep better and have more fun and their consumption of Benzedrine is the lowest of all who shill for profit.

At his best the theatrical press agent is a fusion of smuggler, midwife, hypnotist, confessor and public-address system. He forgoes, if he is wise, the hoaxes which won fame for his ancestors. Anna Held's milk baths, Mrs. Patrick Campbell's insistence that the streets bordering her theatre be strewn with tanbark to muffle traffic noise, are specimens of these classics. Today authors of comparable myths would be drummed out of the regiment. Hyperbole and deception no longer are effective weapons.

In the first quarter of this century white paper was cheaper and editors were more tolerant. Competition from non-theatrical sources had just started to simmer. To survive in New York, the press agent must have the respect, if not the affection, of editors in all communicative media. Out of this respect comes a degree of co-operation. Without this co-operation the press agent is sunk. Clam digging would be more profitable and less perilous. The lost-jewel ruse, the bogus romance and other transparencies are taboo. To gull an editor is to court excommunication. Wild exaggeration and roman-candle rhetoric are condoned only in circus press agents. Though lying is epidemic among theatre people—it's a symbol of bravado or insecurity rather than of malice—press agents skirt it.

As press agents have some skill in hypnotism, so they are susceptible to it. Consider the craftsman who trumpeted *Elmer Gantry,* Sinclair Lewis's attack on religious hypocrisy. Idling in the rear of New York's Playhouse, this romantic became so agitated by the actor impersonating the evangelist that he weaved down to the footlights and clambered up on the stage to confess and seek forgiveness. His intrusion brought a reprimand from the management and the suggestion that he go on the wagon.

Speaking of tippling recalls a morning when I was ruffling the drum for Grace Moore, earlier the Mimi, Manon and Micaela of the Metropolitan Opera. I arrived in my office feeling as if I had swallowed a grenade. Miss Moore, fugitive from Gatti-Casazza that she might regale the lower classes in *The DuBarry,* called me early. She had lost her jade cigarette case in a taxicab. It was a gift from her husband, Valentin Parera, a Spanish screen actor. Miss Moore suggested I broadcast her misfortune and offer a reward large enough to impress editors. Entering her hint in my journal, I was about to take time out for meditation when she called again. Nicholas Murray Butler, president of Columbia University, had asked her to be guest of honor at a Sunday-night gala at the Lotus Club. She would be the first actress ever saluted by this fraternity, she said. I reminded her that Laurette Taylor had waxed convivial at a Lotus Club clambake a few years earlier. Miss Moore hung up. Within the hour, she called again. The Spanish ambassador was to see *The DuBarry* that night. After the performance, she and Valentin were to sup with him at the Pierre. I asked the name of the grandee. She couldn't remember it. "Never mind," I said. "I'll call the Spanish consul's office." I did. The ambassador was in Madrid. I so informed Miss Moore. "How foolish of me," she said. "I meant the Rumanian chargé d'affaires."

Seeking to regain my balance, I composed a digest of Miss Moore's communiqués. It read: "Nicholas Murray Butler, international jewel thief, was arrested in the lobby of the Pierre Hotel early this morning charged with stealing the cigarette case of the Spanish chargé d'affaires. Valentin Parera was booked as an accessory. The modern Raffles was released on $50,000 bail provided by prima donna Grace Moore. Miss Moore, a Del Rio, Tennessee, girl, is presently singing in *The DuBarry.*"

I submitted this to Miss Moore in her dressing room that night. "Mr. Maney is an irresponsible type," she told producer Morris Green. "He doesn't take his work seriously."

An antic release can be misinterpreted. In an attempt to stimulate interest in *Jumbo,* a carnival bearing the crest of Billy Rose, I wrote that the performance would be climaxed by shooting an elephant out of a cannon. This ignited one of the editors of *Vanity Fair.* Over the phone he said Rose might be writing a new chapter in ballistics. When could this feat be photographed? It would make a great spread. Probably a double truck!

Alarmed at his preoccupation with the Russian drama, I was relieved when Jed Harris announced *The Wiser They Are,* a domestic comedy. In a show of elation I wrote eight hundred words for the *Herald Tribune* drama page, commending my patron for renouncing the steppes. His concern with Chekhov and Gogol had worried his friends. "It had been rumored," I wrote, "that Harris was negotiating with Stalin for a joint occupation of the Ukraine. Harris was to hold the bridgeheads and Stalin the bag." In closing I said: "Mr. Harris has combed the last Cossack out of his curls."

Harris applauded my prose, then reprimanded the drama editor for burying the tribute on page 3. This churl was indifferent to style, he snapped. He should be editing a laundry house organ. Three weeks later my employer charged me with giving aid and comfort to the enemy. In retrospect he had come to the conclusion my toast was irreverent. A man of his eminence in the theatre rated more respect from his hireling. He hinted that the Benedict Arnold in me was coming out.

Though twitting the proprietor is a risky gambit, it fascinates me. While chanting the glories of Lillian Hellman's *The Searching Wind* for Herman Shumlin, I received a frantic call from Howard Barnes, drama critic of the *Herald Tribune.* Our mutual friend

Lucius Beebe had been stricken and carted off to Lenox Hill Hospital. Copy for Beebe's syndicated column was overdue. Would I rush over a paragraph or two? My contribution read:

Surely the most startling intelligence of the week was the announcement that, along with Drexel Biddle, Edsel Ford, and other fashion plates, Herman Shumlin had been named one of America's ten best-dressed men by the Merchant Tailor's Association. Mr. Shumlin, on being interviewed, said he detected no new trends in styles. He's in favor of socks, now that he can afford them.

Entering Shumlin's office a week later, I flinched when his secretary asked: "Did you see the nasty crack Beebe took at Herman in his column?"

Yes, I had seen it. Was my master upset? Upset? He was fit to be tied. Herman is a taut, dour man with a low boiling point. He is dedicated to the underprivileged and the oppressed. Beebe was the flower of Boston's Beacon Hill, a symbol of wealth and snobbery, both anathema to my class-conscious employer. I had no option but to confess. Otherwise Shumlin might call Beebe out at dawn. Lillian Hellman agreed to act as intermediary. "I know something you don't know," she said to Herman. "You've been fouled by your own press agent." Once he knew I was the author of the libel, Shumlin's wrath receded. From one of my social standing the sally was a pleasantry, from Beebe, an insult.

Billy Rose was the most jibe-proof of my employers. He didn't care what I wrote about him so long as it ran to half a column and echoed with his name. As Rose sought to become a producer, I stressed his gaucheries and his blunders and christened him "The Mighty Midget." Maurice Evans, accustomed to British decorum, was shocked when I hinted in a *New York Times* essay that Rose's thirst for publicity might prove his undoing. "I thought you were positively rude to Rose," said Evans as he applied the paunch of Falstaff.

An authority shortly came to my defense. Under the heading "Ballyhooey," George Jean Nathan, dean of the drama critics, wrote in his *Encyclopedia of the Theatre*:

The best press agents in the business today are men of wit and humor who are nice hands at literature, students of the more serious side of the theatre, men who appreciate that facts are infinitely more convincing than fiction. Richard Maney's stories about the Mad Mahout of Broadway, Billy Rose, are destined to become classics of the publicity craft. They are immensely amusing, they are adroitly composed; far from making their subject a hero, as the old time press agent would have done, they truthfully make him a slightly absurd but very interesting . . . human being; and they rouse vital curiosity about him and his ventures. Maney's stories about the mock melodramas at the American Music Hall have been similarly humorous, piquant and able performances. They have created the proper air and atmosphere around the productions and their exaggerations have been in strict accordance with the spirit of the enterprise.

Many of the theatre's nobility have found press agentry a springboard from which to arch into more praiseworthy activities. Lillian Hellman, one of our finest playwrights, bugled for *Bunk of 1926*. Ben Hecht, fleeing Chicago, briefly inflated *Captain Jinks* for Schwab and Mandel. On forsaking his post he wrote a bitter valedictory, "Are Press Agents Necessary?" Other dramatists to flee the mimeograph are S. N. Behrman, Arthur Kober, Russel Crouse, and Channing Pollock. Jed Harris, Herman Shumlin, Max Gordon and Brock Pemberton all had a fling at press agentry before becoming producers. The late Lloyd Lewis, Chicago critic and historian, was press agent for Balaban and Katz, picture-house operators, when first I encountered him in Chicago. Though a mercenary for the movies, Lloyd's heart was in the Civil War as his biographies, *Sherman, Fighting Prophet* and *Captain Sam Grant* attest. With Sinclair Lewis, Lloyd wrote *The Jayhawker*. It went down the drain after twenty-four performances. When I called Lloyd to wish him well the day of the opening, Mrs. Lewis said he wasn't in. "Do you know where I can reach him?" I asked. "I think he's up on Lookout Mountain," she said, "and it would be best not to disturb him." When Lloyd and I prowled the Loop in the twenties, our paths frequently crossed in the *Daily News*. While I haggled with drama editor Margaret Mann, Lloyd was badgering the movie editor, Carl Sandburg.

Robert Benchley, wit, critic, stage and screen comedian, briefly press agented the plays of William A. Brady. Benchley later said that Brady was unaware of his aid to *The Man Who Came Back* and *Eve's Daughter,* so furtive was his approach and so irregular his appearances in the office. Novelist John O'Hara, author of the brilliant musical *Pal Joey,* once brooded in Warner Brothers' press department in New York. Finding the experience galling he fled that factory, though penniless. I was with *Take a Chance,* song-and-dance revue with Ethel Merman, when O'Hara put the bite on me for fifty dollars. Not only would he repay me within the month, he said, but I'd get a bonus. He'd write a feature story for *Take a Chance.* At the time the theatres were warring with the stage-hands over salary and other conditions of servitude. Cued by this quarrel, O'Hara started his story: "The most famous stagehand in America was a murderer." He was referring to the homicidal father in Elmer Rice's *Street Scene.* John's tale was superb, but I buried it in my desk. Stagehands are sensitive folk. Had the story appeared, I could never again visit the stage of *Take a Chance.* A sandbag dropped from the fly gallery might have driven me through the floor.

Simply stated it's the press agent's task to circulate reports flattering to his clients. In practice he does many things not touched upon in his contract. He binds those bleeding from critical stabs and calks up injured egos. He consoles those in despair and tries to ease back-stage tensions and mutinies. Most tensions and mutinies are born of the players' scorn for co-workers. I acted as liaison between Tallulah Bankhead and Herman Shumlin through the runs of *The Little Foxes* —star and producer avoided formal conversations—and between Miss Bankhead and Florence Eldridge in *The Skin of Our Teeth.* Their exchanges were confined to the words of Thornton Wilder. Miss Bankhead and producer Myerberg communicated through smoke signals, effective only when the wind was favorable.

When not trying to get his clients into the newspapers, the press agent may be trying to keep them out. Theatrical people are impulsive. They throw caution to the winds when exhilarated. Lunching at Sardi's a producer with an option on a comedy states he'd have a sure hit if he could get Helen Hayes or Shirley Booth to play the role of the coed who renounces love to prospect in the Canadian Rockies for uranium. Glowing under three martinis, he boasts that

Helen or Shirley has all but agreed to terms. His whisper, overheard and garbled, shortly reaches the ear of the *Times's* Sam Zolotow, or the *Herald Tribune's* Bert McCord, the town's top drama reporters. Pinned down, the victim hesitates to deny or affirm the fiction. He resorts to evasive action. If clairvoyant and familiar with the habits of his employer, the press agent may scotch these fables before they get into type.

On an afternoon in the early forties, I was summoned to the studio of Norman Bel Geddes, industrial designer, visionary, producer and father of Barbara Bel Geddes, one of our ablest young actresses. Flanking Bel Geddes were Eddie Dowling, actor and author, and Richard Myers, occasional composer and producer. With Dr. Max Reinhardt, famed for his triumphs in Berlin and Vienna, the trio, said Bel Geddes, would produce a series of notable plays.

"Didn't I read of this pact in this morning's *Times?*" I asked. Norman shrugged his shoulders in annoyance. There'd been a leak in their communications. That's why they'd sent for me. I was to give the world the McCoy on the merger.

What was their first offering? When would it go into rehearsal? Editors are eccentric. They insist on a fact or two even in high-level manifestoes. They didn't have a play yet, said Norman. What's more they weren't going to produce one until the four partners agreed on its merit. (Experience told me this would cause a minimum delay of three years.) "Isn't Thornton Wilder writing a new play?" asked Myers. "Get him on the phone!" The operator reported Wilder was in Italy. I was told to call Dr. Reinhardt the next day. He would have a startling story for me. "I'll call the Doctor at noon," I said. "No! No!" chorused Myers, Bel Geddes and Dowling. "The Doctor doesn't get up until five and doesn't answer telephones until after six."

That night I asked Zolotow about the advance story in the *Times*. It had reached him in an unsigned telegram from "21." Its phrasing indicated the guilt of one of the partners. Bel Geddes knew a leak when he smelled one! I never called the Doctor. Nor did I hear more of the conspiracy. I had worked for Bel Geddes and Dowling before and would work for Myers. I was never ungallant enough to remind them of the only séance I ever attended in broad daylight.

Press agents' dodges sometimes boomerang. Weep for the publicist who sought to profit from the warning issued by the Health Commissioner during the influenza epidemic in 1920. For one edition his ads read: "Take Dr. Copeland's advice. Stay away from crowds. See Alice Delysia in *Afgar* at the Central Theatre." Sigh for the wight who thought "An enervating comedy" flattering and bannered his ad with it. Badgered by the actor playing Judas in *Twentieth Century,* I extolled him for three paragraphs. The story brought a landlady with a long memory storming to the door of the Broadhurst, waving writs which boded ill for her defaulting tenant.

The press agent can write passes. Thus qualified, he becomes the target for crackpots, parasites and imposters. All these are convinced that the purchase of a theatre ticket is the act of a jughead. Clowns who would shrink from asking Stetson for a sample hat think nothing of trying to blackjack two on the aisle. In support of their requests, these chiselers rig up references. Some claim relationship with newspapermen to whom the agent is obligated. The bolder impersonate newspapermen on the telephone. Others plead poverty, hunger or shelter for the night. Some invent theatrical backgrounds. Aliens argue that their attendance will contribute to a better understanding among the democracies.

In the thirty-three years that I have practiced on Manhattan Island, I've hymned 250 shows and plays. Some of these have run as long as three years, some as little as three hours. I've clashed the cymbals for tragedies and comedies, for musical comedies and melodramas, for adaptations from the Chinese, the French, and from Ladislas Bush-Fekete, a hyphenated beaver identified by Brooks Atkinson as "a Hungarian hack."

I've sung the praises of ice shows, water shows, variety shows and ballets, and of *curiosae* which defied classification. I plugged a saloon set up in the old church in which Charles Evans Hughes was baptized, a motion picture made in Astoria, Long Island, and a crystal maze at Grover Whalen's World's Fair. The picture was *Emperor Jones,* with Paul Robeson as the voodoo-crazed Brutus Jones. The maze was the plaything of the aforecited Bel Geddes.

Some paragraphs ago I spoke of solacing the wounded, of easing the last hours of the doomed. Unless supported by evidence, my pose as an altruist is sure to be challenged. At ease, men! Here's a spot of documentation. My motive is suspect? I would bypass the episode had it not brought forth the most discussed advertisement I ever schemed.

After twelve fat years in Hollywood, Fredric March was eager to re-establish himself in the New York theatre. Like all stage players who default, Freddy wanted to prove that his exile among the lotus eaters had not sapped his skill. He longed, too, for applause. Florence Eldridge, Freddy's wife, and a superb actress in her own right, shared his ambition. John Cromwell, an old friend, was to aid them. Long one of New York's top actors, Cromwell was an ace screen director.

For their return the Marches chose *Yr Obedient Husband,* a comedy about Richard Steele, early eighteenth-century essayist and playwright who, with Joseph Addison, had edited the *Tatler* and the *Spectator.* March was to play the rakish Steele, Miss Eldridge his tormented wife, Prue.

Yr Obedient Husband was hoodooed from the start. A ramshackle play, it was flayed by critics in its pre-New York tour. In Pittsburgh, it had to recess for a week when the eighteen-year-old playing Lord Finch came down with the mumps. As subsequent events proved, it took more than mumps to stop Montgomery Clift.

Yr Obedient Husband limped into the Broadhurst Theatre early in '38 and was keelhauled by the reviewers. March, Miss Eldridge and Cromwell bitterly resented their verdict. Like screen players before and since, the trio felt that the critics were against movie actors, regarded them as brash intruders. Crushed, they decided to close the play on Saturday. Deep as was their resentment, Freddie, Florence and Cromwell made no public show of it.

To conceal their hurt, Freddy told me he'd like to take an ad in the *New York Times* to indicate their insouciance. I recalled a *New Yorker* cartoon which illustrated the plight of my clients. Its reproduction, with their names appended, would indicate that even on the scaffold they were capable of a what-the-hell gesture. (See opposite page.)

"Oop—sorry."

The March apology was reproduced in newspapers and magazines all over the country and the signatories saluted for their gallantry under fire.

Above all other people in the theatre, press agents are badgered with advice. Box-office men, backers, ballerinas and ticket scalpers spray them with suggestions. These volunteers have one thing in common. They think editors and others with whom the press agent copes are mental defectives. Though they know less about publicity and its processes than they do about the Norse Eddas, ignorance only spurs their ardor. These aides can be divided into two classes, well-intentioned dopes and kibitzers.

But press agentry is not an exact science. Those engaged in it operate on a slack wire, without net or bamboo pole. Any of a dozen mischances may short circuit the best-laid plan. A coup designed for page 1 of the *New York Times* may wind up in the overset of the *Staats-Zeitung*. The success of the simplest scuffle demands the co-operation of others in the enterprise. Hence the press agent can't be too brusque with those who volunteer advice. He need not follow it but should indicate by occasional nods and clucks that he is listening to it. Such are the wages of good will. It isn't *esprit de corps* that causes a character actor to get up at daylight to appear on Dave Garroway's TV show. It isn't concern with a musical's success that leads a chorus girl to sacrifice her Sunday for a picture stunt at Coney Island. Character actor and chorus girl submit to these indignities because they like to see their names in print, and because, like all Narcissi, they're transported by their own reflections.

The press agent listens to the producer, since the producer is his employer. If provoked this wizard can sack his interpreter on giving him two weeks' notice. Experienced producers give the press agent a free hand. Inexperienced producers come up with proposals that unhinge his mind. The veteran manager has learned from experience what to expect from his press department. The novice, without experience, demands the moon. Trapped in disaster, he goes berserk.

Berserk was the word for Erik Charrell, the Viennese who put on a voodoo variation of *A Midsummer Night's Dream* at the Center Theatre late in '39. Though it had Louis "Satchmo" Armstrong as its Bottom and Benny Goodman and his clarinet in a stage box, *Swingin' the Dream* was lambasted by the critics. No sooner were their verdicts circulated than the Center box office came down with the bends. Desperate, Charrell groped for a device with which to turn the tide.

My suggestions were brushed aside because they involved expenditure of money. The show was already in hock and a troop of process servers circled the Center. I was roused by a Viennese "Eureka!" Erik proposed to fill empty seats with chambermaids from the better hotels. Inflamed by the magic of *Swingin' the Dream,* these gals would return to their bases, corner the occupants of rooms in their patrol, and urge them to buy tickets.

After applauding Charrell for his resource, I pointed out a flaw. Maids and guests rarely meet. When they do, their conversation is confined to the towel shortage and permits no cultural chitchat. Stimulated by Charrell's desperation, I came up with an alternate. Why not cover the ceilings of barber shops with posters showing the *Dream's* delights? Horizontal captives, lathered to the ears, would be obliged to digest them. Charrell was fascinated.

When box-office receipts for revivals of Shakespeare or other dramatic titans bog down, the management seeks the co-operation of colleges and high schools. Stressing the educational value of the classic and their own vast, if sudden, concern with the youth of the nation, these altruists harass the heads of English and speech and drama departments. If the instructors can bully their charges into compulsory culture, the corps may have tickets at half price. The authors of *The Dancer,* a gruesome charade which George Abbott loosed twelve years ago, were somewhat south of Shakespeare. But they'd heard of "school campaigns." When *The Dancer* came a cropper, they suggested the campuses of Columbia, Hunter and N.Y.U. might be invaded with profit. This proposal numbed me. *The Dancer* dwelt on the homosexual relationship of an insane ballet dancer and his patron, and was laced with murder and treachery. Had I so much as mentioned it on Morningside Heights, I might have been jailed.

So experienced a speculator as Howard Cullman, the theatre's

most successful "angel," has come down with press agents' itch.
With a finger in *Arsenic and Old Lace,* he suggested that I pose
Boris Karloff, the farce's menace, and Al Smith on the topmost
ledge of the Empire State Building. Cullman worked up quite a
scenario. In his script, Karloff was a victim of acrophobia. He
argued that a picture of the screen's terror, shrinking in terror from
the Empire State's parapet, would present a memorable paradox,
one sure to ignite picture editors. There was a hurt look in Mr.
Cullman's eyes when I cited the saw about the shoemaker and his last.

    Arsenic and Old Lace brought out the profanity in producer Russel
Crouse, former press agent for the Theatre Guild. I denounced Crouse
when he suggested that the homicidal sisters in the play descend
to the basement of the Fulton Theatre on Memorial Day and strew
the graves of their victims with flowers while their lunatic brother,
who thought he was Teddy Roosevelt, blew taps over the departed.
I would have no part in such an affront. Why didn't he take two
aspirins and lie down until his ague ebbed? Crouse is gnawed by
small anxieties. Woe betide the blunderer who puts a second "l"
in Russel. Katharine Cornell is upset when an "e" instead of a second
"a" intrudes on her given name. The two have terrorized a thousand
proofreaders. As a paronomasiac, Crouse rivals Bennett Cerf. A
sample? Asked if he liked operettas, Crouse replied, "Only telephone
operettas."

    Crouse heads a school dedicated to the delusion that the public
avoids a play sold out weeks in advance. He and his cult claim empty
seats are a sign the "sold out" hex is working. They ignore a universal
truth: the more difficult a thing is to obtain, the more desirable it
becomes and the more frantically it is sought. The spectacular run
of *Oklahoma* was due, in great measure, to tales of the ruses practiced
by those determined to see it, come hell or high water. A sold-out
house is the most potent advertisement in the theatre.

    The quest for *Oklahoma* tickets led to all sorts of strategies. A
young Brooklyn couple received two aisle tickets through the mail.
There was no accompanying letter. Attempts to learn the identity
of their benefactor proved fruitless but they did discover his business.

Returning home after their evening with the lyric Sooners, they found their apartment ransacked, everything of value lugged away.

To my office in the Empire came a beribboned Air Force major. He bore a letter of introduction from St. Clair McKelway, *New Yorker* editor then stationed in Delhi, India. The major was on leave, wrote McKelway. His one ambition was to see *Oklahoma*. If I didn't get two tickets for this warrior he, McKelway, would denounce me in every bar in the Forties on his return. I called Lawrence Langner at The Theatre Guild and told him of the major's plight. Lawrence obliged with a pair of house seats at box-office price. The major saw the musical Tuesday night. Wednesday morning six other majors were lined up outside my door. I denounced McKelway in every bar in the Forties.

Bide Dudley, drama editor and occasional critic of the New York *Evening World,* gave me sound if inelegant advice on my initiation as a press agent in 1919. "Each story should hint that the show you're publicizing is the greatest ever written, and that anyone who doesn't go to see it is a dirty son-of-a-bitch. Your rating as a press agent will depend on the degree to which you can approximate that ultimate."

Press agentry is no business for people with nerves. But it can be a gay life for one with detachment, with sympathy for the deranged, and with an understanding of why the theatre's children behave the way they do. Despite the pettiness, the egomania and the persecution complexes of stage folk, they are more amusing, more generous and more stimulating than any other professional group.

Press agentry is an elusive vocation, defying both definition and analysis. Rarely is a press agent cashiered. It would be next to impossible to itemize charges against him. Only the loosest of codes governs his conduct. Most employers have sketchy notions of what he has done or of what he is up to. Yardsticks with which to measure his output are likely to be misleading. Industry is no substitute for talent. Press agents often lather themselves in missions which, if accomplished, would not bring a sou to the box office. Quality is more to be desired than quantity.

A sense of discrimination is an asset to any press agent. A paragraph in the *New York Times* may have a greater impact on business than a column in a lesser journal. The sane press agent distinguishes between publicity and notoriety. One flatters, one debases, his client. One stresses his virtues and skills, the other his vices. Press agent and producer don't always agree on procedure. On its opening, *Along Fifth Avenue* was mauled by the reviewers. All agreed that it gave off an evil odor. In vain I combed their verdicts for excerpts that might be fused into an ad. When I confessed defeat, producer Arthur Lesser volunteered to help me. Soon he came up with an endorsement from the *Times's* Brooks Atkinson. He had taken a few liberties with the Atkinson prose, distorted a sentence, excised a qualifying phrase.

I protested. "Why?" he said. "It's unethical," I replied. "I'll have no part of it." "Which is more important, your ethics or my $100,000?" he asked. I told him. That's why the ad didn't carry Brooks's benediction.

Along Fifth Avenue had one thing in common with *Artists and Models*, the revue which disillusioned Lou Walters: Jackie Gleason. It's a tribute to Mr. Gleason's fortitude, if not to his judgment, that he survived both disasters to become the Croesus of the twenty-one-inch tubes. It would be pleasant, though false, to say that I detected gold beneath the Gleason dross. To me he was another vulgar fat boy trying too hard to be funny. In my parleys with Gleason, I found him morose and suspicious. In view of his grisly surroundings, his mood was understandable. Necessity, rather than choice, explained his appearance in both *Artists and Models* and *Along Fifth Avenue*. He confessed that his judgment was erratic, then documented the indictment. Heckled by a rowdy while trying to entertain the scum in a Jersey City cavern, Gleason invited his annoyer outside. This challenge was accepted and Gleason was chilled by the first punch. His critic was Tony Galento, the barrel-shaped fighter who once had Joe Louis on the deck.

How did I become a press agent? When? Where? On whose insistence? These are questions calling for sober reflection, for a study of imponderables, for a consideration of the proverb, "Hunger has no conscience." I propose to throw light on these queries in the pages to follow. I may even answer some of them.

Have I a formula for achieving success as a press agent in the theatre? No. But I have a hot tip for those who would avoid disgrace. Insult as few newspapermen as possible.

2

Act I, Scene I

I WAS born on a ranch three miles from Chinook, Montana. Chinook is on the Milk River near the Canadian border. Was I partial to fame by association, however remote, I'd remind the reader that Captain Meriwether Lewis, William Clark and their Shoshone guide, Sacajawea, wound their way through the cottonwoods along the Milk in 1805. It's possible they cantered over the site of Chinook.

My father came to Montana in 1876. That was the year General George Custer and his regiment were massacred on the Little Bighorn. My father was seventeen when he arrived at Fort Benton by steamboat. It would be ten years before the Great Northern Railroad reached this old trading post. More than once on the trip up the Missouri from St. Louis the crew tied up in the shelter of a bluff lest the boat be capsized by buffalo swimming the river. That's what my father told me. The first buffalo I saw were in a corral at the Fort Worth Centennial. They were being directed by the late John Murray Anderson for the glory of Billy Rose.

Fort Benton was a garrison. When Sioux, Blackfoot, Crow, Assiniboin, Cree or Blood Indians would erupt in resentment against the pioneers, the soldiers would sally forth to curb them. I believe my

father was a mess boy in the commissary department of the troops
under Colonel Nelson A. Miles, post-rebellion custodian of Jefferson
Davis, when he chased Sitting Bull into Alberta. That was in 1877.
It's possible Dad was in the audience when Miles bagged the Sioux
chief Crazy Horse, and Chief Joseph of the Nez Percés. Miles was
a born rebellion-smotherer. Seven years later, he subdued the striking
Pullman workers in Illinois.

For four or five years, my father whacked bulls along the Marias
River. For a time, he ran a livery stable. In 1889, he was named
Head Farmer at the Fort Belknap Indian Agency by the Department
of the Interior. He undertook to teach the Indians how to plant and
cultivate corn. This instruction was touched with irony. The Indians
were raising corn when white men first came to the plains.

The redmen at Fort Belknap may have resented my father's cues.
At any rate, he didn't stay there long. In July of 1890, he married
my mother. They met on a train some months earlier when Mother
was en route to Butte from Waseca, Minnesota, to visit a sister.
Elizabeth Bohen was a remarkable woman. Her mother died when
she was eleven. Thereafter she cooked and cared for her six brothers
and sisters, made their clothes, cut their hair. When their father
deserted them, Mother and her sisters and brothers found refuge
with families in and around Waseca. Mother's parents were born in
County Clare, Ireland. Born in Ireland, too, were Richard Maney
and Ann Considine, Father's parents.

After their wedding at Fort Benton, Father and Mother moved
into the four-room log house on the Milk. In this log house my
sister Loretta and I were born. Here we lived until 1900. Life on
the ranch was primitive and vivid. On a clear January night, one
could read a newspaper out of doors. The displays of the aurora
borealis were breathtaking. In the midnight silence the crunch of
a wagon wheel in the crusted snow could be heard for miles. It
sounded like a succession of pistol shots. The more bitter the cold,
the more penetrating the yelps of the coyotes. The Milk River
froze to a depth of three feet. Dad and the hired man sawed out
great cakes, hauled them to the icehouse and stored them between
layers of sawdust. This ice lasted through the following summer.

Part of the ranch was a pasture for the horses and cows, and for a herd of rams after my father went into the sheep business. In the spring there was an epidemic of plowing, planting, sowing, harrowing, hoeing and weeding. This was followed by, or fused with, irrigating, reaping, threshing and storing. In the Montana of the mid-nineties it was fashionable to initiate these ceremonies around five in the morning. Cows were milked in the dark. My sister and I were up at six to be scrubbed, clothed and fed before being driven to school. Father and Mother looked upon attendance at school as a moral obligation. Neither of them had much formal education. Come blizzard, flood or smallpox scare we never missed a day of school save when ill.

As we drove off to school in buggy, spring wagon or sleigh we were tailed by our pet deer. This fawn edged out of the cottonwood grove one morning to sip at the trough in the yard. It was small and timid and lovely. My mother fed and cared for it and it became a dramatic, if capricious, pet. It would scale wire fences. It punctured the window and door screens with its forepaws. Once it treed a book agent on the swinging gate, bounced him off and chased him through the wheat field.

However sketchy Dad's cash position, we never lacked for food. We had an abundance of vegetables throughout the summer. Sacks of these were stored in the root house for winter. Dad bought beef by the quarter, salt mackerel by the keg, whole hams. Chickens flourished despite the hawks. Mother preserved berries, watermelon rinds and cucumbers and put up quarts of chowchow, jam and jelly. The making of a crock of mincemeat took on the guise of a de Mille ritual. Fermented dough filled another crock, the base for hotcakes. Mother did the cooking, the washing and ironing, baked the bread and cookies and pies, made Loretta's clothes, knitted our stockings, made my shirts, cut my hair. She fed the chickens, collected the eggs, made the butter. Twice a year she cleaned the house from cellar to roof. In her leisure moments she went in for fancy work and crazy quilts. She embroidered lace for Loretta's clothes, doilies and centerpieces. My mother was highly emotional. She laughed and cried easily. A devout Catholic, she was a stickler for morality.

As a child she had been shattered by her mother's death and her father's flight. Both events marked her through life.

Dad purchased such food as he didn't raise at O'Hanlon's or Bogy's general merchandise stores. My first oyster came out of a tin can. Customers rarely paid cash at the stores. Everybody charged what they bought and paid up when a crop was sold. The currency was gold and silver. Paper money was suspect. The bit was the monetary unit. Two bits was a quarter, four bits half a dollar. Pockets of the flush were lined with silver dollars, with five-, ten- and twenty-dollar goldpieces.

Dad shriveled our spines with Indian stories and with tales about outlaws holed up in the Bear Paws, thirty miles south. The Curry brothers, bank and train robbers with a price on their heads, were still at large. Dad knew Kid Curry, most notorious of the clan. He also knew Pike Landusky, the Kid's most noted victim. Pike was slow on the draw. There's a town named for him on the edge of the Bear Paws. But there was little violence in the Milk River valley. Charged-up cowboys occasionally exchanged shots but crime was no problem. There was a lot of talk about cattle rustlers and claim jumpers. It was a crime to sell whisky to Indians. The redmen solaced themselves with substitutes—witch hazel, bay rum and varnish.

Most of the Indians in Montana were penned up on reservations. Occasionally a file of braves paraded through the ranch, their covered wagons and travois loaded with squaws, papooses and dogs with the bucks astride grubby cayuses. Mother had been married but a few months when she found a squaw in the kitchen. Alone on the ranch, she was sure she'd be scalped. The squaw carried a bucket of chokecherries. By signs she indicated she wanted to trade the berries for clothes. Dad swore Mother gave the squaw his store suit for a nickel's worth of berries. Mother buried the berries in the ground, certain they were poisoned.

Dad had one gripe against the Indians. They never shut the gates. Because of this omission, the stock would escape to the range. I would be sent off to round up the strays. My pony's name was Billy Barlow and he had a roached mane. I could manage him going away from the house. Once we started home he ran away. Riding bareback I'd have to pull up my leg when rounding a fence corner lest I be scraped off. Loretta had a ten-dollar Indian pony. Everyone in Chinook rode. The ladies rode side saddle in the interests of modesty.

It was my duty to pump water into the horse trough, prime the pump when it balked, thaw it out when it froze. I paged the cows for milking and the chickens for feeding. I gathered eggs from the hens' nests, shut up the chickenhouse at night, filled the coal buckets, prepared kindling for the range. I hoed the berry patch and weeded the vegetable garden. I was moderately skilled at milking if the cow followed stage directions.

Beating the carpet was a frustrating assignment. After it was untacked and heaved on a clothesline, I flayed it with a broom. Even after a six-hour attack every whack set off clouds of dust. To compensate for this indignity, I would be sent into the grove to pick wild berries, or accompany Dad when he went hunting for prairie chicken, sage hens and mallards. Dad was a good shot. Rarely did he return empty-handed. But his skill didn't spur me to imitate him. I winced at the thought of killing any living thing and still do. Chicken was a popular item on our supper table. I'd be told to catch one and cut off its head, that Mother might scald and pluck it. This revolted me. I'd go to considerable lengths to avoid cranking the ice-cream freezer and agitating the churn. Disobedience was not condoned. The penalty for violations was the application of hand, hairbrush or leather strap. The formula instilled in me respect for law and order.

There were no telephones on the ranches. Letters were the only means of communication. To mail or receive one meant a ride to the post office, a cubicle in Bogy's store. When Loretta or I came down with the croup or the chickenpox, we'd be dosed with Jamaica ginger or a hot toddy. In the spring we were drugged with sulphur and molasses, a foul concoction. When one of us became delirious, Dad would set off for Chinook's only doctor, C. F. Hopkins. The nearest hospital was in Great Falls, 150 miles southwest.

Our log house was lit by coal-oil lamps. We carried lanterns when engaged outdoors after dark. By the light of a lamp Mother read me *Robinson Crusoe*. Defoe's tale of the shipwrecked sailor was the first book I remember. It froze my marrow. Thanks to the *Chinook Opinion* we were able to keep track of the neighbors, their comings and goings. This weekly has been published without interruption since 1890.

Dad subscribed to the Sunday edition of James Gordon Bennett's New York *Herald* to keep in touch with the activities of the four Considine brothers, all prominent in the theatrical and sporting world. Their father was Dad's uncle. Dad had met and visited the Considines at their Detroit home in the eighties. George Considine was his idol. For a time George managed James J. Corbett, conqueror of John L. Sullivan, and the crafty Kid McCoy. He was a crony of Tammany Hall sachems and was married to Aimee de Angeles, an actress in Weber and Fields extravaganzas and Charles Hoyt farces.

For ten years George Considine operated the Hotel Metropole at the southwest corner of Broadway and Forty-second Street. It was the headquarters for the stay-up-lates—theatrical folk, gamblers, race-track and prize-ring followers. When the hotel was torn down in 1910, George burned up $60,000 in I.O.U.'s, souvenirs from defaulting friends.

Jimmy was the black sheep of the Considine clan. He was a confidant of Eva Tanguay, a vaudeville headliner famed for her tantrums, her affairs and her "Dance of the Seven Veils." He had charm, swagger and a scorn for convention. Following a brush with the law, Jimmy was tossed into the penitentiary in Columbus, Ohio. While incarcerated he struck up an acquaintance with an inmate who was trying to weave his experiences into short stories. Because of his unsavory address, this hopeful used an alias in addressing editors, substituting O. Henry for William Sydney Porter.

George Considine thought the penalty for Jimmy's prank excessive. He argued the case so eloquently that Theodore Roosevelt pardoned the prankster in 1903. The two had been friends when T.R. was head of New York's police department. To show his gratitude, George supported the Roughrider when he overwhelmed Alton B.

Parker in 1904—the only time a Considine ever voted the Republican ticket.

In 1911 George opened the new Metropole on the present site of Rosoff's Restaurant in West Forty-third Street. The Metropole blazed in the headlines on July 16, 1912. Early that morning gambler Herman Rosenthal walked from it to be mowed down by the guns of "Gyp the Blood" Horowitz, "Lefty Louie" Rosenberg, "Whitey Lewis" Seidensher and "Dago Frank" Cirofici, hired killers of Police Lieutenant Charles Becker. Becker and his agents died in the electric chair at Sing Sing and Charles S. Whitman, the prosecutor who convicted them, went to the Governor's chair in Albany.

Dad envied the Considines. They lived well, dressed well, slept late and associated with celebrities. What's more they led luxurious and exciting lives with a minimum of effort. Dad resented the drudgery which was his lot for most of his eighty-three years. A picture of George Considine and "Big Tim" Sullivan, Tammany brave, centered one wall of our parlor. There was a great to-do on the ranch when Dad learned that Jimmy Considine was the company manager of a show about to play one night in Great Falls. I don't recall its title, but I think Ada Rehan headed the company. Early on this red-letter day, Loretta and I were left with a neighbor and Dad and Mother took off on the great adventure. On their return, Dad gave us a play-by-play account of the excursion. He ignored the drama, save when necessary to establish the nature of Jimmy's job. Mother, as always, was more reticent.

The Maneys had another association with the theatre. Joe Downs, Dad's cousin and a son of a Detroit Considine, was a property man. He frequently crossed the continent with touring plays. Joe had seven sisters. My mother corresponded with the Downs sisters for years though she didn't meet any of them until 1926. Dad thought letter writing effeminate, unworthy of a bullwhacker and buffalo hunter.

True to his Irish background, Dad was fascinated by politics. A lifelong Democrat, he had the misfortune to live in a Republican county. Irked by this anomaly, he tried to split Chouteau County. He spent a month in Helena one winter lobbying for partition. His mission was fruitless but he returned with strange tales of shenanigans in the capital. Most of these concerned William A. Clark, the copper king, who had been trying for a seat in the United States Senate since Montana was admitted to the Union in '89. In those days U.S. Senators were elected by state legislatures. Repeatedly foiled in his quest, it was rumored Clark intended to purchase the post. On the eve of a vote more than one legislator found $500 in gold coin under his bed pillow. This hint put a great strain on a statesman getting $3 a day. All those baited were certain Clark was their benefactor. No other candidate could afford such largess. When Clark went to the Senate in 1901, there was talk his gold had subdued the conscience of more than one solon.

Hazards of travel and communication hobbled our social life. So did Mother's and Dad's devotion to the sixteen-hour-day. A Sunday call on Jim and Fanny Roberts, eight miles downriver, had to be plotted days in advance and presented many problems. Such an excursion could be undertaken only when Dad had a hired man to care for the chickens, milk the cows, feed and water the stock. All of us were implicated in the jaunt since no one could be left behind. Mother wouldn't have tolerated a hired girl if Dad could have afforded one. An aide would have been a slur on her competence. In Mother's judgment all hired girls and cooks were gold-brickers and swindlers.

Getting Loretta, Dad and me ready for such a visit invariably brought Mother down with "a sick headache." That all hands might bathe in the galvanized washtub, the range blazed for hours on the hottest day. Getting us into Sunday clothes was a rough assignment. Even in a new suit, Dad looked as if he had dressed in a cyclone. Loretta and I resented our finery since it cramped our style. But Mother, eager for the esteem of our hosts, insisted that we "look nice." No matter how well we were groomed on departure, we deteriorated in transit. The long ride in buckboard or spring wagon, over treacherous roads and exposed to a boiling sun, took its toll.

An occasional square dance at Chinook's Town Hall, exercises on the last day of school, Fourth of July celebrations and Christmas church entertainments made up our amusements. If any show visited

Chinook while we lived on the ranch, Loretta and I never saw it. But we were deranged for weeks when Dad drove us to Havre, thirty miles west, to see Barnum and Bailey's circus. For months thereafter we risked life and limb trying to emulate the acrobats and wirewalkers.

Dad's income from the sale of wheat, hay, oats and potatoes barely met expenses. He supplemented it with outside work. For a time he operated a butcher shop in Chinook. This failed because he felt it ignoble to bill his customers. In bitter weather Dad hauled silver and copper ore from the Little Rockies to the freight cars on the siding, over roads obscured by snowdrifts. In summer he occasionally worked for the county, repairing roads with plow, scraper and grader.

Around 1897 Dad went into the sheep business. His herd grazed on the range in the summer. In the winter, they munched baled hay in sheds. On May 1, 1899, five feet of snow fell on the prairie and destroyed all the ewes and the lambs they had just dropped. This disaster climaxed a succession of droughts, floods, and blights and caused Dad to cry quits. He sold the ranch and bought a house in Chinook. He had lost his battle with the soil and the weather. Now he hoped to triumph as a merchant.

For the next five years, Dad operated—if I may use that verb so loosely—a hardware store. His approach to trade was heretic. Shortly after he sold his first keg of nails, he came out for self-service, the first merchant in Montana to encourage this practice. Behind a counter, Dad felt trapped. When his phobia became intolerable, he'd bolt for the nearest saloon, leaving the store unattended. Under the Maney honor system, customers were supposed to leave memos itemizing what they had made off with.

Opposed to sin in all forms, Mother was desolated by Dad's defections. Frantic on learning he had deserted the store, she'd send me to find him. This was a delicate errand. A man holding a king-high flush and three belts of Old Crow was in no mood for small talk, even with his son. Though Mother said saloons were sinkholes of iniquity, I found them fascinating. They were masculine and mysterious, cool in summer, warm in winter. Clients were shielded from the curious by whitewashed windows and swinging doors. They were off limits to women. The sawdust in the trough of the bar, the exotic art displays on the walls and the heady aromas were symbols of an adult world. Amid such surroundings Dad was the George Considine of Chinook.

Whatever his flaws as a trader, Dad stopped at nothing to advance me and, in lesser degree, Loretta. I was to compensate for the education denied him, for the ease that eluded him and for the offices he never held. He overlooked no opportunity to push me to the fore. When fate was laggard, he'd invent opportunity.

Learning that the Spanish fleet had been wiped out at Santiago de Cuba on July 3, 1898, Dad piled all of us into the spring wagon the next morning and raced to Chinook for the Independence Day riot. Threatening me with the knout if I failed him, he dragged me to Town Hall and shoved me on the platform to read the Declaration. Numb with fright, I piped Jefferson's words in a weird tremolo. I was still shaking an hour later when I ran fourth in a fifty-yard dash. The day had added significance for my father. He was born on July 4, 1859.

Chinook went all out on the Fourth of July. By noon Main Street was littered with wounded. Cannon crackers as big as fire hydrants were splintering windows. Pistols and shotguns blazed. Dynamite explosions rocked the patriots. By the time the fireworks display started, all the men were plastered, all the children were crying, and all the women had dropped from exhaustion.

Dragooned into a competition to name Chinook's entry in an oratorical contest for Montana High School students, I was disgraced when I omitted the most fervent flight in Henry Ward Beecher's "The Flag." Dad rated this lapse just short of treason. Like all Celts he was a setup for florid speech. Until I fouled up Beecher, he felt I might become another Bourke Cockran, Irish spellbinder then swaying Tammany Hall.

The Beecher scandal had barely simmered down when I was ambushed in another plot to advance me. A chance remark by neighbor Edgar Fuller cued Dad into the delusion that music was my mutton. Fuller had conducted a U.S. Army band at Fort

Assiniboin. He wouldn't be happy until Chinook had a brass band. It would have one, too, he told my father, as soon as he could lay hands on a cornet player. Dad had a quick solution. He'd buy a cornet if Fuller would teach me how to play it. Unaware of the hazards of the assignment, Fuller agreed.

That accursed horn was the symbol of my martyrdom. Its pistons defied me. Its valves mocked me. Sentenced to an hour's practice in my bedroom each day, I'd beat the bugle over the bedstead in protest. This vandalism moved my father to punitive action. A coulee meandered across the fields behind our house. On its banks grew lithe willows. One of these made a satisfactory lash. Dad applied this to me not because he loved me less, but because he loved military marches more.

Each Sunday afternoon I received two hours' instruction from Fuller. To me he was the twentieth-century Torquemada. To him I was the all-time musical misfit. To simplify matters, Fuller explained that the notes bisected by the staff lines could be identified by remembering the initial letters of the mocking adage: "Every good boy deserves favor."

After a year of huffing and puffing and of mutual despair, Fuller said I was ready. It's difficult to explain how a man of his integrity could thus compromise his standards. In my first public demonstration I conspired in the rendition of John Philip Sousa's "Stars and Stripes Forever." Temples bursting, lip paralyzed, I blasted into it when Fuller raised his baton. Almost at once his face started to turn purple. Aware that he heard something that revolted his ear, I began to feel sorry for the trombone player. Only when I played a two-bar solo following the end of the march was I aware of his innocence.

Sporadically I abused the cornet for five years. I committed my last offense while facing eight hundred of my mates at Broadway High School in Seattle. My mayhem on "The Star-Spangled Banner" in the assembly hall caused conductor Nicholas Oeconomacos, clarinetist with the Seattle Symphony, to demand my resignation. It was months before Dad and Mother learned of my digrace. They might never have learned of it had not some Judas tipped them off when I pawned the horn for $6.

Chinook had its first football team in 1905, thanks to my father and Henry Rankin, high-school principal. A squad of twelve turned out for practice. I was named captain by acclamation. Hadn't my father imported the ball from St. Paul? Our rehearsals under Rankin were frustrating because we had no one to scrimmage against. Our plays were run off in slow motion because of our bulky equipment. Our mothers sewed pads and cushions to our uniforms haphazardly. Leather headguards impeded our sight. Rubber noseguards made breathing difficult. We had another problem. We couldn't find a team to play.

After a canvass of Chouteau County, Rankin and Dad discovered that the young bucks at the Fort Belknap Indian Reservation, twenty miles east of Chinook, had a football team. Chinook's challenge was accepted with the proviso that the game be played on the reservation. The Chinook team was jittery at the kickoff. Accompanied by relatives, we had arived at Harlem, a few miles from the field, on the noon local. Many of us had never ridden on a train before.

This was in the five-yards-in-three-downs, pre-forward-pass era. Our opponents wore caps and moccasins. Despite pre-game nerves, Chinook scored first on a criss-cross play called by quarterback Maney and led at the end of the half, 6-0.

Our lead didn't last long. In the second half, the redmen swarmed all over us. Aware we were being outplayed, I had reason to believe we were outnumbered and appealed to the umpire for a recount. My hunch was valid. Twelve Indians were lined up against us. The intruder was easily detected. Loyal to his tribe, he had taken advantage of a play near the sidelines to jump from his horse into the fray. His treachery might have passed unnoticed had he removed his spurs. A brave who had played for Carlisle shucked his blanket to replace an undernourished Blackfoot at halfback. Thanks to his runs we were routed. Final score: 25-6. Chinook went through the next season unbeaten and untied. In our only game we beat Havre, 26-0. The team was photographed around a placard reading,

"Champions of the West." Chinook glowed with civic pride when this hoax was reproduced in the Great Falls *Tribune*.

In 1905 I had three heroes, Michel Ney, Christy Mathewson and Walter Eckersall. The first was a Marshal of France, Duke of Elchingen, Prince of the Moskova and Commander of the Old Guard at Waterloo. Matty was the New York Giant pitcher who blanked Connie Mack's Athletics three times in a row in the World Series that October. Eckersall was the University of Chicago's star kicker and runner. Thanks to him, Chicago tripped up "Hurry Up" Yost's Michigan team, unbeaten in five years. I felt Eckersall and I were kin. He was a quarterback, too, three times on Walter Camp's All-American eleven.

Sometime in 1905 I read *A Page of the First Empire*. I never recovered from it. Overnight I became Montana's leading Francophile. The fourteen-year-old hero of *A Page of the First Empire* served Bonaparte in the Tuileries. He accompanied his master to Moscow and was his aide-de-camp at Waterloo. The book was charged with magic names: Murat, Davout, Bernadotte, Caulaincourt, Berthier, Desaix, Marengo, Austerlitz, Josephine, Talleyrand, Fouché. But of all the warriors who thronged *A Page of the First Empire*, Michel Ney fascinated me most. Above any of his comrades this son of a barrel cooper justified Napoleon's "Every soldier of France carries a Marshal's baton in his knapsack." Properly stimulated, my eyes still moisten at mention of Le Rogueaud's execution by a Bourbon firing squad in the Luxembourg Gardens.

Who brings Ney's name up? I bring it up. At such times I see him, begrimed, epaulettes shot away, beating his sword over a cannon at Waterloo in an attempt to rally the Guard. I have read of him in *Vanity Fair,* in *The Charterhouse of Parma,* in *Les Miserables*. I have pored over Bonaparte and his marshals in dozens of lives, dozens of memoirs. None played such havoc with my emotions as *A Page of the First Empire*.

Napoleon's tomb under the dome of the Invalides was my first stop on reaching Paris in '32. Later I visited another grave in Père-Lachaise. The stone marking it bore a single word, NEY. Nearby were Davout, Masséna and Sérurier. During our stay in

Paris, Betty and I stood in awe before the Arc de Triomphe, on which Napoleon's victories—Wagram, Austerlitz, Jena, Arcola, Borodino—are chiseled in marble. We spent a day at Malmaison, where Napoleon lived with Josephine, another day in Notre Dame, where Bonaparte was crowned Emperor of the French.

During my last two years in Chinook, I picked up a vice which still haunts me, the study of baseball players and their records. I was first exposed to the New York Giants in the pages of the Great Falls *Tribune*. I could pick up a discarded copy of this daily in the lobby of the Chinook House after dinner. Occasionally I bagged a Butte *Miner* or an Anaconda *Standard*. From these I sheared every line and every picture concerned with John McGraw and his men. The Giants of those days had a marked Irish tinge. McGann, McGinnity, Donlin, Dahlen, Devlin and Bresnahan were names to fire my blood. For a time, I clipped Giant news and notes to the exclusion of everything else. That's why I know more about old second basemen than I do about old character actors.

This mania irked my parents. Concentration on Donlin and Devlin and Matty was reflected in my algebra and Latin tests. Hounded, I practiced my rites furtively. I cached my clippings behind the water tank in the attic and pored over them when I was supposed to be taming the trumpet. Acting as lookout, Loretta would warn me of the approach of a hostile. My devotion to baseball was odd because I had never seen a professional game, indeed had seen only occasional games between Chinook and the Harlem or Havre team. I played the game when scrub teams could be assembled. Since eighteen boys were rarely available, we fell back on one-old-cat. My infield career ended when an errant ground ball drove my upper lip through my teeth. Thereafter I found safety behind a catcher's mask or in the outfield.

In the black stole, crimson cape and white surplice of an altar boy, I assisted Reverend Father Fred Eberschweiler, S.J., on the Sundays he sang Mass. There were some five or six towns in his parish stretching from the Canadian border to the Bear Paws. He drove to these in rotation and in all kinds of weather. He was a dedicated and selfless man. Though my responses at the Mass must

have unnerved him, he gave no sign. My sketchy knowledge of
Caesar and his *Commentaries* helped me little with the *Kyrie eleisons*
and the *Christi eleisons, the pax vobiscums* and the *et cum spiritu
tuos.* The vestments of the priest, the aroma of the incense, the
chanting of the choir, the stained-glass windows, the pouring of the
wine into the chalice—all these mystified and intoxicated me.

Dad went to Mass only when Mother shamed him into it. He was
suspicious of any activity that made it necessary to put on a stiff
collar. Mother never missed Mass and she saw to it that Loretta and
I didn't. Father Eberschweiler paid me five cents for each Mass.
There was no additional fee for assisting at vespers. A miscue at
an evening service led to my unfrocking. It was my chore to light
the candles on the altar prior to the priest's entrance. The night of
my mishap I held my taper too high coming from the sacristy and
set fire to the curtains which masked the door. I was mounting the
altar when warned by a cry from the choir loft. Scuttling through
flame and smoke, I summoned Father Eberschweiler. He quenched
the blaze and let me off with a reprimand. His parishioners were
less tolerant. At best I was a security risk, at worst a pyromaniac,
they argued. Placed on parole, I was reduced to tolling the bell.

Montana was and is a state of vast distances and scant population.
Only exceeded in size by Texas and California, Montana has fewer
people than Seattle or Houston. Because of its expanse and scarcity of
customers, few theatrical companies prowled Montana in the 1900's.
Those that invaded Butte, Great Falls and Helena avoided Chinook,
a town of less than a thousand souls. A fugitive *Uncle Tom's Cabin*
company played a night in Chinook. Loretta and I were desolated
at Little Eva's death and outraged at the conduct of Simon Legree.

A hypnotist bewildered the pioneers in a one-night stand at Town
Hall. Lured to the platform, three of Chinook's citizens shortly
were asleep. At the suggestion of the sorcerer, they engaged in
horseplay at odds with their standing in church and community. The
audience resented a character who could befuddle acquaintances with
a wave of his hand. Obviously the intruder was a criminal type. It
would be well to keep an eye on him until he caught the west-bound
local in the morning.

Corrupted by an Eastern college, the daughter of a cattleman touched off a scandal with a dance recital at Town Hall. Chinook's women folk were outraged by the hussy's display of lingerie and ankle. All said she would come to no good end. Maddened by the click of her castanets, the town's males gave her an ovation. They didn't think she would come to any good, either, but any of them would have shared her shame. Observation of *Uncle Tom's Cabin*, the hypnotist and the nautch girl didn't inflame me. A remote and mystic business, the theatre was beyond my dreams.

Shortly after I became a press agent, I loosed the fiction that I had been brought up among Cree Indians, and that I couldn't speak a word of English until I was seven. I resorted to this invention on noting the surprise of co-workers on learning I came from Montana. It seemed a harmless way to embellish my background and sow the seeds of a legend. I lived to rue this boast. Twice I was credited in national magazines with saying that the Chinook of my youth was "a nest of mangy Crees." For this I was denounced by the editors of the Chinook and Havre newspapers. I was branded an ingrate as well as a liar. Here and now I apologize to Chinook and to the Crees, too.

Though it's been fifty years since I left Chinook, my memories of it are warm. I glowed when a story under a Chinook dateline appeared on page 1 of the *New York Times* on a January morning in the mid-forties. The story? Chinook's temperature had dropped to 45 degrees below zero. For one day it was the coldest spot in America. During World War II calves' liver sold for $1.60 a pound in Westport stores. In Chinook, the butcher gave us all the calves' liver we wanted. Thanks to government dams and new methods of irrigation, Chinook's ranchers have some degree of crop insurance. In my childhood the range was cluttered with ant hills, gopher and prairie-dog holes, sagebrush, cactus and splotches of alkali. Dry-land farmers led a perilous existence.

But Chinook was an exciting and healthy home for a boy at the turn of the century. To be sure I was denied space cadets, Hopalong Cassidy and hotrods, but camping on Clear Creek in the Bear Paws made up for these privations. While Dad fished for trout,

Mother, Loretta and I picked chokeberries, wild raspberries and gooseberries. On another vacation I rode with the cowboys as they rounded up cattle on the range, and slept in the chuck wagon. And there were other excitements: searching for beads and arrowheads in the Indian graveyard atop a hill on the Bowes' ranch across the river. Coasting downhill on a home-made sled in brilliant starlight. Skating round a bonfire on the river. Getting through "Hohenlinden" without a stumble at the Christmas entertainment.

Dad finally lost his one-sided duel with the hardware store. It failed him, as had the ranch and the sheep. His heretic notions about self-service, his reluctance to nudge his debtors, his scorn of inventories and other mercantile nonsense proved his undoing. Proud and courageous, generous, resentful of the handicaps which hobbled him, Dad fled West.

There are still Maneys in Chinook. My Uncle Pat, Dad's brother, died there in '54 at the age of eighty-seven. He lived and prospered in Chinook for sixty-five years. I still have leather-bound volumes of the poems of Milton, Pope and Byron, gifts from Uncle Pat, a man without an hour of schooling.

Because he was a member of the minority party, Dad had been thwarted when he sought to become County Clerk, Road Commissioner and County Assessor. His one victory came when he ran for school trustee on a non-partisan ticket. No sooner had Dad fled than Chouteau was split, not into two counties, but three. To add to this mockery, Chinook was named county seat of its subdivision. One detail of this surgery solaced my father. It was perhaps for the best that he had escaped from a community named for James G. Blaine, "the plumed knight" who had outraged all the Irish in the land, when, as he challenged Grover Cleveland for the Presidency, one of his supporters identified the Democrats as the party of "rum, Romanism and rebellion."

3

Scuffles with the Curriculum

THE invitation to attend Seattle's Centennial (1952) was stimulating, though unexpected. In it I was identified as one of her
illustrious sons, along with General Mark Clark and Edward R.
Murrow. In a touch of gallantry the welcoming committee also cited
Ella Raines, screen actress.

The salute was surprising even to one familiar with the excesses
of civic enthusiasm. I was in no sense a native son—nor was Clark
or Murrow. Neither my entrance to, nor exit from, Seattle created
any stir. Nor did my accomplishments in the nine years I lived
there rate a potlatch. The brows of indifferent students, of second-rate
pool and trumpet players, rarely are circled with the bay.

A failure in trade, Dad sought an activity free from bookkeeping.
A week's survey of Seattle converted him to that port. Seattle was
paving the streets which climbed its hills. The base of this operation
was sand and gravel, conveyed from waterfront bunkers in dump
wagons. To Dad hauling sand and gravel was a refinement of one
of his earlier jobs, whacking bulls on the Marias. It would be a
soft touch for a man who had freighted ore from the Little Rockies
through swirling drifts. Snow rarely fell in Seattle. Ice rarely filmed
its lakes.

The boxcar which brought Dad and me to Seattle in the summer of 1906 held eight horses, Loretta's piano, the Maney pots, pans and furnishings, and four stowaways. Not listed on the manifest were Charles Melson and son and two Newbys, smuggled aboard under cover of darkness. Technically I was a stowaway. Dad was the only certified passenger since he fed and watered the horses. To circumvent brakemen and conductors the rest of us burrowed into the furniture, only venturing out when Dad sounded the all clear. Though I slept on the kitchen range, I found the expedition exciting. My standards of travel were sketchy. This was my third train ride. The trip through the Rockies and the Cascades was breathtaking. When our car was sidetracked in Spokane Dad took me to the Davenport Hotel for dinner. This was my first exposure to city life. There was shaved ice on the sliced tomatoes, a touch of elegance that impressed me.

In Seattle Dad and I put up at a small hotel to await Mother and Loretta, luxuriating in a day coach with a stop-over in Great Falls to visit Mother's sister. Fanny Roach, an old Chinook friend, was the proprietor. The hotel faced the Third Avenue Theatre. A stock company was playing there. Admission prices were ten, twenty and thirty cents. A twenty-two-year-old Irish beauty was playing Topsy in *Uncle Tom's Cabin.* When not acting or rehearsing Carmen, Cinderella or Camille she dyed curtains, wheedled props from Seattle merchants and sold tickets. On her death in 1946, the daughter of James and Elizabeth Cooney was rated America's finest actress. The year before the New York drama critics unanimously named her Amanda Wingfield in *The Glass Menagerie* the best performance of the year. In the forty years since I first saw her, Laurette Taylor had come a long and agonizing way.

Because it was larger and because it faced the sea, Seattle awed me even more than Spokane. I ventured only a few blocks from the hotel lest I get lost. I feared that through some gesture, some blunder, I'd be branded a hayseed. The day after our arrival Dad and I saw Seattle play Los Angeles. This was my first professional ball game as well as my first trolley ride.

Nervous on the trolley, I perked up in the park. I knew a lot about the players, thanks to early research. I could rattle off the records of pitchers Rube Vickers and Virgil Garvin, fresh from tryouts with the Brooklyn Trolley Dodgers and the New York Highlanders. Vickers blanked Los Angeles that afternoon. His catcher was Cliff Blankenship. Blankenship is not enshrined in baseball's Hall of Fame at Cooperstown for he played less than one hundred games in the major leagues. But baseball owes him a great debt. Sold to Washington in 1907, Blankenship had played but a few games for the Senators when he was injured. Pending his recovery, manager Joe Cantillon sent him across the continent to inspect a young pitcher. The busher Blankenship brought back from Weiser, Idaho, was Walter Johnson.

In Chinook I had been a hotshot in classroom and sports. At Seattle High School I was a nonentity. Tossed in among strangers, I felt like an alien. I shrank from competitions, fearful my perform-ance would degrade me. I became a spectator rather than a player. I picked up caste and money psychoses. My fears reacted on my classwork. I hesitated to speak even when I knew the answers.

My first term over, I suffered another indignity. Dad decided I should drive a dump wagon during summer vacation. I had to get up at six to curry, brush and feed my horses so that we could be at the bunkers at eight. Each trip to the concrete mixer was an ordeal. The steepness of the hills necessitated a zigzag ascent. My horses slipped and fell straining up Yesler Way, victims of oil slick and the cable-car tracks. Their knees bled. I bled inwardly. Sighting a classmate I'd turn my head and try to recede into the cargo. My plight was comparable to Willie Baxter's in Booth Tarkington's *Seventeen*. With this exception: I had no romantic problems.

Convinced I was outcast, I solaced myself reading. After ten pages of *The Three Musketeers,* my hair was on fire. For months I thrilled over Porthos, Athos, Aramis and Lady de Winter, over Edmond Dantès and his victims in *The Count of Monte Cristo.* Critic Richard Watts of the New York *Post* has called me "the D'Artagnan of the press agents." I rejoice in the epithet. In my private pantheon the Gascon is on the same shelf with Matty and Ney. About this time, I made another hair-raising discovery.

The Sporting News and *Sporting Life,* two weeklies devoted to
baseball, crawled with box scores of the major and minor league
teams, with batting and fielding averages, with reports on twenty
pennant races. My ecstasy approximated that Margaret Webster
might experience on flushing the first folio of *Macbeth.* The time
necessary to memorize and analyze the material in these journals
curtailed my appreciation of French, Cicero, gerunds and gerundives,
and 3.1416.

While I was boning up on third basemen in the Three I League,
my father was working like a coolie that I might have an education.
On my graduation from Seattle High School, I enrolled at the
University of Washington. Dad wished me to become a lawyer.
Most officeholders were lawyers. Brooding over a major, I made
a quick decision when told the curriculum embraced a School of
Journalism. My reasoning was elementary. Qualified to practice
journalism, I might become a sports writer. Sports writers got into
baseball games free. They traveled with the teams.

Startled to learn I had any choice in professions, my father
capitulated. It was a relief to know clipping old newspapers wasn't
to be my life's work. With an A.B. degree as my target, shortly
I was confused by the Malthusian theory, Racine's comedies, and
trigonometry, but was elated by the racy goings-on in *The Canterbury
Tales.* Merle Thorpe, later editor of *The Nation's Business,* headed
the journalism school. One of its courses was devoted to the short
story. Mr. Thorpe read us one of his own compositions, asked us
to criticize it. Eager to oblige, I pointed out its flaws, hinted it
lacked the fevers of Dumas. Thorpe reacted badly. He sought
applause, not analysis. Long since I learned to be wary of producers
and playwrights pleading for "your honest opinion." All wince if
the answer is short of an endorsement.

In my sophomore year, I wore white tie and tails for the first
and last time. This outfit was rented that I might be initiated into
Sigma Delta Chi, honorary journalism fraternity. Since then, I have
been a member of but one other tong, honorary or otherwise—the
American Federation of Labor local which covers the activities
of my craft.

I have said I sought an A.B. degree. I didn't get it, though I pursued it for four years plus. It eluded me, in part, because my academic and poolhall phases conflicted. I spent more time trying to bank the six ball in the side pocket than on homework. I ignored textbooks. I didn't ignore many because I didn't buy many. I could have been jugged for misappropriation of funds. I used my textbook money to improve my drawshot. To prepare for Introduction to Philosophy, I'd borrow the book of a classmate, then skim through the day's assignment. The trick was to avoid being questioned in class, if questioned to confuse the issue with a counter-question. Such strategies delayed exposure. The mid-term tests were my undoing. Then it was learned Descartes and Kant and I were strangers. In these crises I was consoled with the knowledge I had a private cue at Brown and Hulen's Billiard Parlor on Second Avenue.

In turn, I was tripped up in chemistry, economics and French. My marks in English, history and journalism courses were satisfactory. After one semester I had so many conditions I was suspended for a half term. This forced me to lead a double life. Fearing my father's wrath when my nonfeasance was discovered, I left home and returned at the same hours as before my disgrace. My deception was aided by experiments in a new field—the theatre.

Remember my fellow stowaways in the boxcar? One of these, Vernon Melson, told me of a play he had seen at the Moore Theatre. Shocked that a man would squander pool money on such nonsense, I sneered at him. He sneered right back. The show hadn't cost him a cent. He'd seen it from a $2 chair in return for an hour of ushering. For similar service, one night each week, he could see every attraction that visited the Moore.

Melson's disclosure stunned me. How long had this been going on? How could I qualify? If commissioned not only would I see a play each week, but for a night would escape the pretense of homework. In three years in Seattle I had seen but two plays, stock productions of *The Girl of the Golden West* and *The Devil*. The theatre was a luxury the Maneys couldn't afford.

Melson presented my credentials to the Moore's head usher and assured him of my agility and industry. Shortly I was accepted as a volunteer. I was given the Tuesday-night patrol, assigned a locker and fitted into a uniform that included a starched dickey, black bowtie and a jacket with crimson lapels. I had taken the first step in a labyrinth that would lead me to Broadway, Tallulah Bankhead, Billy Rose, Orson Welles and other disorders.

I was not the first man to get his start as an usher, nor would I be the last. Harry Truman once patrolled the aisles of the Orpheum in Kansas City and producer Earl Carroll was a balcony guide in Pittsburgh. Early in their New York phase author-editor E. B. White ushered at the Metropolitan Opera House, playwright Tennessee Williams at the Strand, and Lauren Bacall at the St. James. Bette Davis got her start as an usher in a Cape Cod summer theatre.

My first whiff of the theatre fired me with a new ambition. After two nights on an aisle I was determined to become a full-time operative. Four such stalwarts were necessary because of the erratic attendance of volunteers. My progress at the Moore was spectacular. Within two years I was taking tickets at the main entrance, salary $8 a week. Successively I had been volunteer, full-time usher, head usher, doorman.

Unchallenged by movies, radio or television, the theatre flourished in Seattle and throughout the land. The city had three vaudeville theatres—the Orpheum, the Pantages and the Empress—two stock companies, and the Moore and the Grand Opera House for touring attractions. Today Seattle's only theatre is the Moore, recently reclaimed from the movies.

Most of the stars came to the Moore. There I saw George M. Cohan in *George Washington, Jr.,* David Warfield in *The Music Master,* Forbes-Robertson in *The Passing of the Third Floor Back,* James K. Hackett in *Monsieur Beaucaire,* Henry Miller, whose son Gilbert I would later serve, in *Servant in the House,* Viola Allen in *The White Sister.* While at the Moore, I was entranced by *The Merry Widow, The Chocolate Soldier* and *Madame Sherry.* There I laughed at George Ade's *College Widow, Excuse Me* and *Twin Beds.* There I heard John McCormack, Calvé, Melba and Tetrazzini in concert. Since my high-school contact with Shakespeare I'd been enthralled by his tragedies. Now I saw them acted by Robert Mantell, Sothern and Marlowe, and Fritz Leiber. It's possible I was exposed to more culture at the Moore than I was at the university.

As a member of the Moore's staff and a confidant of manager Carl Reed, I received complimentary tickets to shows in other theatres. I saw Charles Chaplin in Fred Karno's *Night in an English Musical Hall* at the Empress in 1910. I have yet to see his peer on stage, screen or Chautauqua Circuit.

It wasn't only the plays and players that charmed me. With its marble walls, its carpeted ramps and rich furnishings, the Moore was the most luxurious building I'd ever entered. It exuded elegance. So did the voluptuaries who patronized it. Still another thing impressed me. The people who worked in the Moore seemed well paid for doing little, a formula at odds with my experience. They ate in expensive restaurants, stayed at the best hotels, rose late, and went to bed late. Ushering was a setup after service on a dump wagon.

Conditioned to the fourteen-hour day, I marveled at people who telescoped their work into three hours. Only the box-office staff functioned before noon. But the craftsmen who amazed me most were the press agents. These missionaries didn't seem to have working hours. In theory, a press agent traveled two or three weeks in advance of his attraction and loitered in Seattle as many days as it played there. This formula was breached as often as it was observed. Press agents chafed under regimentation. Occasionally one overacted his role and had to hole up for repairs. Rarely was he reprimanded. There were few informers among theatre managers. Managers, too, were subject to occupational mishaps.

The press agents who came to the Moore were gay fellows. They boasted of romantic conquests, of professional coups in Cincinnati and sprees in San Francisco. Widely traveled and handsomely paid, these cavaliers aroused my envy.

The myth persisted that the press agent could so inflame the community that all tickets would be sold before the curtain rose on the first performance. Failure did not disgrace him. He could

cite a dozen circumstances that had thwarted his design. I had yet
to learn that theatre folk are skilled in self-deception, unmatched in
their ability to alibi bad business.

The techniques of press agents varied. They were alike only in
the obscurity of their patterns. Advance men enjoyed many priv-
ileges. They could write passes, leave I.O.U.'s at the box office, and
turn in expense accounts following an evening with newspapermen.
They wenched, gambled and caroused. They came and went as they
pleased. They were responsible only to a remote employer.

I envied press agents for another reason. It was rumored they
could write, that their fictions and inventions stimulated the box-office.
They consorted with newspapermen. Indeed, many of them had been
newspapermen. They had fled that profession to gain more freedom
and make more money. Though most newspapermen looked upon
press agents as panderers, after three drinks together their philosophies
were indistinguishable.

Press agentry, I decided, provided an attractive alternative to
sports writing. Acting on this hunch, I started to peck at an Oliver
typewriter, one of the orneriest machines ever schemed by man. During my suspension, I haunted the Moore. There I tried to tame the
Oliver. It was a lopsided contest.

I slithered through two more years at the university after being
reinstated. My marks continued poor. I enthused only when writing
paragraphs for the University of Washington *Daily*. This experience
might be useful when I started to immortalize actors or outfielders.

A manifesto isued by members of the *Daily* staff led to our
suspension. Colonel C. B. Blethen, editor and publisher of the
Seattle *Times* was the target of our protest. The Colonel, eager
to show his academic muscles, presented the university with a
campanile and a set of musical chimes. The bells could toll the
hours, summon laggards to classes, and ring out for athletic victories.
The faculty was shocked when the rebels demanded that the tower
be uprooted and returned to the Colonel. We hinted that the origin
of the Blethen fortune was reprehensible, that acceptance of the
gongs would amount to an endorsement of the donor, his works
and practices. The Board of Regents was all for sending us to Devil's

Island. But after a lot of palaver we were let off with a warning. All of us felt better for our protest, though chagrined that we were denied the joys of martyrdom. For all I know, the chimes still set the echoes flying. The Seattle *Times* still prevails in spite of Hearst and high water.

A pimply 135-pounder, I did not participate in sports at Washington. During my stay there the football team did not lose a game, nor did it lose one in the college generation that followed. The coach was a lank, dour Scot named Gilmore Dobie. Dobie had been a star quarterback at the University of Minnesota and had coached at North Dakota State for three years. To ensure success at Washington, he brought his Dakota aces with him. A tackle and a halfback who had served him for three years added to their yardage and prestige in their four years on Puget Sound. The tackle could punt sixty yards into the wind. When enrolled as a freshman at Washington, he boasted a mustache, a wife and two children.

Concurrent with, but unrelated to, my stay at Washington, the school's oarsmen gained prominence. The first crew was coached by Hiram Conibear, former trainer for the Chicago White Sox, who had never rowed a stroke. Elmer Leader, who coached Yale's scullers for twenty years, was in that shell, as was Rusty Callow, present coach at Pennsylvania. Nine Washington crews won the four-mile race at the Poughkeepsie regatta in twenty-two starts.

Elmer Leader was one of my classmates, as was his twin brother, Ed. Both played on Dobie's elevens. Another classmate, Charley Mullen, was a part-time first baseman for the New York Yankees for three years. But my association with these and other campus heroes was sketchy. I attended no proms nor hops. No fraternities sought me out. I was a barbarian. Caste-conscious, I shrank from intruding on my betters. It never occurred to me that I might atone for my social inadequacies through academic excellence. I nursed the notion that only the dull studied. Bogged down in this delusion, I decided to survive by my wits.

My father was dismayed by my low marks and my failure to engage in campus activities. Three times he called on my faculty adviser in an effort to find out what ailed me. Each time he threatened

to dismember me if I didn't pull myself together. Any jury in the
land would have acquitted him on the first ballot. My conduct was
oafish—a shameful reward for the sacrifices of my parents.

The hope that I could coast to a degree faded when my class
was graduated. Hobbled by conditions, I was denied a diploma.
But I was indifferent to this disgrace. Shortly I'd be off to New York.
John Cort, proprietor of the Moore, was to send two all-star vaudeville shows on transcontinental tours. One was to be headed by Anna
Held, the other by Lillian Russell. Four of the Moore staff were
to serve with these carnivals. I would be one of three press agents
to precede Miss Held as she stormed from New York to California
and back.

There were theatres named for John Cort in New York, Chicago
and San Francisco. He was a power in the Pacific Northwest. He
booked theatres in Portland, Tacoma and Spokane. From Carl Reed,
manager of the Moore, he learned of my journalistic studies, and of
my experiments with the Oliver. On this evidence he decided I was
qualified to herald Miss Held. There may have been another reason
for his gamble. Of all the employees at the Moore, I was the only
one who had ever been inside a college. Manager Reed, treasurer
Bernard Klawans and Robert Harvey, Reed's secretary by day and
coat-room operator by night, were the others tapped for foreign
service. My salary was to be $40 a week, five times my fee as
ticket taker.

Only because the Considines dabbled in the theatre did Dad condone my employment at the Moore. To a man who had hunted buffalo
and whacked bulls in the Black Hills, the theatre was a sissy business
and its workmen little better than vagrants. Mother was enchanted
by the theatre. She was thrilled by its illusion and excitements, its
color and gaiety. I was able to wangle passes for her and Loretta
and they saw most of the attractions that played the Moore. Dad
scorned them. An evening in the theatre had little appeal to a man
who had to be up at six and work until after dark.

As the time for our departure neared, doubt assailed me. What
were my qualifications for the job I was about to take? I was ill
equipped to tussle with the unknown. A hotshot at Second and

Virginia, I would be a provincial at Forty-second and Broadway. Should I fail, I'd be stranded three thousand miles from my base. The prospect chilled my blood. Seeking a slogan, I found solace in Farragut's "Damn the torpedoes. Go ahead."

4

Me and Anna Held and Izaak Walton

ON the trip to New York I feigned nonchalance though I had never slept or eaten on a train, save on that freight car in our escape from Montana. My ignorance of Pullman practice made my pose transparent. Dining and sleeping cars crawled with booby traps for the inexperienced. Our Sunday stopover in Chicago bucked me up. At Comisky Park, Ty Cobb clubbed Eddie Cicotte for three hits. (That's the Eddie Cicotte who with six mates sold out to the gamblers in the 1919 World Series.) Not until I saw Red Grange race for four touchdowns against Michigan in the first quarter at Champaign in '24 was I so thrilled again.

New York scared me stiff. Its crowds seemed hostile. Alone in its canyons, I felt deserted. What lunacy caused me to think I could be a press agent? I could barely hammer out a sentence on the accursed Oliver. Facing any other typewriter, I blacked out. I knew little of the function of a press agent. In Seattle I had been fascinated by their habits rather than their skills. I scented doom.

The odor sharpened when Richard Lambert, Cort's general press agent, told me to go to the Pennsylvania Station to check my cut trunk. A cut trunk was a multi-trayed chest in which press agents carried electros and matrixes for newspapers without engraving plants.

Lambert's suggestion panicked me. I had never owned a trunk. To question anyone would expose my ignorance. I don't recall how this snafu was solved. Somebody solved it because the trunk was at the theatre in Richmond, Virginia, the scene of my initiation.

I spent a week in New York before being commissioned. At the fabulous Hippodrome I saw fifty chorus girls disappear under water, never to emerge. (Twenty-two years later I would be comforting Billy Rose as he prodded *Jumbo* in this same Hippodrome.) From a gallery seat at Hammerstein's Victoria I saw a variety show. Willie Hammerstein, who managed the Victoria, was the father of Oscar Hammerstein, author of the lyrics for *Oklahoma!* and *South Pacific.* I saw Laurette Taylor in *Peg o' My Heart* at the Cort Theatre.

During my stay in New York I was bleary-eyed, ravaged by hay fever. I asked about the Considine brothers and their saloon. It was across the street from Cort's offices. I loitered in front of it and looked through its swinging doors but never entered. It seemed unlikely men of their note would care to palaver with a second cousin they'd never seen.

I was to be the twenty-four-hour man, last of the three press agents who would precede Anna Held in her *All Star Jubilee.* It was my job to tidy up loose publicity ends initiated by my predecessors and solve last-minute crises. If the ticket sale was sluggish, I was to stimulate it, if possible start a stampede to the box office. The thought of starting a stampede or resolving a crisis numbed me. And I had another fear. Miss Held was highly sensitive to publicity. Wasn't she the heroine of the milk-bath legend? My chill worsened.

Anna Held was forty and fading. She was still singing "I Just Can't Make My Eyes Behave," a ballad she had introduced in *The Little Duchess* twelve years earlier. She was chic and had a French accent. She had come-hither eyes, the remnants of an hourglass figure, and little talent. She was a Paris music-hall singer when Ziegfeld met her in 1895. Aroused by Miss Held's contours and aromas, he brought her to America and starred her in a number of musical comedies. After fifteen years of warfare, the two were divorced in 1912. The trial set a new high in recriminations. It was

Cort's contention, subsequently proved erroneous, that the particulars of the charges would add to Miss Held's box-office might.

Anna Held and Lillian Russell were washed up when John Cort signed them at $3,000 a week each. In their heyday both had been page 1 pets. Cort felt their names would be box-office dynamite in "the sticks." The tours were hit-and-run operations. Grab the loot and get out of town. Half of *Jubilee* was a tabloid musical. In this Miss Held was abetted by six chorus boys, six chorus girls, a leading man and a comic. An olio of variety acts preceded her contribution. This olio embraced an Irish tenor, a Chinese magician, a bicycle act, a dramatic sketch, a piano soloist and a male comedy team. To hasten our getaway after performances, thus avoid reprisals, the company traveled by special train. Miss Held had a private car with bath. In the traditions of major vaudeville the company would play two performances daily.

In keeping with my title of twenty-four-hour man, I was in Richmond on Saturday morning preceding the Monday opening. At the theatre a telegram awaited me. This unnerved me. I had never received a telegram before. I associated such messages with death and disaster. It was from Mr. Cort and it read: "Arrange to have show hauled on Sunday."

The theatre manager told me I'd have to get a permit from the chief of police. Eager to pass my first test, I ran to the police station. The chief had left for a picnic at Jamestown. When was he coming back? No one knew. Desolated, I returned to the theatre. The house manager told me not to worry. He'd get the permit from the chief on his return that night. But he could use a stick of copy on the arrival of Miss Held and company for the *News-Leader*. A "stick" of copy? The term had never turned up at the journalism school. I was victimized by semantics.

Dedicated to my itinerary, I was off for Norfolk at dusk. I didn't explore that port. I was brooding over the Richmond chief of police, off on a picnic on the one day he was needed! Lonely, fearful, I retired early. The telephone rang at midnight. I had another telegram. "Take first train back here," it read. It was from Richmond and was signed "Cort."

The jig was up. I would be cashiered in front of the entire company and sent back to Seattle in disgrace. All because the police chief was picnic-crazy. I pitched and tossed all night. At dawn I retreated to Richmond. My alarms were groundless. I was to remain with the company. It would be my responsibility to see that the special train was ready after each night performance. I was an ex-press agent after one day's service. This demotion didn't grieve me. Traveling with the company would be more exciting and less lonely. I wasn't a transportation expert, but trains would be child's play after those telegrams.

That fifteen-week tour was a rich experience. When it ended I was a wiser young man. Through observation of performers at work and at play, I learned things listed in none of the almanacs. Their tribal customs, sexual practices and conduct under fire marked them as people apart. Travel doubled my knowledge of geography. We ranged as far north as Duluth, as far south as San Antonio. We played San Diego, near the Mexican border, and Vancouver, British Columbia. We played a matinee in Rome, Georgia, that night in Anniston, Alabama. In a day we confused Carolinians in Goldsboro and Wilmington. Together at the theatre and on the train at night, the players reinforced the adage "familiarity breeds contempt." Feuds were a dime a dozen. Intramural romances flared up like brush fires in the Poconos. Most popular member of the company was the stagehand who iced the beer. The chorus men leaned to the epicene. Petulant and peevish, these types held midnight rituals "in drag." Garbed in women's clothes they'd invoke dark curses on fancied enemies. The company's musical headliner was a narcotic addict. When his snow ran low he'd forge a prescription.

Our train was made up of two standard Pullman cars, a drawing-room car, Miss Held's private car, a day coach and two baggage cars. We had the same porters and the same train crew throughout the safari. The day coach was for the bicycle act. Refusing to pay Pullman fares, the Charles Ahern pedalers sat up all night. Civil war raged between the sleepers and the drinkers. All had two problems in common—bathing and laundry. Some of us were a touch gamy on detraining in New York. The pilgrimage lost

$30,000. The company's last jump was from Youngstown, Ohio, to New York. Sometime during the night parties unknown invaded the drawing room of the orchestra leader. While he dreamed of Brahms and Beethoven, they sheared off the exposed half of his beard. His screams in the morning were tonic to the ears of performers whose tempos he had fouled up throughout the tour.

During a two-week trek through Texas, I resumed my post as twenty-four-hour man. I can't remember why. The suspicion that I was expendable mounted. This fear was confirmed in Seattle. Through his manager Cort suggested that I withdraw. The tour was nearing its close. If I resigned in Seattle I'd be saved the return fare from New York. Though shaken by this cue, I ignored it. To be dropped in Seattle would be the crowning indignity. That's what I thought. But a week after the show closed I was foraging at free-lunch counters in Eighth Avenue saloons. Unemployed and under-nourished, I wrote my father. As always he rescued me. I returned to Seattle in a day coach. Soon I was taking tickets again at the Moore.

That summer I worked in a film exchange. Later I prowled small towns in Washington and Oregon with a tin can containing the six reels which made up Rex Beach's screenplay, *The Spoilers*. The picture was shown on a percentage basis. I accompanied it to see that the film company received its share of the receipts. In the spring of 1915, I received another telegram. It was from Carl Reed, former manager of the Moore. He had been named manager of a variety theatre in upper Manhattan. Could I come on to serve as his aide?

His wire found me flat. My father and mother had moved to Corfu, a ghost town in the interior of Washington. Their departure reduced me to vagrancy. Thanks to the Moore's night watchman, I slept on a couch in the ladies' room, covered by ushers' coats. Because of the Japan Current Seattle has a mild winter climate. Loretta, employed as a secretary, gave me eating money. To her I now turned. She loaned me day-coach fare to New York. My re-entry to Manhattan was shabby. On the train I contracted the itch. I had about $5 in cash. The variety theatre which Reed was to manage folded up in a week. I was on the beach again.

That summer was a nightmare. I had no money, no job. I owe my survival to Charley Harris. I met Charley through John McCormick, who had served in my ushers' corps at the Moore. John was in the box office in San Francisco when I arrived with Anna Held. Harris had come to California with Broncho Billy Anderson, first screen cowboy. He and McCormick had bought the Washington and Oregon rights to *Tillie's Punctured Romance* and cleaned up with the Marie Dressler comedy. I had McCormick to thank for the film exchange job and for the expedition with *The Spoilers*. He gave me a letter of introduction to Harris when I fled the ladies' room at the Moore.

On my arrival in New York I found Harris was idle. Gallant and generous, he said I could move in with him. He shared a flat with his brother Dude and his cousin Sidney, on West 110th Street. Technically this flat was Broncho Billy's. Anderson lived at the Claridge but used the hideaway for impulsive trysts. More than once we were routed out in the small hours of the morning to walk the streets until Anderson's ardor abated.

Since he was to manage Anderson's Longacre Theatre that fall Charley could get advances on his salary. He had an office on West Forty-second Street. With Dude he had operated an agency for the screen extras who thronged the ferry to Fort Lee, New Jersey, each morning. The agency foundered but the furniture remained. We loafed here by day and at the Elks Club after dark. We missed few meals. An acquaintance of Charley's was our benefactor that summer. This San Francisco bellboy had $7,500 in cash, a sum he had received in damages after falling down an elevator shaft. Eager to see New York, he chose Charley as his pilot. In doing so he acquired three co-pilots. Dude, Sidney and I tailed him at mealtimes. Lust for survival muted our shame.

For a month Charley and I were self-supporting. Broncho Billy, a rabid baseball fan, was backing the inventor of an electric scoreboard. This contraption was a mess of wires and metal shutters. The shutters popped up in response to impulses tapped on a telegrapher's key. When skillfully operated the board itemized a game convulsively.

The inventor installed a board in the abandoned agency and commissioned Charley to sell duplicates to saloon proprietors. The enactment of a game was calculated to increase consumption among customers. If the prospect showed interest Charley dragged him to the Forty-second Street trap for a demonstration. Because of my knowledge of baseball, and despite my ignorance of mechanics, I was the demonstrator. This led to a lot of confusion. When I miscued every fuse in the building blew out. The other tenants screamed protests. The maintenance company regarded me as a menace. I was sacked when I refused to water the inventor's radiator. Let him fill his own radiator. I had been engaged as a technician, not a caddie.

Shortly after the bellboy limped back to California, Carl Reed sent for me. He was about to publish a magazine, *The American Angler*.

I couldn't have been more surprised had he told me he was to take up basket weaving. He knew as little of the refinements of fishing as I did. The only live fish I'd seen were darting about in a tank in a grill window. Reed knew less about publishing than he did about angling. But there was nothing to worry about, he assured me. Charles Bradford was to be the editor.

Bradford was a press agent. He first visited Seattle in advance of John Mason in *As a Man Thinks*. Hot-tempered, profane and cynical, Bradford was a diabetic wisp of a man dedicated to Izaak Walton and *The Compleat Angler; or, the Contemplative Man's Recreation*. Walton's classic was Bradford's bible. Following a blasphemous tirade, Bradford would cite his hero: "Anglers are men of mild, and sweet and peaceful spirits. Moses and the Prophet Amos were both anglers." That a man could be concerned with both the bluster of the theatre and the simplicities of "the gentle art" was a paradox. The truth was Bradford loathed press agentry. He longed to edit a periodical in which he could worship the Master publicly.

Whatever my fears about fishing and publishing, I couldn't quibble when offered employment. Presently I was up to my ears in Parmachenee Belles and Grizzly Hackles and tossing around "piscatorial," "ichthyological" and other finny adjectives. As aide to Bradford and Reed my activities varied. In the morning, I might compose a plea to subscribers, that afternoon compose a warning: "Keep your fly on the water. Trout don't live in trees." Unable to write technical copy, I became symposium crazy. I badgered anglers about their preferences in dry flies, the relative gameness of black bass and bluefish. Through this ruse I received replies from David Starr Jordan, Cecil B. De Mille, Robert W. Chambers, Gifford Pinchot, Irvin S. Cobb, Ernest Thompson Seton and H. T. Webster.

My wage was sub-coolie. I lived in a rented room in the flat of a seamstress on Washington Heights. To supplement my income I looked for a door to guard at night. Through Reed's pull I was named one of three ticket takers at the Century when it opened with *The Century Girl* in November of 1916. The Century was luxurious. Called the New Theatre when erected by millionaires as a home for repertory, now it was operated by Charles Dillingham and Florenz Ziegfeld. Paintings from the brush of Joseph Urban adorned its walls. My uniform weighed ten pounds and resembled that worn by Murat at Borodino.

I took this assignment in stride. The tickets didn't differ in size or quality from those I had torn in Seattle. Again I was working a fifteen-hour day.

About this time I began heckling Portus Baxter, sports editor of the Seattle *Post-Intelligencer.* My letters covered Pacific Coast ballplayers operating in the big leagues. I was elated when Baxter printed these. I wrote a sonnet to Buck Herzog for columnist Grantland Rice. Herzog, Giant second baseman, was my latest hero. Twice I penetrated F.P.A.'s "Conning Tower." Flushed with success I wrote guest columns for Louis Lee Arms, sports commentator for the *Tribune.* Joseph Mulvaney, later drama editor of Hearst's *American,* summed up my activities thus: "You have touched the nadir in life's cycle, an unpaid columnist."

New York's flower and chivalry turned out for the opening of *The Century Girl.* The Dillingham-Ziegfeld trademark assured a Tiffany production. The cast brimmed with names—Elsie Janis,

Sam Bernard, Frank Tinney, Leon Errol, Hazel Dawn, Maurice and
Walton. The tense ticket takers were drilled for hours lest we curdle
the ceremonies by an awkward act. As we went to our posts these
words rang in our ears: "Under no circumstances, under no pretext,
admit anyone not holding a ticket." Faithful to my oath, I brushed
aside two gentlemen who tried to violate my portal. So they were
Dillingham and Ziegfeld, eh? I wasn't taken in by such a device.
Nor did I flinch on learning they *were* Dillingham and Ziegfeld.
If there were to be exceptions to the edict let them be posted for
all to see.

One of three doormen at the Century, I welcomed solo service
at the Morosco on its opening in 1917. I remained there until
September of 1919. In that interval, I continued to taunt readers
of *The American Angler*. When Bradford died I was named associate
editor. My salary jumped to $40 weekly. I received $12 for my
defense of the Morosco door. These fees enabled me to repay my
sister and lay up a surplus. My Sundays were spent at the Polo
Grounds. I exulted the Saturday afternoon the Giants ran up
their twenty-sixth consecutive victory. I almost died when Heinie
Zimmerman chased Eddie Collins across the plate in the last
game of the 1917 World Series. Baseball was my one extravagance.
I scorned lunch. Later when I could afford lunch I found it made
me ill. To this day I fast from breakfast to dinnertime.

My ignorance of angling proved my undoing. Members of the
fly and bait casting clubs which clutter the land were holding their
annual tournament in Chicago. These purists compete in accuracy
and distance contests with wet fly, dry fly, bait or plug. Weight
of rod, size of line and other tackle twaddle are determining factors.
The high priest of the convention sought to honor me. As editor
of America's only all-angling magazine, wrote this dastard, I should
be the Number 1 judge. A corps of experts would aid me.

This looked like a plot to expose me. Reed and his allies long
had tried to have the *Angler* named the official organ of the fly
and baitcasting clubs. With this goal in their grasp, they would be
fouled by an editor who didn't know a bass bug from a pork strip.
I'd led a charmed life for three years but my luck had run out.

The shadowy figures behind Reed ordered my dismissal. I found consolation in the biblical injunction, "The fishers also shall mourn, and all they that cast an angle into the brooks shall lament, and . . . languish."

My service at Izaak's altar wasn't profitless. I had written thousands of words on a subject I knew nothing about. I had read and edited copy, written heads, wrestled with galley and page proofs. I had publicly apologized to author Zane Grey after a contributor had libeled him. I rejoiced on hearing Robert Davis, famed Munsey editor, swear between syllables, "You're under no obli-goddam-gations to me," he snorted when I sought to thank him for some verse he had written for the *Angler*.

My position was perilous. On leaving college, I was making $8 a week as a ticket taker. Six years and more had elapsed. When *Cappy Ricks* opened at the Morosco in September, I'd be getting $12 a week. In the first flush of employment on the *Angler* I married Frances O'Hara, a girl I met and wooed in Seattle. For months we had shared the seamstress' cell. Now we luxuriated in a four-flight walk-up on West 157th Street. These quarters were modest but their site was magnificent. The flat was five minutes from the Polo Grounds.

5

Coast-to-Coast Crusader

CHARLEY HARRIS, friend of the fortunate who fell down the elevator shaft, was now managing the Longacre Theatre for Broncho Billy Anderson. Anderson had made a fortune as screen actor and producer. He was the "A," George Spoor the "S," in Essanay Films. For them Charles Chaplin made *The Tramp* and *Carmen,* salary $250 a week. Spoor revolted when Anderson suggested they sign Chaplin to a long-term contract at $1,000 a week. So Chaplin went to Mutual Films at $10,000 a week. Incensed at his partner's astigmatism, Anderson sold out to Spoor. Like many another Hollywood nabob, Anderson wished to explore a loftier field—the stage. Even its partisans looked upon the screen as a cheap intruder, a medium for the low-born and the unwashed. (However loudly they protest, most of the screen's anointed are still cursed with variations of this complex.)

Betrayed by the fly casters, with the Morosco dark and the Giants on the road, I sought out Charley. Anderson was about to produce *Frivolities of 1919,* an expensive song-and-dance show. He needed a press agent. Charley was sure I could qualify. If I'd bring him copies of the columns I'd written for Arms, he'd show them to Anderson.

Anderson was a sucker for baseball and for those who wrote about it. I was as good as hired.

I was to meet Anderson Wednesday morning. The Arms columns were on his desk. Charley had briefed him on my background. Anderson didn't look up from his newspaper when I entered his office. Numbed by this reception, I was considering retreat when his phone rang. His chat over, Anderson asked me who I was and what I wanted. I was the young man Harris had suggested as press agent for *Frivolities*. "I don't need a press agent," he said. There didn't seem to be any point in continuing this unilateral argument, so I left. At the elevator I met Charley. "How did you come out?" he asked. I told him. "He's nuts," said Charley. "Wait here a minute." Shortly he returned. "Go in and see him again," he said. Charley had made up Anderson's mind. I was hired.

Was this a delayed dividend on my devotion to baseball? The payoff on my juvenile lunacy? It was ironic that I should be engaged as a press agent because of my skill as a volunteer sports writer. But had I been? It's a moot point. I'm not sure Anderson ever read the columns. But Charley rated me as a lesser Runyon. I have him to thank for my start in the profession I've pursued ever since.

My qualifications for a publicity post? I could tattoo a typewriter. Though my prose was a touch rococo, I could write a readable story. As usher, ticket taker, twenty-four-hour man and transportation expert, I had spent six years in and about the theatre. A soubrette should be no problem to a man lately at grips with muskellunge. I knew little of craft routine. The shop talk of veteran advance men was dismaying. According to them press agentry was a dark and complex art. Years were needed to master its fundamentals. Later I learned that all theatre executives suffer from similar delusions. To a company manager making up a payroll is a feat comparable to squaring the circle. Moving a troupe from Saginaw to Cincinnati, by press-agent standards, paled the ordeal of Hannibal in his passage of the Alps. The more trivial the task, the more awesome the language used to inflate it.

Green and groping, I publicized *Frivolities* in jerky fashion. In one of my first releases I cited Joseph Gallagher as an addition to the cast. This brought a wail from Mr. Gallagher. *Frivolities* was his first New York show and perhaps his last, he said, and I had fouled up his name. He was Edward, not Joseph Gallagher. Edward's pessimism was groundless. Within six years he and his partner would be ruled "unique and extraordinary" by a Supreme Court judge. Remember Gallagher and Shean?

Frivolities' first performance in Providence ran until 12:30 A.M. Had the second act been played it would have lasted until daylight. Stage traffic bogged down shortly after the curtain rose. The massive and clumsy production defied efforts of the crew to manipulate it. Scene changes scheduled to be made in a minute dragged out for five. Successive jams precluded introduction of the last-act lumber.

"It needs a lot of work," chanted the experts. This is the oldest response in the theatre's litany. For lack of a better motto it should be embossed on the theatre's shield. Many a musical show is a shambles in its first out-of-town performance. Costumes aren't finished and shoes don't fit. French horns are flat and prima donnas have laryngitis. Lines are fouled. Fuses are blown. Tempers are frayed. The theatre and its people scorn clock and calendar. Nothing is done on time. Nothing is delivered when promised. Curtains never rise at the advertised hour. As a witness of the Providence fiasco I felt relieved. I wasn't the only fumbler in the house.

Attempts to salvage *Frivolities* were delayed by the Actors Equity strike. On its opening at the Forty-fourth Street Theatre it was a dreary carouse. The critics lambasted the revue. Nettled by this verdict, Anderson retired to his hotel to remain incommunicado throughout the eight-week run.

It would be pleasant to say that I redeemed *Frivolities,* that by zeal and resource I prolonged its life. It would be pleasant, but it would be false. Shortly after the opening Claude Greneker, general press agent for the Shuberts, asked me: "Why doesn't Anderson hire someone to handle the ads?" He had. Me!

Though *Frivolities* was a flop Anderson decided to send it on tour. By this gesture he would confound the critics and recoup his losses. And there was a sentimental reason for this desperate act. *Frivolities* was his challenge to Ziegfeld, admitted Merlin of musical-show producers. It was proof that he was better than a two-reel cowboy. With it he hoped to make a triumphant return to San Francisco, where he owned and operated theatres. He had made his fortune in California. Success of *Frivolities* at the Casino would blot out memories of its New York defeat. But there was a flaw in his strategy. *Frivolities* had to play across the continent. It could lose its shirt before it reached San Francisco.

I didn't grieve over Anderson's gamble because I had a problem of my own. Through an office leak I learned the producer was looking for a more experienced press agent. Though chagrined, I couldn't protest. I was vulnerable, not to say expendable. Again Charley Harris stepped into the breach. With the opening at the Boston Opera House but two weeks away, I was told to continue. The reprieve was welcomed but it caught me unprepared. I set out for Boston with dark misgivings.

In Boston I would have to contend with A. Toxen Worm, press agent for the Shubert theatres there. Earlier Worm had held similar posts in Chicago and New York. Even veteran press agents were awed by Worm. He was a martinet and a perfectionist, bitter and sardonic. His scorn for the profession and for his employers was only exceeded by his contempt for the incompetent. It was an evil twist that made Boston my first port of call. This formidable man would identify me at once as an imposter. Stewing over my plight, I came to a spectacular conclusion. I'd tell him the truth.

A Dane, Worm had a bleak exterior. In a business in which garrulity is often taken for genius, he used words sparingly. Facing him, I confessed my inexperience. I told him of my ordeal in New York, of my lack of material. I was scared, I told him, but I was eager. If he would cue me on protocol and detail the requirements of newspapers, I'd undertake to function.

My confession didn't thaw Worm. Press agents called on drama editors each Tuesday, he said. He would accompany me. All material must be ready Monday evening and approved by him. In that idyllic day newspapers were hungry for theatre copy. The prose for Boston's seven newspapers added up to thousands of words: twenty feature stories, page-long blurbs for the Sunday drama sections, opening night and seat-sale announcements, daily paragraphs for drama columnists, fashion stories, women's page stories, photographs for Sunday layouts, suggestions for feature stories and interviews that might stir city editors. This was the minimum. Off-beat stunts and intrusions on editors of departments indifferent to press agents were so much velvet.

Had I been familiar with craft practice, or had earlier notice of my retention, I could have prepared much of this in New York. Now I must telescope two weeks' work into two days. Worm gave me a key to the press room and indicated a typewriter. His "this will do" after he had glanced through my blood-stained prose Monday evening were the most stimulating words I had heard in the theatre. Occasionally strangers entering the Morosco asked me, "Has anyone told you you look like George M. Cohan?" That had been my only previous caress.

Worm was an iconoclast. He had no illusions about press agentry. When I detailed my frustrations in New York, he dismissed them in cavalier fashion: "If you have a good show it will be showered with publicity if you are strong enough to answer the telephone. If it is inferior, people will shun it even though you hide diamonds under every seat." When Worm reigned in Chicago, a professional trollop achieved stardom in a melodrama. Under her name in the advertisements Worm ran this line: "First Time in a $2.00 House." Listening to me and other press agents pontificate on the fluctuations of the German mark and the French franc, he observed: "I believe, gentlemen, that during the war blood was at par."

The shy young man whom the city editor of the *Transcript* assigned to do a backstage story at *Frivolities* was Brooks Atkinson, then assistant to critic H. T. Parker. Today Atkinson is America's most influential drama critic.

I had come to Boston confused and panicky. Leaving it, I was relaxed, thanks to Worm. Some of Worm's scorn for the shabby and the phony had rubbed off on me. On his death, Worm devoted half his will to excoriating Chicago, waxing bitter over that city's cultural pretensions.

Frivolities limped into San Francisco in June. En route it shed two sister acts, a belly dancer and $20,000 of Anderson's money. Set up in his own theatre, *Frivolities* was panned by the reviewers and ignored by the public. The desperate producer felt all might be redeemed if he could get a star whose name had box office magic.

After a study of available wonder workers, Anderson sent me to Los Angeles to dicker with Will Rogers. Why didn't he go to see Rogers? Why didn't he call him on the telephone? It's unwise to parse the managerial mind. In it one may come upon *curiosae* that will freeze the marrow. Anderson's logic was impeccable, but his timing was atrocious. Over the telephone Rogers told me he had heard of *Frivolities* and had no desire to be immolated in it. His snub capped my despair. On the night ride down, I was flattered when asked to play poker with three strangers in their drawing room. I'll spare the congregation further details.

Frivolities' run at the Casino over, Anderson compounded his folly by inflicting the show on Merced, Stockton, Vallejo, Monterey, Napa and other whistle stops. As the revue began this death march, I received an offer to publicize the touring *Greenwich Village Follies*. This revue was enjoying an all-summer run in Chicago. I was to join it in the Loop, then precede it to California and back to New York. This was the first time a producer had sought my services. I gave Anderson two weeks' notice. If he was desolated, he masked his grief. I was elated. Convivial volunteers helped me celebrate. I awoke in a cell, victim of a policeman's prejudice. I had flouted authority when ordered to pipe down. The fine was nominal, the hangover epochal.

Next to New York San Francisco is my favorite city. It has color and style. Its climate is invigorating and its people civilized. It has excellent restaurants and skilled bartenders. At Herbert's, an all-night stag restaurant on Powell Street, one could breakfast on Persian melon, ham and eggs, toast and coffee for thirty-five cents. During my stay in San Francisco, I guzzled at Coffee Dan's and tippled at Tait's-on-the-Beach. I was trying to live up to my Seattle estimates of press-agent life. San Francisco was an excellent proving ground. Early in January of that year the country had bowed to prohibition. Word of this had not reached San Francisco in mid-July. Gin rickeys were on tap in soda fountains.

I scoured the country ahead of five successive *Greenwich Village Follies*. These tours started around Labor Day and continued into June. Twice I prowled from coast to coast. Each edition spent ten or twelve weeks in Chicago, a violent, noisy city. I brought the first pogo stick to Chicago. Conspiring with the city editor of the *Examiner,* I had *Follies* show girls demonstrate this spine-twister on a high-school playground. Two photographers were recording the exercise and I was dreaming of a page of photographs. Without warning the photographers bolted. Back at the theatre, I learned that Dion O'Banion, one of the city's distinguished hoods, had been shot down in his flower shop. O'Banion got three pages of photos the next morning, and later was given the largest funeral ever to snarl traffic in Cook County. I threw the pogo stick into the Chicago River.

The phone rang at daylight in my room at the Sherman. It was Ethel Davis, the comedienne. With members of the company, she had been whooping it up at Mike Fritzel's joint until the small hours. She was weaving out when two resident thugs intercepted her and volunteered to drive her to the Sherman. Instead they drove her to a South Side apartment, dragged her down a corridor, rifled her purse and stripped her of her jewels.

I accompanied Miss Davis to the LaSalle Street police station. Could Miss Davis identify her assailants? She could. Could she point out the house in which she'd been mugged? Miss Davis said she'd try. We got into a squad car with three detectives, drove to the South Side and started to cruise up and down streets. To our surprise, Miss Davis pointed out the house quickly. We went in and walked down the corridor. On the floor were the receipts for two money orders she had sent her mother in New Rochelle.

"Let's go through this place from cellar to attic," said one of the detectives. His enthusiasm waned when one of his mates asked: "How do you know an alderman doesn't live in this building?" Faced with this awful possibility, they drove us back to the Sherman. Miss Davis never recovered cash or jewels. All she received were threatening phone calls. If she didn't quit blabbing to the police she'd lose more than her diamonds, warned her callers.

I was discussing *l'affaire Davis* with Ed Mahoney, the Chicago

American's city editor. "How would you like to get your show on page 1 of every paper in town?" he asked. The prospect dazzled me. "How?" I asked. "I'll run stories on successive days about these threats," he said. "Then you hide Davis in a Milwaukee rooming house. When she doesn't show up for that night's performance, I'll break the story. She's been done away with. At best, kidnaping; at worst, murder. How about it?"

I thanked Mahoney and fled into the night. He had conceived a thing of beauty. Barring flaws in execution it would stir the nation. I wouldn't get more than five years if convicted as an accessory. The police dredged up two suspects. Miss Davis and others of the company at the Fritzel frolic were summoned to identify them. Will Morrissey, our comedian, was among those subpoenaed. When his name was called out, an attorney arose and said: "Your honor, my client is too drunk to appear in this courtroom."

In Chicago I received my oddest accolade. Gallagher and Shean, fresh from litigation with Florenz Ziegfeld, whose *Follies* they had fled, joined our show at the Garrick. The verses ending "Absolutely Mr. Gallagher, positively Mr. Shean" were known to everyone. The pair were hot copy and I concentrated the publicity on them. After the opening, I had a drink with Gallagher. He was glum. Their reception had been something short of an ovation. After a long silence Ed addressed me: "Know what I think? You overpublicized us."

Five years' exposure to musical-saw players, monologists, adagio dancers, ballerinas, female impersonators, trombone players, acrobats, wire walkers, blues singers, show girls, burnt-cork comics, ingénues and prima donnas convinced me they were all mad as hatters. In a crisis they behaved like Piutes full of vanilla extract. I was convinced of another thing. Association with them forever disqualified me for another trade. Normal conduct would confuse me. I'd survived a civil war involving four stage mothers. Forget the serpent's tooth. Forget the mutineers on the *Bounty*. Four stage mothers can create more havoc and raise more hell in a half hour than all the arsonists and subversives in the land. Perhaps I should define a stage mother. She is the parent of a prodigy who feels that her child will become

the world's youngest martyr unless she, the mother, haunts the
stage through every performance ready to attack with fang, stage
brace and talon those who would violate her sprig's rights. Lacking
such violation, she'll invent one. Most stage children are offensive
little monsters, but compared to their mothers they're seraphim out
of the ceiling of the Sistine Chapel.

Not all the players in those five *Greenwich Village Follies* brought
their mothers with them. The first one sheltered Ted Lewis, "high-
hatted tragedian of song," chanting "When My Baby Smiles at Me,"
as the laughing trombone chortled. Lewis and his band were show-
stoppers, as popular in Walla Walla as in Rector's whence they
came. Bert Savoy, notorious female impersonator, was a riot in
New York and Chicago. His reception in one-night stands couldn't
have been chillier had he been doing his act in Hindustani. Savoy
and his partner, Jay Brennan, were caviar to the general. Bert was
a trial to hotel managers. His suite was open to and prowled by
all comers day or night. When the samples of a shoe salesmen were
found under his cot in the Claypool in Indianapolis, he was suspect
under six statutes but was saved when his opponent turned up full
of aspirin and contrition. All grieved when Bert was killed by
lightning on a New York beach. When the show went on tour, he
was replaced by Karyl Norman, billed as "The Creole Fashion Plate."
The stagehands called him "The Creole Chafing Dish."

Those musical-saw players? Maddened by the scent of gin, the
smaller of the pair tried to force the lock on the room of the company
bootlegger in Minneapolis. Failing, he tried to crawl through the
transom. When he recovered consciousness, it was found he would
be unable to ply his blade for two weeks. His lower vertebrae had
been scrambled. He incurred no penalties. By theatrical standards,
he had been wounded while carrying out a dangerous mission. He
might be in line for a decoration.

As courier for these revues, I visited most of the larger cities of
the nation, and Toronto, too. I became familiar with the customs
and folklore of many communities. The manager of the theatre in
Bismark, North Dakota, received me in the Western Union office.
At the Garrick in Detroit, the stairs to the executive roost could

be raised and lowered by pulleys, thus assure press agents and thirsty newspaper and railroad men privacy during their devotions. A departing publicist, unaware the drawbridge was up, stepped off into space and plummeted to the concrete pit below.

Press agents ran risks consuming native broths. In Billings, Montana, awaiting the midnight train to Butte, I felt it would be churlish to refuse the tonic offered me by the house manager. He had an author's pride in it. First he bought a gallon of grape juice. Then he removed the cork and let fermentation rage.

When I came to, I was sharing a cell with a Chinese vagrant. The turnkey agreed to let me telephone the theatre manager. After a long wait, the porter who answered told me his master was asleep on the floor of a balcony box and couldn't be wakened. I was fined $25 for unseemly conduct. As I fled this jug I was grabbed by two strangers and hauled back before the judge. My captors were from an insurance company. They demanded $75 for the plate-glass window in the Masonic Temple Building.

This charge lifted my scalp! I didn't know Billings had a Masonic Temple. They reassured me. I had been knocked through it by the arresting officer. He had resented my advice or something. I demanded my accuser be produced. He didn't report until six that night, I was told. Pending his return, I could return to the dungeon. Already late for Butte, with my character witness dreaming in a balcony box, I paid the $75.

A touring press agent led a salty, carefree life, so long as his attraction prospered. Most of his traffic was with newspaper and railroad men and other press agents. "Entertaining Press" was a standard item on expense accounts. Producers condoned the practice. Some thought editors might be more generous with space and critics less caustic, if wined and dined. It was a shabby suspicion. I have yet to meet a critic who could be decoyed by a quart of Canadian Club. Though contemptuous of so patent a slander, press agents found "Entertaining Press" an acceptable fiction under which to group nonprofessional outlays. The term might embrace crap-game losses, wenching, or a detour from the show's route. I drank with dramatic editors only when I found them stimulating. I had a block against

"Entertaining Press." I concentrated on entertaining myself. There was no reason the management should be clipped for my indulgence.

Road press agents loafed during July and August. One summer I was lured to Los Angeles by my old Seattle friend, John McCormick, then with First National Pictures. He brought me on, so he said, to supervise the page ads his company ran each Sunday in the Los Angeles *Times*. My friend was wooing star Colleen Moore by mail. She was on location in the High Sierras and John was doing a lot of hand wringing. To allay his anguish we'd mix a pint of gin with a pint of orange ice, stir vigorously, and swill down. Thus soothed we'd drive to Buster Keaton's studio to play scrub baseball, or to a cabin on the beach. This was my first association with screen and camera. It was also my first association with earthquakes. It was considered poor form to mention tremors. Only when my couch was showered with plaster, when my hotel buckled and shuddered, was I convinced.

In another July I was solicited by Herman Mankiewicz, assistant to drama editor George S. Kaufman on the *New York Times*. An occasional critic, Mr. Mankiewicz was eager to become a producer. He was about to try out *Love 'Em and Leave 'Em* at Asbury Park. If it came up to expectations, he'd present it in New York. Herman's budget was leaking. He couldn't afford to hire a manager. Would I serve him during the tryout? The suggestion that I function without fee was proof of his affection. The bathing was wonderful. The sea air would do me good. Herman was a gay fellow with a sharp wit. I consented.

Love 'Em and Leave 'Em was a comedy by John V. A. Weaver. It created no stir at the beach. Box-office trade was anemic. Empty seats posed problems for Herman. How was he going to pay the actors Saturday night? If he paid them, how was he going to get them back to New York? His third problem was even graver. In defiance of all codes he hadn't paid author Weaver his $500 advance royalty. He could delay this obligation no longer. Anticipating the denouement, I hastened to tell Herman I barely had enough to get through the summer. But Herman was resourceful. The next evening he told me he had paid Weaver his delayed advance. Where did he get the money? He had borrowed it from his old friend, actress Peggy Wood. Miss Wood, in private life, was Mrs. John V. A. Weaver.

Though it failed Mankiewicz, *Love 'Em and Leave 'Em* touched off the career of another young man fated for the heights. When first I met Jed Harris, he was the press agent for *Apple Sauce*. Seething with ambition, he looked upon press agentry as a frowzy activity. You'll hear more about Mr. Harris, but not until I have saluted a few heretics with whom I have reveled, and not until I have submitted testimony to support my conviction that the people of the theatre are prone to error.

6

Off Limits and After Hours

NOT one theatre goer in a thousand could have identified Bernie McDonald, or the nature of his work, at the peak of his career. He was unknown to the critics. In theatre programs his name appeared in the clutter marked "Credits," following "Synopsis of Scenes," lumped with wigmakers, dressmakers, shoemakers, florists and other technicians and tradesmen. Despite his anonymity Bernie was one of the theatre's most skilled craftsmen. As head of the T. B. McDonald Construction Company he built the scenery for hundreds of plays and musical shows. No matter how involved or defiant the décor it functioned if carpentered by McDonald. He was tops in his calling, with prices to match.

I first met Bernie McDonald in the Artist and Writers' Club, a saloon which flourished in the shadow of the *Herald Tribune* throughout prohibition. To the inmates the club was known as Bleeck's pronounced to rhyme with "shakes," in tribute to its gray-haired proprietor. It was patronized by newspaper and theatrical people, strays from the Metropolitan Opera House, and the garment center, from Wall Street, the pulpit and the police department. Its furnishings were rugged and primitive, as was the food. A visored knight in gorget, brassart, jambs and sollerets flanked the entrance to the back room. Weaving to his table one night, Bernie charged the robot with jostling him. When the warrior showed no sign of repentance, Bernie belted him in the breastplate. His right hook put a dent in the mute but two of his knuckles retreated half an inch. In the club minutes it was scored as a technical knockout.

"What's the hour?" I asked Bernie one midnight. "Guess what this watch cost," he replied, crooking his wrist. "About $250," I said. "It's the most expensive watch in America," he snorted. "Cost me $50,000. It's what Ziegfeld gave me instead of what he owed me."

Token payments were standard practice with the *Follies* impresario. Curious why experts submitted to such nonsense, I queried costumer Charles LeMaire. By theatrical logic his defense was valid. The Ziegfeld revues and musical comedies provided him with a handsome showcase. Excited on seeing LeMaire's creations in the *Follies,* rival producers bid high for his services. Even though Ziegfeld defaulted, LeMaire would profit. LeMaire did think Ziggy was laying it on a bit thick when he requested an extra dress or two for a noncombatant, Mrs. Ziegfeld, née Billie Burke.

McDonald delighted in baiting friends. Summoned to the office of Guthrie McClintic to discuss publicizing *Star-Wagon,* I found the producer-director seated with author Maxwell Anderson, scene designer Jo Mielziner and the ubiquitous McDonald. Before I could be introduced to McClintic, Bernie barked, "Hello, Dick! It's good to see you sober again." Later in Bleeck's, I denounced him for this salute. "Take off your glasses, you wretched old man," I said, rising from the table. Instead McDonald took out his upper bridge and dropped it into a convenient ashtray.

Mention of *Star-Wagon* recalls Burgess Meredith, a sawed-off pixie with whom I used to roister. *Star-Wagon* was a poetic tussle with time. Meredith, acting president of Actors' Equity Association, was its hero. In the first and third act, he was an aged inventor, in the second act a stripling in a bicycle shop. Buzz, as Meredith is known to his friends, was then twenty-eight. To counterfeit the dotard he applied wrinkles and sideburns and whitened his mane.

At a midweek matinee, my friend was repenting the gala which had kept us up until dawn. Spent by his first-act exertions, he sent his dresser, Malcolm, for a bucket of Coca-Cola with which to extinguish his inner fires, then started to strip off the symbols of senility. The call boy's "Five minutes, Mr. Meredith" jarred him. With Malcolm missing Buzz had to dress himself, no easy task in his condition. Confused, Buzz reapplied the whiskers and wrinkles he had just removed. In his delirium, he had hurdled the second act.

Meredith was forty years too old when he stepped into the first entrance. On seeing him, the stage manager flung himself on the premature gaffer and hustled him to his dressing room, all the while crying "Malcolm! Malcolm!" This aroused another Malcolm, Lillian Gish's West Highland terrier. Hearing his name, he darted into the corridor to see Meredith being undressed on the run. At that moment his namesake entered the corridor. Something snapped in both Malcolms. Lillian's nipped the stage manager in the ankle while Buzz's ripped a swatch from his master's lip in his haste to rejuvenate him.

The curtain is now lowered to denote the lapse of four years. The telephone rings in my office in the Empire. The call is from Meredith. He's in Boston. He must see me at once. It's a matter of life and death. He couldn't tell me the reason for his agitation. The details were too grisly. When could I come up? I couldn't. Why didn't he take the midnight train to New York? Reluctantly, he agreed.

When Buzz entered my office the next morning, he looked as if he'd been hit over the head with a blunt instrument. His eyes were glazed, and his necktie was knotted under his ear.

While in a state of euphoria, he said, he had agreed to play Prince Hal and Henry V in *The Five Kings*. *The Five Kings* was Orson Welles's corruption of Shakespeare. Fascinated by Falstaff, Welles had telescoped four of the Bard's chronicle plays into one so that he might play the fat knight throughout. To expedite scene changes Welles employed two revolving stages. It was the eccentric action of these turntables which unhinged Buzz's mind.

In theory these stages were to circle only at the end of one scene and the start of another. But Buzz swore each platform whirled continuously while he was aboard. He muttered something about centrifugal and centripetal forces. He had to speak his lines on the gallop, said Buzz, lest he be whipped into the orchestra pit or spattered against the proscenium. And that wasn't all. As often as not, these stages spun in contrary directions. This resulted in collisions not indicated in Welles's truncated script.

Buzz was convinced there was a conspiracy to humiliate him, perhaps ruin him. But who were its authors? The stagehands? Some of his best friends were grips and clearers. Was Welles using the perverse platforms to break his spirit? Or, worse yet, his contract? Whoever the guilty, Buzz wanted out. And he wanted out while he was all in one piece. He wanted my advice. How could he retire? When?

I counseled fortitude. If he took a powder, he might be broken by Equity, the union he had headed. His fears were phantoms, I argued. Welles was as careless about revolving stages as he was about money. He was being victimized by Welles's infatuation with trial and error. Where was his loyalty? His *esprit de corps?* Had a Meredith ever capitulated in a crisis? Hadn't we survived a summer tryout that opened and closed in Westport, Connecticut, and *Battleship Gertie,* a naval farce which opened on Friday night and closed after the Saturday matinee? A man dedicated to the classics must be conditioned to hunger and torture.

I was spraying Buzz with these and other do-or-die bromides when José Ferrer, then playing in *Mamba's Daughters* downstairs, entered. I introduced the pair, briefed each on the current activities of the other. "What's your role in *The Five Kings?*" asked José. "I'm Henry V," said Buzz, "and it's too bad I didn't perish at Agincourt."

Buzz had cooled off when he took the two o'clock for Boston. His ordeal lasted five weeks. Audiences in Boston, Washington and Philadelphia scorned Welles's classic stew. His ally, The Theatre Guild, went A.W.O.L. after its brass read the Boston reviews. In desperation Welles tried to float a loan that his hybrid might have a New York showing. Prodded by Welles, the play's Hotspur sent Tallulah Bankhead a wire for help. Though prospering in *The Little Foxes* Tallulah couldn't oblige, much as she wanted to. It would take a year to repay the debts she had incurred in six successive flops. Hotspur was John Emery, Tallulah's first husband. There are those who say that he, rather than Ney, rates *"Le plus brave des braves."*

Though I sympathized with Welles I had a Falstaff of my own to worry about. Maurice Evans was playing Sir John in *Henry IV, Part I* at the St. James. Evans was not at his best in paunch and haunch. He lacked the juices and vulgarities that are the essence of Shakespeare's obese braggart. Bellies being equal, I'm sure Welles was the more satisfactory knight.

Ferrer and I prospered together only in *Mamba's Daughters,* a play memorable for Ethel Waters' terrifying performance of a vengeful mother. But *In Clover, How to Get Tough About It, Missouri Legend* and *Vicki* fouled us both. Though *Missouri Legend* boasted such prodigies as Ferrer, Karl Malden, Dean Jagger and Dan Duryea —to say nothing of such veterans as Dorothy Gish, Mildred Natwick and Joseph Sweeney—it was shuttered after six weeks. Not content with appearing in *Vicki,* Ferrer directed it. This absurdity was sponsored by Frank Mandel, librettist for *The New Moon, No, No, Nanette* and *The Desert Song.* Mandel coddled *Vicki* for four weeks before conceding defeat. I came to condole him on the closing night. Deep in despair, he paced the lobby throughout the performance. Occasionally he paused to read the text of a framed poster:

"THE FUNNIEST PLAY IN TOWN"
                     —Arthur Pollock, *Brooklyn Eagle*

Just before the final curtain, he turned to me and said: "Two people were badly fooled by *Vicki*. Me and Arthur Pollock."

My associations with Myron McCormick were as barren as those with Ferrer. Though we were together in five different plays, only in *State of the Union* was our alliance profitable. Don't tell me you don't know Myron, the original belly dancer in *South Pacific.* McCormick is a salty fellow in the Meredith tradition. He is a product of Princeton, as is lank James Stewart. I first encountered Stewart in *All Good Americans,* Sid and Laura Perelman's tribute to Americans loose on the Left Bank. The twenty-two-year-old was upset when in his biographical program note I wrote: "He played the concertina in *Spring in Autumn* while Beckhardt burned."

Beckhardt had been the producer of *Spring in Autumn.* Stewart thought I taunted him needlessly. He couldn't afford to needle ex-employers, he protested. Jobs were too hard to get. When I encountered

Stewart in *Page Miss Glory* a year later, I recited his past in solemn terms. I didn't want a juvenile's vagrancy on my conscience.

Elsewhere I've said that I've joined but two tongs, an AFL local and an honorary fraternity. I was a bit hasty. I'm also a member of The Formerly Club, thanks to my long support of Bleeck and his wares. When this canteen opened in '25, Bleeck wangled a club charter out of an Albany bureaucrat. This enabled him to circumvent enforcement snoopers. Overnight the membership jumped to six thousand, any one of whom could get in on being identified through a slit in the door. Officers were named and minutes of meetings ad libbed. To carry out the hoax of legality, Bleeck christened his oasis the Artist and Writers' Club. (Punctuation was not the proprietor's forte.) Walter Davenport, Elmer Davis, Heywood Broun and Gene Fowler were initiated in 1929.

No woman set foot in the Artist and Writers' Club until 1934, a year after repeal. With this surrender the legend on the sign which jutted out from the entrance was altered to read:

ARTIST AND WRITERS' RESTAURANT
(FORMERLY CLUB)

The words parenthetically embraced assured patrons the change was chiefly one of semantics, regardless of the girlish laughter which rattled the chandeliers and the collapse of communications once the nymphs monopolized the phone booths.

Bleeck's had been called "man's last citadel" and "the Fortieth Street version of The Mermaid Tavern." Assigned by *Life* to survey it, I wrote:

Bleeck's has more individuality, more uninhibited gaiety, and permits its inmates greater latitude of expression and conduct than any other deadfall on Manhattan Island. It scorns chichi and tablecloths, its decorative scheme suggests early Butte, Montana, the service ranges from lax to sketchy, but the food is masculine and inexpensive, the drinks authoritative and free of seaweed, and a veteran may loiter at a table for hours without raising the pulse of the management.

The customers were devoted to drink, debate, gaming and food, in that order. No juke box or other mechanical noisemaker was

tolerated. Membership provided the floor show. In Bleeck's I first saw
Wendell Willkie, enjoying a bourbon with Alva Johnston, one of the
great reporters of our time. It was there Beverly Smith, now Washington editor of *The Saturday Evening Post,* rescued a publisher
from drowning. The opinion molder had skidded face down into a
tureen of lentil soup. Bubbles were coming up when Smith won his
medal.

During prohibition, the New York *Telegram* assigned Courtney
Terrett to case New York's leading speakeasies. He was to report on
the quality of the liquor sold in them and the devices employed to
thwart revenuers. Agitated by this treachery, Ogden Reid, publisher
of the *Herald Tribune,* acted with dispatch. Fearful his staff's lounge
might be closed he summoned Sam Koenig, Republican leader. To
this statesman he delivered an ultimatum. The *Herald Tribune* was the
voice of the Republican party in New York. If Koenig permitted any
interference with Bleeck's, official or otherwise, the paper would go
Democratic. Apocryphal? Perhaps! Thanks to its charter, the
vigilance of its owner, and its proximity to the *Herald Tribune,*
Bleeck's ran without interruption through the eight years of prohibition.

Conversation among its tipplers was edged and truculent, but never
bawdy. In all the years I worshiped there, I didn't hear a half-dozen
off-color stories. It differed from "21," the Stork Club and other
boorish bivouacs in its scorn for reputations. Café society vagrants
and Hollywood hotshots were tolerated only if they stayed off the
trapeze. Conditioned to fame and its alloys, the members could spot
a phony at forty paces. Unlike caste-stricken East Side taverns,
Bleeck's had no blacklist. Occasionally a brave was waved to the
sidelines for overestimating his capacity. Community singing which
ended late at night was condoned. A novelist who took a nap in an
order of sauerbraten escaped with a tut. Bleeck took a dim view of
clients who tanked up at "21," then came to his hearth to heckle.

In Bleeck's the clock stood still. Engaged in debate with sports
writer Caswell Adams late one afternoon, I was irked when he left
to make a phone call. It seemed an uncommonly long call but other

debates and debaters took up the slack. On Caswell's return I questioned him. "Where have you been?" I asked. "Why don't you marry the girl?" Caswell had nothing to hide. He had been to Philadelphia, covered a night football game, had returned and typed his story upstairs. In this seven-hour absence, I had drifted but five feet.

"I don't want any publicity," Bleeck protested when first I approached him about the *Life* tribute. I ignored this rebuff. I have yet to meet acrobat, bartender or banjo player who doesn't glow on seeing his name in print. Bleeck thawed out so thoroughly I missed three trains to Westport. But he professed indignation when the report appeared. "You've ruined the joint," he cried. "Every lug in Horn and Hardart's will be barging in here now."

In 1940 Bleeck was feted in the *Herald Tribune's* private dining room by publisher and Mrs. Ogden Reid. It was an affectionate salute to their neighbor. The guest of honor had served and soothed most of the editors and executives present. He had placed them in cabs and retrieved their overcoats and manuscripts, he had listened to their gripes and cashed their checks. At the end of the luncheon, the ensemble arose and sang "Shall We Gather at the River," the favorite hymn of syndicate editor Harry Staton. It had warped Bleeck's rafters on many a midnight.

I took Tallulah to Bleeck's early in the run of *The Little Foxes*. The rear wall of the National Theatre abutted that of Bleeck's in the next street. Tallulah liked its informal atmosphere. Competition with rival monologists edged her output. On her first visit, she beggared city editor Stanley Walker in the match game, a form of gambling in which guests persisted.

Weary and dazed, I left Miss Bankhead there one morning at four, deep in debate with A. J. Liebling and Joseph Mitchell, two of *The New Yorker's* ablest writers. At noon the next day I remembered Tallulah was to be guest of the Dutch Treat Club that day. This was a pretty kettle of fish. I had sworn to critic John Chapman that she'd be on the dais. Press agents can't afford to stiff-arm critics. Contrite, at three I called Chapman to explain. Before I could start, he interrupted: "Tallulah was wonderful. She challenged Morris

Ernst on sex, led an open forum and told two hilarious stories." I was awed by Tallulah's vitality. "What time did you get to bed this morning?" I asked her that night. "I didn't," she said.

Though Tallulah flourished in Bleeck's, most women loathed it. Wives of addicts complained of the food, the lack of tablecloths, the service, and their mates' preoccupation with drink and match games. And they were sure their husbands regretted repeal of the Eighteenth Amendment, the reversal which made their invasion possible.

Chatting with Helen Hayes in her dressing room during the run of *Harriet,* I was chilled when she said, "I've heard a lot about the goings-on in Bleeck's. You take Tallulah there. Why don't you take me some night?"

I never thought of Helen in terms of saloons. Husband Charlie MacArthur did the drinking for the family. Helen was a one-martini girl. "How about tonight?" I said.

On the way to Bleeck's, I elaborated on its charm and the distinction and flavor of its customers. On our entrance the place was empty. The bartender was polishing glasses. A stranger was reading the *World Almanac.* The resort editor of the *Herald Tribune* was telling a waiter a pointless story about life in a duck blind.

Why had I given the place such a build-up? Helen must think I had quaint standards of gaiety. I sought to create a diversion. Bolting down a highball while Helen toyed with a cordial, I pointed out the James Thurber mural, the Clare Briggs cartoon, the swordfish caught by J. P. Morgan, Sr., off Newport, Rhode Island, and a radiogram from Russell Owen at the South Pole. This was the room in which Humphrey Bogart, Pat O'Brien and Tommy Mitchell pranked when in town, I said.

By this time things had calmed down. The resort editor had gone home and the almanac reader was asleep. A ten-year-old girl came to our table and asked for Helen's autograph. She was the first tot I'd ever seen in the place. A fine hour for a moppet to be bouncing about in a saloon, I thought. It developed she was the daughter of drama critic Howard Barnes. Fearing to expose Miss Hayes to further rioting, I took her home. Helen's a gallant woman. She never mentioned Bleeck's to me again.

Helen and Charlie MacArthur were married while she was playing in *Coquette,* and *The Front Page,* by Charlie and Ben Hecht, was selling out at the Times-Square. I publicized both plays. Things weren't always serene when I tippled with Charlie. When first I met him I had an odd distinction. I had been barred from "21," fashionable speakeasy, before it opened. Prior to their mint in Fifty-second Street, the brothers Kriendler and Charley Birns had operated at 42 West Forty-ninth Street. Jack Kriendler had outlawed me when I denounced a visiting wine buyer too vehemently. In keeping with my offense the ban was for life.

When I bumped into MacArthur on Broadway one afternoon he suggested a drink. Climbing into a cab, he told the driver to take us to "21." I remonstrated. Didn't he know I was among the proscribed? We'd better go elsewhere. MacArthur dismissed my protests with a wave of the hand. I had taken the verdict too literally, he said. My civil rights were outraged. I'd paid my debt to society hence rated another chance. He was going to see I got it.

Jack Kriendler was not easily swayed. But Charlie was charming and persuasive. Reluctantly Kriendler lifted the ban, then said, "I'm sure it's a great mistake." This was the soundest observation Mr. Kriendler ever made. Hours passed. Seven o'clock found Charlie and me in the men's room. Kriendler entered and went to the mirror to adjust his tie. While he was thus occupied, MacArthur maneuvered me behind the host. Then he kicked him in the seat of the pants. Kriendler wheeled to face me. In vain Charlie conceded his guilt. I was rebarred forthwith.

Association with Miss Hayes, a model of deportment in private and professional life, seemed to cue me into excesses. After *Coquette* closed at Maxine Elliott's, it toured for a year, then jumped from New York to the Pacific Coast for a summer engagement. I headed the expedition. Early I detected omens of trouble. In San Francisco one gawker piped up in the Curran Theatre lobby: "Look! They've made a play out of that picture Mary Pickford was in." In a moment of lunacy Harris had agreed to the release of the film version while the original company was still playing.

In Los Angeles, I looked up Lee Tracy. The critics had been

ecstatic about his Roy Lane in *Broadway* and his Hildy Johnson in *The Front Page*. His characterizations of both hoofer and reporter crackled. He was the most exciting young actor of the day. Baited by Hollywood, he succumbed to Fox Films. On my arrival he was making something called *Big Time*. I had difficulty in finding Tracy. He moved so often the studio couldn't keep track of him. He had a ready explanation for his frequent shifts. The landlords were prudish. They didn't share Lee's Halloween approach to life. They frowned on fun. His current address was satisfactory. Only one tenant ever had been ousted. Her indiscretion? Smoking opium in the lobby.

I met Tracy on a Saturday afternoon and we toasted each other into Sunday. That night I shared his quarters. In the morning, we decided to invade Mexico. At ten-thirty we took off in a trimotored plane for Agua Caliente. Thirsty picture folk swarmed to this resort on weekends. It consisted of a hotel, casino and bar, sprawled in the cactus ten miles from Tijuana.

After registering we went to the Casino. There Tracy's roulette system was our undoing. Within an hour we were without a peso. We went to the bar to restore our morale. We'd loiter there until we could put the bite on an acquaintance. If no acquaintance showed up perhaps a stranger might bail us out.

First candidate was Gus Edwards, vaudeville veteran, who had profited from the juvenile skills of Eddie Cantor, George Jessel and Walter Winchell. We raised our glasses to him. He took one look at us and bolted into the mesquite. We had no better luck with Mark Kelly, Los Angeles sports writer. Briefly we were joined by a squaw of such provocative design it wasn't until she left we discovered our tab carried the cost of a quart of Château Gringo '29.

Betrayed, we charged our drinks to our rooms and retreated to them to reassess our position. We couldn't get money from Los Angeles before Monday. We couldn't eat in the patio. In the confusion leading to our departure we'd forgotten neckties. The necktie stores were closed in Agua Caliente on Sunday.

Confined to quarters, we dined and drank in camera. Ransomed on Monday through the co-operation of Western Union, we flew back to Glendale. At my hotel I found three calls from the Fox Studios. The Fox foremen were furious. I was the last man seen with Lee Tracy. Where was he? We'd certainly gone to a lot of trouble for thirty minutes of roulette.

It must not be inferred from the alcoholic scent of this canto that all theatre folk find surcease in the sauce. But I find the company of tipplers less trying. Bent on a convivial evening, I seek out newspapermen rather than impersonators of Rozencrantz and Guildenstern. The conversation of pressmen is less parochial and so is their point of view. There's another reason I prefer the festive to the formal. Tallulah makes better copy than Katharine Cornell.

Don't think that carousing is a requisite of employment in my craft. There are sixty theatrical press agents in New York, most of them as sober and reliable as so many Congressmen. This, I think, is unfortunate. In achieving respectability and recognition, the theatre has lost something. It was a more fascinating profession when its agents were outlaw. There's too much decorum in the world, too little fun. Humor, along with those who practice it, is about to go the way of glass blowing and the antimacassar. Humor smacks of dissent. By current standards, dissent is a synonym for treason. The humorists and the hellions are hiding under culverts. When conformity becomes the law of the land, their heads will be the first to roll.

The increasingly stuffy conduct of actors, authors and producers is reflected in the pages of the Sunday newspapers devoted to the theatre and kindred distractions. Identified as "The Amusement Section," these pages are often as drab and morose as an actuary's report. The editors of these sections are suspicious of humor. They associate gaiety with irresponsibility. Funny men are likely to be untrustworthy, perhaps even subversive. It would be folly to encourage such eccentrics.

Editors, actors and press agents would do well to recall the admonition of George Bernard Shaw: "Always take your work seriously, but never yourself."

7

To Err Is Human

THERE are no invincibles in the theatre and there are no pat formulas for success in it. Even its elite are guilty of fantastic errors in judgment. Most of these stem from their inability to predict critical or box-office reaction to a play from reading a manuscript. Actors scorn roles in long-run successes to perish in a New Haven tryout. Producers bypass hits, then squander a fortune on a play that would shrivel the nose of a barge captain. There are chinks in the armor of the ablest playwrights. Brilliant talent may blush unseen under the nose of a swami credited with 20/20 vision. Theatre owners are vulnerable, too. They often stiff-arm hits to shelter stinkers. Intangibles rule the roost.

As art or business, the theatre is a fusion of a Chinese lottery, a seance and a course in economics under the late Charles Ponzi.

When Roland Young complained of his inability to get a role in an enduring play, I wasn't sympathetic. I reminded him he had turned down Elwood Dowd in *Harvey* and Father Day in *Life with Father,* assignments which would have given him twelve years' employment. Roland was quick to defend his evasion of *Harvey.* "I wasn't going to be upstaged by a seven-foot rabbit," said the sixty-five-inch comedian. In the original manuscript the rabbit which haunted Elwood was visible. Only during rehearsals did he become a phantom.

From wartime London author Emlyn Williams sent a copy of *The Corn Is Green* to Helen Hayes. She would make an ideal Miss Moffat, its schoolmistress heroine, he said. Miss Hayes had misgivings though she liked play and role enormously. In London Miss Moffat had been played by Dame Sybil Thorndike. Dame Sybil is majestic in mien and impressive in stature. Miss Hayes is smallish. Dismayed by their discrepancy in tonnage and altitude, Helen rejected the role. Her daffy decision dismayed me. Hadn't she played the six-foot heroine of *Mary of Scotland?*

Victor Payne-Jennings, an Englishman, had the American rights to *The Corn Is Green*. In his New York bow he came a cropper with *Farm of Three Echoes,* with Ethel Barrymore as its star. Miss Barrymore hadn't had a hit since *The Constant Wife,* twelve years earlier. Payne-Jennings pleaded with her to play Miss Moffat, but she brushed him off to play fifteen performances in Vincent Sheean's *International Incident.*

Unable to cast the play, Payne-Jennings sold his rights to Herman Shumlin. Shumlin's conviction that she would be a superb Miss Moffat broke down Miss Barrymore's resistance. *The Corn Is Green* provided the star with her most successful play in her fifty years in the theatre just as Miss Moffat was her most moving role. These verdicts are mine. Miss Barrymore bristled when I suggested that her roles in *Farm of Three Echoes, International Incident* and earlier mishaps were unworthy of her. All her plays were excellent, all her roles satisfactory, otherwise she wouldn't have undertaken them, she said. Beyond any star I know Miss Barrymore is reluctant to concede fallibility.

But Helen Hayes and Ethel Barrymore weren't the only ones suspicious of *The Corn Is Green*. Despite its long run in London and the note of its author, the play was spurned by The Theatre Guild, John Golden, the Shuberts, Guthrie McClintic, John C. Wilson and Robert Montgomery. Some were scared off by the occasional Welsh dialogue. Some thought the play presented unsolvable casting problems. Others felt it wise to await the end of the war, then import Dame Sybil and the original company. Their myopia cost each of these sages $300,000.

Shirley Booth's Lola Delaney in *Come Back, Little Sheba* won her the cheers of the New York critics and an Academy Oscar. But when *Sheba* was tried out in Westport, Connecticut, author William Inge and director Daniel Mann pleaded with The Theatre Guild to sack Shirley and engage Joan Blondell. Inge and Mann were depressed by "Shirley's stock-company approach to rehearsals." She shuffled through the role and mumbled her lines, they complained. In a rare spasm of sanity the Guild hierarchy vetoed the proposal and Shirley and Lola went on to win practically every plaque and medal in competition.

Consider the sagacity of Billy Rose, confessed sorcerer. Imported by Fort Worth's city fathers to stage its Frontier Centennial, memorial to Sam Houston's rout of Santa Anna on the San Jacinto, Rose recruited a corps of Texas beauties to sing and dance in the carouse. To his tryout came a gamine from the University of Texas. Rose scrutinized her, listened to her sing, then dismissed her with a shrug. Two years later Mary Martin captivated New York singing "My Heart Belongs to Daddy" in *Leave It to Me*. I was Rose's New York shill during the two summers he bemused the Texans. I had been his spokesman when Benny Goodman failed to meet his musical standards at the Casino de Paree, a peasant trap he operated on the Broadway periphery in the early thirties.

Members of the staff, investors in the melodrama and friends and relatives of the management were the only witnesses to a preview performance of *Arsenic and Old Lace* on a January night in '41. Shortly after the final curtain, I was discussing the opening-night ticket shortage with co-producer Russel Crouse when Marc Connelly, veteran playwright, bore down on us. "When do you open, Buck?" asked Marc. "Tomorrow night," said Crouse, "Too bad! Too bad!" replied Marc, shaking his head. "If you could keep it out of town another two weeks, I think you'd have something." *Arsenic and Old Lace* ran for more than three years. The fortunates who invested in it profited to the tune of 1800 per cent. How do I know? I was one of the fortunates.

There is evidence that Lindsay and Crouse were as doubtful of *Arsenic* as Connelly. The day after the opening, thousands stormed to the Fulton Theatre to buy tickets. The supply was exhausted within an hour. The producers had ordered tickets for one week only, a shocking exhibition of caution. A week's set of tickets cost $40. No use running up unnecessary expense. Given the option of *Snafu* or *Harvey* as a tenant for the Hudson Theatre some years later, Lindsay and Crouse elected the first. *Snafu* groped through twenty weeks; *Harvey* ran for two hundred.

If Lindsay and Crouse scouted the success of *Arsenic* so Brock Pemberton was skeptical of *Harvey*. The production would have disgraced a Duluth stock company. Seeking Josephine Hull, Pemberton cringed when she named her salary. He regarded *Harvey* in terms of *Janie,* an innocuous comedy which had stumbled along for a year and a half, thanks to its microscopic payroll. *Janie's* life had been prolonged through two-for-one tickets and other odious stimuli. Content if *Harvey* could take in a modest $10,000 a week, Pemberton cooed when Miss Hull agreed to his offer of a percentage of the gross receipts. His elation was short lived. Since *Harvey* was an immediate sellout—$23,000 a week—he had to pay Miss Hull twice what she'd asked.

Pemberton's chagrin over this miscalculation was tempered by the knowledge that other managers were guilty of similar faux pas. Ten years earlier he'd tried to get John Golden, a producer credited with the Midas touch, to invest in *Personal Appearance,* a comedy lampooning the life of a screen star. Golden not only turned Brock down, but begged him to abandon the comedy. *Personal Appearance* would alienate everyone in Hollywood, he said, and ruin him financially. It would destroy his prestige in the theatre. For years thereafter Brock laughed like a hyena each time he saw Golden. *Personal Appearance* ran for sixty-three weeks to capacity trade.

The customers also nod. I'm among those who believe Thornton Wilder's *Our Town* may be the best play written by an American. But when it opened in Boston its reception was so chilly, and attendance so wretched, that the two-week engagement was pared to one. The American Athens wanted no truck with a play without scenery. To Beacon Hill Brahmins, such an omission was as confusing as tackling a grapefruit without a spoon.

Consider the aversion of Broadway's pundits for *Life with Father* and *Oklahoma!*, the greatest hits of the century. Clarence Day's comedy about his crusty sire played for eight years at the Empire, longest run ever enjoyed by a play in the English-speaking theatre. The five-year stay of *Oklahoma!* at the St. James created an all-time record for a musical show. Investors in *Oklahoma!* have been rewarded fifty-fold. *Life with Father* stockholders received $25 for every dollar they risked. Yet for months sponsors of *Oklahoma!* and *Life with Father* despaired of getting them on a stage. Trying to finance them, The Theatre Guild and Oscar Serlin resorted to every device save a house-to-house canvass of the Bronx.

Singed by experience and aware of the odds against success, few producers will risk a sou in play or musical. Their timidity was vividly illustrated by Max Gordon as his production of *The Great Waltz* was about to open at the Center Theatre. Though the Center was but two years old, its stage had to be radically altered to encompass the scenic wonders of *The Great Waltz*. This was an expensive operation. Staggered at this outlay, a friend cornered the producer. "Max, you must have terrific confidence in this show." "Confidence in it?" shouted Max. "I've got $900 of my own money in it."

In 1943 The Theatre Guild was ready to give up the ghost. Only two of its last sixteen productions, Robert Sherwood's *There Shall Be No Night* and a revival of *Twelfth Night* with Helen Hayes and Maurice Evans, had made a nickel. Most of the Guild's surplus had evaporated along with its theatre on Fifty-second Street and many of its backers. When the Lunts failed in *The Pirates,* when Helen Hayes couldn't redeem *Candle in the Wind,* the Guild's goose seemed cooked. The coterie which had underwritten the Guild's efforts over the years took to the hills.

In this crisis Theresa Helburn, with Lawrence Langner, executive head of the Guild, suggested a musical version of *Green Grow the*

Lilacs might halt their losing streak. The proposal shocked her associates. If the Guild couldn't produce a successful play, how
could it hope to put on a successful musical? Drama, not song and
dance, was its forte, if it had a forte.

Suspicions about Terry's sanity increased when the history of
Green Grow the Lilacs was bared. Written by Lynn Riggs, it had
expired after an eight-week run in '34. There was another problem.
The Guild didn't own the screen rights to *Green Grow the Lilacs.*
Eager to salvage something from its failure, it had sold these rights
to RKO Pictures for $7,500. RKO later sold the rights to Metro for
$10,000.

The potential loot from the picture sale of a stage hit is one of the
lures dangled before prospective backers. If the Guild hoped to
recruit a new set of angels it must regain the screen rights. There
was another alternative—persuade Metro to finance the musical. This
last seemed a plausible solution. Metro owned only the dramatic
rights, thus had no equity in music or lyrics of the proposed variation.

Metro wanted no part of *Green Grow the Lilacs,* with or without
tunes. Prior to production, the Guild could regain the rights for
$40,000. The price would be tilted to $50,000 if it delayed its
verdict until after production.

Scouring the community for partners, the Guild received its
first rebuff from Paramount Pictures. The picture rights were too
involved, said its swamis. Howard Cullman, chairman of the Port
of New York Authority, tobacco prince and the most successful play
backer in the business, dismissed Miss Helburn's nightmare with a
wave of the hand. In desperation the Guild sweetened the bait. Cus-
tomarily backers put up all the money in return for 50 per cent of
the profits. The Guild raised the backers' cut to 60 per cent.
Prospects remained wary.

The Guild gave three frantic cocktail parties for hand-picked
speculators. At these auditions the show's songs and snatches of
dialogue were heard. With Richard Rodgers at the piano, and
Oscar Hammerstein singing in a cracked baritone, each gathering
heard "Oh, What a Beautiful Morning" and "The Surrey with the
Fringe on Top." One of these levees was at the home of Jules

Glaenzer, head of Cartier's, another in the lean-to of Mrs. Natalie Spencer.

When the concert was over the guests murmured tributes to Rodgers and Hammerstein, nibbled at the canapés, tossed off their martinis, and departed—checkbooks unsullied.

Among those who resisted seduction were actress Lillian Gish, the social Mrs. Byron Foy, Lorraine Dresselhuys, sister of Tommy Manville, producer Vinton Freedley, William Zeckendorf, real-estate tycoon, picture executive Hal Horne, Carleton Palmer, head of the house of Squibb, Pam Blumenthal and wealthy Horace Schmidlapp.

Over the protests of an associate who called it "just another goddamned horse opera," Harry Cohn of Columbia Pictures chipped in $15,000, thus became the largest investor. S. N. Behrman's gallantry caused him to take a $5,000 slice. In happier days, the Guild had mounted many of his comedies. He could not resist Miss Helburn's cry for help. Aware of the Guild's distress, Alfred Lunt and Lynn Fontanne offered to put money in the venture. Mr. Langner bid them nay. He feared a fiasco might jeopardize the Guild's relationship with its top stars. Langner's caution cost Lunt and Fontanne a fortune.

The Guild was in such straits it offered Lemuel Ayres an interest in the show instead of his customary fee for designing the settings. He accepted and thus became the highest-paid designer in history. My friend T. B. McDonald turned down a similar offer to build the settings, thus ducked a handsome annuity. When the show opened in New Haven as *Away We Go,* it was still in trouble. So evil was its plight the Guild was soliciting the cast. Joseph Buloff, the musical's Ali Hakim, consulted Jed Harris, his adviser in such matters. Mr. Harris, in New Haven for Twentieth Century-Fox, thumbed it down. He found the exercises trivial and voiced his dissent with characteristic vehemence.

Harris wasn't the only bigwig to reject *Oklahoma!* after seeing it. "Are they going to ask $3.60 for that?" jeered Michael Todd, even then identified as a genius by the illuminati in Lindy's. "No legs, no jokes, no chance!" was the verdict of a Broadway ticket broker credited with occult powers. Lee Shubert frowned on the proceedings. No musical could prosper in which a character was killed, he said. He urged the Guild to have the show rewritten forthwith and the corpse revived.

Lawrence Langner was leery of *Oklahoma!'s* success seven months after it opened. While a dinner guest at the Langners' town house, an investor with a 2½ per cent share said he wanted to sell—for tax purposes and because he thought the Germans would bomb New York. Over the protests of her mate, Armina Marshall (Mrs. Langner) took an option on the stock for $15,000. To avoid domestic debate she turned to an old friend, Fania Marinoff. Miss Marinoff raised $6,000 and Miss Marshall the balance. *Oklahoma!* was in its infancy, picture and foreign rights yet unsold. Thanks to her furtively acquired share, Miss Marshall has lived on the fat of the land ever since. Mr. Langner would like to drop the whole subject.

Oscar Serlin thought he was hoodooed before he started to raise the $35,000 necessary to produce *Life with Father.* He had held options on *Once in a Lifetime, The Vinegar Tree* and *Grand Hotel,* and had to drop all three through inability to incite investors. On getting the consent of the Clarence Day family to make a play of their sire's sketches in *The New Yorker,* Serlin gave up his Hollywood job and headed for New York in a day coach. While conducting his fund-raising drive he shared a warren on Christopher Street with his brother. He was on the dole—$20 a week from that same brother.

The elite of the theatrical and publishing worlds yawned in Serlin's face as he flourished his prospectus. Rowland Stebbins, banker friend of the Day family who had produced *The Green Pastures,* thought the play "too light." Alfred Knopf, Day's publisher, shied away. Harry Scherman, President of The Book-of-the-Month Club, was immune to his pleas, as were Cary Grant, Alice Duer Miller, Max Marcin, Benny Goodman and Goodman Ace.

Serlin relentlessly tailed millionaire John Hay Whitney, presently our Ambassador at the Court of St. James's. Jock had squandered $200,000 on Billy Rose's *Jumbo* and had sunk a bale in Peter Arno's *There Goes the Bride.* Whitney had shared the losses of *Broken Dishes,* Serlin's first production. Unable to penetrate the Whitney offices, Serlin concentrated on Whitney's comptroller, Francis Allstock. Learning Whitney was taking off for Europe, Serlin persuaded Allstock to smuggle the *Father* script into Whitney's bag. It would greet him as he reached for his razor.

Whitney ignored the script. On his return he sent it to his friend, Robert Benchley, wit and recent drama critic for *The New Yorker.* Benchley's report was a model of brevity: "I could smell it as the postman came whistling down the lane," he wrote. "Don't put a dime in it."

But Whitney was to profit from *Life with Father.* Martin Gabel and Carly Wharton, who represented him in theatrical activities, overruled Benchley and tossed $15,000 into the hopper.

Serlin's troubles weren't all fiscal. He couldn't get a desirable actor to play Father Day. Roland Young, John Halliday and Walter Connolly scorned the role. Alfred Lunt read the play, liked it, and suggested it to Lynn Fontanne as a joint starring vehicle. Miss Fontanne didn't take him seriously. "I don't think I'd want to spend every night worrying about getting you baptized," she bantered. Lunt bantered right back: "I've been seducing you in the theatre for twenty years. Here's a chance to marry, settle down and have children. Don't you think it about time?" Serlin was in no mood for such badinage. He blanched on recalling that the class of '24 at DePaul University had named him "the most likely to succeed."

Confident the nabobs he wooed would unbelt if he had a star for Father, Serlin trained his guns on Walter Huston. Huston didn't enthuse. When treed by Serlin, he hinted he might play Father if Max Gordon approved. He had faith in Gordon's judgment because of his success in *Dodsworth.* Secretaries and other hindrances kept Serlin from Gordon, but he cornered Ben Boyer, Gordon's general manager. Gordon could have a quarter of his share in *Life with Father,* he said, if he could persuade Huston to play Father. Though he could ill afford it, Serlin called a messenger and sent the script to Gordon that afternoon.

There is no evidence Gordon ever read the play, or heard of

Serlin's offer. On the opening night at the Empire, he nudged a friend. "This is a pretty funny play. Has the script been around long?" Had he given a pep talk to Huston, Gordon would have picked up a million.

Sixty-three of the anointed of stage, screen and letters spurned chances to invest in *Life with Father*. Among these loons were B. P. Schulberg, screen mogul; Messmore Kendall, who would later dodge *Oklahoma!;* publisher Lincoln Schuster; author Sigourney Thayer; toy manufacturer Dave Marx; Mrs. Otto Kahn; agents Frank Orsatti and Leland Hayward; costumer Jimmy Stroock; tycoon Jules Brulatour. When Serlin was starving in Christopher Street, he solicited Arthur Mayer, operator of the Rialto Theatre. "I'll loan you as much as you want," said Mayer, "but I won't put a penny in the play."

Don't assume that Serlin is gifted beyond his fellows in detecting long-run plays. Two years after the launching of *Father* Serlin looked the other way when Lindsay and Crouse, who had adapted the Day sketches, offered him a piece of *Arsenic and Old Lace*. And Benchley proved as errant in judging a role as a play. Brock Pemberton thought the actor to play Elwood P. Dowd in *Harvey* should have Benchley's exuberance and *joie de vivre*. Why not get Benchley to play it? Hadn't he convulsed audiences with his *Treasurer's Report* in a *Music Box Revue?* Benchley declined, said he couldn't act. He could be taught to act, argued Pemberton. Benchley said no.

Braves lacking Benchley's modesty shunned the dipsomaniac. Harold Lloyd, silent screen comic, for one, Jack Haley and Edward Everett Horton for two others. Frank Fay, bellicose Celt who took the part, was a vaudeville and musical-comedy star. He had never acted in a straight play. Among the knowing he was looked upon as a dangerous risk. Fay foiled these carpers by giving a great performance, and got the best notices of his stormy life.

Pemberton had fey experiences rounding up backers for *Harvey*. Marcus Heiman, head of the United Booking Office, turned the play over to his psychiatrist. That headshrinker said a play glorifying a drunkard conflicted with public interest. All for law and order, Heiman sent *Harvey* back to Pemberton. Harold Staley had no such scruples. Staley was a mousy little man who had saved $3,000 from his wages as a ticket seller. Staley admired the Pemberton technique. He was fascinated by the producer's dodges to keep *Janie* alive. Knowing it represented his life savings, Pemberton hesitated to accept Staley's bid. In the end he capitulated, and Staley went on to fortune. Did this prove Staley knew more about the theatre than Heiman? I have no quarrel with those who argue the affirmative.

Scouting prospects for Pemberton, ticket broker Louis Schonceit flushed a Lou Klein. Mr. Klein, to use a trade name, was loaded. He said he'd invest $7,500 in *Harvey* if he liked it. Klein fell asleep reading the first act. He was awakened by Mrs. Klein, hysterical. "So you like it?" said Klein. "Which would you rather have, a piece of this play or a mink coat?" Defying the adages, Mrs. Klein chose *Harvey* and netted enough to buy twenty mink coats. A notable dissenter was Preston Sturges. His *Strictly Dishonorable* made a fortune for Pemberton. When Brock asked him to invest in *Harvey,* Sturges warned him, "If you produce this you should have your head examined." Picture producer Sol Lesser was just as pessimistic. "I can't see anything in it," he wrote Pemberton. "You find out what a pukka is, but what else?"

Was I the press agent for *Oklahoma?* For *Life with Father?* For *Harvey?* Would that I had been. Long-run hits are a press agent's safe-conduct certificate. Then how do I know so much about the travails which attended their birth?

It all started with a phone call from Richard Aldrich in the summer of '52. With Richard Myers, Aldrich, husband of Gertrude Lawrence, was the producer of *The Moon Is Blue,* a sex-scented lark then midway in its three-year run. I was their press agent. Aldrich asked me to have cocktails with him and Gardner and Fleur Cowles at the Algonquin. Aldrich and Mike Cowles were classmates ('25) at Harvard. Cowles was the publisher of *Look.* Fleur (Mrs. Cowles) was one of *Look's* editors.

Fleur Cowles, said Aldrich, thought *Look* was inept in its handling of amusements. For weeks, she'd prodded her mate about its lapses and missed opportunities. Though concerned with weightier affairs— he was a director for R. H. Macy & Company, and had flown round the world with Wendell Willkie in '42—Cowles agreed to consult authorities in the theatre. He sought advice from Aldrich. Aldrich suggested the pair talk to me and to William Fields, press agent for the playwrights.

I welcomed this opportunity to pontificate. I didn't often have a chance to counsel a publisher. The martinis were excellent. Fleur Cowles asked me what I thought of *Look's* treatment of stage and screen. "Juvenile," I replied. This verdict cheered her up since it confirmed her own suspicion. Cowles frowned. Stimulated by the martinis, and cued by questions, I volunteered a lot of suggestions. Cowles said there should be a good story in the people who made fortunes through investments in plays. "That story's been written repeatedly," I said. "There's a better story in the Broadway know-it-alls who have passed up chances to participate in hits. The productions of *Oklahoma!, Life with Father* and *Harvey* were delayed interminably," I said, "because speculators were allergic to their merit."

After one more martini, Cowles asked me if I'd write this story of the blind for *Look*—and for $750. I was his man. Shortly I cross-examined Serlin, Armina Marshall and other Guild zouaves, and Pemberton. All were eager to recite the terror and privation they'd suffered in attempts to finance their shows. After I turned the story in, I received a note from Cowles. He thought it was fine. Shortly I got a *Look* check for $750. When did the story appear? It never appeared. That explains why I'm so familiar with the birth of three unwanted bonanzas.

Some paragraphs back, I mentioned Frank Fay, the Elwood P. Dowd of *Harvey*. It was poetic irony that Fay play this genial tosspot. A teetotaler when tapped for *Harvey,* and ever since, for years Fay was a dedicated drinker. Though difficult and arrogant, Frank is a magnificent performer. He is also a devout Catholic. During *Harvey's* run, a fellow player sought to ingratiate himself with the star by going to Mass every morning. With the closing of the comedy his devotions ceased. Sighting this renegade at the Lambs Club bar, Fay cried, "Look at that bastard. A run-of-the-play Catholic."

Failure of stage-struck gamblers to sense a hit is a commonplace. These same noodleheads slough off millions on turkeys. The judgment of players is just as faulty. Helen Hayes, Margaret Sullavan, and Katharine Hepburn all passed up the chance to play the leading role in *State of the Union*. Their veto assured Ruth Hussey a two-year run in her first Broadway play. Miss Hayes's dissent was noteworthy. The play had been written for her. More! She had outlined the plot to the authors.

If some go to extravagant lengths to avoid success, others have success thrust upon them. *Tobacco Road* opened at the pit of the depression. It was savagely assailed by the critics, and the management was ready to cry quits at the end of the second week. A clause in the contract with the Masque Theatre stayed its hand. To indicate the poverty and depravity of the white trash who peopled the play, the stage was covered with dirt and refuse. The theatre had frowned on this vandalism. Stirred up by the shiftless Lester family, the soil would seep into the auditorium and befoul seats and draperies. The theatre demanded an $800 deposit to cover cost of a vacuum-cleaning job when the work folded.

During rehearsals a succession of crises sapped the play's budget. Faced with a last-minute emergency, Sam Grisman, one of the producer's aides, persuaded the theatre to return the $800. In agreeing to this breach, the theatre management stipulated fearful penalties should producer and cast try to sneak out without tidying up—or returning the deposit.

Aware continuance would multiply their obligations, Grisman tried to borrow $800 from Joe Greenwald when that comedian ventured into the Masque lobby. If Joe loaned him the $800 the play could adjourn without disgrace. When Greenwald shied away the *Tobacco Road* boys were in a pickle. Lacking the $800, they couldn't afford to close. Nor could they afford to stay open. So they resorted to the classic theatre tactic—delay.

Driven into a third week, a miracle started to unfold. Business bounced. *Tobacco Road* ran for seven years, wore out Henry Hull,

James Barton, James Bell, Eddie Garr and Will Geer—Jeeter Lesters all. If Greenwald had forked up $800, *Tobacco Road* would have had a run of fourteen performances instead of 3,182.

An unlikely story? It couldn't happen? True! It couldn't happen except in the theatre.

8

My Liege Lords

IN the thirty years I've practiced in New York, I have worked for seventy producers. Sometimes I've performed for six prospectors simultaneously, a feat comparable to shooting Niagara in a canoe. Some of my employers were the toast of Dun and Bradstreet, while others haggled from pay stations in the corridor. Some were sybarites, welcomed at "21," the Colony and other fashionable grills. Others operated from fleabags in the Forties. Some were men of lofty ideals who thought in terms of Aeschylus and Ben Jonson. Others were sharpers, their goal a quick buck. Some were dedicated to a revival of *Titus Andronicus,* some to mention in Winchell's column and some to the blonde show girl in the Byzantine number. In taste, background and competence they varied widely.

Consider Robert Reud, sometime press agent for Jed Harris and Gilbert Miller and a confidant of Greta Garbo. About to present *Ramshackle Inn,* Mr. Reud mulled my astral status for a week before engaging me. Some dastard had told him I was a Gemini and that my aspects were malefic. I must have passed the zodiac test because *Ramshackle Inn,* one of the corniest melodramas of all time, prospered for six months. Despite Reud's verdict, I always felt Zasu Pitts' performance had more to do with the run of this mishmash than the position of the planets at its birth or mine— or Reud's.

I shall long remember Erik Charrell, the Viennese vagrant who produced *Swingin' the Dream.* Assigned by the *Times's* drama editor to capture the background and design of my employer in twelve hundred words, I approached him at a rehearsal. Beset by trouble, Charrell pleaded for delay. Couldn't we meet at dinner? At the appointed hour he took me to his office above the auditorium. Pulling out a desk drawer, he unwrapped a meat loaf that had accompanied him from the Danube, sliced off a slab and handed it to me. *"Gut nein?"* he asked, as I took a cautious nibble. Later he wept on learning I had reported his attempt to poison me to his manager.

When E. Ray Goetz, mask for an assortment of Warner Brothers, produced *Fifty Million Frenchmen,* I could consult him only in his suite at the Savoy Plaza, so alert were the process servers who ringed his office in the Empire Theatre. Suave, nonchalant in adversity, Goetz was a voluptuary. He lived like a king even when tailed by the sheriff. Most of our parleys were conducted over the telephone. Rarely did he rise before dusk or retire before daylight.

The day I announced *Blood Stream* as the first production of youthful Sidney Harmon, an outraged dentist called me. Actors had been streaming through his office since dawn, he cried; they had laid it waste. When I learned my caller's name, I understood his plight. The dentist was the only Sidney Harmon listed in the Manhattan telephone directory. My Harmon operated from a Forty-second Street curb. Did *Blood Stream* and Harmon defy these evil auguries and career on to glory? They did not. The critics jeered the collusion and my client took off for Hollywood the day after the inquest. Then as now, Hollywood was a haven for the haunted and the hunted.

The theatre is the most contrary of the arts. Black omens do not always mean disaster. The success of *Richard II* made theatrical history. In doing so, it confounded the skeptics, outraged precedent and rewarded as odd and conflicting a set of partners as ever schemed a coup.

Early in '37, Eddie Dowling, reformed song-and-dance man,

phoned to ask if I'd publicize this rarely seen chronicle play. He and Robinson Smith, a neophyte from the Social Register, were to star Maurice Evans in it. Could I meet with him and his partner and Evans that afternoon?

Though I muted my pessimism in talking to Dowling, I thought the prospects for *Richard* drab. I doubted New York could absorb any more Shakespeare that season. It had seen the Hamlets of John Gielgud and Leslie Howard, and the ill-advised Othello of Walter Huston. And *Richard II* seemed a capricious choice. There hadn't been a professional performance of the play in New York since Edwin Booth's sixty years earlier. Indeed, the play hadn't had over half a dozen performances in New York's stage history. Because Richard is on stage at the play's start, Booth, who reveled in a built-up entrance, prefaced it with a fragment from *Henry IV,* a play which follows it chronologically. The play has no romantic interest. Richard's Queen, Anne of Bohemia, is little better than a walk-on.

Other considerations troubled me. A classic revival cannot hope to prosper without a star. Evans had yet to achieve this status. He was almost a stranger to New York audiences. The critics had cheered his Dauphin in Katharine Cornell's *St. Joan* the previous March and his Bonaparte in *St. Helena* in October. But business for the R. C. Sherriff play—the same Sherriff who wrote *Journey's End*—had been so wretched that Evans wound up playing the exiled Emperor for the Equity minimum wage—$50 a week—in an effort to keep the play open. And the enterprise clashed with the calendar. February was an unfortunate month for such a gamble. Essential patronage from schools and colleges would shrivel with the start of Lent. I wasn't impressed when Dowling told me that Evans had played Richard at London's Old Vic two years earlier. London has more reverence for the classics than New York and honors them more frequently.

Weighing my qualms, I decided to bypass Dowling's offer. To screen my doubts I told him I'd been called for jury duty. This invention backfired. Dowling was chummy with the town's politicos and welcomed an opportunity to display his influence. "Forget that jury summons," he said. "Who's the judge? I'll square it with a phone call." Hoist on my own petard, I capitulated.

Evans and his director, Peggy Webster, were charming, modest and intelligent. They'd be content with a six-week run, they said; *Richard* could break even if the weekly receipts averaged $8,000. The role and the play would establish Evans' worth in classic parts. They'd get their rewards in other seasons with others of Shakespeare's plays. The production would be inexpensive. From a Chicago storehouse they salvaged crown and scepter worn by Dennis King in *Richard of Bordeaux* three years before, and the regalia of Bolingbroke, Thomas Mowbray, the Dukes of York and Lancaster, and other personages common to both plays.

Most of the funds for the revival had been provided by Joseph Verner Reed. Reed was a wealthy young idealist who had produced four plays with Kenneth MacGowan. Trying to cope with the vagaries of his partner, with the heresies of Jane Cowl and Pauline Lord and the confusions created by Mary Ellis and Basil Sydney had been a shattering experience. *The Curtain Falls,* his book on his frustrations, is one of the most honest and amusing books ever written about the lunacies and extravagancies of the theatre.

Impressed by Evans' Napoleon, Reed sent for the star and asked him what he would like to do in the theatre. Evans cited his success with *Richard* in London and his desire to test it in New York. When he left Reed's hotel he had a check for $25,000. This sum would cover the cost of the physical production, Evans and Dowling assured me, and would leave a small surplus to cover possible operating losses. Boris Said would post the Equity bond covering two weeks' salary for the cast, they said.

Boris Said? This was the first time his name had come up in the dialogue. With Dowling, he was proprietor of the St. James Theatre, where the tragedy was to be shown. After wangling a lease for the St. James from Vincent Astor, Dowling had needed Said's fiscal aid to validate it. Hence the presence of this corporate Cossack.

Some strange characters wriggle into the theatre, but none was so ill equipped to wrestle it as Boris Said. A White Russian with Standard Oil affiliations and chummy with Amtorg, Soviet Trading cartel, Said waged relentless war on the English language. An international speculator, he could scent a dollar seven versts away. His risk in the revival was slight. His staff manned the box office. He could recover his guaranty from the first monies taken in, regardless of the play's reception. Even then he was trying to muscle Dowling out of the entente.

Without out-of-town trials, *Richard II* opened at the St. James on February 5, 1937. When it closed on the last day of May, it had played 133 performances, the longest run ever achieved by the play in its 340 years. On the final day, three hundred standees crowded the rear of the theatre and paid $2.20 each for this privilege. Weekly box-office receipts frequently topped $20,000. When they slumped to $17,000 in the twelfth week, Dowling and Evans were alarmed. "What's happened to business?" they chorused. I reminded them that *Richard* had surpassed their wildest expectations. Hadn't their goal been a six-week run and average receipts of $8,000? I shouldn't have been astonished. Perspectives fluctuate wildly in the theatre. A whiff of success can distort the criteria of any sage in it. Nothing so unhinges the judgment of its craftsmen as a succession of sellouts. The delusions born of these phenomena transform the faint into the ferocious overnight.

With the success of *Richard,* Said went haywire. Eager to be recognized as one of the authors of this miracle, but aware that his sole contribution was the Equity bond, he sought to arrogate the functions and roles of his colleagues. By the end of the first week, he was an authority on iambic pentameter and the Ben Day technique in engraving, the history of the Plantagenets, four-color lithography, and ticket scalping.

I resented Said's intrusions and challenged his qualifications when he tried to advise me on advertising, the press list, syntax and other esoterica. He told Dowling and Evans that I was insolent and suggested that I be disciplined or confined to quarters. But those gentlemen were too intoxicated with the play's success to give ear to the moujik.

The only thing Said brought to the theatre was the conviction that everyone in it was a crook, out to rook him of his share of the swag. Convinced that the ushers were smuggling Bardolators through the side exits and that others were getting in through chicanery and collusion, Said set up an espionage system at the St. James. His agents clocked all entrants. After each performance, these totals were checked with the ticket stubs and complimentary chits taken up by the doorman. The two items never matched and the discrepancy brought Said to the edge of lunacy.

The explanation was simple. Staff members, program men, firemen, attachés, concessionaires and understudies entered the theatre before and during the performance in line of duty. But Said's henchmen drew no distinction between a customer and a coat-room boy. They clocked them all. Awash with suspicion, Said hinted that I was at the head of a conspiracy to upend him. I took no steps to disillusion him. To me he was an obnoxious oaf, a regrettable fly in a miraculous ointment.

My final clash with Said came after Evans set himself up in the four-hour, uncut *Hamlet* in October of '38. This was the first time that the tragedy, in its entirety, had ever been played in this country. The curtain rose at 6:45 and came down at 8:15. After a half-hour interval for dinner it resumed at 8:45 and continued until 11:15. This setup precluded matinees, but cued Said into a masterstroke. Since *Hamlet* was giving six performances instead of the conventional eight, he cut the wage of the matron in the ladies' room 25 per cent. Following the critical ovation given Evans and play, the dialectician numbed the company with a gala in the men's lounge in the St. James basement. To climax the carouse the host toasted Evans and his comrades in domestic champagne, at room temperature or higher.

Said had liquidated Dowling, and now was the sole operator of the St. James. He was also allied with Evans and Reed in the presentation of *Hamlet*. I spread the rumor he was having both Laertes and the night watchman shadowed. As my fractional employer, Said questioned my expenditures for photographs. Why did I need so many? What happened to those I purchased? Outraged by the implications of these queries, I told the Slav I was hawking 8 x 10 glossies in the subway during rush hours. It was a nice side line,

I added. When Said protested the cost of the canvas posters on which
I flaunted the verdicts of the critics, I had these judgments limned
on the marble façade of the theatre in letters of gold.

Screaming that I had defaced his temple, that I was guilty of
vandalism, Said rushed to Evans with an ultimatum. Unless I was
sacked forthwith he'd withdraw every kopeck he had put into the
venture. He was fed up with me. No press agent could tell him he
didn't know a couplet from a can opener and remain in his employ.
In language consonant with his station in the theatre, Evans told
the Muscovite what to do with his marbles. Said's defection had
no impact on the box office. *Hamlet* went right on selling out. What
would have happened had I been fired? *Hamlet* would have continued
to sell out. Once a hit gets up momentum, nothing can derail it.

Not all my masters thirsted for recognition. Some were masked and
functioned behind false fronts. Engaged by Richard Aldrich to
publicize the American Lyric Theatre, I discovered that he was
fronting for a passel of Rockefellers. Hired by Louis Lotito to
promote *Another Love Story,* it developed he was the proxy for
Joseph P. Kennedy, our Ambassador to the Court of St. James's.
I was elated when Lew Brown and Ray Henderson asked me to press
agent their revue, *Strike Me Pink,* with Lupe Velez and Jimmy
Durante. With Buddy De Sylva, Brown and Henderson had written
Good News, Manhattan Mary and *Flying High.* Meeting them in a
cubbyhole at the Majestic Theatre, salary and other terms of enslave-
ment were agreed upon quickly. There remained one formality,
they said, the approval of their partner.

I didn't know they had a partner. He wasn't listed in the billing.
But I recognized him on his entrance. He squashed into a chair,
then discussed "a rap from the D.A.'s office" over the telephone.
Though prohibition was still in flower, he told me of his beer business
in Jersey. I fled this fat man at the first opportunity. In the foyer
Detective James Coy pointed out four young men loitering behind
pillars. They were Mr. Wexler's bodyguards, he said. Each carried
a rod. Mr. Wexler, Brown and Henderson's silent partner, was better
known as Waxey Gordon, notorious hoodlum, income-tax evader
and narcotics peddler.

Edgar Selwyn was an alias for Metro-Goldwyn-Mayer Pictures when he engaged me for *The Wookey,* with Edmund Gwenn in the title role. *The Wookey* was about a British tugboat captain, veteran of World War I, and his heroic conduct at Dunkerque and under the blitz. Mr. Wookey was a symbol of Britain's little man and his stubbornness and fortitude in extremity. I stressed these virtues in ads and press copy. Two weeks after the opening, Selwyn told me to cease plucking "the little man" string, to concentrate on the play's "love story." "What love story?" I asked Edgar. He shrugged his shoulders in resignation.

A congressional committee was about to investigate pro-Ally propaganda. This scared the daylights out of Metro. As producer, director and author, Edgar Selwyn, who started as an usher at the old Herald Square Theatre in the nineties, had made and lost millions. The spineless conduct of his sponsors nauseated him, as it did me.

Screen companies commonly affect a disguise when they invade the theatre. In an attack of culture, Warner Brothers footed the bills for the revival of *Romeo and Juliet* which I tried to exalt in May of '40, though the ads read, "Laurence Olivier presents." Olivier was an attractive façade behind which to operate. He had created a furore in *Rebecca* while Vivian Leigh, his Juliet, was known to New Yorkers as Scarlett O'Hara.

Olivier overestimated his prowess. Not content with being the play's titular producer, he acted the moon-struck Montague, directed the doings at Verona, and wrote part of the score. The result was messy and confusing, though Miss Leigh was a radiant Juliet. May 10 was a tragic morning for the English stars. The revival was drubbed on the drama pages and page 1 reported German parachutists darkening the skies over the Low Countries. The families of both were imperiled. *Romeo and Juliet* eked out a month's stay at the vast Fifty-first Street. Why had the Warner Brothers jeopardized the venture by installing it in this arena? The Warners owned the Fifty-first Street. Such procedure was a variation of the screen's scourge, nepotism.

I haven't had much truck with distaff producers. In three assignments for The Theatre Guild, I found Terry Helburn less discursive and more decorative than Lawrence Langner. Rose Franken, creator of the *Claudia* sweepstakes, inherited me when she decided to bring *Outrageous Fortune* to New York over Gilbert Miller's veto. Following the play's frigid reception in Baltimore, author and producer agreed to call it quits if the Boston reviews were sour. Sour they were. On a Tuesday noon, Miller phoned me from Boston to cease and desist. Later that day the *Christian Science Monitor* hailed *Outrageous Fortune* as a dramatic gem. Miller was unmoved by this dissent. but Miss Franken waxed defiant and announced she would bring the play to New York.

I was summoned to her Washington Square home for questioning the following Sunday. Miss Franken had heard that I didn't like her play, that I thought its chances slim. This troubled her. "Have you ever publicized a play you didn't like?" she asked. Her query floored me. If I confined my efforts to plays I liked, I assured her, I would have starved long since. Consoled by my confession, Miss Franken re-engaged me. Though Elsie Ferguson, the toast of the town in the twenties, had emerged from a thirteen-year retirement to play the leading role, *Outrageous Fortune* was shuttered after ten weeks. The *Monitor* reviewer cost Miss Franken a pretty penny.

While *Outrageous Fortune* was in its final throes, I was engaged by Margaret Webster and Carly Wharton, two gay and gallant ladies about to defy the record with a revival of *The Cherry Orchard*. Two phenomena attend every renewal of the Chekhov drama: the critics praise it to the sky and the public avoids it in droves. I'm on the side of the stay-at-homes. Though most authorities, including G. B. Shaw, hail it as a masterpiece, when Americanized and retitled *The Wisteria Trees* by Joshua Logan, it stupefied its beholders. One scoffer identified this variation as "Southern Fried Chekhov."

Despite her predilection for *The Cherry Orchard*, Peggy Webster is one of the most versatile women I've encountered in the theatre. Though this was the first time I had worked for her, it was not the first time I'd worked with her. To a great degree, she was responsible for the success of Maurice Evans in his revivals of *Richard II, Hamlet, Henry IV Part I* and *Macbeth,* all of which she edited and directed and all of which I publicized. Intelligent and courageous,

Peggy Webster lived up to the traditions of a great theatrical family.

Starting with Captain John Frederick Webster, Conductor of Amusements at Bath at the tag end of the seventeenth century, there have been Websters in the English theatre for over 250 years without interruption. Peggy was the daughter of the fourth Ben Webster and Dame May Whitty and she was born in New York in 1905. Her father, who had toured America with Irving ten years earlier, had returned to play in *The Marriage of William Asche.* Peggy wasn't to visit our shores again until she staged Evans' *Richard.* By that time she had twenty years in the London theatre behind her. When John Barrymore played *Hamlet* at the Haymarket in London, Peggy was his Gentlewoman. She's been up to her ears in Shakespeare most of her life. With Paul Robeson as the Moor and José Ferrer as Iago, her production of *Othello* enjoyed the longest run of any Shakespearean play anywhere, any time.

A year after *The Cherry Orchard* had been quelled, I was allied with Peggy again. She was directing *Thérèse Raquin* in a contraction of one of Emile Zola's minor works. Peggy's mother, Dame May Whitty, then eighty, was coming on from California to play in it. Considerate of her parent's comfort, Peggy wired her not to worry about hotel reservations. She had taken care of everything. Dame May's reply startled her daughter: "Forget about the hotel. What about the gin?" Despite its short life and my pessimism, Peggy and Carly's *Cherry Orchard* was not without its excitements. Joseph Schildkraut's ex-wife invaded the theatre one night. On Joe's first entrance she hissed him. After his first speech she saluted him with a Bronx cheer, then thumbed her nose at him as ushers hustled her toward an exit. Pepi's fortitude during this ordeal won the admiration of one and all.

The fortunes of producers fluctuate wildly. One season they feast on terrapin and truffles, the next they're reduced to hardtack and pemmican. Consider the zigs and zags of Herman Levin, just now the envy of his fellows as the producer of *My Fair Lady.* Levin got a spectacular start with *Call Me Mister.* This revue netted him $200,000. A year later he undertook an encore with *Bonanza Bound.* A deceptively titled musical, *Bonanza Bound* opened and closed in

Philadelphia. Cost of disaster, $200,000. Tussles with Jean Paul Sartre and William Shakespeare further depleted Herman's surplus. When he opened *Gentlemen Prefer Blondes* in December of '49 he was down to his last subway token.

With *Blondes* Herman hit the jackpot again. His share of the swag was $250,000. Yet when the curtain went up on the first performance of *My Fair Lady* in New Haven, he was $50,000 in arrears. Factors in his fiscal decline were *Bless You All,* a $250,000 bust, ill-advised investments at Belmont Park and Jamaica and midnight surveys of El Morocco and the Copacabana.

Two months after *My Fair Lady* opened in New York, Levin sold two-thirds of his 20 per cent share for $450,000. On this he paid a capital gains tax of $112,500, leaving him a $337,500 nest egg. How long will this last him? No man knoweth. He's still going to Belmont, and he's deep in blueprints of two more musicals.

Though I've had my share of crackpots, of fugitives from the Morris Plan, most of the producers I have served have been men whose affection and respect for the theatre has ripened through experience. All have put on resounding hits. All have had disastrous failures. Though they know the dice are loaded, the theatre continues to fascinate them. Aside from the risks of producing there is another circumstance which attracts them. In what other trade could they sleep until ten?

The ups and downs of the late Arthur Hopkins point up the perils of producing. I press agented two of his failures in '31 and his last success in '46. Hopkins was a man of taste and intelligence. An able director, a skilled writer, he scorned the cheap and the shabby. Once dedicated to a play, he ignored kibitzers and critics. In this respect he differed from most of his colleagues. The theatre crawls with authorities and with victims of these volunteers. Something of a mystic, Hopkins was sparing with words. In a loquacious business, his reticence marked him a heretic.

Hopkins' fortunes were at a low ebb when he engaged me for the ill-fated *Man on Stilts* and *The Passing Present. On Trial* had enriched him and twenty-one-year-old author Elmer Rice back in 1914. Since that time he had made and lost four or five fortunes.

Ethel, John and Lionel Barrymore had prospered under his management. He had given New York Eugene O'Neill's *Anna Christie* and
The Hairy Ape, notable revivals of Shakespeare and Ibsen, and such
bristling successes as *What Price Glory?, Burlesque, Holiday* and
Paris Bound. Later, *The Petrified Forest* and *The Magnificent Yankee*
would add to his note. He did not strut in victory nor whimper
in defeat. Neither wealth nor poverty altered his habits. For twenty
years he operated from a cell abutting the balcony in the Plymouth.

In common with everyone in the theatre, I had great respect for
Arthur Hopkins. He did not encourage familiarity. He was Mr.
Hopkins when first I worked for him and he was Mr. Hopkins
when I met him on a crosstown bus, shortly before his death. His
humor was curt and trenchant. One of his major mishaps was *Deep
River,* a folk operetta with Jules Bledsoe, Negro baritone, in the
leading role. Bledsoe was a stranger to the theatre. A concert singer,
he persisted in singing directly to the audience, instead of his stage
companions. Hopkins tried for weeks to correct his solo tendencies.
Came the opening night in New Haven. Apprehensive, Hopkins sat
in the last row. On Bledsoe's first entrance, he reverted to his concert
style. Ignoring his colleagues, he strode to the footlights and let fly.

In his anguish, Hopkins muttered an oath. The woman in front
of him turned and barked, "If you don't like the show, why don't
you go to the box office and get your money back?" Anguished
over the $60,000 he had spent on the production, he replied:
"Madam, I wish to God I could."

Veterans are the most satisfactory employers. Their standards
may be rigid, but they distinguish between the possible and the
impossible. The theatre boils with shoestring operators and stage-
struck dilettantes attracted by its get-rich-quick legends. These
upstarts are the despair of press agents. They heckle their betters,
look for news of their blunders on page 1, and parade their ignorance
at every opportunity.

Piccolo players and press agents, adagio dancers and ingenues,
even female impersonators, serve an apprenticeship before they work
in a New York stage attraction. Craft unions covering everyone
from wardrobe woman to scene designer set up qualifications for

membership. One requisite is experience. Producers are exempt. Any adventurer with $60,000 and a manuscript can call himself a producer without penalty. Reputable managers complain that the demands of theatrical unions make presentation of plays prohibitive. They would be better employed screening applicants to their own guild. All suffer for the offenses of these chiselers.

Because of the libel law, I cannot identify the hit-and-run dodger who, after years of shady practice, came up with a hit. "Success hasn't changed him a bit," remarked a Broadway veteran. "He's still a son-of-a-bitch."

Save when immobilized by defaulting authors or investors, some twenty producers put on plays or musicals year after year. To these loyalists, the theatre is a career rather than a crap shooter's picnic. As I write this, they include, but are not confined to, Gilbert Miller, The Theatre Guild, John C. Wilson, Kermit Bloomgarden, Guthrie McClintic, Sidney Kingsley, Maurice Evans, Courtney Burr, George Abbott, Aldrich and Myers, Herman Levin and Herman Shumlin. I cite only those I have served. These gallants have devoted most of their lives to the theatre. It has enriched them one season, all but beggared them the next. Come weal or woe, they're true to it. They have no other option. Their devotion to the hussy disqualifies them for other activities.

Gilbert Miller is the most reliable of my clients. He is also the wealthiest and the most accomplished linguist. Since he reproduced *Daddy Long-Legs* in London in 1916, he has functioned on both sides of the Atlantic as producer, director and theatre operator. Miller had a sound schooling. His father, Henry Miller, was one of our leading actor-managers for thirty years. Matilda Heron, his maternal grandmother, was a skilled actress. She played in her own adaptation of *Camille* with marked success. Miller had played small roles in London and New York and had toured as company manager for his father's attractions before he set up *Daddy Long-Legs*.

Since 1938, I have hymned more than twenty plays bearing Miller's crest. First of these was *Oscar Wilde*. It was produced at the Gate in London by Norman Marshall. The Gate was a club theatre, admission by subscription only. Public performances of *Oscar Wilde* in London were taboo. A long interval must elapse before the deceased notable can be animated. The play dwelt on Wilde's relationship with Sir Alfred Douglas, his trial and conviction for sodomy, and his tragic end in a tawdry hotel.

No such restrictions menaced the play in New York. Our respect for the departed fades rapidly. But Miller had qualms about its production. Twelve years earlier he had presented *The Captive,* a powerful play about Lesbianism. Though expertly staged and played, *The Captive* shocked the bluenoses. Their screams intimidated the District Attorney. At the peak of the run, a patrol car backed up to the stage door of the Empire and carted the cast off to the Forty-seventh Street police station. Miller was all for fighting this action in the courts, but Famous Players—Lasky, the firm cartel for which Miller managed the Empire and Charles Frohman, Inc., flinched. *The Captive* was closed by official edict and Miller placed under bond not to revive it.

Oscar Wilde was to open at the Fulton Theatre. While chatting with Miller at a dress rehearsal the day before the opening, a police squad car drew up in front of the theatre. From it spewed fifteen patrolmen. Miller's eyebrows shot up. "Could they pinch us before we open?" he asked. His fear was groundless. The clutter in front of the Fulton was routine—one set of cops relieving another.

In his first appearance in America, Robert Morley gave a bravura performance in the title role. His characterization of the wayward wit, poet and dramatist was voted the finest of the year by the New York critics. Miller elevated Morley to stardom the day after the opening. I have seen many actors impersonate men of genius on the stage. Rarely is the illusion fulfilled. As Wilde in the dock, badgered, humiliated and bewildered, Morley was superb. I forgot he was an actor. He was Wilde. An aged lady was similarly convinced. She had met Wilde when he visited America in 1882. She asked Morley to tea to re-create that meeting. Morley was fascinated in the hour he spent with Mrs. Cornelius W. Vanderbilt, long arbiter of New York society.

Oscar Wilde flourished for thirty weeks, without so much as a whimper from a prude. Long after it had closed came a repercussion. Its authors, Leslie and Sewell Stokes, were haled into court by the widow of Frank Harris, braggart editor who boasted he had discovered H. G. Wells and Bernard Shaw. She charged that they had lifted much of the plot and dialogue of *Oscar Wilde* from her husband's biography of Wilde. A judgment was returned in her favor and the errant brothers had to disgorge their royalties. Charges of literary larceny haunt producers. To appropriate data from ten authors is research, from one author, plagiarism, some sage has said.

Morley did not visit New York again for ten years. I was in his dressing room at the Martin Beck Theatre when, shortly before a matinee performance of *Edward, My Son,* a clubwoman barged in to say that her sorority had named him as the season's best actor. When could they present him with their testimonial? Mulling over a likely day, Morley was brought up short when the invader whispered, "We're all Christians, you know."

That evening Morley sent his benefactress this note:

I hope you will not think me ungracious if I decline your citation. I am not unaware of the support which your club affords the theatre in New York and the honour you have done me, but after you left my dressing room, your fiercely whispered aside rang in my ears all afternoon. Your members may indeed be all you claim for them, but I have never inquired too closely into my own lineage which may, for all I know, be partially Jewish, nor have I much regard for those who covertly exclude from their organizations the non-Aryan. Holding your views, my dear Madam, you should change your club's name to the Christian Matinee Club which would give you a standard by which to judge and be judged. Perhaps it is because I am an Englishman, a race so constantly accused of anti-Semitism, that I am particularly sensitive to this form of nonsense.

Morley wasn't the only brilliant alien I met while in Miller's service. His efforts to present Terence Rattigan's *Flare Path,* late in '42, were delayed through his inability to find a satisfactory actor to impersonate Flight Lieutenant Graham. Learning that a young Englishman, lately commissioned in the Royal Navy, was in New York awaiting delivery of his ship, Miller pulled international wires. Admiralty bigwigs ruled the idle sailor could play the airman until his craft materialized. That's how I met Alec Guinness. We renewed our acquaintance seven years later when he played Sir Henry Harcourt Reilly in *The Cocktail Party*. The T. S. Eliot play was a press agent's dream. Its partisans called it a masterpiece. Dissenters jeered it as poetic balderdash. It wasn't difficult to fan these conflicting judgments into a box-office flame. The play became a social must. Failure to see it disqualified delinquents from after-dinner forums.

I think Alec Guinness is the best actor alive. He also may be the bravest. Who else would have risked the wrath of the London reviewers by playing Hamlet with a beard? One can't play ducks and drakes with tradition in London. Beerbohm Tree, Irving, John Barrymore, Garrick, Gielgud, Salvini, Sarah Bernhardt—none of these had dared a whiskered Dane. Nor had Burbage, creator of the role. What did Mr. Guinness think he was up to?

Prowling two continents in search of a *gamine* for the title role in *Gigi,* Anita Loos's variation of a Colette novel, Miller relaxed when Collette cabled she had chanced upon a proper Gigi while watching the shooting of a British picture at Monte Carlo. The candidate's qualifications were slender, said Colette. She had never played a dramatic role. Her stage experience consisted of dancing roles in small London revues and of chorus work in the London production of *High Button Shoes*.

The day after *Gigi* opened in New York, Audrey Hepburn's name went up in lights above the comedy's title, the most rapid rise to stardom in theatrical history. Though she had much to learn about acting, Audrey was so lovely and refreshing, so coltish and eager, that she enchanted critics. That's more than *Gigi* did. Played and directed in three or four different styles, it was doomed unless the box office received a quick stimulant. If audiences shared the critics' enthusiasm for this radiant newcomer, a solution was at hand. But starring Audrey on such slight evidence was revolutionary and ironic. This eminence commonly is achieved only after years of struggle and mischance. With a hundred plays and forty years in the theatre behind her, so skilled and incisive an actress as Cathleen

Nesbitt, Audrey's great aunt in the play, would be cited below the title. Discussing tactics the morning after the opening, Miller and I agreed that this was no time to quibble over tradition. We must strike while the iron, i.e., Audrey, was hot. Miss Nesbitt concurred.

All publicity was focused on Audrey. Alert and articulate, she was a joy to interviewers and editors. She had an exciting background and an exotic origin. Daughter of an Irish father and a Dutch mother, throughout World War II she had lived in Arnheim, Holland, under the Nazis. Often she went hungry. Her male relatives were dragged off to labor camps. When she danced, it was to raise funds for the Dutch underground. All this made copy.

Thanks to Audrey, *Gigi* flourished for six months. It would have flourished throughout the summer had not Paramount Pictures, inflamed by the furore she created in the play, exercised the option it had taken on her services after seeing her in *Nous Irons à Monte Carlo,* the picture she was making when Colette first glimpsed her. Off she went to Italy—to Gregory Peck and *Roman Holiday.* Few of the stage's children can resist Hollywood moolah. It's unfortunate that so many young players flee to the cameras before they achieve their acting potential. Their movie salaries will dwarf their stage pay, but they'll learn little about acting among the lotus eaters.

But this is no time to explore the screen's sins. I'd better get back on the chronological rails. When I interrupted this saga to salute the eccentrics and producers, I was scouting ahead of the *Greenwich Village Follies* and my tourist status threatened to become chronic. Though not spurred by ambition, sporadically I mulled the disadvantages of nomadic practice. A road press agent was an anonymous guerrilla, known only to newspapermen and theatre managers in the cities he visited. Only in New York could a press agent hope for recognition. It would be pleasant to operate from a permanent base. Any curiosity I'd had about Butte and Indianapolis and Fresno had been sated. George M. Cohan voiced the creed of his craft when he said, "If you're out of New York, you might as well be in Bridgeport."

Though I little suspected it, the hour of deliverance was at hand. I had surveyed the country in advance of four *Greenwich Village*

Follies when A. L. Jones and Morris Green, producers of that annual, named me their New York press agent in the spring of '25. I wasn't summoned because of my exceptional conduct in the field. Richard Richards, my predecessor in the post, had died.

9

Resident in Manhattan

NAMED Jones and Green's general press agent, I came down with misgivings. One minute exhilarated, the next I'd be gnawed by doubt. With *Frivolities* I'd laid an egg. What if I took an encore? In competition with eighty other press agents, I might be lost in the shuffle. As the firm's roving deputy, I was subject to little discipline. In Times Square, I'd be under the gun, my employers at my elbow. Against these alarms was the promise of comfort.

A road agent led a gypsy existence. Willard Keefe has described the tribe as "salaried Okies." Trains arrived in towns I visited at seven in the morning. The hotel room assigned me rarely was made up. Often it reeked of the caprices of the previous guest. My room in Walla Walla lacked a window. The hutch I drew in Wichita had no fire escape. If awakened by smoke, I was to lower myself from the window on a knotted rope. Eating was a hazard. Standards of cooking ranged from exceptional (San Francisco) to soggy (Middle West). In Provo, Utah, the theatre manager reprimanded me for smoking. The illumination in hotel cells discouraged reading.

My economic position was touch and go. My salary was $150 a week. Out of this sum, I paid all my traveling expenses save transportation and kept up an establishment for my wife in New York. I was idle for three months each summer. Establishment is a pretty flossy word for a four-room flat in a fifth-floor walk-up on Washington Heights. But budgetary problems were my least concern. Compared to my pre-*Frivolities* phase, I was living in luxury. At my peak on *The American Angler,* I was paid $40 a week, a wage augmented by the $12 I received for taking tickets at the Morosco.

But I should profit from the experience gained in five years on the road. No longer was I awed by the *mystique* of press agentry. Equipped with some resource and intelligence, the ability to write a declarative sentence and some understanding of good will, what had I to fear?

On taking office, my first assignment was *Desire Under the Elms,* perhaps Eugene O'Neill's most powerful play. It had been produced at the Greenwich Village Theatre the previous November by O'Neill, designer Robert Edmond Jones and Kenneth MacGowan, a reformed drama critic. Acclaimed there, it had been brought uptown and installed at the George M. Cohan Theatre by Jones and Green. This is the common fate of off-Broadway productions blessed with critical acclaim. Few managements can resist the call of commerce, however lofty their ideals.

Press agenting a drama was a new experience. My prior scuffles had been with song-and-dance shows. Because of the note of the author and the grimness of the plot, *Desire Under the Elms* must be publicized with dignity. The raffish inventions used to inflate a *Greenwich Village Follies,* and its adagio dancers, clowns and acrobats, were taboo. *Desire* made few demands on my resources. In the fourth month of its run when I joined it, the play was no longer news. My work was routine, bulletins about the play's progress and popularity, feature stories about its players and an occasional newspaper ad. Taking over in mid-term worked to my advantage. Spared the complications of an opening night, of christening a new play, I was under no pressure. I could familiarize myself with tactics at leisure. No miracles were expected of me. I didn't volunteer any. Eased into an established hit, my alarms ebbed. Relaxed, I rejoiced in New York.

I remember *Desire Under the Elms* best for Walter Huston. His performance of the seventy-five-year-old Ephraim Cabot, gaunt and bitter New England farmer, was superb. Aside from his performance, Huston inspired me. Then forty, Huston had prowled the country in vaudeville for fifteen years before gaining recognition in O'Neill's tragedy. A vivid actor, Walter was a vivid companion. He introduced me to Greenwich Village deadfalls. Riding uptown in his Ford at four in the morning was an exciting experience. He was partial to the route under the Sixth Avenue El and was expert in caroming from pillar to pillar. Twenty-one years later I was the press agent for Jean Paul Sartre's *No Exit*—the scene was laid in hell—directed by Walter's son John.

On Christmas Eve of '25, I presided at the opening of the new *Greenwich Village Follies*. Conforming with tribal custom, I wore my first dinner coat. The revue limped along for twenty weeks. In a desperate, if unworthy, effort to bolster the box office, Jones and Green signed Joyce Hawley. Miss Hawley was untalented but notorious. For a fee she had stripped and dunked herself in a tub of champagne to climax a rout touched off by Earl Carroll for the edification of one of the backers of his *Vanities*.

When news of this escapade leaked out—most of the town's gossip columnists were among the guests—the sanctified screamed protests. Carroll was a scofflaw, they cried. He should swing from a gibbet. Rival producers were nettled. They envied the newspaper space the Carroll circus received. Charged with violation of the Eighteenth Amendment, of thumbing his nose at enforcement, Carroll went on trial in General Sessions for perjury. Miss Hawley was the prosecution's star witness.

I had some sympathy for Carroll. He, too, had started as an usher. He had written the lyrics and music for *Canary Cottage,* a tenant of the Morosco during my tenure as ticket taker. Carroll wore a smock, a world-weary smile, and other trappings of genius. Back in 1916, he made the feature pages as the occupant of Manhattan's first penthouse. He, too, aspired to the throne of Ziegfeld.

Trussed up in our Sunday finery, Dad, Mother, Loretta and I faced a camera together for the first and only time. The ordeal behind us, we bolted back to the ranch.

Chinook's challenge to Bix Beiderbecke and Louis Armstrong. I'm holding the horn with which I mutilated the marches of John Philip Sousa and laid waste the national anthem.

Dad, my Uncle Dick (standing) and a pioneer unknown to your correspondent. Derbies, opera hats and cigars were de rigueur in Montana saloon society in the 1890's.

Twelve iron men made up the Chinook High School football team of 1906, which went through the season unbeaten, untied and unscored on. In our only game we clobbered Havre 26-0. The triple-threat man clutching ball is captain and quarterback Maney.

Head usher at Seattle's Moore Theatre, circa 1912. Though under an academic cloud I had run 14 at straight pool and could give names and batting averages of all second basemen in Three-I League.

Palavering with Lillian Gish and her West Highland white terrier in the star's dressing room at the historic Empire during the run of Maxwell Anderson's The Star Wagon.

Jed Harris eyes me cynically as I outline a publicity coup calculated to confuse the enemy and stimulate business for Coquette. The man in the middle is Paul Streger, casting director.

Eileen Darby—Graphic House

During a rehearsal of Jumbo at the Hippodrome, Billy Rose hums a Rodgers and Hart song to angel Jock Whitney. I'm in front pew flanked by co-author Charlie MacArthur.

Eileen Darby—Graphic House

The mustached man is producer Herman Shumlin. Whatever amused me and Kermit Bloomgarden at a dress rehearsal of The Great Big Doorstep in Boston failed to thaw out our master.

Bantering with Shirley Booth during a picture call for A Tree Grows in Brooklyn. The critics voted Shirley's Aunt Cissy the best musical comedy performance of the year.

Vandamm Studio

Gilbert Miller, for whom I've press agented thirty plays, regards Al Hirschfeld, caricaturist whose witty drawings of stage folk decorate page 1 of the Times's Sunday drama section.

I'm the stiff in the window seat, understudy to one of the thirteen victims of the gentle Brewster sisters and their lethal elderberry wine in Arsenic and Old Lace.

Richard Avedon—Harper's Bazaar

At the request of Harper's Bazaar, I provide the background for Tallulah Bankhead and her Maltese poodle, Doloras, in a feature story dedicated to the stars and the men who hymn them. Because of Tallulah's iron whim I've publicized all but one of her New York engagements over the last eighteen years.

I confront Bill Frawley, who played Owen O'Malley, disillusioned press agent in Twentieth Century. Hecht and MacArthur modeled O'Malley after me.

Betty airs Dark Boy, a gift from "Tex" O'Reilly and the pride of the Maney stable, at our Westport home a few months before Pearl Harbor.

The press agent, director Elia Kazan, scene designer Albert Johnson and producer Michael Myerberg in a dress-rehearsal huddle on the eve of the opening of Thornton Wilder's salute to mankind, The Skin of Our Teeth.

Eileen Darby—Graphic House

clining Figure was Harry Kurnitz's comedy about a wealthy art collector bamozled by a bogus Renoir. To hop up the ads, producers Martin Gabel and nry Margolis commissioned artist Tully Filmus to paint a wench in the Renoir nner. Though faithfully limned, Filmus' belle (left) seemed a touch grim for box-ice purposes. We needed a more provocative nude to bait the peasants. From nus' original, caricaturist Al Hirschfeld sketched a more knowing nymph. The ad h the revised figure blazed in the Herald Tribune's drama section, but the Times ected the sylph as too brazen in her exposures. When we protested, the Times npromised. It would run Hirschfeld's hussy if she was brassièred. Al obliged wer right) and Broadway roared with laughter on viewing the conflicting treat-nts. Life, Time, Newsweek and Editor and Publisher memorialized the controversy h illustrations. In this crisis the Times reassessed its position, then rescinded the n on the babe's breasts.

George Karger—Pix

o humor a Life editor I model the ghoul-sh vest which Mrs. Theodore Roosevelt, r., embroidered for Alexander Woollcott. 3ack of vest carried verse (Psalms 17:10) o fit portly critic.

Albert Fenn—courtesy *Life*, © 1945, Time, Inc.

The barroom of Bleeck's, throughout prohibition known as "man's last citadel" since the gentler sex was outlawed. Here I tippled for twenty-five years. Match-game players in foreground: Lucius Beebe, William Houghton and Joseph Driscoll, all *Herald Tribune* men, plus author. Leo and Henry are the martyrs behind the counter.

On the opening day of the trial, I ran this ad in the morning
papers:

2 PUBLIC APPEARANCES TODAY!

J O Y C E   H A W L E Y

(The Porcelain Prankster)

at 10:30 in

JUSTICE GODDART'S COURT

at 2:30 in

GREENWICH VILLAGE FOLLIES

My office telephone rang early that morning. Was I the author
of the Joyce Hawley ad? Anticipating applause, I confessed. My
caller was a bailiff in Justice Goddart's court. He didn't beat about
the bush. A repetition of the ad and I'd be jugged for contempt, he
warned. I took the hint. The sequel? Carroll did a year in Atlanta.
Miss Hawley went over the hill to oblivion.

This ecdysiast behind me, my standards sagged. By such dodges
as matinees "For Women Only," and by stressing its carnal content,
I contributed to the twenty-week run of *One Man's Woman,* one
of the most odious plays ever loosed on Manhattan Island. Why
did I exploit so offensive a work? I couldn't afford to be idle.
Indeed I was about to compound my delinquency.

The Squall was the sordid recital of the havoc wrought by a
gypsy waif afflicted with pidgin English. Nubi—that was the name
of the Jezebel—seduced every male in the household of her benefactor. Charged with malpractice, she sought a stay of execution.
"Nubi good girl. Nubi stay?" she implored. This plea routed Robert
Benchley, critic of the year-old *New Yorker.* Citing the deplorable
events which had preceded it, Benchley fled the theatre. He explained
to his readers, "Benchley bad boy. Benchley go."

Seeking to capitalize on this rebuke, I inserted "the Play that
made a Street-Walker of Robert Benchley" in the daily ads. The
New York Times rejected this flippancy. It relented when I changed
"street-walker" to "nocturnal nomad." To further inflame the
community, I identified *The Squall* as "a passionate drama of the
sexes." The implication that there were more than two sexes was a

taunt the curious could not withstand. Appealing to the baser side
of pedestrians, I plastered the front of the theatre with enlarged photographs of the play's sinful episodes. These bared Nubi's sultry
charms to a degree not approximated in the three-act horror. *The
Squall* prospered for eight months, thanks to Benchley and a relentless
airing of its sexual heresies. Though I gained a shabby triumph,
I did not exult. I had conspired in a swindle. I had some notable
conspirators, among them Dorothy Stickney, Sylvia Sidney, Blanche
Yurka and Romney Brent. Actors must eat, too.

My success in tricking slummers into *One Man's Woman* and
The Squall, my ability to catch the eye of a judge in General Sessions
gained me momentary renown in Times Square. For the first time
I sipped fame or its Broadway counterfeit. Though it was heady
stuff, I was not deluded. Such recognition as I had won sprang
from service to stinkers. I would welcome the opportunity to practice
on a play of merit, one with critical approval. Save for *Desire Under
the Elms,* I had not represented a work of consequence. I couldn't
take any bows for the O'Neill play. It was an established success
when I joined it.

Nothing so enhances a press agent's note as a sellout. A succession
of hits and he is hailed as another Aladdin. In no other activity
does the fame-by-association sophistry flourish as it does in the
theatre. But my seedy status was self-imposed. I didn't need to look
for a hit. A spectacular one had been beckoning to me for weeks.
Fittingly enough it was called *Broadway.* Its producer was Jed Harris,
the truculent young man with whom I had shared so many dawns
in Chicago.

10

The Gitano

"**W**HO'S that bird?" a friend asked screen writer Henry Myers, pointing me out at the opening of *Serena Blandish.* "Don't tell me you don't know," said Henry, arching his eyebrows. "That's Jed Harris' representative on earth." Noel Coward dubbed Harris *Destiny's Tot.* The observations of Myers and Coward were testimonials to Harris' eminence at the end of the twenties. In less than two years, he had produced *Broadway, Coquette, The Royal Family* and *The Front Page,* all resounding hits. Addicted to hyperbole, theatre folk hailed Harris as a genius. Genius is not a word to bandy about. I have yet to meet anyone in the amusement world who rates this accolade save Charles Chaplin. But beyond any of his rivals, Harris had symptoms of genius.

There is evidence that eccentricity is the complement of genius. Men of rare gifts often flout conformity. Their revolt may be expressed in attire, speech or conduct. Though most geniuses are eccentric, few eccentrics qualify as geniuses. If genius and eccentricity were synonymous, the theatre would be crawling with supermen. Though a demi-genius, Harris was a top-flight eccentric.

As noted earlier, I first met Harris in Chicago in '24 when I was publicizing my fifth *Greenwich Village Follies* and he was the courier for *Apple Sauce*. Harris was lean, dark and hungry looking. Then but twenty-four, he had a remarkable set of phobias. Scorched with ambition, he felt he had a higher destiny than eulogizing Alan Dinehart, star of *Apple Sauce*. He fumed at the circumstances which prevented him from producing plays in New York. He was convinced he was better equipped than those thus engaged. After listening to him for twenty minutes, I was convinced, too. He discussed the theatre more intelligently and eloquently than anyone I had met. True, I had met few stage oracles. But in the past thirty years I have met most of the theatre's wizards and my opinion of Harris still stands.

Jed and I hit it off from the start. He didn't like to go to bed either. We shared a suspicion of the theatre's anointed. We had another common interest: Jacques Fournier. Jacques was a left-handed first baseman, a wicked hitter but confused when trying to subdue a ground ball. Jacques once tried to murder Jed. The scene was Newark. When a soft hopper slithered through Fournier's ankles letting in the winning run, Jed denounced the bungler from the front row of the bleachers. Ignited by Jed's invective, Jacques leaped into the stands to dismember him. Following the precepts of J. Caesar, Harris sought safety in flight. I had seen Jacques perform in Seattle. Our mutual interest in Jacques was the base for a warm friendship.

Harris was a more stimulating companion than any press agent I had met. While his mates talked about sniping three-sheets, planting layouts and circumventing the drama editor of the *Chicago Tribune,* Harris carried on about Stanislavsky, Meyerhold and Gordon Craig. While they studied the overnight entries at Jamaica, Harris rhapsodized over Max Beerbohm's *Zuleika Dobson*. After a couple of swigs of the varnish then popular on Randolph Street, Jed would wax voluble. He could play the fiddle. He had spent two unhappy years at Yale. He had worked on the New York *Clipper*, theatrical trade weekly. He had bummed his way across the continent, riding the rods. During his hobo phase, he had been mistaken for a returned war hero while shuffling into a Colorado town. A cheering throng picked him up and carried him through the streets on their shoulders.

When I hinted that this tale could do with a little documentation, Harris got apoplectic.

In Chicago, Jed was known as "the horizontal press agent," because of his reluctance to get up once he'd retired. Most workers in the theatre are late risers, but only actors can luxuriate beyond noon. Jed would turn up bright and brisk when his opponents were ready to go home. This led to a lot of acrimony.

Charged with industry when vertical, Jed rarely found time to shave. This omission, plus spontaneous whiskers, contributed to his menace. Shaved or bristled, he was acid and truculent. Night after night he'd pontificate in one-armed beaneries in the Loop. We grieved when disaster overtook the New York Giants in the final game of the World Series. About to catch a pop foul from the bat of Washington's Muddy Ruel, catcher Hank Gowdy stepped into his own mask. Reprieved, Ruel hit a double to left, and shortly scored the decisive run when a bounder from McNeeley's bat struck a pebble and hopped over Lindstrom's head. (My ability to remember trivia like this is phenomenal.)

Jed had an exclusive grief. A month before Gowdy was booby-trapped, *What Price Glory?* opened in New York. Written by Maxwell Anderson and Laurence Stallings, it seethed with profanity and tough doughboy talk. Louis Wolheim's Captain Flagg and William Boyd's Sergeant Quirt were the talk of the town. *What Price Glory?*, Jed told me, was to have been his first production. He had worked on it with Anderson, then on the staff of the New York *World,* and Anderson had promised him he could produce it. Enter now the villain, Alexander Woollcott, critic of the *Sun.* A crony of Stallings, Woollcott warned him against giving the play to an unknown. Only Arthur Hopkins, argued Woollcott, could give *What Price Glory?* the eloquent, sensitive treatment it demanded.

Stallings was a swashbuckler with an overwhelming personality. A Marine in World War I, he had lost a leg at Belleau Wood. Cued by Woollcott, he insisted on Hopkins. If Anderson argued Harris' case, it was to no avail. That's why Hopkins had a hit in New York, why Jed writhed in Chicago.

But Jed was going to be a producer or perish. *Apple Sauce* was his last stand as a press agent. About the time I was assigned to *Desire Under the Elms,* Jed opened an office in New York. His aide and confidant was Herman Shumlin, a Newark schoolmate.

Jed's first two ventures fizzled. *Weak Sisters,* in a singular sense, affirmed its title. *Love 'Em and Leave 'Em,* Mankiewicz' betrayer, had a tantalizing run, but added neither to his repute nor his purse. But Jed was not easily discouraged. He learned much from these trial heats. The production of *Broadway* in September of '26 confirmed his conviction that he was the peer of any living producer. Overnight, he became the theatre's wonder boy.

The history of *Broadway* is a cockeyed variation of a Horatio Alger theme. Written by an unknown, produced by an unknown, it became the outstanding melodramatic hit of the century. Though *Broadway* was fated to make millions, and in its adaptations cheer theatre goers in every European capital, it was scorned by almost every producer in New York. Its pre-production ordeals illustrated the vulnerability of the theatre's sages.

Broadway was the work of Philip Dunning, stage manager for William A. Brady. Under the title *White Little Guy,* he completed it in the summer of '24. Within the year, and under a variety of titles, it was read by the Shuberts, George M. Cohan, the Selwyns, Rufus LeMaire, Oliver Morosco, Kilbourne Gordon, Jones and Green, Mike Goldreyer and lesser fry. They hemmed, they hawed and they quibbled, but none of them would risk a dime on it.

The play pivoted about the tribulations of Roy Lane, brash young hoofer, in the Paradise Night Club. In turn, Dunning persuaded Skeets Gallagher, Eddie Buzzell, Hal Skelly and Joe Laurie, Jr., to read it. They were comedians of consequence. If one of these clowns liked it, he might persuade a producer to put it on. Since Roy Lane was a fat role, they all liked it. But nothing happened. Dunning changed the title to *Bright Lights.*

Brady, Dunning's employer, gave him $500 for a six-month option on *Bright Lights* in July, '25. Cheered by this vote of confidence, the author was confused when next day's newspapers said Brady was to produce *So This Is New York,* a play by Philip Dunning. Brady was a violent Celt with an insatiable thirst and a flair for controversy. His wife was Grace George, brilliant comedienne. His daughter, Alice, was a superb dramatic actress. In his forty years in the theatre, he had been actor, director, producer and theatre operator. He had managed heavyweight champion James J. Corbett. He was an expert on parliamentary law and a master of billingsgate.

I first saw Brady at an emergency meeting of producers. Playwright George Broadhurst was temporary chairman. Before he could raise his gavel, Brady chilled him with a ten-minute tirade. Bracing himself on the backs of two chairs and weaving like a cobra, he snorted defiance. Failing to quell Brady, Broadhurst ordered the sergeant-at-arms to eject him. Brady whipped out Roberts' Rules of Order and challenged the ruling. In a speech reminiscent of Cicero's oration against Catiline, he convinced the stunned assembly that, as temporary chairman, Broadhurst lacked authority to name a sergeant-at-arms. Whatever crisis menaced the managers went unresolved. When I left Brady was still fulminating. Broadhurst and his appointee had taken to the hills.

Writing out the advance royalty check exhausted Brady. He went to Atlantic City to recuperate, and remained there incommunicado for weeks. Desperate, Dunning tracked him down. Irritated by his intrusion, Brady told Dunning to produce the play himself. "But don't pay any actor over $200 a week," he said. It would be impossible to get proper actors for the roles of Roy Lane and gangster Steve Crandall at that figure, Dunning protested. "You can get English actors for $200, can't you?" snorted Brady.

In January, Brady gave Dunning another $500 check to extend his option for six months. A month later, a young actor named James Cagney read the Roy Lane role for him. Unimpressed, the producer turned the play over to William Brady, Jr. Young Bill was a frustrated cavalry officer. He didn't like the theatre. What's more, he didn't like *Bright Lights*. Dunning couldn't afford to needle Brady. He might needle himself out of a job. In despair, Dunning picked up the copies of the play in Brady's office and set out to tree another producer.

He recalled a press agent named Harris he had met a year earlier in Detroit while stage manager for a Brady play. Harris had read

Bright Lights and enthused over the Paradise entertainers and the hoodlums who applauded them. Inquiry revealed this was the Harris about to produce *Love 'Em and Leave 'Em.* Grasping at straws, Dunning sent Harris one of the scripts he had salvaged from the Brady office.

Two days later Harris called Dunning, his hair on fire. He didn't have the money to produce the play, but he swore he'd get it. Harris persuaded Crosby Gaige to read the melodrama. Gaige agreed to finance the play in return for half the producer's profits. Gaige was "loaded," thanks to association with producers Edgar and Archie Selwyn. Harris found Gaige a desirable colleague for other reasons. Gaige played poker with Heywood Broun and Herbert Bayard Swope and was a first-edition collector. He had a country estate in Westchester and was an authority on vintage wine and Basque cooking. Harris was a Western-sandwich man.

Dunning concurring, Harris called in George Abbott, a reformed actor, to direct the play and to help rewrite some of its scenes. Abbott had performed similarly for *Love 'Em and Leave 'Em.*

With Lee Tracy as Roy Lane, *Bright Lights* played its first performance at the Apollo Theatre, Atlantic City, on July 5. The audience was scant and the play was panned by Philadelphia critics. Alarmed, Harris developed buck fever. He suggested Hugh Ford be called in to rewrite the second act. Dunning dissented. The ensuing debate rocked the boardwalk. It reached a crescendo the following week in Asbury Park and Long Branch. But Dunning stuck to his guns. Rechristened during its skirmishes on the shore, *Broadway* was unaltered when it opened at the Broadhurst in New York. It remained there for seventy-six weeks.

Dunning didn't see the curtain rise on *Broadway's* opening. He had to get the curtain up at the New Amsterdam where he was stage manager for *Sunny.* Outraged he couldn't see the opening of his first play, *Sunny's* stars chased Dunning out of the theatre at nine o'clock. The stars? Marilyn Miller, Jack Donahue and Clifton Webb. Rarely has a stage manager been routed by so celebrated a trio.

Though the first-night audience cheered *Broadway,* those rancid

Philadelphia reviews still echoed in Dunning's ears. It wasn't until he read Percy Hammond in the *Tribune* that he relaxed. Wrote Mr. Hammond: " 'Broadway' is the most completely acted and perfectly directed hall show I have seen in thirty years of professional play-going." Harris' nemesis, Alexander Woollcott, waxed hysterical in the *World*. "The official hat of this department, which has almost forgotten how it feels to leave the departmental head, is hereby sent into the air for 'Broadway.' "

As Dunning's ears tingled, Brady's face turned red. So did the kissers of other producers who spurned *Broadway*. Scarlet, too, were the pans of the Philadelphia reviewers. Hawked up and down the street for which it was named for two years, *Broadway* was a monument to the fallibility of the theatre's high brass. When the original company rounded out its first year at the Broadhurst, six duplications of *Broadway* were scouring the country. One copy played twenty-two weeks in Detroit. The troupe which opened at the Strand Theatre, London, three nights before Christmas, stayed for forty weeks. Translations raged in Vienna, Berlin, Budapest, Sofia, Bucharest and Leningrad. When Universal Pictures bought the silent-screen rights for $235,000, one of its brass suggested this sum should embrace "talking-picture" rights. He was hushed as a heretic. Had Universal heeded this visionary, it would have saved $55,000, the sum it had to fork over when it decided on a vocal version. Silent firms started to dissolve when Al Jolson appeared in *The Jazz Singer* (1927). Remember?

Harris and Gaige whacked up better than $2,000,000. A sentimentalist, Dunning parted with Marilyn Miller and Jack Donahue reluctantly. His chagrin was tempered by the $450,000 he received in royalties.

Success didn't rob Jed of his hatreds. It sharpened them and provided him with a larger arena in which to exercise them. Hailed as a magician, he demonstrated a rare talent for hostility. His candor shocked those conditioned to twaddle from the theatre's bigshots. Successively, he lashed out at critics, producers, playwrights and actors. Convinced the theatre was his oyster, he hosed down all comers with his scorn.

Although he had loathed being a press agent, Jed was sensitive to the rewards of publicity. Seeking a literate crier, he tapped S. N. Behrman. Behrman had degrees from Harvard and Columbia. He had reviewed books for the *New York Times* and the *New Republic,* and had written two plays. Shy and sensitive, he couldn't cope with the bluster and confusion of his office. Infatuated with the Restoration dramatists, and enslaved by Richard Brinsley Sheridan, Behrman became nauseated when harried about three-sheet locations, ads in hotel guides, coarse-screen mats and other craft matters. Still another thing contributed to Berry's vertigo: the fey deportment of his master.

In Jed's hands the telephone was an instrument of torture. He thought nothing of paging an aide at three in the morning. A sun dodger, he tried to conduct his affairs from his couch. This tactic preyed on Behrman's mind. Slinking from his cell at five-thirty, Berry would be appalled when Jed burst from the elevator fresh as a daisy.

Shortly after *Broadway's* opening, Behrman decided press agentry was too rowdy a trade. He sought a cloistered profession. Those familiar with the wit and gaiety of *The Second Man, Brief Moment, Biography* and *Jacobowsky and the Colonel* know of his success. Famed as a playwright, applauded for brilliant profiles of Ferenc Molnár and Joseph Duveen in *The New Yorker,* Behrman still cringes at sight of a telephone. Only a handful of intimates have his private number. Others trying to communicate with him must use the mails or apply for a court writ.

When Behrman went over the hill, Arthur Kober succeeded him in the Harris cabinet. Kober, too, was shy and sensitive. But he had the advantage of prior practice. Attempting to adjust himself to the caprices of the proprietor, Kober came down with the fantods. He felt he could recuperate only in the quiet of a Hollywood studio. He was prepared to make any sacrifice to become a screen writer.

Periodically Harris asked me to join his staff. To publicize *Broadway* after exposure to *One Man's Woman* and *The Squall* was tempting. Two things stayed me. I had a sentimental loyalty to Jones and Green. They had rescued me from the road. Working for Harris might breach our friendship. I was aware of his flaws as an employer. My scruples evaporated in May of '27 when he tilted the salary figure.

When I enrolled with Harris, Herman Shumlin, later to achieve note as director and producer, was his general manager, Paul Streger his casting director. Earle McGill, classmate of Jed's at Yale, acted as liaison officer and pinch hitter. In between times, he understudied Luigi Bardi, the coin-clinking waiter in *Broadway*. McGill later was cited for distinguished service in radio. Eddie Blatt, subsequent stage producer and screen executive, doubled as office boy and spy. Whittaker Ray, an affable outlaw from Philadelphia, was awaiting assignment. He became general manager when Shumlin found irreconcilable chinks in his schoolmate's armor.

Shortly after I signed with Jed, Shumlin, seeking to abate the din and traffic in the corridor, ordered stacks of interoffice communications. When filled out, this listed the name of the petitioner, his target, and a clue to his quest. I addressed my first chit to Harris. It read, "What time is it?" After an interval I sent him a second: "Whatever happened to Dorothy Arnold?" Miss Arnold, an heiress, had vanished into thin air on Fifth Avenue in the 1880's. Mr. Harris didn't vouchsafe me a reply. Instead he summoned Shumlin and ordered him to consign the forms to the flames.

Broadway's success enabled Jed to indulge an old ambition. Eager to plow the deep, he purchased a fifty-foot sloop with auxiliary motor. Because of his nautical bent, trusties could be observed fleeing down fire escapes of late afternoons. Any minute one of us might be nominated for overnight duty on the yacht. To escape this fate, we'd risk life and limb.

Harris was intimidated by his crew. If he suggested a sail at sunset, the captain would scan the sky and say a blow was coming up. They'd better batten down the hatches. A guest aboard the lugger would have been as comfortable sitting in a stalled taxicab in Central Park on a hot afternoon. The boiled chicken and Jello which came out of the galley didn't cheer the shanghaied. In all my nights on this clipper, it never moved a foot. My only cruise was in its dory. To thwart the crew, thus get a breeze in his mane, Jed bought

an outboard motor. At dusk we clambered into the dory. Harris
screwed the motor to the rear of the craft and yanked the starting
rope. The motor snorted. We had putt-putted about fifty feet when
it arched into the air, then plummeted to the bottom of Long Island
Sound. Concentrating on the fiddle in his childhood, Jed had bypassed
swimming. There were no oars. Very awkward!

When in the clutch of Conrad, Jed wasn't easy to circumvent.
A night I shared on his craft with Warren Nolan and Ed Hughes
still haunts my dreams. Jed promised us a sail out of City Island
and all the martinis we could hold. We'd have a night under the
stars with a breeze whipping us along at ten knots. The martini
gambit proved the greatest hoax since the invention of the shell
game. There wasn't a jigger of gin in the galley. Tinkering with his
second act, the cook had charred the chicken. When Jed suggested
a spin the captain scowled and said the craft might suffer the fate
of the *Hesperus* if he so much as raised the anchor. At nine o'clock
the coward came out in Hughes. An artist on the *Telegram,* Hughes
said he had to get back to draw tomorrow's cartoon. Nolan and
I volunteered to go with him. A frown from my liege lord stayed us.

Hesitating to rouse the crew, Harris said he'd row Hughes ashore.
It was pitch dark. As soon as Hughes and Harris lowered the dory
from its davits and clambered in, Nolan and I dashed below to
ransack crannies and closets for the gin. A cry of terror stabbed
the night. We rushed on deck to see Harris rowing furiously toward
us, a geyser spouting from the dory's floor. In the nick of time, we
dragged the derelicts aboard. Despite his years before the mast,
Harris had forgotten that the cork in the bottom of a dory is
removed at night to prevent accumulation of rainwater. He still
couldn't swim. Nor could Hughes.

Though mastery of the crawl eluded him, though the crew foiled
his marine urges, the theatre presented no hurdles Harris couldn't
skim. Within a six-week span he produced *Coquette* and *The Royal
Family*. Both were immediate sellouts. Both showed the Harris
touch, said the reviewers. This vague salute nettled him. Aware
few producers contributed much beyond money, Jed crackled with
suggestions for revisions in plot and dialogue.

George Abbott had directed *Coquette,* and was its co-author. *The Royal Family,* a caricature of the home life of the Barrymores, was the work of George S. Kaufman and Edna Ferber. It was staged by David Butler.

Though eager to direct, Jed contented himself with spraying Abbott and Butler with advice. Because many of his cues were inspired, and all presented with vigor, they were woven into the play. Since none of the reviewers were clairvoyant, they did not recognize and identify these golden threads in the fabric of the play, an omission that devastated Jed.

My two years with Harris were the most outrageous and hilarious I've spent in the theatre. Harris moved to the Sardi Building in West Forty-fourth Street in the fall of 1928. This shift from the Selwyn on Forty-second Street was necessitated by the increased activities of the mahatma, the intrusion of secretaries, office boys, telephone operators and visitors come to pay him reverence.

The office lacked one piece of equipment it sorely needed—a ticker. Every inmate was in the market. The office boy had twenty shares of Bank of America on margin. The proprietor was loaded with Radio Corporation. This author leaned toward the red metal— Anaconda Copper—on the strength of a hot tip from Ann Andrews and Roger Pryor, in the cast of *The Royal Family*. General manager Whittaker Ray scorned the big board for the curb. The auditor was trying to corner International Knickknacks. When a quorum was needed a messenger was dispatched to the brokerage office in the Astor Hotel fifty yards northeast of headquarters. Barring a crisis, business was suspended from ten to three.

Harris scorned competitors and people tactless enough to work for them. Poltroons with whom he disagreed, who were rash enough to traffic with the enemy, or who did not concede his pre-eminence, were identified as sons-of-bitches. It was no secret that many of the theatre's nobility were thus stigmatized. For corporate reasons, each Harris hit had its own bank account, hence its own checkbook. "S.O.B. Local No. 1" was engraved on *Coquette* checks, "S.O.B. Local No. 2" on those of *The Royal Family*. Lest he be charged with discrimination, the *Front Page* certificates bore the inscription

"S.O.B. Ladies Auxiliary." When the three-year-old son of George Brooks, co-author of *Spread Eagle,* started to caper in the hall while Mr. Harris was deep in meditation, there was talk of a Boy Scout chapter. This simmered down when Jed's fire was diverted by a necktie peddler who had penetrated the blockade.

Feuds with the Shuberts, who operated most of the theatres in New York, with newspapermen, critics, waiters, playwrights, night watchmen and cab drivers raged. In tribute to Jed's talent in this field, I hung a sign from his door, which read: WHERE THE GRAPES OF WRATH ARE STORED. The staff identified our employer as "the Earth Shaker" and "the Gitano." This last was inspired by a painting of a Spanish gypsy, the image of our mentor. Years later, an authority identified the Harris of this era as "the old non-appeaser, berater, and all-time, All-American uncompromising megalomaniac." The authority? Jed Harris.

Starting with a Chicago playwright, a column writer and a tardy guest at the opening of *Spread Eagle,* membership in the S.O.B.'s mushroomed. The club went international in January of '28, and at the same time enjoyed its largest initiation. When *Broadway* opened in Budapest, Alexander Ince, Harris' Balkan agent, cabled that the play had taken the town by storm, that it would run until the Danube dried up. Elation over this triumph ebbed when weeks passed without word from Ince. A letter with a Budapest stamp brought all hands to the throne room to hear Ince's tardy report. Harris opened the dispatch, scanned the enclosure, then announced: "Ince is a son-of-a-bitch." No word broke the hush until Harris spoke again: "All Hungarians are sons-of-bitches." He was provoked to this verdict by the profit check. It was for 500 pengö, roughly $85.

The Front Page was written by Ben Hecht and Charles MacArthur out of their experiences in the Cook County Criminal Courts' Building in Chicago. Profane and irreverent, it was a brilliant cartoon of reporters assigned to cover the activities of the jailed and the jailors. Magnificently directed by George Kaufman, blessed with vivid performances by Lee Tracy, as a fanatic reporter, and Osgood Perkins, as a maniacal city editor, *The Front Page* was violent and uproarious.

Brooks Atkinson, *New York Times* critic, found it exhilarating. But Adolph Ochs, the *Times's* owner and publisher, was shocked. His attorney, George Gordon Battle, wrote a letter of protest to the *Times* Sunday editor. George Kaufman, then drama editor of the *Times,* warned me our ads might be tossed out of his newspaper. Mr. Ochs considered the play a libel of the Fourth Estate. In it, a reporter was described as "a cross between a bellboy and a whore." Another of the play's reporters, who had once served the *Times,* said: "It was like working in a bank."

The cast of *The Front Page* shrank at the dress rehearsal. Harris, the authors, Kaufman and I sat in on this run-through at Maxine Elliott's Theatre. Charles Gilpin, the original Brutus Jones in *Emperor Jones,* was impersonating Alderman Willoughby. On his first entrance, Gilpin struck a dramatic stance, but no words came from him. "Throw him a line," Kaufman yelled to the stage manager. Mr. Gilpin bristled. "It isn't words I lack, it's feeling," he said. "Take the entrance again," said Kaufman. Mr. Gilpin exited, re-entered and remained mute. Signaling for a recess, Kaufman vaulted to the stage and huddled with the Alderman. Shortly he dismissed him and returned to us. "He's full of gin," said George. "Tight as a coot. Someone had better pedal up to Harlem for another Willoughby."

"Why doesn't Jed play him?" asked MacArthur.

"If he does, we'll have to change the name of the character to Erastus Goldberg," added Hecht. That night Willoughby was excised from the script.

Bluenoses charged that the play's dialogue poisoned the ear. They pelted District Attorney Joab Banton with protests. Rumors reached Harris that official action against the play might ensue. This galvanized Hecht, the Anse Hatfield of Nyack, into action. He ordered sandwich signs carrying these questions: WHERE WAS JOAB BANTON ON THE NIGHT OF MAY 14? WHAT DOES JOAB BANTON KNOW ABOUT THE DOT KING MURDER? Stenographers from the Police Department dropped into the theatre to jot down samples of the dialogue. A friend at headquarters tipped us off to these visits, thus enabling the stage manager to perfume the dialogue for the night.

Two of these sleuths called on Tracy in his dressing room before a matinee. Tracy plied them with illegal beverages. So great was his hospitality they slept through the last two acts.

Hecht rushed into my office one afternoon boiling with anger. He had just had a call from his mother. Over the radio she had heard that the police were going to raid the play that night and jug all the actors. I tried to reason with Ben. If the police were going to make a pinch, it seemed unlikely they would broadcast a warning.

"Are you calling my mother a liar?" he roared.

St. John Ervine, distinguished playwright and critic of the London *Observer,* was exchange critic on the New York *World* in 1927. For reasons that now escape me, Hecht and MacArthur resented the invader. Learning he was about to see *The Front Page,* the pair conspired with the company electrician and property man to so rig his seat that the flick of a switch would cause it to collapse and roll him into the aisle. This plot never got off the drawing board. Harris pointed out that Herbert Bayard Swope, editor of the *World,* might take umbrage and resort to retaliatory action.

Once street fighting simmered down, intramural strife broke out. Leo Marsh, drama editor of Hearst's *American,* was the innocent cause of a fine donnybrook. He called me one morning to say that Gilbert Gabriel, the *American's* drama critic, was ill and unable to write his syndicated column for Sunday. A by-line piece by one of Harris' authors would be a fine substitute, he said. Could he have eight hundred words by Tuesday noon? No restriction on theme. Eager for this space, I canvassed prospects. Hecht volunteered. He smiled sardonically when I asked him his topic. He was going to toast Harris, he said.

In a deranged moment, I told Jed Hecht was going to parse him. His temperature shot up three degrees. He must see Hecht's copy before it went to Marsh, he said. In an attempt to dissuade him, I cited the freedom-of-speech clause in the Bill of Rights. Jed was adamant. When I told Hecht of Jed's ultimatum he erupted, then resumed his indictment.

Harris blanched when he read Hecht's lead. "We are sitting around the office, a worldly crew, when Ariel enters," it started. There was no denying the identity of Ariel. Warming to his work, Hecht called his colleague a frustrated writer and a busybody dedicated to reshaping the lives of friends and acquaintances. There were two Harrises, he said. One was fashioned after an English dandy of the Victorian era, bowing from the waist and full of punctilio; another was reminiscent of Rasputin, the Mad Monk who destroyed Nicholas II.

Harris delivered another ultimatum. If the Hecht tribute appeared in the *American,* he must have equal space for rebuttal in a parallel column. Marsh might resent my attempt to usurp his office, I said. He wasn't in need of a co-editor. Wasn't it bad practice to look a gift horse in the mouth? Harris shrugged me off. Rashly, I had sent Hecht's piece to Marsh. Granted Marsh fell in with Jed's proposal, when would his counter-attack be ready? This was an awkward question. In the throes of composition, Harris often got bogged down in symbolism, vituperation and circumlocution. He had insisted on writing the preface to the printed edition of *The Front Page.* None of six versions pleased him. The book went to press without a preface. The second edition carried Harris' attack on Bartlett Cormack, author of *The Racket.* In a careless moment, Cormack had permitted an untouchable to produce his play.

While Harris wrestled with his prose, I called Marsh. He told me what to do with Hecht's piece, which he liked, and with Harris' phantom dissent. The furious Hecht threatened to print his tribute to Jed in the form of an ad. Shortly, Jed and Ben were distracted by a mutual enemy.

As *Serena Blandish* was about to open at the Morosco, I reminded Jed that Walter Winchell could not see the première. He had been barred from Shubert houses for saying one of their musicals was malodorous. Jed chortled defiantly. He'd teach Lee and Jake a lesson they'd not forget. He dispatched attorney Joseph Bickerton to court for a restraining order. The judge said he would pass on the plea the following Thursday. This would be two days after the opening. Shortly we learned that the judge had a relative in a Shubert box office. Jed screamed collusion, then played his ace. If Winchell was denied entrance, the curtain wouldn't go up. Faced with the refund of a soldout house, the Shuberts' mercenaries looked the other way as I escorted Walter through the Morosco's portals. All hands exulted at this great victory for the free press.

Jed's former press agent, S. N. Behrman, had adapted *Serena Blandish* from a novel by "A Lady of Quality." The anonymous author was Lady Jones, wife of the head of Reuter's. Years later, I learned she was Enid Bagnold, author of *National Velvet*. Aside from Winchell's presence, the opening was remembered for the conduct of Constance Collier. As Countess Flor di Folio, Miss Collier made her first entrance carrying a marmoset. Before she could utter a line, the monkey nipped her, whereupon she belted the simian silly.

Following *The Front Page,* Harris was singled out for cover treatment by *Time.* Researchers sought out his friends and enemies for anecdotes and libels which, when fused, would give a well-rounded picture of the victim. Earle McGill and I were examined. I was counting up at a matinee of *Coquette* the day Jed's face appeared on the newsstands. A snide caption was ribboned beneath it. The text dwelt on Jed's origin and youth, his spectacular rise in the theatre, his gifts and his flaws, his enthusiasms and his phobias. A fair estimate, I thought, though in it were items sure to infuriate my master.

This suspicion was confirmed by a call from Jed. Who was responsible for this outrage? I resorted to evasive action. It had been a big operation. A lot of authorities had been grilled. *Time's* authors were anonymous. Cornered, I confessed that Noel Busch had co-ordinated the salute. "Drop everything you're doing and bring Busch to my hotel immediately," rasped Jed.

Nonchalantly, I agreed. A *Time* editor would have better things to do than placating a wounded ego on a warm Saturday afternoon. To avoid charges of nonfeasance, I called Busch and told him of Jed's rage and demand. To my surprise, Busch agreed to the rendezvous. I picked him up in a cab and took him to Jed's suite at the Buckingham. I rang the bell. No answer. I pushed open the door. The living room was empty. Bidding Busch be seated, I entered Jed's chamber. Prone, covered by a single sheet, he fixed me with a maniacal glare.

"Mr. Busch is without, sire," I said.

Jed eyed me accusingly for a good two minutes. "Take him away," he whispered hoarsely. "I can't trust myself. Were I to face him, I might do something I'd regret all my life."

Harris, and in lesser degree his staff, were caught up in half a dozen brouhahas at once. During the tryout of *The Gaoler's Wench* in Newark, Ina Claire replied to a Harris jibe by kicking him in the stomach.

Jed ordered Archie Selwyn drawn and quartered when I reported that Archie's nephew, Solly Tepper, had opened a ticket scalper's office on the stage of the Times Square Theatre, where *The Front Page* was to open two nights hence. A blacklist of those denied access to Harris plays was headed by Morris Gest and Sidney Skolsky. I've forgotten the nature of their crimes.

Observing that Lee Shubert aired himself on the roof of the Shubert Theatre at noon each day, we dubbed him "The Priest of Apollo," with a bow to G. K. Chesterton. From our office across Forty-fourth Street, we could look down on the little man as he scowled at the sun. McGill and I commissioned the property man to construct a giant peashooter that we might pepper Jake's brother at will. We never scored a hit—faulty trajectory.

I was named an honorary vice-president of the S.O.B.'s when the proprietor learned Ring Lardner had been in my office for two hours, discussing the purchase of the Boston Red Sox. Fanatic in his worship of Lardner, Jed never forgave me.

To validate his position in the theatre, Jed spent the 1929 holidays in Palm Beach. Before he departed, he summoned Whittaker Ray, now his general manager. "Give Dick anything he wants for Christmas up to $5,000," he told him. An hour after his departure, Whit asked me to name my figure.

"Give me the five grand?" I said. Whit feared the order had been impulsive, that it might be subject to revision. He didn't want to be caught in the middle. "Better wait until he gets back," he said. A bronzed Harris greeted me three weeks later. "Money is bad for you," he said. "You don't know how to handle it. I'm going to get you a grand piano."

"I couldn't get a grand piano into our apartment," I protested. "How about a baby grand?" he asked.

The bonus petered out into the suggestion I take a two-week vacation in Maine at the end of August. Harris said I could hole up in Whit Ray's cabin on Rangeley Lake, in that pollen-free paradise avert the ravages of hay fever. Starting August 20 of that year, I sneezed right up to the first frost in West Forty-fourth Street.

Weary of attacking individuals, Harris went in for group insults. In a manifesto, he announced intelligence was a handicap to an actor. One of the most skilled players on the stage had never understood a line he uttered, he said. Still concerned with IQ's, he stated all current producers were noodleheads, save two. He broke with George Kaufman after the opening of *Serena Blandish*. The news story in the *Times* reporting the Philadelphia opening had not been flattering. Harris felt that Kaufman, the *Times's* drama editor, should have edited or eliminated the bulletin. His rage, voiced in sulphurous terms, created a schism that was never bridged.

Harris dodged an opportunity to produce *The Green Pastures*, Pulitzer Prize play of 1930, which Marc Connelly had adapted from Roark Bradford's *Old Man Adam an' His Chillun*. Connelly insisted on directing the play, but Jed had another man in mind—himself. Connelly was a Celt, therefore a sentimentalist, said Jed. The play would be curdled by his romantic touch. So Connelly directed *The Green Pastures* for Rowland Stebbins, and both were enriched during its seventy-week run.

Twenty-five-year-old Moss Hart brought the first draft of *Once in a Lifetime* to Jed. He told Hart it had great potentials, but the plot needed tightening and better organization. He suggested Moss seek the aid of George Kaufman. Kaufman had been brilliant in collaborations with Marc Connelly, Edna Ferber and Ring Lardner. Hart took Jed's advice. Fashioned by Kaufman and Hart, *Once in a Lifetime* was an uproarious hit in its year's run at the Music Box. But because of Jed's row with Kaufman, it was produced by another Harris—Sam H.

Though denied *Once in a Lifetime* and *The Green Pastures,*
Jed knew where his next Cadillac was coming from. During the golden
days of 1927-28, his profits often ran to $20,000 a week. He paid
me well. The office operated in informal fashion. Members of the
staff came and went as they pleased. There were no penalties for
disagreeing with the foreman. Occasional two-week binges by his
top executive were condoned or ignored. Reflecting the credo of
our employer, the office crawled with iconoclasts.

With the closing of *Serena Blandish,* New York was without a
Harris play. It would be a year before he resumed practice with
Chekhov's *Uncle Vanya.* He spent this leave in London. It was
rumored he was about to emulate Disraeli, become a British citizen,
and stand for Parliament from Upper Tooting. To encourage this
nonsense, he bought a house in Cheyne Walk.

When Jed took off for England, I jumped to San Francisco, where
Helen Hayes was to start a California engagement in *Coquette.*
This junket terminated in Los Angeles, when Helen announced she
would soon be a mother. With characteristic gallantry, some of
the players protested the condition of the star should in no way
curtail the engagement. Helen could play until two weeks before
her accouchement, said these stoics. By that time, Harris must find
a substitute. They were entitled to a season's pay under the terms
of their run-of-the-play contracts.

The resulting hassle between Harris and the cast stirred as much
bitterness as the Dreyfus case. I was a witness when the controversy
was threshed out before the Actors' Equity Association. Witnesses
for the defense argued the birth of Mary MacArthur was "an act
of God," hence relieved the management of obligations. A verdict
was found for the cast. Mary received more publicity before she was
born than most players do in their lifetime.

On my return to New York, the Harris office was closed. There
were indications that the Darkling, as he was known to the irreverent,
had forsaken the theatre for higher things. Since our funds were
tied up in the market, Whittaker Ray and I had to find employment
elsewhere. Shortly he was general manager and I was the press agent

for *Fifty Million Frenchmen* and *Top Speed,* musicals produced, respectively, by E. Ray Goetz and Bolton, Kalmar and Ruby, Ltd., for the Warner Brothers.

Ray Goetz was a voluptuary. Beyond any producer I have known, he had insouciance. The heavens might yawn, the stagehands revolt and the ingénue report stiff, but Goetz remained unruffled. He inserted Ravel's "Bolero" into the Cole Porter score of *Fifty Million Frenchmen* without the consent of its composer, only shrugged when lawyers bore down on him waiving writs. *Fifty Million Frenchmen* rehearsed under Monty Woolley, lately assistant professor of the drama at Yale. This was Woolley's first theatre assignment.

Woolley's vocabulary confused the actors. The first rehearsal I saw at the Manhattan Opera House was devoted to a scene at Longchamps, racetrack outside Paris. Mr. Woolley was urging the cast to greater vocal efforts. "I want pandemonium to reign until the curtain hits the floor," he said. Pleased by the elegance of this order, he repeated it, while the cast eyed him suspiciously. The stage manager, an experienced gnome named Murry Queen, destroyed Monty's aplomb when he piped up, "Mr. Woolley, this is a blackout."

The show was to play two weeks in Boston before opening at the Lyric. I went there three weeks in advance. Before leaving, I cornered Goetz. I wanted to be briefed on billing—the size, position and prominence of the names of all listed in advertisements. William Gaxton and Genevieve Tobin were the featured players. Whose name would come first? I asked Mr. Goetz. "Don't you think it would be gallant to run the lady's name first?" asked Mr. Goetz.

I wasn't interested in such chivalrous tosh. When their names are juggled in ads or on theatre marquees, actors run amok. I asked Goetz to write down the names of his headliners in the order he desired. The chit would come in handy later if I was charged with treason. He obliged. Under the title he wrote:

with

GENEVIEVE TOBIN and WILLIAM GAXTON

On my return from Boston following publication of the first ad I had an indignant call from Goetz. "Why don't you follow instructions, Maney? You get me in more trouble. How many times have I told you that Mr. Gaxton's name must precede that of all other players?" I caught on rapidly. "Is Mr. Gaxton with you perhaps?" I asked. "Yes! Yes!" he barked. "I understand perfectly," I replied. "I shall sin no more."

Then and thereafter, Mr. Gaxton bewildered me.

No one with so little talent ever rose so high in the theatre. An indifferent dancer and singer, he had the nerve of Willie Sutton and an excellent set of teeth. Of a midnight in Goetz's suite at the Ritz in Boston, I listened to Gaxton argue that he, and he alone, should be on the stage at the finale of the first act. Though there were fifty people in the company, he felt they should be demobilized while he had his lyric fling. This was Gaxton's notion of pandemonium.

The inscrutable Goetz peered at his opponent over his champagne glass, fascinated by the range of his paranoia. Gaxton pleaded his case for an hour without interruption. When he had finished, Goetz raised his glass to Gaxton, smiled and uttered a single word, "No."

Three days before *Fifty Million Frenchmen* was to open in New York, I called Goetz at his hotel to ask about possible last-minute changes in the program copy. Preparing, editing and correcting programs is one of the press agent's routine chores. Prior to opening in New York, revue programs change from day to day. The running order of scenes is constantly altered in an effort to give the work pace or to appease complaining players.

"I don't think you need worry about the programs," said Goetz, "because I don't think we're going to open."

His reply stunned me. "What's happened?" I gasped. The tale he unfolded shriveled my spine.

Betty Compton was the show's leading dancer, but Gaxton, Miss Tobin and Helen Broderick outranked her in salary and billing. While the show was in Boston, I read with amusement that New York's Mayor James J. Walker was spending a well-earned vacation in New England. I knew better. He was spending his vacation at the Colonial Theatre, hard by the Common. He had put aside civic cares to watch and encourage the frisky Miss Compton.

Boston behind them, the players reported at the Lyric in New York at noon on Monday. The dressing rooms assigned them by the stage manager were listed on the callboard. The room given Miss Compton was short of her desire. Scorning appeal to the stage manager, she raced to a pay station at the stage door and dialed City Hall. "Jimmy! You should see the lousy dressing room they've given me. It's a disgrace. You must do something about it." Thus testified the stage doorman.

Although a notorious procrastinator, Mayor Walker acted with speed. Before the drops were hung, he had slapped six violations on the Lyric, any one of which would preclude the rise of the curtain two nights hence. That's why Goetz thought my mumble about the program academic. Eventually Ray saw the light. In the interests of amity, politics and the Warner Brothers money, Miss Broderick bowed to a reshuffle of dressing rooms.

When *Fifty Million Frenchmen* opened, hundreds of people in the theatre were still stunned and bleeding from the disaster of a month earlier—the stock market crash. Overnight producers, actors, press agents and playwrights were beggared. Bert Kalmar, lyricist and co-author of *Top Speed,* came into my office, took off his pants and shirt, asked me to send them to his broker, then started to crawl out on the window ledge. He said he was going to make a trial jump. Sam Harris, A. H. Woods and hundreds of others in the theatre's peerage were flattened. The author of this monograph was reduced to rubble. When the market started its dive, I phoned my curb broker to sell my hundred shares of American Founders. That morning I had a paper profit of $5,000 in the stock. The ticker still was spitting out disaster an hour after the market's close, when my broker called. One of his aides and a friend of mine had pledged my American Founders to cover a margin call. This Achates, along with my Founders, had been wiped out before I phoned the order to sell. But the broker reassured me. My friend was bonded, he said. I'd get my money back. Of course the bonding company would toss the book at the hypothecator. He might get off with five years.

What was I doing in the market? I had caught the national disease: the desire to get something for nothing. I knew less about stocks, bonds and debentures than I did about Saturn's rings. A more addle-headed ape never scanned closing prices. Trying to become a Wall Street wolf I gained a Mexican stand-off, lost my money but saved my life. I haven't bought a share of stock since.

Returning to my office in the Bond Building one afternoon, I found it bare. Without warning Warner Brothers had moved my equipment to their factory on Forty-fourth Street. Entering this hive the next morning, I discovered my desk in an open field surrounded by forty other desks. While surveying this clutter, a page handed me a note. It was from Percy Waxman, Warners' general press agent. Hereafter, it said, I was to submit all copy on *Fifty Million Frenchmen* and *Top Speed* for his approval before sending it out. I halted the messenger and scribbled across the bottom of the memo: "I'm not submitting any copy. What's more, I'm not writing any. Good bye." With that, I walked out. I hadn't taken my hat off.

In retrospect I marvel at my audacity. Flat broke because of my speculations, I could ill afford idleness. There was no clamor for my services. In my years in the theatre, I've never asked for a job. This reluctance is a hangover from my youth rather than a boast. In Seattle, my father often urged me to find summer work to bolster up the family budget. He'd dig up prospects and instruct me to explore them. My investigations were slipshod. Nearing the office of my potential employer, I'd panic. That night I'd tell Dad I'd just missed out. The opening had been filled. I had the delusion that job hunting was debasing.

Before I could be penalized for my revolt, Harris returned from London and resumed practice atop the Morosco Theatre, where I had torn tickets thirteen years earlier. Within two years, he gave New York a memorable revival of Chekhov's *Uncle Vanya; Mr. Gilhooley,* an adaptation of a Liam O'Flaherty novel; Gogol's *The Inspector General; The Wiser They Are,* a foolish comedy involving Ruth Gordon and Osgood Perkins; and *The Fatal Alibi.* Lillian Gish was the wraithlike Helena of *Uncle Vanya,* returned to the theatre after seventeen years on the screen.

The critics cheered this revival. Harris was still invincible, they said. This theory was jarred by *Mr. Gilhooley.* Harris' partisans

shrugged off this indiscretion. Even Homer nodded, they said. But
when *The Inspector General* folded after seven performances, heads
started to wag all the way from the Battery to Spuyten Duyvil.
Had the master lost his touch? *The Wiser They Are* indicated that
if he hadn't lost it, he had mislaid it. Graver suspicions flared up
when *The Fatal Alibi,* with so skilled a scoundrel as Charles Laughton, was flattened in three weeks. This setback refuted George Jean
Nathan, a practicing seer who assured Harris no play with "fatal"
in its title had ever failed.

Ben Hecht had a theory about Harris' lapses. "He's on an *Uncle
Vanya* bender," said the pamphleteer, when Harris announced his
intention to revive Schnitzler's *Reigen,* an adulterous Viennese
comedy. "*Gilhooley?* That's Uncle Vanya in Dublin. *Reigen?* That's
Uncle Vanya in bed."

The short life of *Mr. Gilhooley* toppled two critics from their
pedestals. In the O'Flaherty play, Helen Hayes was a Dublin tart.
I am among those who think Miss Hayes is one of our finest actresses.
But for all her magic, she cannot simulate a tramp. Both Alexander
Woollcott and Thornton Wilder had told Helen *Gilhooley* provided
her with her finest role. So stout was her faith in these oracles, she
expected an ovation at the play's end. Modestly she planned three
or four curtain calls with other members of the cast before she exercised the star's prerogative and stepped to the footlights alone. Her
confidence had infected the stage manager. He felt it would add to
the suspense and increase the applause if a thirty-second wait
preceded the rise of the first curtain.

Helen was victimized. When the curtain rose to a spatter of
applause, all she saw were the backs of her admirers, headed for
the exits.

Maire O'Neill, sister of Sara Allgood, fared better. In casting
Gilhooley, Harris' choice for the title role was Arthur Sinclair,
veteran star of Dublin's Abbey Theatre. In transatlantic telephone
talks, Sinclair received Harris' bid casually. He'd risk another trip
to America only if his wife, Maire O'Neill, might play with him.
Was there a role for her in *Gilhooley?* Nothing worthy of her, Harris
told him. There was a two-minute bit for a landlady, little better

than a walk-on. Sinclair said Miss O'Neill would welcome this bit that they might be together. Harris, apologetic for so trivial an assignment for so skilled an actress, agreed. On opening night, Maire O'Neill walked down a stairway, paused in a room, delivered four or five short speeches and exited. In that interval, she performed a minor miracle, picked up the entire play and made it something far better than it was. Electrifying!

Even the matchless Sinclair, associate of Barry Fitzgerald, William George Fay, Sara Allgood, McCormick and Dudley Digges, at the Abbey in plays of O'Casey, Synge, A.E., and Yeats, could not redeem *Mr. Gilhooley*. But he and I were to meet again. When next I saw him, he was astride an elephant in *Jumbo*.

When *The Fatal Alibi* succumbed to public apathy, Jed and I parted without recriminations. Eleven years elapsed before he paged me to press agent *Dark Eyes*. Over that interval, he produced but six plays. Three of these, a revival of *A Doll's House, The Green Bay Tree* and Thornton Wilder's *Our Town,* were cast and directed superbly, and gave eloquent evidence that Jed still had the magic touch. Though his productions were infrequent, Harris was far from idle. In between presentations, he negotiated fruitlessly with the screen's sachems, prowled Europe and jeered at the ineptitude of his contemporaries.

If I have dwelt overlong on associations with Harris, it is because he is the most stimulating and the most exciting of my employers. Great as were, and are, his talents, just as great was his skill at making enemies. Whatever demons have pursued him, he has a knowledge of the theatre and a skill in it unmatched by any of his fellows. There are no peaks he might not have scaled had he cared to muffle his malice. The obstacles which stymied him were his own creations. He will reappear in this narrative from time to time, always in character, his dirk unsheathed.

11

The Bantam Barnum

WHEN I first met Billy Rose, he was smoldering in the shadow of Fanny Brice. Fanny had married Rose to pique Nicky Arnstein, handsome crook and gambler whom she had divorced. A zany comedienne, Fanny was one of the theatre's elite. She had starred in seven Ziegfeld *Follies.* She was the pet of critics, racketeers and Park Avenue swells. Rose had rhymed four or five popular songs but, save in Lindy's restaurant and Tin Pan Alley, was as anonymous as a subway guard. Identified as "that little guy Fanny Brice married," he writhed. Aware of his zombie status in Fanny's world, he knew he would continue to writhe unless he achieved note comparable to hers. Seeking a trapeze on which to demonstrate, he decided to make his bid for immortality in the theatre. He was lured into this ambush while hypnotized—by Jed Harris.

Returning from London to start rehearsals of *Uncle Vanya,* Jed met Fanny on the *Europa.* Immediately they formed a mutual admiration society. Jed was fascinated by Fanny's gaiety and earthy candor, while Fanny was enthralled by Jed's eloquence and his contempt for the mighty. Accompanying Jed to Fanny's home, I discovered that if Fanny was enthralled by my lord, Rose was bewitched. Jed's conversation, his knowledge of the theatre, and the million dollars he had made from *Broadway, Coquette, The Royal Family* and *The Front Page* numbed the neophyte. Spellbound by Harris' airy references to the theatre's aristocrats, Rose sought to emulate him. In short order, he devoured Bernard Shaw's *Prefaces,* Stanislavsky's *My Life in Art,* Ibsen's *Naar vi Dode Vaagner* and the last issue of *Variety,* all touched upon by Harris in his monologues.

Eager to test the dogmas he had gulped, Rose decided to make his bid with *Corn Beef and Roses,* a revue which would have the services of George Jessel, Jim Barton and Miss Brice. To ensure success, Rose persuaded Harris to direct the dialogue, then compounded the seduction by getting Harris to invest $10,000 in the rumpus. This alliance collapsed even before *Corn Beef and Roses* could be christened. Deep in his Russian phase, Harris approached the musical's sketches as he would Gorki's *Lower Depths.* It was his first skirmish with a song-and-dance show, and it would be his last. Harris' scorn for Rose's blunders, his taste and his delusions was monumental.

Though feigning bravado, Rose was jumpy. Arriving at the Philadelphia theatre in which *Corn Beef and Roses* was to open, he raged on finding the alley abutting the stage cluttered with scenery and properties. He assumed that this mountain of canvas and lumber belonged to the previous attraction, that its tardy exit had delayed the entrance of his show. The theatre manager disillusioned him. The litter in the alley was that part of *Corn Beef and Roses* which the theatre couldn't accommodate. Designer Jo Mielziner's sketches had confused the novice. "I never thought they'd build a lamppost forty feet high," he wailed. "It was only an inch high on the blueprint."

Rose and *Corn Beef and Roses* narrowly escaped lynching in Philadelphia. "The producer's name is Rose," wrote one reviewer. "He's a rose that does not smell so sweet." "A downright and undeniable black eye for the theatre," reported *Variety's* correspondent. Other appraisals were equally bitter and a blight hit the box office. In the four weeks before *Corn Beef and Roses* opened in New York, Rose lost $36,000. Seeking to throw the posse off the scent, he changed the title to *Sweet and Low.*

Sweet and Low was hooted by the New York critics. An experienced gnome would have taken his losses and bolted. Outwardly defiant, Rose swore he would redeem the fiasco. He excised offensive material, reduced his "nut" through hair-raising economies, and rehearsed new scenes until the company was dizzy. This action was born of desperation, he told me later. If *Sweet and Low* was a quick flop, he would be broke and discredited on the street whose cheers he craved.

Rose was $150,000 in the red before *Sweet and Low* had its first profitable week. As business bettered, he cocked his ear to catch the applause due his spectacular salvage. It wasn't forthcoming. By Broadway standards, *Sweet and Low* was still a bust. Dismayed, Rose hired and fired four press agents.

Rose's anguish was eased on discovering a new source of income. Banker Otto Kahn's son, Roger Wolfe, was betrothed to Hannah Williams, the show's soubrette who sang its "Cheerful Little Earful." Young Kahn was hellbent on an immediate wedding and on Miss Williams' retirement from the theatre. But she was bound to Rose by a run-of-the-play contract. Banker Kahn solved this jam with a $7,500 check. Rose next sold chorus girl June McCloy's contract to Paramount Pictures for $5,000. Paramount felt her presence in *Reaching for the Moon* vital.

With the close of *Sweet and Low,* I became Rose's Boswell and apologist. His awe of Harris ebbing, Rose came to the conclusion that much of Harris' success had been due to the sorceries of his publicist. Amused by Rose's naïveté, I tried to disillusion him. In the clutch of an *idée fixe,* he attributed my disclaimers to modesty.

When *The Wiser They Are* started to turn blue, Harris chucked the theatre under the chin and took off for Europe again. He would be back in September, he said, eager to resume warfare. But I couldn't afford to speculate on his whims. What if he decided to stand for Parliament? I accepted Rose's bid with the understanding I might serve other producers.

My first assignment was *Crazy Quilt.* Only a week intervened between its opening and *Sweet and Low's* closing. This operation was an optical illusion. *Crazy Quilt* was *Sweet and Low* retitled.

Rose replaced Jessel and Barton with Phil Baker and Ted Healy. He popped "I Found a Million-Dollar Baby in a Five and Ten Cent Store" into the proceedings. He threw away most of the scenery to reduce stagehand expense. Tolerant of this chicanery, the critics found the hybrid noisy and moderately funny. It stayed on for two months, and the following year made a small fortune touring one-night stands, thanks to the delirious boasts of Ned Alvord, the press agent who preceded it.

Sixteen months elapsed before Rose again assaulted the drama. In that interval, and for five years thereafter, I operated from his office. A penthouse atop a Forty-second Street skyscraper, it crawled with canvas and chromium chairs, Venetian blinds, privet hedges, tropical flora and concealed gadgets. Centered under a forty-foot ceiling, Rose's desk was as big as a billiard table. An enormous black block in the Delft-blue carpet bore his initials.

With Harris and Rose becalmed, in the fall of '31 I went in for multiple employment. In the next fifteen months, I publicized thirteen plays and musicals for ten different producers. Working for one producer has its compensations, provided he produces. But few producers can assure a press agent, or a wardrobe mistress, continuity of employment. If I continued to put all my eggs in one basket, I'd wind up behind the eight ball, a metaphor which I will not defend. Working for three or four producers simultaneously called for dexterity, but after my three years with Harris, I felt I could cope with any conflicts that might arise.

Of the thirteen attractions I inflated before Rose resumed practice, only three, *Ed Wynn's Laugh Parade,* J. B. Priestley's *Dangerous Corner* and Schwab and DeSylva's *Take a Chance,* were hits. Had I paused to reflect, I might have shied from a profession in which failure so outweighed success. But the theatre is no place for reflection. The treachery of my calling is one of its greatest lures.

It was in this interval that I first worked for Arthur Hopkins. I didn't work for him long. *The Man on Stilts* was shuttered after six performances, *The Passing Present* after sixteen. But in the theatre defeat whets desire. Hopkins would triumph again, as he had before, hence wasted no time in lamentation.

Failure can serve the young and the dedicated as a springboard. As a $75-a-week Antiope in *The Warrior's Husband,* a freckled redhead named Katharine Hepburn raised the temperature of the critics. I had noted this hoyden loitering around the Harris office two years earlier. Indifferent to dress, scorning make-up, she had an air. Even to my untutored eye, she seemed fated for the marquees. Her determination to succeed brushed all obstacles aside. At twenty, she had already served as understudy and walk-on and had explored Baltimore, Great Neck and Ivorytown, Connecticut, in summer stock.

Solvent since the touring *Crazy Quilt* had recouped the losses of *Sweet and Low,* Rose looked about for another windmill. He didn't have long to wait. Ben Hecht and Gene Fowler brought him *The Great Magoo.* Recognition by these titans touched off gongs in his skull. Entranced, he agreed to produce what the authors called "a love-sick charade, a drama full of passion and bird calls, something like *Romeo and Juliet,*" before he read it.

Three or four days later, Rose handed me the play. Would I read it and let him know what I thought of it? My opinion would be for his ears alone. On reading it, I told Rose he'd better arrange for bail in advance of the opening. He and the authors were headed for the Tombs. The dialogue covering the romance of a flagpole sitter and a Coney Island hussy was shockingly frank. The crone who had plotted the union of the crazed pair delivered the play's last line. As the bride-to-be was about to exit with her weather-beaten bum, this harridan stayed her. Holding aloft a douche bag she cried, "Wait a minute, Cinderella! You've forgot your pumpkin."

Rose greeted my verdict with a false chuckle. Two days later he summoned me again. Ben and Gene were with him. "Tell the boys what you thought of the play," he said. This treachery outraged me. I first met Ben when he interviewed a covey of Berkoffs (Russian dancers) for me in Chicago eight years earlier. Ben and Gene were my friends long before Rose met either. Trapped, I saw no point in evading the issue. I told them what I had told Rose. "We live in a democracy," said Ben. "Every man is entitled to an opinion." Fowler didn't say anything.

Since my office in the Rose roost flanked the switchboard, I was

exposed to those seeking audience with my betrayer. The next time
Fowler called on Rose he paused, pointed a finger at me, and
yelled, "Judas Iscariot!" His maniacal roar routed a character actress
and a female impersonator browsing nearby and caused the telephone
boy to short-circuit the switchboard. Fowler repeated the denunciation
at each subsequent visit.

The Great Magoo was blackjacked by the critics. The enraged
Hecht flung himself on his typewriter and bombarded his tormentors
with invective. The greats of the world had all been hounded and per-
secuted by envious clods, he cried. He cited Rousseau, Benvenuto
Cellini, François Villon, Ben Jonson, Voltaire, Victor Hugo, Dostoy-
evsky, Francis Bacon, O. Henry, Spinoza, Franz Kafka, Oscar Wilde
and Joan of Arc. "I didn't see you at the tar barrels Friday night,"
he started his letter to Percy Hammond. "Fowler and I are hiding
out in an abandoned silo up near Port Chester until the baying of
the bloodhounds dies down," he confided to another.

Knowing less about the drama than he knew about the migrations
of the Arctic tern, Rose couldn't cope with The Great Magoo
once it had been bludgeoned. People to whom he gave passes didn't
show up. He glowered when I suggested we resort to subpoenas.
When The Great Magoo folded after eleven repetitions, Hecht and
Fowler had runs in their prestige, and Rose had gashes in his wallet.
He was $40,000 lighter. Seeking to laugh off misfortune, Hecht
and Fowler started negotiations with Frank Campbell's Funeral
Parlor. What would the mortician charge to wax their faces, rig
them out in the habiliments of death and permit them to lie in
open coffins for an hour on Friday afternoon?

If the undertaker agreed, I was to bid the critics to come and view
the remains. This prank bogged down when the Poillion Sisters,
tall and muscular, treed Fowler and charged him with libeling them
in The Great Mouthpiece. Gene took off for the border. Hecht wasn't
up to a solo in a shroud. Rose began to suspect the tenets of Shaw,
Ibsen and Stanislavsky.

Proximity to, and palaver with, Hecht and Fowler had convinced
Rose The Great Magoo might win him parity with Fanny Brice.
That no neglect of his might foul the formula, Rose sought a top-

notch director. He asked me to feel out George Abbott. Abbott and
Phil Dunning were my clients. They were fumbling with *Lilly Turner,*
and George wasn't eager for outside trouble. Despite this, he said,
he'd direct Rose's play if Hecht would finish *Twentieth Century*
and let him and Dunning produce it.

Let's retreat to a July morning in 1930. A phone bell stabs my
dreams. It is my employer, Harris.

"Get $5,000 in cash from the dike-mender and lay it in Ben
Hecht's lap before noon," he said. ("Dike-mender" was the office
pet name for Hugo Schaaf, the auditor.) Prone, the significance
of this order escaped me. Harris enlightened me. He had read in
the *Times* that Hecht was to write a play for Chester Erskin. Erskin
had achieved genius rating for staging *The Last Mile.* Hecht must
be in desperate circumstances to thus play the apostate, said
Harris. It was less than two years since Harris had enriched him
and MacArthur with his production of *The Front Page.* It was less
than four months since he cheered Rose Caylor (Mrs. Hecht) for
her adaptation of *Uncle Vanya.* What ingratitude!

I tracked Hecht down in an East Side hotel. He was playing gin
with MacArthur. I pressed the $5,000 into his hand. "A token
from the Darkling," I said. "For what?" asked Hecht. "Advance
royalty on your next play." "What next play?" they chorused. "And
where's my five grand?" chirped MacArthur. "Looks like discrimination!"

Having accepted a fat advance on a phantom play, Hecht's
conscience started to gnaw him. To appease Harris, he and Mac-
Arthur wrote a fifteen-page synopsis of the life and times of Big
Jim Colisimo, a Chicago hoodlum recently ventilated in his own
saloon. This outline could be spun into a three-act melodrama if
Harris found the sample to his liking. Harris wanted no part of a
Cook County hood. He resorted to a pocket veto.

During the Colisimo debate, Charles Bruce Milholland came to
Harris with *The Napoleon of Broadway.* Milholland had been Morris
Gest's press agent when that dreamer set up the Fassnacht Family
in the Freiburg Passion Play at the Hippodrome. Exposure to Gest
all but demented Milholland.

The central character in *The Napoleon of Broadway* was a lunatic producer, a paraphrase of Gest. Harris was fascinated with this maniac, but found the other characters tiresome. He persuaded Milholland to let Hecht and MacArthur coin a new plot. Ten days later, Hecht and MacArthur were cloistered in a Charleston hotel. Three weeks later they laid two acts of *Twentieth Century* on Harris' desk.

From Helen Hayes I learned that I was on the brink of immortality. "Charlie and Ben have written you into the play," she phoned. "The boys have done you proud. You're Owen O'Malley, a truculent press agent. They've caught your fevers, your epithets, your skepticism."

This was pretty heady stuff. When applauded I can purr as loudly as an adagio dancer. Few of us are dramatized in our lifetime. To be etched by these braves was a rare distinction. I had a single qualm. I hoped Ben and Charlie didn't tell everything they knew about me.

Whittaker Ray, Harris' general manager, was also in the script. And so was Harris. Oscar Jaffe, the moody producer about whom the plot swirled, was a composite of Belasco, Morris Gest and the Gitano, with all of whom the authors were familiar.

Harris found the two acts very funny. Impulsively he started to cast the play. He offered the Jaffe role to Alexander Carr, Arthur Byron and Ferdinand Gottschalk. All declined. Harris next tried to bag Morris Gest. A reformed ticket scalper and Belasco's son-in-law, Gest was a spectacular showman and eccentric, given to bravura performances offstage. Gest had imported the Moscow Art Theatre and the moon-faced Balieff and his "Chauve-Souris." Though tempted, Gest ducked the chance to animate both himself and his wife's father.

Lilly Garland was the comedy's heroine. Lilly was a temperamental witch and a smoldering beauty. Jaffe had brought her from obscurity to stardom. He swore she would make the hit of her career as Mary Magdalene in *The Passion Play*. She was fed up with his fakery, his visions and his bogus martyrdom. Harris sent the script to Tallulah Bankhead, a young actress just returned from eight spectacular years in London. After she held the play a month,

Harris instructed me to call her. "Tell your Mr. Harris I gave up playing this kind of a role years ago," she said.

Tallulah was then in the coils of a two-year contract with Paramount. She couldn't have recessed to play the role even had she liked it—even if Harris had had a third act. That was unfortunate. She would have made a superb Lilly.

Two of the characters on the New York Central's crack train were identified in the manuscript as First Beard and Second Beard. Eager for action, Harris instructed two idle actors to forgo shaving until they heard from him again. He'd tolerate no false whiskers.

Scorning caution, Harris announced *Twentieth Century* would open on August 15, 1931. Shortly thereafter, he learned Hecht and MacArthur were off for Hollywood to prepare an epic for Ronald Colman. What about the third act? He had nothing to worry about, said the authors. It would be in his hands before rehearsals started.

Things worsened rapidly. The Colman colossus finished, Hecht returned to his estate on the Hudson, but MacArthur became involved in *The Sin of Madelon Claudet,* Helen Hayes's first picture. On MacArthur's return, Hecht took off for the West Coast. August 15 came and went. Without a third act, unable to reach Hecht or MacArthur, Harris cried quits. Con McSunday, cited for First Beard six months earlier, parted with his two feet of whiskers.

A half-dozen producers tried to get Hecht and MacArthur to finish the comedy. There was a snag. The Hecht-MacArthur-Milholland alliance was valid only if Harris was the producer. Even if Ben and Charlie finished the play, the producer must have Milholland's approval. Abbott's provisional consent to direct *The Great Magoo* goaded Hecht into action. From a synopsis written by Dunning, he wrote the third act in ten days. A very funny third act it was. Dunning and Abbott repaid Harris the $5,000 he had forced on Hecht two years earlier. With Milholland's blessing, Abbott started to rehearse *Twentieth Century* the day after *The Great Magoo* came a cropper. It would be a month before Rose discovered Hecht had sold him the wrong play.

Abbott, too, had casting problems. Moffat Johnson played the deranged producer with a Scotch accent, while Eugenie Leontovich's

Lilly had a Russian flavor. As the disillusioned press agent, Bill Frawley was superb.

Twentieth Century was an immediate hit. But business wilted when banks started to explode like Chinese firecrackers. During Franklin Roosevelt's Bank Holiday, the Broadhurst accepted checks from strangers from Bismarck and Terre Haute. Fortunately, Dunning, Frawley and I could sign tabs at Frankie and Johnny's, a speakeasy half a block from the stage door.

Routed by the theatre, Rose took refuge in night clubs. Mobsters engaged him to operate the Casino de Paree, a theatre-restaurant. Shortly, these outlaws took over the Hammerstein Theatre. Aware of his weakness, they named it Billy Rose's Music Hall. Rose's name towered twelve stories high. Because of this display, his employers didn't think it necessary to pay him his $1,000 weekly wage. Familiar with their homicidal tendencies when irked, Rose didn't nudge them.

Though I publicized Rose's activities in these canteens, I did so from afar. Our pact provided that I never need enter either. I insisted on this proviso after tossing off one Scotch highball in the Casino de Paree. Devoted as I was to the Mahatma, I wasn't going to risk blindness to prove it.

After twenty weeks without fee, Rose went over the hill. To recover his *sang-froid,* or something, he fled to Europe. In Czechoslovakia, he was a guest at Bernard Baruch's shooting lodge. Rose had been Baruch's stenographer when that volunteer statesman was chairman of the War Industries Board in 1918. If Rose bagged any grouse, the cable editors ignored it. But he didn't return to Times Square empty-handed. In Bucharest he had seen an al fresco fantasy in which a zoo was imposed on a boy-meets-girl plot. An elaboration of this idyl in New York might remove the bushel from his light, he reasoned.

On his return to Manhattan, Rose ran wild. Impressed by the reception of *Twentieth Century,* he commissioned Hecht and MacArthur to write the book for the saturnalia. Richard Rodgers and Lorenz Hart were assigned the music and lyrics.

Haggling with wire walkers, midgets, acrobats, prima donnas, daredevils and the man who owned Rosie, the elephant in the title role, Rose's delirium reached such a pitch he started to rehearse before he had a theatre or the funds to animate his hallucination. So vast would be this carouse, he shouted, that the Hippodrome was the only amphitheatre large enough to contain it. This confession brought the Hippodrome's banker-proprietors from their vaults chanting hallelujahs.

Once New York's best-known theatre and still its largest, the Hippodrome was dark for weeks on end. Vagrant opera companies, an occasional protest meeting, political rally or wrestling match— that was its shabby fare. Had Rose been less hasty, he might have rented it for $1,000 a week. With the knowledge it was vital to his jamboree, the figure skyrocketed. Victimized by his own brashness, Rose capitulated. The financiers had a rake-off of $6,000 a week at the peak of *Jumbo's* run. Even while haggling for the Hippodrome, Rose couldn't restrain himself. He had gutted it six weeks before he had a right to enter the building.

Sections of *Jumbo* had been in rehearsal for two months in a Brooklyn riding academy, in a deserted church on Forty-eighth Street and on the stage of the Manhattan Opera House, when Rose developed budgetary cramps. He had spent $35,000 of his own money. He needed another $200,000. This crisis waned when multimillionaire Jock Whitney agreed to pick up most of the tab. Baruch and Herbert Bayard Swope made token contributions. Though Swope knew Rose slightly, he was impressed by his ego. After one huddle with him, he told a friend, "I'm willing to wager Rose thinks he won the World War."

Jumbo became a legend before it opened. The theatre's spectacles are permitted five weeks' rehearsals by Equity. If the drills exceed that, all players must receive full salary. Because no one could define his exhibit, most of Rose's serfs lacked the protection of a performers' union. Astride horses for the first time, twenty-four girls rehearsed "The Cossack Drag," "The Whiparound" and other equine ballets in a dirt ring for six months. For this exhausting and dangerous training, none of them received a sou.

Early in the campaign, Rose announced that *Jumbo* would have its première on Labor Day. He missed the target by eleven weeks and set a record for postponements that will endure through the ages. Seven times the opening was set back for periods ranging from four days to four weeks. These delays were grist to our mill. Rose and I used them to build up suspense. I coined a slogan for Rose: "*Jumbo* will make me or break Whitney." Prodded by my employer, I composed ads that were now contrite, now defiant. "Rome wasn't built in a day," read one. In another Rose sought a wealthy eccentric who might like to see a full dress rehearsal in private. The necessary credentials? $10,000 in cash. A distiller rose to this bait. He was about to descend upon the Hippodrome in an Inverness cape, with an escort of photographers, when the Alcoholic Control Board in Washington flagged him down. The prohibitionists, they warned, would renew their attack on our liberties if the bottler paraded his profits.

Rose plastered the side of a building with a sign which read: SH-H-H-H! JUMBO IS IN REHEARSAL! This sign was still up three months after *Jumbo* opened, a symbol of Rose's thrift.

With each postponement speculation mounted. Kiviette, the costumer, bought tickets for the opening in August, canceled them after two postponements, made a trip to Europe, returned in time for three more postponements. MacArthur said the opening was being delayed because everyone in town hadn't seen it. This observation had point.

Dress rehearsals, waged day and night for six weeks, drew crowds of the curious despite Rose's efforts to bar intruders. Slumming parties from Harlem and Greenwich Village often dropped into the Hippodrome around two in the morning to watch an hour's drill. Joan Crawford and Franchot Tone, preceded by native beaters, made it a port of call on their honeymoon. Candid cameramen swooped down on the place like seven-year locusts. There were more gate-crashers in the balcony than there were animals in the cellar. Hecht suggested the final ad be headed:

GRAND RE-OPENING BY POPULAR DEMAND!!

"There are thousands of people who think we've opened, gone on tour, and are back for a return engagement," he said.

A preview performance revealed a fatal flaw. The Hippodrome was no place for the spoken word. In its vast recesses dialogue was reduced to feeble echoes. The Hecht-MacArthur book ran a hundred pages in manuscript. Torn between reverence for the authors and a yen for survival, Rose shredded the text. Outraged at this vandalism, Hecht never entered the Hippodrome again. I received a telegram from him on the opening night which mirrored his mood. "It should never have opened and it would have been a great hit, thanks to you."

Summoned to Rose's chambers at dawn, I found him immersed in his bath. His face was lathered. Through the suds, I detected a man at bay. This was the morning following the preview. "You'll have to kill the Sunday ads," he said. "Are you familiar with the last meeting of Marat and Charlotte Corday?" I asked. "This is no time for riddles," he said. "Charlotte went to the guillotine wearing a smile of satisfaction," I continued. "Marat had it coming to him. Ask any Jacobin." "You shouldn't start drinking so early," said Rose. "How about some coffee?"

The ads for *Jumbo* on November 17, 1935, were in the form of a sworn affidavit, signed by the suspect. Under oath, Rose swore *Jumbo* would open that night. And open it did to the city's surprise and delight. It was worth the delay, the critics agreed. It was an entrancing spectacle, a miraculous fusion of fantasy, fun and menagerie. It burst with wonderful Rodgers and Hart songs—"The Most Beautiful Girl in the World," "Swing High, Swing Low," "Song of the Roustabouts," "Little Girl Blue," and "Over and Over Again." Pivotal in the plot was Claudius P. Bowers, a circus press agent, impersonated by Jimmy Durante. The role provided Schnozzola with one of the funniest lines ever uttered in a theatre. When the circus was attached, Durante tried to smuggle Jumbo through the sheriff's roadblock. When detected, Jimmy froze in his tracks. "Where are you going with that elephant?" bawled the law. "What elephant?" said the fugitive as he ducked a caress from his companion's trunk.

Jumbo was a wonderland, a place of magic and enchantment for young and old. Where else could one see Paul Whiteman directing

his band from a snow-white charger? Arthur Sinclair, pride of
Dublin's Abbey Theatre, entering atop an elephant? The great clown
A. Robins fumbling with miles of bananas? A lion lying down with
a lamb?

A wonderland? A place of magic? *Jumbo* was also a press agent's
dream of paradise and Rose his beau ideal. Rose prodded me into
a ruffle on the drum before he had signed cheetah or camel. The
musical circus was no more than a mote in his eye when I circled
a cable dispatch from Sofia. Boris of Bulgaria wanted to get rid of
three royal elephants. Their upkeep, he said, was beggaring the court.
I cabled Boris Rose's bid within the hour. Boris gave him the brushoff.
A week later I showed Rose another dispatch from Sofia. Boris
had decided to keep his monsters "despite a handsome offer from
an American theatrical producer." Outraged because his identity
was masked, Rose clobbered his opponent. "Boris was popping off,"
he shouted. "He's just another publicity hound."

Early I decided the truth about Rose was more exciting and
amusing than any fables I might concoct. In the tradition of his
brazen ancestor, Phineas T. Barnum, Rose didn't care what I wrote
about him so long as his name was spelled right. Fearless when
facing a camera, a geyser when probed by an interviewer, he placed
no restrictions on my boasts.

Untethered, I made capital of his blunders, of his naïveté in the
theatre, of his financial problems. To counteract these smudges, I
cited his nonchalance in adversity, his energy and his disdain of
convention. Hewing to this line, Rose emerged a fellow of frightening
candor, ready wit and little or no dignity. In turn he was racy,
boastful, a brave insensitive to his limitations and quick to jeer
his betters.

When the plot called for a direct quote, a blast of rhetoric erupted
from my client. A sucker for salty phrases and bizarre invective,
he rejoiced. His appreciation took permanent form. He incorporated
these purple patches in his conversation. Starting his siege of the
theatre, he had but one figure of speech. Everything that offended
his eye looked "like the inside of Earl Carroll's stomach."

My press releases ran to levity and mockery. All had a tongue-in-cheek flavor. Bored by the stuffy statements of Rose's rivals, editors found this tactic diverting. Rose cooed over the sub-titles I lavished on him. At one time or another he was "The Bantam Barnum," "The Mighty Midget," "The Basement Belasco," "The Mad Mahout." He didn't wince when I termed him "the deflated midget" following "The Great Magoo." He found no flaw in *"Multum in Parvo."*

If Rose resented my derisive tributes, he gave no sign. Curious about his prototype when I greeted him as "the penthouse Cagliostro," he chuckled when I told him the Italian scamp was "an eighteenth-century charlatan."

Under Rose's by-line, the souvenir program for *Jumbo* itemized the ordeals he had survived and the doubts he had muted in creating this, his *chef d'oeuvre*. He had kept the faith. His lot and that of *Jumbo* were now in the lap of the critics. "I am adrift in a cockleshell between Scylla and Charybdis," he explained, then concluded with a classic variant: "I stand on the Rubicon rattling the dice." As he beamed on the congregation pouring into the Hippodrome the opening night, he was accosted by columnist Leonard Lyons. "How do you feel, Billy?" asked that prowler. "I stand on the Rubicon rattling the dice," he quipped. Lyons didn't understand it either.

Despite the hullabaloo it raised and the unions it instigated, *Jumbo* was a box-office bust. Though it rehearsed six months, it played only five. On its closing, it lacked $160,000 of recovering its cost. But by trade standards, Rose had scored a triumph. Standing on a stool, he could look Fanny Brice in the eye. Intoxicated by applause, he declared war on the ticket brokers. Each week he wiped out his box-office staff in an effort to get an equitable distribution of "the ice." In the theatre, ice is the generic term for the largess paid theatre treasurers by ticket scalpers that they may get choice seats. In the twenties, it was not uncommon for box-office men to whack up as much as $5,000 a week if the theatre in which they worked sheltered a hit.

Focusing publicity on Rose, I bypassed the experts who made *Jumbo* the wonder it was. Long before its christening, Richard Rodgers cornered me in "21." "Has anyone told you Larry and I are doing the lyrics and music for the show?" he asked. The implication was not wasted on me. He and Hart were incomparable in their field. By comparison Rose was a brash upstart. My reply will never make any anthology of epigrams. Rodgers knew the reason for my delinquency. The sorcerer I served was no man to split a spotlight.

In the three years between the closing of *Twentieth Century* and *Jumbo's* last trumpet, I fried other fish than Rose. I was with George Abbott when he made his last stand as an actor, a bewhiskered Osawatomie Brown capitulating to Colonel Robert E. Lee at Harpers Ferry. A competent actor in less rugged roles, George was miscast. His is not the mettle of the martyr.

Dance with Your Gods, a voodoo confusion, gave up the ghost after nine performances, *Ladies' Money* after thirty-six. The first-named concealed a girl named Lena Horne and the second a bit player named Garson Kanin. Both were fated for the laurel.

The Broderick Crawford whose mother was ousted by Betty Compton in *Fifty Million Frenchmen* could not redeem *Sweet Mystery of Life,* scuttled after eight repetitions. Producer Herman Shumlin winced when, in a post-mortem statement, I identified *Mystery* as the triumph of lumber over imagination.

After a disastrous tryout in Westport, Dunning and Abbott agreed to store the scenery for *Heat Lightning* in Dunning's barn and turn to other things. But Lee Shubert popped up at the last performance and hailed *Heat Lightning* as a masterpiece. Learning they meant to abandon the play, Lee insisted they bring it into the Booth. As an inducement, he guaranteed the partners against loss. Mr. Shubert made but one request. One of the love scenes should be rewritten. When Dunning questioned him about the proposed revision, Shubert pounced upon Matty Zimmerman, head of Leblang's Cutrate Ticket Agency.

After a five-minute huddle, the pair acted out the variation Shubert felt would ensure success. Dunning's play-by-play account of this demonstration had Abbott and me in convulsions. The myth of Lee Shubert's talent for scenting success persisted to his death. Never did a legend have so feeble a foundation. Mr. Lee, as he was known to both relatives and enemies, couldn't tell a hit from a handsaw at twenty paces.

Trying to revive *New Faces* through artificial respiration in the spring of '36, I was barely conscious of two unknowns scrambling for recognition—Imogene Coca and Van Johnson. Miss Coca was a chronic newcomer. She had threshed around in Heywood Broun's *Shoot the Works* five years earlier. It would be fifteen years before she was rescued from oblivion by television. Johnson went West years ago. Wonder what happened to him?

Though this three-year interlude was cluttered with mishaps, I was constantly employed. Indeed, I tattooed the timpani for two long-run successes, *The Children's Hour* by Lillian Hellman, and *Sailor, Beware.* " 'The Children's Hour' will make your eyes start from their sockets as its agitating tale unfolds," wrote Percy Hammond in the *Herald Tribune.* Based on a case famous in Scotch jurisprudence, Miss Hellman's play told of a vengeful child who destroyed her school and ruined two of her teachers by whispering they were Lesbians.

Because of the charge against the teachers, producer Shumlin had difficulty getting actresses to play them. Alice Brady, Katherine Alexander, Margalo Gillmore, Kay Johnson, Beth Merrill and Sally Bates shunned the roles. Fresh in their memory was the fate of the players of *The Captive* at the Empire eight years earlier.

The Children's Hour stressed the evil implicit in a lie. The play had greater impact on its revival in '52. Then character assassination was rampant.

Though considered the season's best play by most New York reviewers, Mayor Mansfield of Boston felt *The Children's Hour* would corrupt his constituency. In ruling it objectionable, Mansfield climaxed a season in which he had outlawed O'Neill's *Strange Interlude* and Sean O'Casey's *Within the Gates.* His attempt to win the title of all-time, all-American noodlehead didn't go unchallenged. Seemingly envious of Mansfield's headlines, Chicago's Mayor Kelly banned the play on the ground that it might impair the morals of his community. Kelly's action was the ultimate in hypocrisy. Chicago was then the criminal's paradise. To their credit, Boston and Chicago critics were unanimous in flaying the city fathers for their idiocy.

On its revival, *The Children's Hour* played Chicago and was cheered by the *Tribune's* Claudia Cassidy and colleagues. *The Chil-*

dren's Hour has yet to play Boston. Prior to the revival in New York, producer Bloomgarden tried to book the play for two weeks in the American Athens. Walter R. Milliken, Chief of the Licensing Bureau in the office of Mayor John B. Hynes, handed down this verdict:

> I have read the script of "The Children's Hour," with the possible view of permitting this show to play in Boston. In addition to reading the script, I have made extensive investigation relative to the history of the play. I have submitted my report to His Honor the Mayor.
>
> The Mayor is of the opinion, as am I, after carefully considering all the facts, that it would not be judicious to book this show to play in Boston.

It was something more than a coincidence, I think, that beyond any city in the nation, Boston applauded the demagoguery of Joseph R. McCarthy, the Wisconsin yahoo.

The civic alarms about *The Children's Hour* reminded me of an observation made by George Moore, author of *A Mummer's Wife.* Prudes and hypocrites, he wrote, profess to be shocked at any hint of adultery in the theatre, yet cheer murder melodramas. To Moore, this seemed a paradox. Adultery, in most civilized countries, is no more than a misdemeanor, while murder is punishable by death.

Adultery was the theme of *Sailor, Beware.* Every gob in the Canal Zone wagered Dynamite Jones would overcome the scruples of Stonewall Jackson. Dynamite was famed for his conquests, Stonewall for her chastity. This rumpus ran over a year and made a fortune, after one of the most stumbling starts in theatrical history.

Authors Kenyon Nicholson and Charles Robinson were elated when Courtney Burr agreed to produce their "variation on a familiar theme" in the summer of '32. Burr had been a classmate of Monty Woolley and Cole Porter at Yale. He was full of the amenities and knew the best vintage years. He had been an ally of E. Ray Goetz when that boulevardier set up *The New Yorkers,* first show to employ Jimmy Durante, Lou Clayton and Eddie Jackson. The year before Burr had aided and abetted Norman Bel Geddes in a revival of *Hamlet.*

Sailor, Beware was about to go into rehearsal when Nicholson

and Robinson discovered that Burr didn't have a dime. Worse! He
was reduced to making his own gin. Momentarily stunned, the authors
quickly regained their composure. Solvent producers were rare in
the thirties. The theatre was bursting with Burrs.

Three times that summer, Burr summoned me to his cell in the
New Amsterdam, which served as office and distillery, and offered
me the press-agent portfolio. Aware of his shaky fiscal condition,
I shied away.

Nicholson had a stage-struck friend who said he'd invest in the
farce provided it met with the approval of a Baltimore critic whose
judgment he trusted. Burr and the authors gave a private performance
for this alien. It was wasted. At the final curtain, he approached
Nicholson, shook hands, and said, "Well, it was nice to have met
you anyway."

Burr had a large and undernourished staff, all named Harris.
Dude, a skilled crapshooter, was his general manager. Charley,
Broncho Billy Anderson's former adjutant, was to manage the
Lyceum Theatre where the farce would play, when and if it opened.
Sidney would preside in the box office.

The desperate Burr was about to abandon the play when he was
rescued by Evelyn Hoey, a lovely young actress who had danced
and sung in *Fifty Million Frenchmen*. Miss Hoey had just received
a handsome sum for damages to her scalp while getting a permanent
wave in a beauty parlor. Learning of her windfall, Burr persuaded
Miss Hoey to lend him enough money to pay two weeks' rent on
the Lyceum. This coup provided him and his staff with a shelter.

In cleaning out the box-office safe, Sidney Harris found a twenty-
dollar bill clipped to a laundry charge for *Berkeley Square,* earlier
tenant of the Lyceum. This trove enabled Burr and the Harrises to
break a two-day fast, with enough left over to get three quarts of gin
from Moe Ducore's pharmacy on Broadway. Still without funds,
Burr couldn't advertise the opening of the play in the newspapers.
This crisis was solved by author Nicholson's nephew. Awaiting his
uncle in the lobby one afternoon, the young man was surrounded
by Burr and a posse of Harrises. Before he could escape, he was
a partner in the play and $1,500 lighter.

By hocking a week's supply of tickets with a broker, Burr raised enough money to open the farce. *Sailor, Beware* sold out on its second night. It ran for sixty weeks. A one-set show with a low-salaried cast, it was a mint.

The day after the opening, the exultant Burr again offered me the press-agent job. Now that he was paying off in cash rather than in trinkets and colored beads, I signed up for the duration.

In defiance of the law—it would be a year before the Eighteenth Amendment was repealed—Burr opened a twenty-foot bar in the smoking room. There a Klabiach game raged from dusk to midnight. Guests allergic to cards could throw darts. An errant arrow penetrated the derby of a Boston critic on his way to the toilet, creasing his skull. The theatre was as informal as an Elks' picnic. Ticket scalpers rented hallways on either side of the entrance. From these nooks, they darted out to waylay customers turned away from the box office. Burr kidnaped a bartender from a downtown club that he might be served proper cocktails. Every night was Mardi Gras. Nicholson's nephew started a lawsuit for an accounting of profits. Burr retaliated by charging him $4 for a pony of brandy when he sought surcease at the bar.

Shortly after *Jumbo* was subdued I issued a bulletin stating Rose was a victim of claustrophobia. The theatre was too confining for a man of his awesome visions. He needed room to lash about. He could function best with the sky for a roof and the sod for a floor. This manifesto prefaced the announcement that he was to get $1,000 a day for a hundred days to help Fort Worth celebrate its centennial. What's more, he'd hypnotized the management into hiring me to publicize his Texas activities in New York.

Eager to vindicate my engagement, I asked Rose to send me pictures of his inauguration. He didn't fail me. Shortly I had the likenesses, the al fresco Frohman in chaps, spurs and sombrero. As a bonus, I received stills of my hero instructing dazed Indians in the use of bow and arrow.

Throughout the summer of '36, I shuttled between New York and Fort Worth. On these flights, I was accompanied by gaggles of drama critics and reporters, and feature writers from magazines, syndicates and wire services. Never had so many flown so high and so far for so little. For by metropolitan standards, Rose's carnival was tawdry. His arena was a ten-acre stockade. Within it, he set up *Jumbo,* minus Durante, Whiteman and many of its fauna, in a papier-mâché *palestra.* Also available to the fun starved were Sally Rand and a retinue of ecdysiasts behind a barbed-wire fence, a snake pit, a dance hall, and other flimflams.

Fortunately for my master, the newsmen whom I dragooned to these demonstrations left their standards behind them. On their return to New York, they wrote of Rose's capers in the desert in glowing terms.

Although these tributes were widely circulated, their impact on the Centennial box office was negligible. In July and August Fort Worth is no summer resort. The evening breeze is like a gust from a blast furnace. Air conditioning was confined to the coffee shop in the Texas Hotel. On my first visit to the transplanted Jumbo, five stage hands and six customers were prostrated by the heat. A journalist who sat through the performance said the experience shamed Dante's Inferno. Many of my companions settled for a token visit to the jamboree, then bolted to the Crown Bar in downtown Fort Worth. At this canteen Scotch drinkers were considered effeminate. Bourbon was Fort Worth's *vin du pays.*

Amon Carter, owner and publisher of the Fort Worth *Star Telegram,* and other bigwigs were delighted with Rose's contribution to the celebration. They liked, even envied him. Despite his brevity Rose talked bigger than the Texans. The fiction that Rose had struck oil within his enclosure led a Dallas columnist to observe that Rose would probably charge the natives to watch his drillers. Such procedure, commented this dyspeptic, would be comparable to taxing a Waxahachie farmer to watch a Negro pick cotton. Dallas, thirty miles away, had its own Centennial carouse. The oil jibe was a symbol of its envy. Rose rebutted with "Go to Dallas for culture, come to Fort Worth for fun."

When the Frontier Centennial Celebration adjourned in October the city fathers presented Rose with a loving cup, and asked him to return for an encore in '37. Rose accepted and I was engaged for a second term. The chef-d'oeuvre of the revival was Rose's Casa Manana, an elaborate open-air theatre-restaurant.

In this terraced coliseum, he bemused the diners with a variety show and platoons of girls in song, dance and tableau. In New York we recruited thirty fugitive noblemen as dancing partners for unattached but eager matrons of Tarrant County. The ad through which I assembled these peers excited wide comment. It read:

WANTED!!

100 bonafide noblemen to serve as dancing partners at the Frontier Centennial at Fort Worth. In answering submit photographs in uniform, with orders, ribbons and decorations evident. . . . Bogus counts, masqueraders and descendants of the Dauphin will get short shrift.

Prey to his own enthusiasm, Rose put on a musical version of *Gone with the Wind*. This salute to *belles-lettres* was muted following dissents from Margaret Mitchell and her publisher.

Though in his press releases Rose professed his infatuation with Texas, Fort Worth and Sam Houston, he was desolated. He longed for New York. Only there could his thirst for recognition be slaked. His position was similar to Napoleon's at Elba. His only solace was Winchell's Sunday-night broadcast. The Casa Manana was as alien to Fort Worth as the World Series to Duluth.

Noting Rose's triumphs in Texas, the management of Cleveland's Great Lakes Exposition summoned him to redeem that disaster. This carnival was plucking at the counterpane when Rose, now confused with Merlin, arrived. Shortly it was on its fiscal feet, thanks to his Pioneer Palace and *Aquacade*. This last was a marine rumpus on Lake Erie, shoals of girls swimming in rhythmic formations. Rose's dive into the deep was accompanied by an ear-splitting ballyhoo. I found it easier to entice newsmen to Cleveland than to Fort Worth. It was cooler and its steaks weren't as tough.

Back on Broadway after three years' exile, Rose touched off a second Casa Manana in the Earl Carroll Theatre, then started to plot the entrapment of Grover Whalen.

Smartly mustached and erect as a Grenadier Guard, Whalen long had been New York's official host. He flanked every channel swimmer, flyer and visiting potentate given parade treatment on Fifth Avenue. Though he had been an executive for Wanamaker's, secretary to "Red Mike" Hylan, for seven years Mayor of New York, and Police Commissioner, to Rose Whalen was just another dude in top hat and cutaway who fouled up traffic five or six times each year. But his indifference changed to fascination when Whalen was named president of the New York World's Fair, to be loosed on the Flushing Meadows in the spring of '39.

Still quivering from his victories in Texas and Ohio, Rose felt he was the only showman qualified to preside over the Fair's amusement section. He was also certain that those who financed this folly would rather put it to the torch than permit him to operate a shooting gallery in it. With his talent for self-effacement, reasoned the sponsors, Rose's name would be blazing from the peak of the seven-hundred-foot Trylon if ever he got his toe in the door. How to circumvent these hostiles? How to break down their resistance? Rose mulled these problems day and night.

Ignored by the Fair's hierarchy, Rose resorted to threat. Cued by the conspirator, I raised a din about his plans for the summer of '39. Here are specimens. He proposed to open a block-long museum on Broadway, jammed with wax monuments of its famed and notorious and with souvenirs and relics of all its magnificoes from Peter Stuyvesant to David Belasco. He would duplicate the "Pioneer Palace" with which he had stunned beholders in Fort Worth and Cleveland. He had blueprints for an Ice Palace. This would house a skating carnival to shame Sonja Henie. His Summer Rodeo would be sheltered by Madison Square Garden. With Ripley, the Believe-It-or-Not conjurer, he was scheming a Broadway Odditorium. The tired and thirsty could revel after dark in his Diamond Horseshoe.

This barrage worried the Fair's moguls. If all materialized, they'd dampen the Fair's box office. Having menaced his opponents, Rose now turned the other cheek. In the Casa Manana he revealed *Let's Play Fair*. This handsome show was a tribute to Whalen. On Rose's invitation, Whalen and suite were guests of honor at the opening performance. Flattered and intimidated, the enemy capitulated. I put the cover back on the mimeograph machine. Museum, Ice Palace,

Odditorium, Summer Rodeo and other fictions in Rose's arsenal evaporated over night.

The Fair, subsequently known as Whalen's Folly, lost its shirt, and so did every concessionaire in it. Every concessionaire save one. Rose's *Aquacade* netted him over $1,000,000. There was justice in this audit. *Aquacade* was a brilliant and exciting water show. He duplicated *Aquacade* at San Francisco's Golden Gate Exposition and was similarly rewarded. To this day, Rose shudders on recalling that for a time he thought of setting up a historical pageant in the Fair's marine amphitheatre. To a man, New York's drama critics braved a bus ride to Flushing to see *Aquacade's* christening. I was touched by their co-operation, by their willingness to endure hardship. Rose was stoic. What had held them up?

There may be something in Rose's claustrophobia complex. He functions best out of doors. He's kin to the circus rather than to Corneille or George M. Cohan. He has neither the taste nor the talent to triumph in the theatre. Save for *Carmen Jones,* schemed by Oscar Hammerstein, all his stage offerings have curdled.

Beyond any of his competitors, Rose has a talent for making money and for hanging on to it once he gets it. Rarely in the theatre are these two gifts fused in one person. He has skill at selling his product, regardless of its merit. When night clubs were starving, his Casa Manana and Diamond Horseshoe ran up fantastic profits. Both were havens for impoverished headliners of yesterday. In engaging them, he was swayed by the minimum wage rather than sentiment. He purchased the Ziegfeld Theatre for a pittance, could have doubled his investment within a week. In its operation, he has made a fortune. Gilbert Miller did little more than break even when he brought Vivien Leigh and Laurence Olivier to the Ziegfeld in the two *Cleopatras.* Rose made $100,000 on the fifteen-week engagement, without investing a cent.

Though Ziegfeld's crown never fit him, Billy has had extraordinary success—by his standards.

12

Meet the Press

ELSEWHERE in this odyssey I have said that the theatre's nobility are wayward in their judgments, that often they dodge success to grapple with disaster. But these peers have no monopoly on myopia. The critics, too, are prone to error. Though accepted as connoisseurs, not all of them are cast in the image of Bernard Shaw or Max Beerbohm. Frequently they gain office through circumstance or expedience. Seeking a wizard to cope with the poetry of T. S. Eliot and the prose of Tennessee Williams, with the lilts of Jerome Kern and the rhymes of Alan Lerner, with Pinza's bass, Bolger's grace and the arabesques of Agnes de Mille, editors may explore the qualifications of the candidate sketchily. Though few aspirants to so sensitive a post can meet its demands, none shrinks from it. The man is yet to be born who will confess inadequacy if challenged by *Macbeth, The Mikado* or Orson Welles.

Critics have but one thing in common, suspicion of the sanity of their fellows. Some are under the spell of Ibsen and Chekhov, others are happiest at a leg show. Some favor the inaudible school of acting, others the chilly technique of Katharine Cornell. In lofty or gruesome fashion, their reviews reflect their prejudices, their taste and their familiarity with, or scorn for, the English language. In the twenty years that the New York Drama Critics' Circle has been voting awards to the best play and the best musical of the season, only once have its members been unanimous in their choice. It pleases me to report that the show which charmed one and all was *My Fair Lady,* musical variation of Shaw's *Pygmalion* in whose success I'm still basking.

When the musical version of Voltaire's *Candide* opened, Brooks Atkinson wrote that it was "a brilliant musical satire." The *Herald Tribune's* Walter Kerr said it was "a spectacular disaster." To further befog the issue, columnist Leonard Lyons confused it with *Candida* and credited its authorship to Bernard Shaw through all editions.

While such critical discords taunt the customer, they're healthy and honest. If all conformed, the theatre would be a dull devotion. Much of its fascination lies in the perils which beset its workers and the speed with which they rocket from pit to peak. In the pursuit of their calling, the theatre's braves are driven by the same compulsions which cause a man to essay Niagara Falls in a barrel. Economically the theatre operates in a straitjacket. Only one attraction in seven recovers its cost. Only sellout hits survive. A set of sour notices is a death sentence. In an earlier day, a play charged with hokum and heroics, however poisonous to the reviewers, might develop into a mint. Today recovery from critical cudgeling is all but impossible.

Consider a hypothetical case. *Free and Easy,* a one-set comedy with a small cast, though keelhauled by the critics, shows signs of popularity. Ticket sales slowly mount. The producer is courageous and solvent, the actors defiant and co-operative. Weekly receipts of $12,000 will meet expenses. Slight losses may be incurred for a few weeks, but these deficits will be absorbed as business improves.

Slight losses, did I say? A hurdle intrudes. The contract with the theatre provides that *Free and Easy* can be tossed out on its ear on a week's notice any time business falls below $14,000. This ambush is known as "the stop clause." Barring a truce, the comedy is smothered even as it starts to recover.

Why the discrepancy between the sum cited in the stop clause and the figure at which *Free and Easy* can survive? At the season's

peak, there are three candidates for every theatre. The theatre operator prefers to gamble on a new attraction rather than harbor a
cripple. His devotion to profit outweighs his concern for the distressed.

Producers sometimes buy tickets to their own show in an effort
to escape or delay eviction. This tactic is touched with fraud. But
the practice is reciprocal. Theatre proprietors have been known to
curb ticket sales to hasten the departure of their tenant.

Crises brought on by the conflict of supply and demand could be
obviated were there more theatres. But the number of theatres
has shrunk alarmingly since the thirties. Then there were seventy.
Today there are thirty.

Both *Abie's Irish Rose* and *Tobacco Road* were scalped by the
critics. Nursed by tenacious managements, both ran for years. Of
all the plays presented in New York since Hallams played *The
Conscious Lovers* in the Nassau Street Theatre in 1753, only *Life
with Father* had a longer run than these two. Cramped by a stop
clause, neither would have lasted two weeks.

Is the theatre engaged in a dance macabre? The omens are grisly.
I was the press agent for *The Children's Hour* when the Lillian Hellman play ran for eighty-six weeks at Maxine Elliott's Theatre during
Franklin Roosevelt's first term. I was its press agent when it was
revived nineteen years later. The first production cost Herman
Shumlin $10,000, the revival nicked Kermit Bloomgarden for
$35,000. In only one week did the original play to as much as
$14,000. It averaged $11,500. On its reproduction at the Forrest,
the stop clause was $14,000. In its twenty-three-week run there,
business was as much as $21,000 in a week. But it didn't recover
its cost. The original made a small fortune.

The plight of the theatre cannot be charged to the critics. They're
opposed to the cheap, the vulgar and the shoddy—when they recognize it. They wish the theatre well and, within their limitations, try
to improve it. When they sin it's on the side of indulgence. There
may be flaws in their judgments, but it is rubbish to charge, as
do some peevish victims, that they seek to destroy the art and/or
industry which makes their luxuriant life possible.

Unless pushed off a pier, the critics die in office. None has given a thought to vacating his seat for a life of ease. He's living a life of ease.

Seeking a critic in the fall of '51, the *Herald Tribune* baited John Mason Brown, Thornton Wilder, Cornelia Otis Skinner and other literates. All spurned the assignment. So did staffmen John Crosby and John Hutchens. The list of applicants embraced ex-critics, ersatz critics and embryonic critics, drama reporters and drama editors and malcontents from the music, sport and rewrite desks. I was flattered when Geoffrey Parsons, then the *Herald Tribune's* chief editorial writer, asked me to the Century Club to discuss the candidates. I was gratified when the *Herald Tribune* tapped Walter Kerr. Kerr's reviews in *Commonweal*, liberal Catholic weekly, were stimulating, authoritative and free of craft clichés.

Two years earlier, editor Ted Thackrey had offered me the reviewer's chair on the New York *Post,* vacant through the death of Wilella Waldorf. Though thrilled by this bid—a rare compliment to a man of my cloth—I rejected it. Acceptance would have curdled my *modus vivendi.* And there were other considerations. Neither a by-line nor after-dark employment could compensate for the wage differential. Then, too, I had qualms about my ability to execute such a switch.

Although his critical gifts were known to few, Kerr was no stranger to the theatre or its people. As head of the Drama and Speech Department at Catholic University, Washington, D.C., he had won attention. I met Kerr in 1943. He was on leave from the campus to sit in on the Baltimore tryout of *Star Dust,* his comedy about a movie trollop and the havoc she loosed at a girls' school. Michael Myerberg, intoxicated by the success of *The Skin of Our Teeth,* dragged me into a booth at Sardi's after the first rehearsal to assure me that *Star Dust* would be his "bread and butter play." It would run for years and enrich us all, he swore. Mike was disillusioned four weeks later when *Star Dust* was buried on the shores of the Patapsco without benefit of clergy.

Kerr was unchastened by this mishap. Six years later I publicized *Touch and Go,* a fresh and witty revue he had written with his wife, Jean. A half-dozen producers stormed down to see it played at Catholic University. George Abbott won the rights for its Broadway reproduction. Though one of the theatre's top directors, Abbott left its staging to Kerr. He had no reason to regret this decision even though Kerr dismissed Ray Walston that he might put one of his sophomores in the leading male role. This maneuver confused me. It seemed unlikely that a sophomore could have the experience necessary for so demanding a part. I voiced my suspicion to Abbott. "You don't understand," said George. "He's been a sophomore for five years."

Kerr's appointment to the *Herald Tribune* post caused a wagging of heads. Who was this unknown who would succeed William Winter, Percy Hammond, Heywood Broun and Richard Watts? The carpers were muted when Kerr started to function. His experience as playwright, director, producer and instructor, fused with his style and judgment, equipped him for the assignment. Today he is as pungent and gifted a reviewer as is to be found in our land.

With the inauguration of its new critic, the *Herald Tribune* had two Walter Kerrs. The prior W. K. had been its Paris correspondent throughout World War II and was now its foreign editor. The conflicting Kerrs led to a lot of confusion, much of it in the mind of Lucius Beebe. After twenty years' service to the *Herald Tribune* as columnist and reporter, Beebe had fled Forty-first Street in 1951 to publish the *Territorial Enterprise,* Virginia City, Nevada, newspaper which once sheltered Mark Twain. Seeing "By Walter Kerr" over a review, Beebe jumped to the conclusion that his old friend had forsaken international affairs for the drama. Outraged, Beebe wrote his former associate to rebuke him for his perfidy. To complicate matters critic Kerr received the letter meant for the foreign editor.

In his years on the *Herald Tribune* Beebe interviewed dozens of actors and producers for me. Some of these seances were hedged with incidents at odds with his intent, and mine. At the funeral services of Ogden Reid, publisher of the *Herald Tribune,* Beebe lost his notes on Philip Dorn, Dutch actor he had explored earlier that day, and had to put him through the wringer a second time. His skirmish with Beth Merrill was more confusing. Miss Merrill, sometime Belasco star, had emerged from retirement to have a baby, stage center, in *Christmas Eve,* a curious play by a professor of zoology.

Beebe and Miss Merrill were to meet in the lobby of Henry Miller's Theatre during a rehearsal break. When her opponent failed to show up at the appointed hour, Miss Merrill called me. No sooner had she hung up than I had a call from Beebe. Miss Merrill had stood him up, he complained. How about a little co-operation? Baffled by this mixup, I questioned Beebe. Where was he? In the engine room at Maxine Elliott's Theatre. "What are you doing down there?" I asked. "The Maxine Elliott has been closed for five years. How did you get in? Bribe the engineer?" Beebe pleaded amnesia. He recalled that he was to meet Miss Merrill in a theatre named for a deceased player. This miscalculation had brought him to Maxine Elliott's and the fireman's grotto.

Beebe, a millionaire from Beacon Hill, had laid waste the curricula of both Yale and Harvard. To prepare himself for the rigors of the evening, he held court each afternoon in the Biltmore Baths. Given to garish dress, skilled in invective, a fusion of François Villon and Beau Brummel, Beebe was a raffish companion and, paradoxically, a rowdy reactionary. New York is duller since he departed for Virginia City in his private railway car.

Before he became a columnist for the New York *World,* Heywood Broun served the *Tribune* as sports writer and drama critic, hence won my envy. This Harvard graduate who organized the Newspaper Guild was once sued for libel by an actor whose performance, he wrote, was the worst he'd ever seen. The actor lost his suit. Shortly Broun sat in judgment on the unfortunate again. His comment? "Mr. Doe's performance was not up to his usual standard."

I attended a Broun rally at the Selwyn Theatre on a Sunday night in October of 1930. Heywood was running for Congress from New York's Seventeenth District. His opponent was Mrs. Ruth Pratt. All the theatre turned out to cheer its champion. Alexander Woollcott presided. For two hours Broun was eulogized. As Woollcott raised his gavel to rap adjournment, he was checked by Groucho Marx. "The fine flower of the theatre has met here tonight to honor

Heywood Broun," he started. "This is fitting and proper. But before we leave, I'd like to ask one question. How many here live in Broun's district?" Only three of two thousand qualified.

Beaten by Mrs. Pratt, Broun sought solace in the theatre. In July of '31, he opened a revue, *Shoot the Works,* to provide employment for hungry actors. Ira Gershwin, Yip Harburg, E. B. White, Dorothy Fields, Vernon Duke, Peter Arno and Jimmy McHugh were among its authors. Broun's vaudeville and musical-comedy friends thronged his dressing room. It served them as mail drop, comfort station and bar. Night after night a visiting headliner would strut out on the stage and, without fee, do a fifteen-minute specialty for which he got $5,000 a week at the Palace. Despite these spectacular interruptions, business was squalid. But a speakeasy around the corner started playing to capacity. Broun and his cast were responsible. They used the hideaway as rehearsal hall, club and gymnasium.

When Broun left the *Tribune* for the *World,* he was succeeded by Percy Hammond, long the pride of the Chicago *Tribune.* Percy's review of Broun's performance in *Shoot the Works* serves both critics, as it does me. It read:

HEYWOOD BROUN—A SHY ACTOR

With Mr. Heywood Broun's prowess in many arts, the world is familiar. Renowned as a journalist, essayist, novelist, painter and orator, his name is blest in the rolls of fame, and he needs no eulogy from this quarter to establish him as one of the most brilliant and versatile of our public men.

Mr. Broun is also gifted with the large heart of the humanitarian. Soft pity fills his ample bosom whenever he meets another's woes, and he is quick to extend the helping hand of compassion to the unfortunate. This sympathy for his crushed fellows now leads him to become an actor and an impresario, as it led him into a candidacy for Congress. He comes to the rescue of the unemployed folk by producing and starring in a cooperative revue entitled "Shoot the Works." It was presented last night at the Cohan Theatre, a disheveled informality, as genial and full of fun as a Socialist's picnic. At times it was wide awake, occasionally it was drowsy; but there were songs, skits, and satires in it, and also Mr. Broun.

The philanthropies of others are always appreciated by me, and when I see a Titan slowly stirring from his comfortable couch in order to ameliorate the distresses of others, I am overcome by a desire to applaud. Also I take an ignoble pleasure in the discomfiture of a colossus trying to be a clown. It seemed to me that Mr. Broun suffered last night more agonies than many of his brother almsmen have ever suffered; by these convulsions he gave entertainment to scores of less benevolent friends and admirers.

As the dominating person of the revue Mr. Broun seemed afraid and retiring, proud only of his baggy trousers, his wrinkled socks, his unshaven jowls and the shirttails oozing from his liberal waistline. To his dignified brothers-journalist therefore, he was an enjoyable sight as, bulky, perspiring and cumbersome, he accepted the warm caresses of his cool chorus girls— a timid Silenus frisking bashfully with a bevy of Times Square nymphs. Though Mr. Broun's eager diffidences are most affecting, it is possible to hint that he is more proficient in the other arts than he is in that of the revue. I, for one, prefer his painting to his acting, and I have no doubt that so does he.

Milton Raison, press agent for *Shoot the Works,* was an old friend. A frustrated Keats, Milton was happiest when reading his sonnets to bewildered chorus girls. He and Broun used to come to our walk-up for gin and controversy. Often they were accompanied by William O'Neill, baritone in *Shoot the Works.* After each O'Neill visit our landlady would give us warning: another two-in-the-morning concert and she'd start ejection proceedings. O'Neill favored "On the Road to Mandalay." In full voice, he could cause a hundred heads to pop from windows of the San Remo, the apartment house in whose shadow we caterwauled. Broun contended he could make a fortune if O'Neill would co-operate: Hire him out as a lease breaker.

I was startled on meeting Hammond at a tryout performance of *The Royal Family* in Newark. Plays are edited, sandpapered and paced in these pre-Broadway performances. For a critic to inspect one during this warm-up period is considered a violation of privacy. I was more surprised when movie critic Richard Watts told me Hammond was writing about the comedy in Sunday's *Tribune.* What was he writing? Watts clammed up. He had said too much already.

Alarmed, I alerted Jed Harris and co-author Kaufman. Kaufman called Hammond to protest. At the *Tribune* that night, Hammond growled that the drama department harbored a Judas. Watts withdrew to Bleeck's to avoid questioning. Hammond pulled his *Royal Family* essay out of the paper. Piqued at Kaufman's protest, Hammond did not review the comedy when it opened in New York. Ironically, Watts drew the assignment.

Though his judgment was erratic, Hammond was the most entertaining critic I have known. A brilliant stylist and a devastating
phrasemaker, he slaved like a coolie in his search for *le mot juste.*
Once finished, his verdict was sacrosanct. No copy reader, no editor
dared correct it, even when Percy confused Osgood Perkins and
Roland Young.

During prohibition, I occasionally tippled with Hammond at The
Type and Print Club, a scabby speakeasy favored by newsmen
because it stayed open all night. Percy was highly sensitive. He was
convinced that his fellow critics regarded him as an intruder and were
out to discredit him. Stimulated by shellac, he would break into tears
as he detailed his persecution.

I exulted when I could insinuate a client into Percy's Sunday
column. I sent him a letter arguing that *Sailor, Beware* should get the
Pulitzer Prize. He printed this blasphemy in full and identified its
author as a man with "a voodoo personality who fears neither God,
man nor the *New York Times.*" Pre-empting Hammond's column, by
craft standards, was a triumph. Rarely does a man of my kidney
intrude on a critic's meditations.

Though thin-skinned, Percy could jeer at himself. Reviewing
But—Is It Art?, a collection of his judgments, he appraised his style
and influence thus:

> During the period of what may be referred to as his incumbency he
> [Hammond] has tried to wag his tongue while keeping it in his cheek,
> which is a feat only to be performed by the maestros. The result has
> been a muddle of confused irony and candor practically worthless to
> those who love the Drama. . . . Nevertheless, it may be contended on
> behalf of Mr. Hammond that he is glib. He can say nothing in more
> words than any musical comedy librettist, and he can say it again and
> again. Polysyllables gush from his calligraph like carbonized water from
> a siphon, diluting and adulterating their subject with effervescent bubbles.
> Forgetting for the nonce a hesitancy to hurt an author's feelings, this
> commentator can now say for the benefit of the bookworms that "But—
> Is It Art?" is only a printed museum of piffling affectation and that it
> adds nothing of value to the literature of show business.

The 1927 holiday week which saw the christening of *The Royal
Family* was the most crowded in New York's theatrical history.
In a six-day span, seventeen plays and musicals opened. (Only sixty

were set up in the entire 1956-57 season.) Eleven opened the night after Christmas. Trying to cope with this clutter, drama editors impressed music critics, movie critics and dance critics. Some of the exhibits were judged by volunteers from the financial, maritime and garden desks and by reporters and rewrite men, all eager to air long-supressed "evocatives," "adequates" and "poignants."

Though deft with the dirk, critics bleed easily and heal slowly. They wince when the wounded strike back. Identified as "the Jukes family of journalism" by Maxwell Anderson after they had pilloried his *Truckline Cafe,* they wailed like banshees. George Jean Nathan has flayed all his brothers impartially. Nathan dubbed Alexander Woollcott "the Seidlitz Powder of Times Square" and jeered George Bernard Shaw because he rated Joseph Jefferson with such immortals as Salvini and Coquelin.

Critic baiting is as old a sport as falconry.

"A man must serve his time to every trade save censure—critics all are ready made," wrote Lord Byron. Disraeli identified them as "men who have failed in literature and art." "Reviewers are usually people who would have been poets, historians, biographers, etc., if they could; they have tried their talents at the one or at the other, and have failed; therefore they turn critics," wrote Coleridge. "Criticism is the device by which one may grow important and formidable at the expense of others," said Boswell's Dr. Johnson.

Though they resent attacks on their products, playwrights and producers rarely resort to counter-attack, lest their tormentors enlarge on the original indictment. The few who risk it make headlines. Audacious Jed Harris ridiculed the reviewers after they castigated his revival of *A Doll's House.* "There is no man in New York writing dramatic criticism today [1938] who has any creative force; they are critics only because they have jobs. When their papers fold, they are no longer critics. I've never seen so many men so ill-equipped for their jobs as the boys now reviewing for the New York dailies."

Angered when the critics tomahawked two of his three-act sermons, Elmer Rice castigated them in a paid ad in the *Times.* "For the most part they are men without intellect, perception, sensitivity or background. They pander to the tastes of the empty-head, the bored, the insensitive and the complacent," said Elmer. He repeated much of this charge in an address to Columbia's Journalism School. In this he identified one of the enemy as "a senile alcoholic." In his rebuttal the following Sunday in the *Tribune* Percy Hammond wrote, "Mr. Rice hasn't told all he knows about us."

Indignant because Richard Watts damned his adaptation of John Steinbeck's *Tortilla Flat,* Jack Kirkland sought out the critic in Bleeck's Artist and Writers' Club and swung from the floor. Kirkland's choice of an arena was unfortunate. Bleeck's was Watts's other home. It crawled with his cronies and they all but decimated the irate author. Watts and Kirkland had been classmates at Columbia. Their scuffle further frayed the old-school-tie tradition.

Incensed over a hostile report, the Shuberts sometimes retaliated by barring its author from their theatres. At various times, Percy Hammond, Alexander Woollcott, *Variety's* reviewers, columnists Leonard Lyons and Walter Winchell were outlawed by Lee and J. J. To this day, the names of Lyons and the *Variety* reviewer cannot appear on the first-night press list for an opening in a Shubert theatre. Press agents circumvent the Shubert lookouts by striking out the names of the condemned and replacing them with proxies. The deception is condoned by the Shubert serfs.

Critics occasionally are trapped in their own folly. Theodore Dreiser's phantom review is still talked about in St. Louis. Yet to achieve note as a novelist, Dreiser was to report on one of Shakespeare's tragedies. Beset by some occupational miasma, but familiar with the plot, he reviewed the work *in absentia.* Judiciously mixing censure and praise, his finding ran to half a column. But the actors and their scenery and their properties betrayed him. All were snowbound in Joplin.

Similarly confused was the critic who tottered into Forty-eighth Street during an intermission at the Cort. Seeking to smother the flames that consumed him, he entered a nearby fountain. Slaked, he decided to return to his task. A half hour elapsed before he discovered he was watching a radio program at the Vanderbilt, adjoining the Cort.

Press agents have little traffic with critics save those who double as drama editors. Respecting their integrity, even when suspicious of their judgment, we never try to sway them. Indirectly we try to ease their ordeals, ensure their comfort. When Maurice Evans presented his four-hour, uncut *Hamlet,* the curtain rose at five-thirty, with an hour's recess at seven for dinner. That they might dine leisurely, and escape jostling at nearby restaurants, I had them served in a private dining room across the street. Though most of them welcomed this maneuver, two revolted. One cried out that he couldn't be bribed with a two-dollar table d'hôte. Another said it was an attempt to regiment them. This rebel lost two buttons off his jerkin in the crush at Sardi's.

Mrs. Maney has not always shared my convictions about the sanctity of critics. She registered a notable dissent on the night of February 1, 1936. The locale was the American Music Hall, a reclaimed chapel in which the brothers Krimsky, Lucius Beebe and Harry Bannister had set up *Murder in the Old Red Barn,* mock melodrama.

The Music Hall operated on two levels. On the upper deck the thriller was overacted before an audience seated at tables. The customers, warmed by grog, cheered the heroine, hissed the villain and shouted advice to the players. To compensate for flaws in the performance, each critic was faced by a fifth of his favorite sauce. All had a fine time save the sober and stoics who thought the proceedings juvenile.

After the performance, the audience descended to the Beachcomber Bar for community singing and dancing. Volunteer magicians, acrobats and exhibitionists were encouraged.

To carry out the Beachcomber illusion, the proprietors rigged up a Pago-Pago. This device fascinated my wife. To satisfy her curiosity, I explained its mechanics. In memory of *Rain,* streams from a garden hose played on a pane of plate glass. About to enlarge on the sham, I was distracted by a group mutilating "Slaughter on Tenth Avenue," the ballet Vera Zorina and Ray Bolger danced in *On Your Toes.*

During my absence, Betty fled. When next I sighted her, she was headed for the bar, snaking the hose behind her. My wife is an

impulsive type. When elated she may flout Emily Post. On a June
night in London, she captured and, for half an hour, operated an
elevator in the Savoy. Rocketing from cellar to roof, she sought to
emulate Paul Revere, in a vertical rather than a horizontal plane.

In debate with the bartender, Robert Garland offered an attractive
target. Betty agrees with Oscar Wilde that the only way to get rid
of a temptation is to yield to it. She gave the *Telegram's* sage the
works, i.e. the water works.

Garland was infuriated. Never had he been subjected to such
an indignity, he cried. But vengeance was at hand. His review of
Murder in the Old Red Barn would be a lesson to all press agents,
to their wives and heirs. Betty's sacrilege whitened my mane. It
was comparable to giving a bishop the hotfoot as he intoned the
marriage service.

The night was bitter cold. In his review, the *Journal's* John Anderson wrote that one of his colleagues, on returning to his "digs," had
to be chipped out of his cab with a chisel. The Critics' Circle
named Betty "Lady Precious Stream," after a Chinese charade
which had puzzled them earlier. A motion to cite her for "the best
performance" of the year lost by a narrow margin.

Once he'd thawed out, Garland's rage abated. So did his memory.
In his review he said *Murder in the Old Red Barn* offered one of the
most satisfying nights in the theatre since the invention of the
footlight.

Reviewers seldom prod press agents. Burton Rascoe was an exception. He was named drama critic of the *World-Telegram* in '42 after
fifteen years' service as a literary critic. Rascoe had eccentric notions
about the theatre and boiled with suggestions for its improvement.
On seeing *Ramshackle Inn,* his agitation soared.

Ramshackle Inn was reminiscent of *Arsenic and Old Lace, The
Cat and the Canary, The Bat* and other whodunits of the last half
century. The author's memory atoned for his lack of invention. The
critics hooted the play but cheered its heroine, Zasu Pitts. The day
after the opening I was numbed by this note from Rascoe:

"I think Reud [the producer] has a potential goldmine in 'Ramshackle Inn,' though, privately, I think Sircom should direct Zasu

to play the part much straighter and omit, or trim down, some of the comic business with the pink wrap and the handbag; she'll be funnier without that. In fact the play would be funnier without her because she's known as a comic and depends upon her movie technique too much."

If it hadn't been for Miss Pitts and her pantomime, the whole company might have been lynched during the Boston tryout. Only when she was on the stage alone, unencumbered by words or actors, did the customers perk up. Rascoe was mad as a xylophone player. By plugging Miss Pitts shamelessly, by excising lines and players, this atrocity ran for six months. If ever a woman triumphed over material, it was Zasu Pitts in *Ramshackle Inn*.

Rioting broke out when *The Old Maid* was voted the Pulitzer Prize in 1935. There was talk of jailing members of the Advisory Committee who recommended the play to the trustees of Columbia University. Their choice climaxed a series of daffy decisions. Lillian Hellman's *The Children's Hour*, Maxwell Anderson's *Valley Forge*, Robert Sherwood's *The Petrified Forest* and Clifford Odets' *Awake and Sing*, all produced the same season, were infinitely better.

The will of Joseph Pulitzer, owner and publisher of the St. Louis *Post-Dispatch* and the New York *World*, provided annual cash awards for achievements in American journalism and letters. The drama award was to go to "the original American play performed in New York City which shall best represent the standard of good morals, good taste and good manners." Exercising discretion granted to them in the will, in 1929 the Advisory Board changed the requirements to read: "To an original American play performed in New York which shall represent in marked fashion the educational value and power of the stage, preferably dealing with American life."

In citing *The Old Maid*, the Committee violated its own rule. It was not an original play. Zoë Akins had adapted it from an Edith Wharton novelette. The guilty men were never brought to justice. The Advisory Board had masked its members after Walter Prichard Eaton, Clayton Hamilton and Austin Strong resigned in disgust, a year earlier.

Fuming over the choice of *The Old Maid*, the critics jumped at

Helen Deutsch's suggestion that they offer a prize for the best
American play of each season. To earn their medal, a play must
receive three-fourths of the votes cast. Fearful a cash prize might
be thought vulgar, the viewers settled for a silver plaque designed
by Henry Varnum Poor. The first token went to Maxwell Anderson
for *Winterset*. Anderson and Poor were Nyack, New York, neighbors,
Anderson and Miss Deutsch old friends. Indeed, Miss Deutsch was
something more than an old friend. She was the press agent for
Winterset.

Trying to determine the best play of 1938-39, the critics were
thwarted because no candidate could get three-fourths of the votes.
Lillian Hellman's *Little Foxes* led the field, followed by Sherwood's
Abe Lincoln in Illinois.

Denied in '39, Miss Hellman bagged the plaque in '41 with *Watch
on the Rhine*. When the reviewers voted Emlyn Williams' *The Corn
Is Green* the best foreign play of the year, Herman Shumlin's cup
overflowed. He had produced both plays. In proof of their good
will, the critics were to entertain the prize-winning casts and authors
Sunday night at the Algonquin. The winners would be announced
in a fifteen-minute radio program preceding the festivities. Since
author Williams was trapped in war-torn London, Shumlin was to
reply for him. Joseph Wood Krutch, president of the Drama Critics'
Circle, would preside.

Since the critics' treasury resembled Mother Hubbard's cupboard,
guests were warned to leave mates, caddies and co-makers at home.
Paul Lukas, the Kurt Müller of *Watch on the Rhine,* ignored this
cue. The other players fumed when the émigré entered with Mrs.
Lukas on his arm. They were about to mutiny when Ethel Barrymore,
star of *The Corn Is Green,* stilled them. Mr. Lukas was only observing
an old Hungarian custom, she said.

As the press agent for both plays, I, too, was a guest. On my
arrival, a donnybrook was raging. During a rehearsal of the radio
program, Krutch hinted that Saroyan's *Love's Old Sweet Song* was
the season's best play. Shumlin was fit to be tied. His indignation
mounted with the entrance of Saroyan. He demanded that Krutch's
address be revised. His anger was justified. The rules provided for

one winner in each category. Krutch should be impeached if he voiced his dissent over the air.

Krutch's colleagues ruled him out of order and his presentation speech was rewritten by John Anderson and Richard Watts. During this melee, Miss Hellman and I took Shumlin into protective custody. He was ready to destroy Krutch with his bare hands. The bitterness born of Krutch's heresy ebbed during supper. Everyone got pleasantly high save Ethel Barrymore. Sipping lemon juice and seltzer, from the head of the table she looked down upon the celebrants with characteristic scorn. Early in the evening, she warned me that if two of the reviewers so much as spoke to her, she would caress them with a carafe. When one of the condemned weaved toward her, I turned my head in dismay, awaiting the glass crash. But Miss Barrymore was too great a lady to strike down her foe before his fellows. She swept him with a radiant smile, giving no sign of her homicidal urge.

In the twenty-one years that they have functioned simultaneously, only seven times have the critics and the Pulitzer committee seen eye to eye. They were in agreement on *The Time of Your Life, A Streetcar Named Desire, Death of a Salesman, Picnic, Teahouse of the August Moon, Diary of Anne Frank* and *Long Day's Journey into Night.* Ironically, *The Time of Your Life* received the twin citations posthumously. Its burial preceded the citations by three weeks.

Fanatic in their devotion to the drama, the critics will endure hunger and hardship to do it reverence. Shortly after the opening of *Richard II,* I received a telegram from Mordaunt Hall requesting two seats for Friday night's performance. Formerly motion picture critic of the *New York Times,* Hall was then drama critic for the Boston *Transcript.* Mr. Hall addressed me at the theatre. I sent him a confirming wire. Then, confronted by crises, I forgot his request.

The following Saturday I was awakened by a call from Eddie Dowling, co-producer of *Richard II.* "Take my advice," he said. "Stay out of Boston. Hall will have you jugged on sight." Then he detailed the nature and scope of my crime.

Mr. Hall had driven to New York. On arrival he picked up Mrs.

Hall, donned black tie and dinner jacket, dined modestly and at eight-twenty tripped into the St. James lobby. Elbowing his way to the wicket, he asked for his tickets. The treasurer fumbled in the rack, riffled envelopes, then asked, "What was the name again?"

"Mordaunt Hall of the Boston *Transcript*." The treasurer riffled again. With the arrogant smile affected by box-office men when they command a sellout, he dismissed Mr. Hall with "Nothing in your name."

"There must be some mistake," said the critic. "Will you look again? Mr. Maney wired he was leaving them."

"Nothing in your name," repeated the box-office man. "Please step aside!"

Mr. Hall turned to the crowd and announced that Dick Maney was the all-American bastard. Mr. Dowling, loitering in the box office, sought to placate him. Worming his way through the crowd, he held out his hand. "I am Eddie Dowling." Hall drew back as if facing a cobra. "I remember you," he shouted. "You used to sing. I heard you in *Thumbs Up* and you were lousy."

Ignoring this insult, Dowling explained that the house had been sold out for days. He was sure Mr. Maney could explain when and if found. Though it violated fire rules, he'd be glad to place chairs in an aisle for him and his wife. This infuriated Hall further. Stabbing Dowling with a forefinger he shouted, "You know what I think? Maney left the tickets for me and you have sold them." With that, he strode from the lobby, spitting invective.

"I didn't mind him calling you a bastard," said Dowling, "but when he smeared my singing I wanted to slug him. How are you going to wriggle out of this fix? I'm curious."

I wired Mr. Hall my regrets. Owing to a clerical error, the tickets had been left for Saturday night rather than Friday. When could he drive down again? Hall accepted this fiction and a week later thrilled at the conflicts of Bolingbroke and John of Gaunt, or King Richard and Hotspur.

On the night of Hall's second visit, I called the theatre shortly after the curtain's rise. Disguising my voice I asked for Dowling. "This is Mordaunt Hall's father," I said. "I understand my son is having trouble getting into the play. I—" Dowling's denial shattered my eardrum. "No! No! No!" he cried. "That was *last* Friday. Mordaunt's sitting in the fourth row on the aisle, happy as a lark."

Producers are sensitive to the conduct of critics on opening night. They watch their comings and goings like hawks. They are desolated if one arrives late or departs before the final curtain. If Brooks Atkinson is smiling at the end of the second act, they're transported. If Kerr or Watts or Chapman seems grim they're ready to drain the hemlock cup. Beset by vapors, often they attribute base motives to innocent men.

Producer John Krimsky was fuming when I encountered him in front of the Vanderbilt on the opening night of *In Clover*. The reason for his rancor? Though the second act was four minutes old, three critics loitered in the tavern next door. "Whether they like it or not, they should sit through it," John protested to me. Just then the trio emerged and entered the theatre. They were accompanied by George Atwell. Mr. Atwell was Krimsky's father-in-law and the play's chief backer. He had been host to the reviewers.

When drama critic of the *World-Telegram*, Robert Garland was obliged to write a column on days when there was no opening to review. Premières were scarce in the spring. Often he found a theme for a sermon elusive. In such extremities he occasionally reviewed an attraction a second time. Garland had enthused over Ethel Merman, Jack Haley and Sid Silvers when *Take a Chance* opened the previous winter. "Why not review it a second time?" I asked.

Garland agreed. I left tickets for him for Saturday night's performance. His reappraisal would appear Monday. On Friday, Garland called to say he couldn't go Saturday night. Why didn't I write a review of *Take a Chance,* echoing his original estimate? He would use it under his by-line, provided my prose didn't get out of hand. I promised to use discretion. That's more than Garland used.

The salute to *Take a Chance* appeared as I had written it, with one exception. In the months that had elapsed since the musical's opening, Garland had changed his mind about singer June Knight. He struck out my tribute to her and inserted a slap. This gratuitous dig aroused one of Miss Knight's remote admirers, an outlaw who cheered her every Saturday night from the fifth row. On the Saturday night covered in Garland's report, this Launcelot fled the theatre in dismay on learning that Miss Knight was indisposed and that her understudy would sing her role. His anguish changed to fury on learning that Garland had condemned his dream girl *in absentia*. Tightening up his holster, he announced he'd destroy Garland on sight. This threat reached the critic. It was days before he ventured from his chambers.

At my suggestion, one of Garland's successors agreed to interview Guthrie McClintic, director-producer. The powwow was set for noon. At ten that morning, an aide phoned me at home. He had received a call from a Harlem bagnio. My friend was held as a hostage until arrears of $21.35 were cleared up. Did I want the McClintic interview? Then I'd better spring him. I did. What's more, the captive's report was printed though it read like an excerpt from *Finnegans Wake*.

On the whole critics are a sober and scrupulous crew. Just as umpires shun outfielders off the field, few critics consort with actors, producers or directors. Most of them lead secluded lives. Only when they invade a theatre as jurors are they spotlighted.

At every New York first night 130 orchestra seats are filled by what is loosely called "the press." The list of eligibles, barring extensions or deletions by producer or theatre owner, is made up by the press agent. Rigid protocol is observed in assigning pews. Priority rights, service records and intramural vendettas are weighed in determining who shall sit where. Each of the anointed receives two tickets. They're all in "on the cuff."

The sixty-five who make up this elite corps include the critics of New York's newspapers, their drama editors and drama reporters and, save in the case of the *New York Times,* their gossip columnists. The seven dailies average thirty-five representatives at each première. The remaining thirty? Critics of dailies dedicated to horse racing, finance, commerce and the garment industry. Critics of Newark dailies and wire services. Commentators from TV and radio stations. Critics from *Time, Life, The New Yorker, Variety* and *Newsweek.* A few defy classification. Their presence is due to their skill at intimidation and nagging.

Enrollment on a first-night list is an approximation of immortality. It's comparable to being named to the French Academy or being decorated on the field of battle. It confirms the prestige or nerve of the candidate. A virago of my acquaintance has sought certification for ten years. Her qualifications are microscopic—an occasional radio bleat. But so ceaselessly does she badger manager, stars and theatre proprietors, few openings are without her. More than one reviewer has tried to retain his first-night chairs after being sacked, even after he's been buried. Pleas of relicts are rarely honored.

Periodically a producer demands that I trim the press list. With fewer newspapers each year, he can't understand why it grows. Trying to riddle this paradox, I cite the inroads of television and radio know-it-alls and the epidemic of columnists. The press agent shrinks from playing pioneer. The first suspect dropped from the rolls will scream like a fishwife. The producer is fortunate if he can keep the list within its present limits, I argue. There are fifty critics, representing everything from annuals to almanacs, smoldering with resentment on the second-night list. A revolt by these brooders could be an ugly business.

It's to my advantage to have drama editors and drama reporters, picture editors and feature editors strategically seated at such performances as they elect. My traffic is with them rather than critics. They rule the space to which I aspire. Without their good will, men of my cloth would be well advised to take up crocheting or serendipity. (Serendipity? Vivien Leigh lists it and flower arranging as her hobbies.) It's up to me to get tickets for qualified newsmen and out-of-town critics even if I have to burgle a ticket broker or twist the arm of the producer for house seats.

House seats are the symbol of the sellout. The more spectacular the hit, the more frantically they are sought. Located within the first eight rows, from fifty to eighty seats are earmarked for the producer, theatre owner, authors, stars and director, that they may oblige associates, friends and people to whom they are indebted, or flatter visiting headliners. The number of these seats is constant. So is their location in the theatre. They are issued on presentation of a requisition signed by the person to whom they have been issued. Unless picked up at least twenty-four hours before the performance, they are released for public sale.

House seats for *My Fair Lady,* judged by me and higher authorities as the greatest musical of all time, rapidly acquired the status of Kohinoors. The quest for them dimmed the ordeal of Jason as he sought the Golden Fleece. Fanatics who wangled them experienced an ecstasy comparable to that of Captain Hillary and his Sherpa guide as they looked down from the crest of Everest. *Fair Lady* folk with house seats at their disposal led hunted lives. Their phones rang day and night. They were sprayed with telegrams and cablegrams, with threats, prayers and charges of treachery.

Weighing intangibles, pressures and the potential for intramural strife, Herman Levin set aside seventy house seats. Twenty of these were for his own use and a like number went to Anthony Farrell, owner of the theatre. Six were credited to the Columbia Broadcasting System, the radio and television cartel which put up the $400,000 necessary to produce the show in return for 40 per cent of the profits. Alan Jay Lerner and Frederick Loewe, authors of the words, lyrics and music, and director Moss Hart had two pairs. Rex Harrison and Julie Andrews and Stanley Holloway, designer Oliver Smith and choreographer Hanya Holm had two seats each.

I had two pairs with which to cope with requests from newspaper and magazine editors, wire and syndicate editors, radio and television experts, and agents of other media. Of all *My Fair Lady's* staff, I alone could write a pass. Producer Levin ruled that visiting critics rated complimentary seats, however remote their base, however small their circulation. I could also frank feature writers and interviewers whose words mushroomed the musical's fame. Mr. Levin is sensitive to good will and the potential of reciprocity.

Starting March 16, 1956—the day following the show's opening— I was running a branch box office. My phone rang incessantly. Incoming mail reached new highs. Word of *My Fair Lady's* success, of its rapturous reception by the reviewers, spread like fire in a confetti factory. Editors once frigid to my advances now caressed me. Long the hunter, I was now the hunted. Badgered with bids to exalt Rex Harrison and Julie Andrews, I could practice discrimination. Purring over this paradox, shortly I was buried under ticket requests. There were twenty applicants for each of my seats. My allotment for April and May was wiped out in two weeks. Thereafter the clamor crescendoed.

I wasn't the only man with ticket trouble. The drama critics, editors and reporters on New York's seven newspapers were deluged with requests, requests they couldn't ignore. These came from their publishers, from their managing editors, executive editors, foreign editors, their aides and equerries, from the editors of the fashion, book, sports, marine, music, news and crossword departments. None of these braves cared to stand in line at the Hellinger, sold out for months in advance. None deigned to order tickets by mail. Instead they heckled the drama department. They knew it had access to house seats—my house seats.

The *New York Times* and the *Daily News* were my best customers, *The New Yorker* a close third. It was a dull day that I didn't get a half-dozen requests from the *Times*. I obliged a slew of Adlers and Sulzbergers, the *Times's* top brass, and Sunday editor Lester Markel and his aides. I'm partial to Markel and his staff. I've written some thirty stories for the *Times Magazine*—the most literate and topical Sunday supplement in the land. Many of these pieces concerned my clients. For them I was paid the *Times* fee. To a press agent, this is comparable to winning the Nobel Prize for Literature.

As the press agent needs the co-operation of the press, so drama editors and critics need the co-operation of make-up men, copyreaders, the foreman of the composing room and the head of the art department. Without it their chores may become unduly sticky. Thus they go to great lengths to humor these craftsmen. In the spring of '56, the easiest way to humor them was to get them house seats for *My Fair Lady*. This caused demands on me to snowball. Irked by a constant busy signal when he tried to call me, producer Levin had our offices connected with a direct wire. This device led to further confusion. The bells on my office phones purred.

The one on the direct wire went off like a gong. On first hearing it, visitors bolted. Some thought the building was on fire. Others felt the joint was being raided.

Though I feigned dismay, the ticket tumult was music to my ears. The unprecedented demand proved that I was linked with the greatest hit of my life. I had hit the press agent's jackpot. Temple bells jangled in my noggin.

The success of *My Fair Lady* revived a lost art—letter writing. Some of the appeals for tickets were eloquent and some emotional; some humorous and some acrimonious. Ogden Nash addressed me in fractured rhyme. "Pretend I'm your mother, then act like a dutiful son," wrote a retired librarian from Memphis. A soldier addressed me from Thule, Greenland. After two years on the ice, his first night back in New York must be memorable. How about two on the aisle for August 13 for him and his fiancée?

When I honored a request from Phyllis McGinley, she acknowledged it in rhyme:

> THIS IS (I QUOTE) A THANK-YOU NOTE
>
> Whenever skies are rainy
> Or hope has taken flight,
> I'll think on Richard Maney
> With wonder and delight;
> I'll muse on Richard Maney
> Whose like I seldom see
> For deeds urbane but brainy
> And warm philanthropy;
> Who even solves such zany
> Predicaments as mine.
> Oh! *darling* Mr. Maney
> Wilt be my Valentine?

Then there was Mrs. Moore, for five years exiled in Saudi Arabia. From Medina or Riad she airmailed a letter to the Hellinger. She was returning to the States for a month's vacation in the fall. Could she have two for any night in the week of October 15? She enclosed the necessary $16.10, plus a dollar for airmail reply.

Charles Walters, treasurer at the Hellinger, beamed as he showed me a second letter from Mrs. Moore. She had received her tickets three weeks after mailing her request. This, she said, was a record

for an exchange of letters with the States. Her gratitude was bound-
less. She thanked Mr. Walters for noteworthy service.

Box-office men for hits get a lot of abuse. They're harassed
through the mail, over the telephone and at the window. They're
accused of collusion with the brokers and black-market activities.

Mrs. Moore provided me with evidence to refute slanders on
the Hellinger's ticket sellers. Both her letters were printed in the
Times drama section. Their publication touched off a storm of
protest. People unable to get tickets seethed with indignation. "What
do we have to do to get tickets," they screamed, "move to Saudi
Arabia?" Walters called me Monday morning. "Do me a favor," he
pleaded. "Don't publish any more compliments to the box-office staff.
You've stirred up a hornet's nest."

Because of its title, *My Fair Lady* brought the chivalry in newsmen to a boil. The night for which they wished tickets invariably
was their wife's birthday or their wedding anniversary. "The little
woman" would be desolated if I failed them.

On assignment, I wrote pieces for the Sunday drama pages of both
the *Times* and the *Herald Tribune,* accenting the ticket problems
of a press agent with a hit. These brought an avalanche of requests
from laymen, previously unaware of my existence. I was victimized
by my own industry.

The *Times's* Sam Zolotow has been New York's top drama
reporter for thirty years. Feared by many, disliked by some, Zolotow
is respected by all for his competence and diligence. When Zolotow
questions a producer about a play or a star he seeks, he is relentless.
He mousetraps the naïve and bludgeons the hard-boiled. He knows
more theatre people than anyone else in the business. He is awed
by none of them. He'll challenge Gilbert Miller as quickly as a
freshman playwright. Alexander Woollcott memorialized Zolotow in
a *New Yorker* profile in 1928.

Under the title "Office-Boy of Destiny," Woollcott said in part:

In December, 1919, the dramatic department of the *New York Times*
acquired a new office-boy, the previous incumbent having heard the
clarion call of the jewelry business. The newcomer's name was Sam
Zolotow.

From the first there was something in his breezy manner of taking pos-
session which suggested a not implausible intention to own the newspaper
itself at his earliest convenience. Indeed the various members of the department felt their natural ferocity towards any office-boy tempered by an
uneasy and propitiatory feeling that some day they would all be working
for this one.

Doubtless some early observers based their sense of Sam as an office
boy of destiny on the circumstance that, while pocketing affably the
weekly stipend on which Mr. Ochs thought he was living, he was at
some pains to augment that sum by running a horse-racing book among
the compositors and circulation men in the office, thereby cleaning up
an extra forty dollars a day.

. . . Recently at the pretty wedding of Charles MacArthur and Helen
Hayes, the first of the thirty uninvited guests to arrive at Judge Ober-
wager's bower was none other than Samuel Zolotow, Esq., wearing a simple
business suit of unobtrusive gray, plus a determined expression which suggested that, without his sanctioning presence, the marriage would hardly
be legal.

Because of his lust for exclusive news, the prestige of his newspaper and his sources of information, Zolotow is the despair of
drama reporters on other newspapers. Thanks to Zolotow, theatrical
reporting has improved throughout his reign. Only a noodlehead
tries to hoax Sam. He has a long memory. Frequently Zolotow
knows more about my employers and their activities than I do, and
before I do.

Of all New York newspapermen, Ward Morehouse is most devoted
to the theatre. At sixteen he had written sixteen plays. In his first
three months on the Savannah *Press,* he interviewed Billie Burke,
Raymond Hitchcock and Margaret Illington on the veranda of the
De Soto Hotel, an experience from which he never recovered. Since
that winter of 1915, he's interviewed most of the theatre's famous
and infamous. He has treed them in Soho and in the Bois de
Boulogne; in Chicago's Loop, San Francisco's Market Street and
Tokyo's Ginza. The more remote his prey, the more ardently Ward
pursues it.

I have flown with Ward to Buffalo that he might interview Ina
Claire, and to Fort Worth to palaver with Billy Rose. For me he's
sought out Tallulah in Boston, Lillian Hellman in Philadelphia and

Helen Hayes in Baltimore. Ward has given me some anxious moments, none more anxious than when I found him trying to pat a black panther in the basement of the Hippodrome during the run of *Jumbo.* "Pretty kitty, pretty kitty," he intoned.

Gifted with total recall, Ward can remember the name of every actress he ever glimpsed and the play in which he saw her. He's seen and adored thousands. He has another talent which endears him to me: He can give the complete line-up of the New York Giants in 1905, and name the outfielders who supported Grover Cleveland Alexander when he won a pennant for the Phillies ten years later.

Setting up interviews for actors, authors and producers is press agent routine. Since stage folk are reputed to lead colorful, off-beat lives, the legend persists that they make good copy. They rarely do. Questioned for publication, they muffle their phobias and prejudices. Hellions talk like missionaries. They publicly praise those they privately curse. With few exceptions, headliners are sanctimonious and mealy-mouthed under cross-examination. Why? Insecurity! Since jobs are few and hard to get, actors must be careful whom they hiss in type.

Trying to get fire or fun into an interview, newspapermen sometimes worry actors into statements that match their convictions. Seeing his words in type, the actor screams he's been misquoted. Misquoting actors is an obsession with newsmen, if you can believe Equity's rank and file.

Sir Laurence Olivier would rather submit to the rack than to an interview. When I tried to break down his resistance, he took refuge in Garson Kanin's quip: "No one ever won an interview." Olivier grows vehement in defending his allergy. Who's interested in what he thinks of the United Nations, Britain's Labour party or ructions in Pakistan? The reader is as indifferent to an analysis of an actor's technique as he is to the mechanism of a watch when all he wants to know is the time. If he's curt, he's called rude. If he is flippant, he's branded as a showoff. He was still crushed by the reception given his Romeo when I persuaded him to talk to a syndicate feature writer. During the exchange, Olivier cited his inadequacy in these duels. By way of explanation, he said he feared he was a dull fellow. The published story had him saying all English actors were dull fellows. Mr. Olivier has communicated his misgivings to his wife, Vivien Leigh. When Miss Leigh visited us to play the Cleopatra of both Shaw and Shakespeare, she was so alarmed by Maurice Zolotow's questions that she demanded approval of his copy before it went to the *Times*. Such veto power is frowned upon by reporters, editors and me. Were the practice common, the interview business would bog down in protests and delays.

Players pop up with howlers during interviews, and so do their inquisitors. While in *Watch on the Rhine*, Lucile Watson told a *World-Telegram* man World War II could have been averted had women worn more clothes. In his talk with Raymond Massey (*Abe Lincoln in Illinois*), Lucius Beebe cited the entrance of Mrs. Massey. To show he was *au courant*, Lucius identified her as the former Adrianne Allen. His conclusion was faulty. The Mrs. Massey who interrupted the powwow was the successor to Miss Allen. On reading Beebe's gaffe, I phoned him: "There's a banana boat leaving for Guatemala in the morning. I'd advise you to get on it. In Champerico you can defy the posse. Extradition laws do not cover your offense."

When Ethel Barrymore was starring in *The Corn Is Green*, her friend Joseph Medill Patterson, editor and publisher of the *Daily News*, instructed his Inquiring Photographer, Jimmy Jemail, to submit this question to the top players in New York:

"Who was—or is—the greatest actress of all time?"

When I relayed the question to Miss Barrymore, she gave me a withering glance. "Patterson is giving the feature two pages in the Sunday *News*," I added. Another withering glance. I reported both glances to Jemail and suggested that Patterson put the question to her. Miss Barrymore's silence didn't disturb me. She doesn't waste time cheering contemporaries. To Patterson, Miss B. vouchsafed this reply:

"Certainly Mme. Modjeska and Ellen Terry were among the greatest actresses who ever lived. Every real student of the theatre must include them in his list of all-time greats. Of the two, Mme. Modjeska was greater. She was an American actress of Polish

ancestry and she used to act with my father. I had many opportunities
to observe her greatness."

Too gallant, or too careless, Patterson didn't challenge Miss
Barrymore's identification of Modjeska as "an American actress."
Mme. Modjeska had been married twice and was thirty-two before
she set foot on our shores.

In voting for Modjeska, and ignoring her co-nationalists living
or dead, Miss Barrymore masked her modesty. I'm sure she had
little doubt who deserved the bay. In citing her father, she dropped
a clue. Though Maurice Barrymore flourished before my time, I
treasured his observation on tippling. "Staggering is a sign of
strength," he told a reporter. "Weak men are carried home."

Tallulah Bankhead pulls no punches when interviewed. She has
vivid opinions about everyone in the theatre and spits them out.
Following a Bankhead soliloquy, the moans of the maimed echo
in Sardi's, the Algonquin and other theatrical roosts. While in *Clash
by Night,* she denounced producer Billy Rose as "a filthy little
bully." On withdrawing from *The Skin of Our Teeth,* Pulitzer Prize
play, she voiced her scorn of manager Michael Myerberg in rich,
ripe terms. Eager to have Miss Bankhead tour in Thornton Wilder's
cosmic farce, Myerberg tried to bludgeon her into consent. This was
a blunder. Miss B. doesn't intimidate easily. The dimensions of
Myerberg's folly developed quickly. With Gladys George—an in-
credible choice—as Tallulah's and Miriam Hopkins' successor, *The
Skin of Our Teeth* opened its tour in Boston and ended it there a
week later. Myerberg's fumble cost him a fortune. With Tallulah,
the play would have toured all season to sellout business.

Dedicated to unilateral debate, Tallulah is the delight and despair
of the interviewer. Getting her to talk is no problem. The trick is
to stop her. In full cry, she can cover six topics and three centuries
in a sentence, then top off the tirade with a quatrain from Omar.
The survivor of a Bankhead broadside is likely to emerge numbed,
eyes glazed, notes scrambled and listing to port. One victim went
into shock on discovering Gaylord, her budgereegah, in his brandy
tumbler. A second was gnawed by her lion cub, named for Winston
Churchill. Senegas, her marmoset, perforated the pelt of another.

Since she's a prodigal hostess, no reporter flees Tallulah's roof thirsty. Occasionally one has been unable to flee, so excessive is her bounty.

Let's consider the case of Micky Murphy. On the staff of *Time,* Miss Murphy undertook a close-up of screen actor Paul Douglas for another magazine. Eager to present a well-rounded portrait, Micky sought out authorities on the actor, friendly and hostile. Learning Tallulah was a Douglas partisan, Micky asked me to arrange an appointment. She'd see the star at her Pound Ridge home any hour or day that was agreeable, she said.

Tallulah gave me a quick brushoff. Like most of her craft, she gets depressed at the prospect of discussing another performer. Conditioned to her quirks, I tacked and luffed, absorbed a Willie Mays routine, then renewed the request. After denouncing me for intruding on her reveries, she agreed to see Micky at four-thirty Friday afternoon. "Tell this dame she'd better be on time," warned Tallulah. "I can only give her half an hour." Could Sylvester, her chauffeur, pick Miss Murphy up on her arrival at the Pound River station? He could not. "Tell her to take a cab. That driver with the red mustache knows how to get to my house."

Pursued by four dogs, Micky popped into Tallulah's living room at the appointed hour. Eager to observe protocol, at five she rose to depart. Tallulah protested. "Why, you've only just got here," she said. "What is it you want to know about Marlene Dietrich? She's an old friend of mine." Micky's attempt to bring Douglas into the conversation was smothered by Tallulah's impersonation of Marlene singing "See What the Boys in the Backroom Will Have."

Conviviality mounted over the next three hours. On Tallulah's insistence, Micky phoned her husband, Marc, at eight to say that she was going to stay the night at Windows. At noon the next day, Tallulah learned that Micky had two children, left in Marc's charge in a Greenwich Village apartment. "What a shame," she said. "Why didn't you tell me? Get Marc on the phone immediately. I'll have Sylvester pick him and the children up at Stamford."

Micky protested. Marc had things to do. Trapped with two children, he would be in no mood for banter.

"Get him on the phone," barked the hostess. "I'll talk to him. The kids can spend the day in the pool."

The interview developed into a three-day carnival. The four Murphys didn't get back to New York until late Monday. The children said they hadn't had so much fun since the Ringling Circus. I never heard what happened to the Douglas survey.

Despite the commotions which attend it, reporters who survive a Bankhead barrage, who catch its flavor and decode its substance, have a gay and racy feature—not the one they sought, to be sure— even after it has been fumigated by the libel editor.

Carol Channing, who caricatured Lorelei Lee in *Gentlemen Prefer Blondes,* hoodooed newsmen who tried to analyze her. While the Anita Loos musical was trying out in Philadelphia, the *Times's* drama editor assigned Lewis Nichols to sound her out after a Saturday matinee. At noon on the appointed day, I learned that Nichols had debouched on Boston Common instead of Rittenhouse Square. Not since "Wrong Way" Corrigan confused Ireland and California had a traveler been so disoriented.

Fearful this contretemps might negate the Channing story, I called Nichols at his Nyack home Sunday afternoon. Though shaken by his fruitless foray, he agreed to meet Carol Monday afternoon at the Ziegfeld Theatre where *Blondes* was going through its final paces prior to its opening three days hence. Monday morning I checked with Biff Liff, stage manager for the musical. The principals were called for a one o'clock rehearsal. Nichols could question Carol then. To avoid a second foul-up, I accompanied Nichols to the theatre. Miss Channing had just left, reported Liff. She was having costumes altered in a dressmaker's loft near the Hudson. On our arrival, Carol was naked. She answered Nichols from behind a Japanese screen. The exchange was brief. She had to leave for rehearsals as soon as she could dress. Thanks to snail-like crosstown traffic, Nichols got his interview in the six-block ride to the theatre. Those who read his Sunday report recked little of his ordeals.

Carol had demonstrated her skill as a dodger earlier. Her first victim was Frank Brookhauser of the Philadelphia *Inquirer*. A week before *Blondes* invaded Philadelphia, Brookhauser agreed to see her in New York. We were to meet in the Algonquin lobby at three. Brookhauser and I arrived on the dot. Carol was missing. I had her paged, then I phoned the doorman at the rehearsal hall. She had left fifteen minutes earlier, destination the Algonquin. After I assured Brookhauser that Carol was a paragon of punctuality, we started our vigil. An hour and four highballs later, no Channing. In desperation I prowled the dark and empty dining room. It wasn't quite empty. Carol was cowering behind a pillar. She'd been there since 2:55.

Gentlemen Prefer Blondes was a bonanza, thanks to Carol's raffish performance and the gusto with which she delivered "Diamonds Are a Girl's Best Friend" and "A Little Girl from Little Rock." Mark Barron, critic for the Associated Press, agreed that a wire story on her success and her reactions to it was in order.

"Would six-thirty be agreeable to Mr. Barron?" Carol asked. "Perhaps he'd like to have dinner with me." I said I'd have Barron call her. Later he reported that Carol was going to cook and serve dinner in her apartment. This domestic switch seemed a touch off key, but I made no comment.

"I'm curious to know how the dinner came out," I asked Mark the day after the interview. "I didn't know Carol could cook."

"She can't," he said. Barron had cooked the dinner. First fascinated, then alarmed by her fumbles, he manned the gas range after the first five minutes. Within a week, hundreds of thousands of readers from coast to coast were acquainted with Carol's acting and culinary achievements. Mark is the only drama critic ever decorated by Mussolini—while an A.P. correspondent covering the rape of Abyssinia.

If I've twitted my employers for their pretensions, I have also flouted their orders when I felt they might boomerang. Shortly before the opening of *The Front Page,* Ward Morehouse asked Jed Harris to delay its première that his *Gentlemen of the Press* might be reviewed first. *The Front Page* was a certain hit, argued Ward. But *Gentlemen of the Press* was a gamble. Both plays dealt with newspapermen, their follies and fevers. If *Gentlemen of the Press* could escape comparison with *The Front Page,* it would fare better and last longer. Harris dismissed the proposal with a shrug.

The Front Page was an immediate sellout. Ward's play faltered. Victimized by fate, Morehouse pondered reprisals. In his *Sun* column he listed notables seen at the hits. As a token of his distemper, he ignored bigwigs cheering *The Front Page.* Though I twitted him about this omission, he continued to brood. While Ward brooded, my sovereign seethed. When two weeks passed without the citation of a *Front Page* caller, Harris instructed me to write Keats Speed, the *Sun's* managing editor, and complain of Morehouse's neglect. I demurred. Harris insisted. Recalling the strategy of Quintus Fabius Maximus, I sought solution in delay. Though I had no intention of denouncing Morehouse, I agreed to write the letter. I was sure Harris would forget his gripe, once diverted by a new offender. Jed heckled me about my indictment of Morehouse for a week. In desperation I wrote it. I flayed Ward as an apostate, as a man who violated his office in his lust for vengeance.

I showed this to Harris. "That's something like it," he said. "Get it off to Speed special delivery." I returned to my desk, tore up the letter and awaited developments.

Daily, Harris asked if I'd heard from Speed. Following my sixth "No," Speed was voted life membership in the S.O.B.'s. Morehouse had preceded him into Jed's Hall of Infamy by three weeks.

Though I have never tried to sway a critic, I have fraternized with most of them. John Chapman is my Westport neighbor. As critic of the New York *Daily News,* he has an audience of over three million, the nation's largest. Though he thinks *Kiss Me Kate* a better musical than *South Pacific,* he is a sound reviewer. A newspaperman since 1917, he had been photographer, reporter, columnist and drama editor before he succeeded Burns Mantle in 1943.

Chapman has many talents. He can wire a house, adjust a carburetor and turn out a lime chiffon pie. He can face a woman's club without flinching. He is a man of courage. In the summer of '55, with his wife, Georgia, he piloted twenty culture-mad excursionists in a six-week tour of Europe's odeons and was as sane on his return as when he started.

Chapman is the only critic with a swimming pool and the only one I have seen in white tie and tails. He has spent evenings at the Metropolitan Opera House voluntarily. Hard by his pool is a converted barn, with bar and footrail. Its walls are covered with photographs of deceased stars, faded theatrical posters and programs, a furred fish and other trophies. There, spent from their efforts in the pool, his guests find peace, perhaps oblivion. Partial to rye and bourbon, the host makes no concessions to Scotch drinkers. This lapse has led to mutinies, even to smuggling.

The *Times's* Brooks Atkinson is our most influential critic since he speaks for America's best and most distinguished newspaper. An adverse report by Brooks is regarded as the kiss of death, while his benediction enhances prospects of success. Many critics are nettled by the theatre's concern with an Atkinson review. They point out that Brooks slated such successes as *The Cocktail Party, The Heiress, Kismet* and *Anniversary Waltz,* and eulogized such short-lived specimens as *The Grass Harp,* Michael Redgrave and Flora Robson's *Macbeth, By the Beautiful Sea* and *Billy Budd.* Because of Atkinson, opening-night curtains rise at eight o'clock or earlier instead of eight-forty. Brooks has a midnight deadline. He writes in longhand, hence must leave the theatre by ten-thirty. Atkinson's opposites on evening papers complain that the early start fouls up their eating habits and leads to digestive disorders. But authors and producers are so awed by the *Times* and its reporter they'd agree on a six o'clock curtain if Brooks suggested it.

Consistent with the paper he represents, Atkinson leans to decorum. He engages in few pyrotechnics. He scorns purple patches, puns and gags. His "this is not for the dopes" in his review of Maurice Evans' uncut *Hamlet* startled the town. While press agenting *Arsenic and Old Lace,* I lured Atkinson into a mock feud which he lived to regret.

Clare Boothe Luce, playwright, diplomat and mate of the publisher of *Life, Time* and *Fortune,* and Frank Sullivan, humorist and hypochondriac, were among those who invested in the melodrama.

I first met Sullivan at Chez Florence, a pre-dawn deadfall of the twenties. We were brought together by the plight of a mutual friend,

John O'Hara. John had been bounced by host Tommy Guinan for
an infraction of the ground rules. So eloquently did Sullivan and
I plead his case that O'Hara was readmitted. O'Hara was ousted a
second time and Guinan told Sullivan and me to pipe down lest we
join him in exile. Playing Zola and Clemenceau to O'Hara's Dreyfus,
Sullivan and I found we had a common thirst, and a common irreverence for the dull and the dignified.

Co-investors in *Arsenic and Old Lace,* we plugged the melodrama
through a sham feud. The column of Richard Watts, *Herald Tribune*
critic, provided a forum for our bluster. In his column in *PM,* Sullivan
charged me with dawdling, with tricking him and other stockholders
into doing my work. Feigning indignation, I addressed my reply to
Watts. He printed it in full after this observation:

The playwright is presumably the most important man in the theatre,
and the actor is the one who gets the most publicity. Producers, who
pay their publicity representatives princely salaries, naturally get their
names in the papers from time to time, too. Even stage directors and
scene designers, comparatively retiring fellows, achieve a certain minor
attention. This is the customary order of things. When such lowly objects
as a press agent and a mere angel attract more public attention than
anyone else in their shows, something unusual enough to warrant investigation is taking place. Once the investigation has started, it is only
fair to admit that the matter becomes less sensational than it had first
appeared. For the gentlemen getting the publicity are Richard Maney,
the D'Artagnan of press agents, who generally attracts more attention
than the plays he is publicizing, and Frank Sullivan, the sage, not a forgotten man in these parts either.

It seems that Mr. Sullivan and Mr. Maney are at war and, since I like
to see more war in the theatre and less in the outside world, I am for
egging them on. Permit me, then, to publish my Gascon friend's gage
of battle as valiantly hurled at the feet of Mr. Sullivan.

I had addressed Watts thus:

I'd like a little elbow room to air a grievance. Mr. Frank Sullivan,
the Celtic cliché trapper and man-about-Saratoga, has been boasting that,
thanks to the whimsies he whips up about the appetites and lusts of the
twenty-odd backers of "Arsenic and Old Lace," I'm luxuriating on a
bed of roses and twanging my zither.

Sullivan's attempts to sully my industry are as scurvy a piece of skul-
duggery as I've encountered since Billy Rose wanted me to play the
ram to his Abraham. Sullivan had better keep a civil tongue in his head
or I'll reveal his recent attempt to touch off a mutiny among the Lindsay

and Crouse partners, a plot so base as to freeze your marrow. I'd have him know that last season when I was reduced to a wraith by my efforts in behalf of Herman Shumlin and "The Male Animal," James Thurber not only wrote all the publicity pieces, but illustrated them as well. Did I hear a whimper out of Thurber? It was more like a bellow. Too late I learned that Thurber could cook.

I have trouble enough circumventing Crouse, an unhorsed press agent, without having to ward off Sullivan. The man has no ethics! Only a week or two ago that he tried to compromise me by slurring the millinery of the aforecited Shumlin and branding my client a capitalist. Do such didoes make for an *entente cordiale?* Howard Lindsay takes Sullivan's charges against me with a grain of salt. Lindsay thinks I'm a fusion of the bee and the beaver.

After expressing the hope that Mr. Sullivan would not let my accusation go unchallenged, Mr. Watts added:

If Mr. Maney's communication is a trifle long, it is also educational. Not only is it conducive to the best interests of belligerency in these parts, but it may prove to be of help to all young press agents. In the first place, the letter mentions all the writer's clients. In the second place it gives away some of his professional technique. The system is to get others to do your work. Exploit the exploiters. Not only did Maney get Thurber to write and draw for him, but he forced his collaborator, Elliott Nugent, to write pieces about Thurber, and now is putting Sullivan, who is merely an angel, to labor in what might roughly be called his vineyards. He also went after S. J. Perelman. And last season, when Vincent Sheean, poised between wars, had written a play and was preparing to set off for London, the eminent Broadway Gascon made him stay around to grind out essays for the dramatic sections. And here am I helping him out with his chores. I hope at least I get to see a fight out of it.

Watts didn't have long to wait. Sullivan's counter-attack filled his column two days later. It read:

It is painful for one who has a passion for anonymity equal to that of Miss Maude Adams to reply to Richard Maney's garland of old eggs printed in your column. I fear not Mr. Maney nor any man, yet I am not skilled in the use of his favorite weapons, the bludgeon, the knee, the kick from behind, the hired assassin, the disrespectful gesture with the thumb and the custard pie. I prefer the rapier. Yet I shall do my best.

Let me say at the outset that Richard Maney, although possessing many of the less winning qualities of the *cobra de capello,* does have a certain charm, which, however gossamer, must be admitted in any fair

appraisal of the man. He also has integrity of a sort. Doubtless this quality led him to protest vehemently when, after the opening of "Arsenic
and Old Lace" in January, I suggested that, as a mark of simple gratitude,
a one per centum share of the play be given to each New York critic.
I argued that this would give the fraternity a certain economic security,
make the chips on their shoulders seem less like Yule logs, and make
the critics as persons seem more winsome.

You should have heard Mr. Maney scream. He said it would be
unethical to give you or Mr. Brown, or Mr. Anderson, or Mr. Krutch
five grand apiece. He swore and cursed and said that if he had his way,
no critic would even be fed for two days before being let out of his cage
to review a play. Mr. Maney's wails at the very thought that anyone
should be kind to a critic, or treat one as a human being with hopes and
fears and emotions just like ours, sounded like our old family banshee,
whom we had to fire several centuries ago because her voice had changed
and she got to drinking. Mr. Maney's behavior on this occasion seemed
rather quixotic for an entrepreneur who is constantly bragging that he
has inherited the mantle of Phineas T. Barnum.

Mr. Maney waxed gabby about some recent remarks of mine on
Herman Shumlin as a well-dressed man, but he does not state who egged
me on to that attack. I met Mr. Shumlin for the first time a week ago,
and he was a veritable poem in a new checked Easter suit. I felt rather
a fool for having accepted Richard Maney's word about Shumlin's taste
in dress. To me, it seemed that Mr. Shumlin out-goadbied William Goadby
Loew at his goadbiest, and made Russel McKinley Crouse, that road
company Lucius Beebe, look like Jeeter Lester. I apologize to Mr. Shumlin.
My theory is that the fuss you scribes have raised over Mr. Maney has
spoiled him. He dines at Sardi's nowadays with rich producers like
Lindsay, Crouse and Shumlin, on canvasback duck and larks-wing fritters.
He has lost touch with the common actor, on whom, in the last analysis,
his fame rests.

Contrast that behavior with mine. Not an evening passes that I do
not visit the Fulton Theatre, West 46th Street just west of Broadway, box
office open at 10 A.M., to cheer up the actors. I pass from dressing room to
dressing room, with a kind word for one and all, chucking Josie Hull
under the chin, caressing dear Jean Adair, soothing Joslyn, stroking
Karloff, buckling on Tony Ross's cop's harness for him. Of course, I am
not fooled by Maney's antics. I am aware that he is only a tool in the
hands of Jake Lindsay and Lee Crouse, that they hope through him to
goad me into such a rage that I'll tear up, or return to them, my dividend
checks. They are barking up the wrong tree. I am an oak, Mr. Maney
is a shrub.

No sooner had Sullivan's riposte appeared in Watts's column than
Atkinson got into our act. Under the heading:

FEUD BETWEEN RICHARD MANEY AND FRANK SULLIVAN
EXTENDS TO THIS COLUMN IN SIMPLE JUSTICE TO CRITICS

he wrote:

When an injustice has been committed, it clears the air to come out and say so, in public. I am referring to the venal attitude of Richard Maney towards critics as disclosed by Frank Sullivan yesterday morning in Richard Watts, Jr.'s column in the *Herald Tribune*. When the thundering good notices of "Arsenic and Old Lace" appeared in the newspapers last January, Mr. Sullivan, who is the great heart behind that drama, suggested to Mr. Maney, counselor of public relations, that "as a mark of simple gratitude a one percentum (sic) share of the play be given to each New York critic."

This is the first time that a Broadway banker has suggested paying critics on a piece work basis for their services to a successful play, although everyone knows that critics have to make up out of their private resources the cost of failures—an arrangement, incidentally, that becomes more and more exhausting. But what was Mr. Maney's response to this business-like proposal? "You should have heard him scream," writes honest Frank Sullivan. "He said it would be unethical to give Mr. Watts or Mr. Anderson or Mr. Brown or Mr. Krutch five grand apiece." When you consider that nearly everyone else in New York is being supported on a technicality by "Arsenic and Old Lace," including Gilbert Gabriel, who spent the winter in Venice, Florida and is now Springing in Towners, New York, Mr. Maney's attitude boils down to one of willful and partisan meanness.

Mr. Sullivan is the salt of the earth. Whenever he meets an old friend these days, he pulls out his wallet, and says, "Have some money." Not a very practical social attitude, perhaps, but it is winning. All things considered, however, an attitude of persecution towards critics comes with particularly bad grace from Mr. Maney. For years he has masqueraded as the critics' best friend. As Mr. Sullivan says, he has a superficial charm. He occasionally comes into this office and tries to break down professional resistance with humorous stories and clever phrases suited to the occasion. He writes well—fairly well. He is also forever cadging drinks at Bleeck's with his disarming affability. When I think of the number of times I have gone up to the old American Music Hall to listen to Mr. Maney's fanatic attacks on the novels of Joseph Conrad and to let him dance with my wife, although he is clumsy on his feet, it is impossible for me to contemplate this example of wanton treachery without formally protesting.

It is not the principle of the thing that rankles; it is the money. In all fairness, I believe I have a special claim on the unwholesome profits of "Arsenic and Old Lace." Nearly everyone except the patrons of that play knows that the fascinating character of the drama critic is a composite portrait of Watts and myself. The line about going to China is

Watts; the line about looking at some purely imaginary bird and writing a chapter on Thoreau is me, and a pretty lame joke, too.

The composite photograph also extends to Allyn Joslyn's acting of the stellar part; the charm is Watts; the mustache is me. When John Byram, Howard Cullman, Clare Boothe and nearly every other New York freebooter is getting a regular dividend check, why should Maney draw the line at me? For I assume that Watts is being taken care of in the usual undercover fashion. Notice that on a morning when he should be commenting on the opening of "Texas Town" at 108 West 16th Street, he sits back and lets chivalrous Frank Sullivan write his entire column. He is also talking about going to China next month—an expensive journey. And here is the crusher: After living on Riverside Drive for years without a squawk, he is now talking of moving to Fifth Avenue where he can be among his own kind. Not a very pretty picture. In fact, the entire episode of the financial arrangements behind "Arsenic and Old Lace" begins to smell.

Atkinson's seeming concern with our bickering agitated some of his readers. The spoof appeared on a weekday morning in the space invariably filled by his report on the play opening the night before. Never, save on Sunday, had Brooks' by-line appeared over anything but a review. To further befuddle his followers, his jest appeared under "The Play," standard head for reviews of stage attractions. The findings which appeared under this head were studied and sedate. Rarely were they touched with levity. Hence Brooks' raillery caught his audience by surprise. Some of them jumped at conclusions that chilled his blood. Atkinson had publicly admitted what they had long suspected, said these oafs. Good reviews could be bought. Critics were as venal as Congressmen. They were as shocked as if their bishop had endorsed the striptease.

This adventure taught Brooks a lesson. Never again did he pull the leg of his congregation or try to amuse it with an off-beat prank. *Times* readers expect its authorities to be solemn. Any deviation from the norm will backfire on its author, perhaps ignite his beard.

Gentle, sober and self-effacing, Atkinson reflects the character and standards of his newspaper. Once in his seat at an opening, he does not leave it until the final curtain. Don't think that critics who take advantage of the intermission for a smoke or a breath of fresh air are derelict. Nor do they meet between acts to compare notes and agree on a verdict, as wounded producers and actors

occasionally charge. Critics are models of punctuality. It's the relatives and friends of the management who stumble in fifteen minutes
late.

Only once has Atkinson wavered in his devotion to the theatre.
During World War II, he was a correspondent for the *Times* in
Chungking and Moscow. On his return to New York, he remarked
to an interviewer that "dramatic criticism is an ignoble profession."
This observation, I suspect, was born of the dramatic events he had
witnessed overseas.

Richard Watts has been my friend for over thirty years. With him
I've prowled ballparks and football stadia. I've tippled with him in
Bleeck's, "21," and the Oak Social Club, one of the twenty-five
thousand speakeasies which festered in New York in the twenties.
Since Watts is a resolute traveler, it was easy to lure him to Fort
Worth, Cleveland and the Flushing Meadows to inspect Billy Rose's
spectacles. Watts is partial to Irish playwrights and Irish whisky.
He's also partial to comely young ingénues. Though he's a chronic
bachelor, in many of these nymphs he detects symptoms of Duse.

Urbane, sensitive and waspish, Watts delights me and other readers
of the New York *Post* with pithy columns headed "Random Notes
on This and That." In these he lauds or damns figures in the amusement, literary or political world whose activities have thrilled or
nauseated him. In one sentence he may cheer James Fenimore Cooper
for Natty Bumppo, in the next pillory Senator Joseph McCarthy
or his Dixie duplicate, Senator James O. Eastland. His observations
on friend and foe have spice and brevity. He's at his best when
belaboring a controversial reactionary.

In line of duty—this was in the thirties—occasionally I put to
sea. Having bagged Noel Coward, Laurence Olivier or another alien
star for a New York play, my employer, in the interests of good
will, would suggest I greet the invader aboard ship. This involved
getting up at dawn and hastening to the Battery. There, armed
with credentials from a friendly city editor, I would board the
revenue cutter which carried customs officials and ships' newsmen
down the bay.

These excursions were fraught with excitement and peril. If the weather was foggy, the departure of the cutter might be delayed for hours. During these delays, the reporters holed up in nearby saloons to fortify themselves for the rigors of the journey ahead. Since I'm a gregarious type, I would accompany them. The cargo taken on in these waits stood me in good stead when the cutter rendezvoused with the liner. To get aboard, we had to scale its side by a Jacob's ladder. Once on deck, I recovered quickly. As a temporary newsman, I had access to the tonics made available to reporters by the line's press agent.

This marine episode serves to introduce John McClain, drama critic for the New York *Journal-American.* When I first met McClain, he was ship's newsman for the New York *American,* now defunct. Affable, nonchalant and amusing, McClain, despite his lowly post, was a man-about-town. He consorted with wealthy toffs. Among his chums was Jock Whitney. Then, as now, McClain had expensive tastes and thirsts and knew the areas in which they could be gratified with minimum damage to his budget.

The weird hours of a ship's newsman appalled McClain. He didn't mind staying up until six, but rising at that hour unnerved him. Early in the thirties, he fled the deep to become a columnist and radio script writer. He served a brief sentence as press agent for *Trader Horn.* In 1938, he gave up writing to become a screen scenarist. When I prodded him into a salute to a playwright at the fag end of '56, he described his adventures thus: "Dropping into Sardi's for my midnight noggin of Kickapoo Indian joy juice the other evening, I fell in with my old friend, Harry Kurnitz. We once occupied elbow positions in Hollywood's Willow Run, putting rivets in old scripts at the M-G-M celluloid scatter."

McClain's stay in Hollywood ended with the outbreak of World War II. After five years in the Navy, he returned to column writing. Since 1951, he has been the *Journal-American's* drama judge. McClain is tolerant of error in actor and author. "I try to keep in mind, even when viewing the dreariest efforts, that the people involved are not criminals," he has said. "Even an I.B.M. machine blows a gasket now and then."

I visited the Racquet and Tennis Club, exclusive citadel of the

swells, for the first and only time in '55. How did I get in? As a
guest of McClain. He can also sign tabs at The Brook Club in
New York and at Buck's in London. To repeat a Broadway epigram,
McClain doesn't want to be a millionaire, he just likes to live like one.

The *Mirror's* Robert Coleman, possessed of sideburns that are
the envy of every actor who would play Gaylord Ravenal in a
revival of *Show Boat,* is the dean of the New York critics. He's
served that tabloid since 1924. Coleman's infatuation with the
theatre borders on the masochistic. Since there are few New York
openings between June 1 and Labor Day, most of the critics enjoy
summer-long vacations. Only such cultural eruptions as the Shakespeare Festival at Stratford, Ontario, or its echo at Stratford, Connecticut, can lure them from their retreats. Coleman is the exception.
Indifferent to heat, humidity or ptomaine, he scours the rural theatres
which clutter the Atlantic seaboard from Maine to Virginia. What's
more, he reports on the horrors he sees in them.

Originally schemed as incubators for young authors and players,
the strawhat theatres were commendable. Too soon they were taken
over by sharpsters. By professional standards, most of the offerings
on the Citronella Circuit are clumsily acted, sloppily directed revivals
of Broadway successes. There's but one justification for these three-act
bores. They provide employment for hundreds of actors who otherwise might starve. Some summer theatres prosper, not because of
the quality of their fare, but because they provide social escape for
vacationists. They also provide escape for residents overexposed
to weekend guests. The Westport Country Playhouse is the oldest
and best of the summer theatres—but I visit it only under duress.

Though now he seldom reviews a play because of his preoccupation
with vendettas and cosmic crises, in his heyday Walter Winchell
redeemed more than one show after it had been clawed by the critics.
Hellzapoppin, a noisy, witless revue of the thirties, was turning up its
toes when Winchell first cheered it. In his column and in his radio
show, Winchell flayed the clods who condemned it and urged the
millions who read and heard him to see it forthwith. So effective was
his crusade that *Hellzapoppin* ran for three years. Never before or

since has the silk purse and sow's ear adage been so thoroughly refuted.

In the spring of 1948, I loosed the rumor that *Command Decision* was a dark-horse contender for the Pulitzer Prize play award. I confided my suspicion to Irving Hoffman, who funneled it to Winchell. Walter printed this invention in his column and echoed it in his radio program. In the half hour following his broadcast, Kermit Bloomgarden, producer of *Command Decision,* received a dozen calls congratulating him on winning the Pulitzer citation. One was from his mother. There are as many careless listeners as there are careless readers. To confirm this, *Command Decision's* box-office trade boomed.

Winchell's enthusiasms have worked magic in other fields. His manifestoes have stimulated stock-market prices and sales of second-rate books. His plugging transformed the Stork Club from an obscure speakeasy into the nation's most notorious saloon and celebrity haunt. In appreciation, proprietor Sherman Billingsley named Winchell head of his cabinet and vested him with pardon and veto powers. For years, Winchell held court in the Stork's Cub Room. Many delinquents regarded entrance to this saloon as the equivalent of winning the Distinguished Service Cross. To his throne in search of counsel, approval or recognition, came statesmen and sycophants, the publicity-crazed and J. Edgar Hoover. The relationship of Winchell and Billingsley dimmed the duet of Damon and Pythias. The country couldn't have been more stunned had McCarthy denounced Jenner when Billingsley removed Winchell's likeness from his walls in the spring of '56. Winchell retaliated by installing his partisans and penates in El Morocco.

I am not familiar with the circumstances which brought about this schism. It was bruited on Broadway that it had its origin in a clash of cigarettes. Winchell's TV program was dedicated to Old Golds, while in his half hour before the cameras Billingsley extolled Chesterfields. I'm foggy about the circumstances because I'm barred from the Stork Club. Billingsley long rated me an untouchable. Only once since my excommunication have I violated his doors. My entrance was condoned because I was flanked by Arthur Godfrey and columnist John Crosby. I couldn't run the blockade today even in their company. Since my last visit, Crosby, too, has been barred.

Though it's been ten years since I profaned the Cub Room, as late as 1955 Billingsley rebarred me, *in absentia*. Interviewing Martha Raye on his TV show, he bracketed Tallulah Bankhead and me as pariahs. With characteristic scorn for syntax, Sherman told Martha, "I had to bar that Dick Maney out of here." What brought about this affirmation of my exile? At the request of the *American Weekly,* Hearst syndicated Sunday supplement, Tallulah and I wrote a tribute to Mr. Billingsley. We touched on his gaucheries, his war on the English language and his malapropisms. We cited the question which ended his TV talk with Admiral "Bull" Halsey: "Admiral, tell me. What year did you graduate from West Point?" We also quoted the *Times* critic Jack Gould, who dubbed Billingsley's TV show "the greatest argument for home-cooking in American history." Our salute to Sherman had not yet appeared on the day he chatted with Miss Raye. But he had learned we were writing it. Vulnerable and suspicious, he jumped to the conclusion that our panegyric would not enhance his fame.

"Maney is the only guy ever barred from the Stork Club with an oakleaf cluster," commented comedian Henry Morgan on learning my banishment had been reaffirmed.

How and when did I first incur Mr. Billingsley's displeasure? It was a winter's morning in '39. Following a damp evening in Bleeck's, Jim and Helen Thurber and I fared to the Stork to observe the anointed at play. Certified as pure by one of the proprietor's adjutants, on the way to our table I paused to greet Lewis Edward Lawes, then Warden of Sing Sing Prison. I had met the eminent turnkey in the company of Elise Chisholm, press agent for Brady and Wiman, whom he subsequently married. About to rejoin the Thurbers, the Warden and I got bogged down in a debate about James J. Hines, a Tammany Hall statesman then on trial for grafting. The Warden thought Hines was a martyr; I thought he was guilty as Cain. This led to high words. The next afternoon, a story on page 1 of the *World-Telegram* said that the Warden and I had slugged it out in

Mr. Billingsley's *boîte* early that morning. There was a movement
afoot to rematch us for a bout in Madison Square Garden, the
report read. In it, Mr. Billingsley stated that I had violated his pot-
house for the last time.

Was my memory so treacherous that I couldn't recall the scuffle?
Shaken, I called Thurber. Jim and Helen reassured me. The fracas
was a phantom, they swore. I was the victim of a hoax, coined by
a cove who confused debate and battery. Fights in the Stork Club,
genuine or feigned, always got space in first editions because of
the elegance of the arena and the note of the duelists, added Thurber.
"You and Lawes should be gratified," said Jim. "You've joined the
immortals. Now you're one with Hemingway and Max Eastman."
This pair had exchanged jabs in the Stork when Max said the hair
on the novelist's chest was bogus.

Though whitewashed by the Thurbers, not everyone thought I
was innocent. High among the skeptics was Billingsley. Though
a sporadic shopper in his shebeens since he opened his first
Stork Club in 1928, my respect for the proprietor was dim. I
loathed the caste system which governed entrance requirements; I
also deplored his efforts to curb guests who grew giddy after three
or four swigs. Such snobbery ill became a man who got his start,
at seven, selling firewater to the Cherokees in Oklahoma. By Sherman's standards, I was a calculated risk, insensitive to the distinction
implicit in admission to his fountain. The Lawes hoax climaxed his
suspicions. I joined the Legion of the Damned.

But enough of the Stork. Let's get back to the critics. In their
judgment, industry and devotion to the theatre, the New York
reviewers rank with any group of the past half century, save in one
item: entertainment. Their prose lacks salt, style and irreverence.
Because of this lack, they're not as readable as were Woollcott,
Hammond, Broun, Nathan, Brown, John Anderson and Gilbert
Gabriel, who functioned in the thirties. Salt, style and irreverence
are suspect by New York publishers. They would do well to recall
Bernard Shaw's dictum: "My method is to take the utmost trouble
to find the right thing to say and then to say it with the utmost
levity."

As becomes a man who genuflects to Max Beerbohm, Wolcott
Gibbs is the only critic who is consistently entertaining. "Not edited
for the old lady in Dubuque" is the slogan of *The New Yorker,*
the weekly he serves. Alone among our periodicals it welcomes satire,
irony, humor and scorn of conformity. Its dedication to the light,
deft touch is reflected in its art, its profiles, its fiction and its comment
on current convulsions. Gibbs was at his best in describing *The
Cocktail Party,* T. S. Eliot's controversial play: "It's partly the kind
of thing that Noel Coward might have turned out if that fashionable
elf had enjoyed the benefits of a classical education and some decent
intellectual companionship."

In common with Shaw, Gibbs is suspicious of Shakespeare's
comedies. His judgments can be wayward. In a blasphemous moment
he once identified me as "the most articulate press agent since St.
Paul." As long ago as 1941, he profiled me in *The New Yorker.*
Though Gibbs's close-ups of Henry Luce, Thomas E. Dewey and
Alexander Woollcott raised the hackles of those nobles, I emerged
"a repository of charm, learning and fury . . . perhaps the most
contented man in New York."

In the forty years that he has scoffed at its frauds and its flap-
doodle, George Jean Nathan has been our theatre's most stimulating
critic and its most feared one. A gay iconoclast, skilled with the stiletto,
Nathan has debunked most of the theatre's great. His ridicule has
loosed the homicidal urge in hundreds of victims. Nathan's influence
on drama criticism was as marked as that of his long-time associate,
H. L. Mencken, on American letters.

Nathan hasn't winged all his barbs at players, playwrights and
producers. He delights in castigating his colleagues, and at one time
or another has clobbered all of them for their errant judgments.
As recently as 1955, he reprimanded me in the *Journal-American*:

The trouble with Richard Maney, the Cy Young of current theatrical
publicity pitchers, is that he usually knows so much more and is so
much more literate than many of his playwright, actor and producer
clients, and concocts such educated articles and interviews for them
to sign and pass off as their own that when one subsequently sees their
dumb performance one is twice as let down as one otherwise might be.
The late Toxen Worm and his fellow press agents of another day operated

contrarily. They deliberately made their clients seem so innocent of learning that it flattered readers into a feeling of comparative superiority and sympathy for the poor dolts. This was particularly true of reviewers. Maney reduces them to the state of intellectual snails when they compare themselves to the intellectual gianthood of his clients. Worm and those other old boys worked in reverse, and the reviewers preened themselves, with the result that whereas today they jump to put the loftily intellectualized clients in their places, they used to pat the derogated clients on the head affectionately and charitably toss them juicy bones.

13

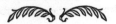

Hocus-Pocus

ACTORS and actresses revel in applause. They tingle to critical cheers. Save for these ecstasies, they're happiest when looking into a mirror. Since they're all descendants of Narcissus, photographs are key weapons in the press agent's arsenal. Paradoxically, performers regard photographers as the common enemy. They're convinced the lens is yet to be ground that can snare their contour, their beauty and their concealed fires.

If they wince on reading their words in an interview, they shudder when confronting their likeness or its rough approximation. No sane press agent shows an actress over thirty an unretouched proof lest she fall on the floor in convulsions. Presented with thirty studio poses, free of the wens, scars and structural flaws evident on the negative, she may approve three or four with sullen reservations. But she's sure to add, "Photography isn't what it used to be." She's partial to pictures taken ten years earlier when she was younger and slimmer. Males are less picayune. They're aware that the odds are against them, that Marilyn Monroe, Jayne Mansfield and other maids of spectacular design outscore Alfred Lunt and Laurence Olivier in the half-tone contest, 100 to 1.

Editors are susceptible to girlish knolls and nooks. So are their subscribers. All echo Mark Twain's "I'd rather see Lillian Russell naked than General Ulysses S. Grant in full dress uniform."

Despite their distrust of photographers, practically all Equity's members are camera crazed. Rarely do they resist a studio sitting. Alerted for such a session, actresses plead for a three-day delay that they may have their hair washed, waved, set and lacquered.

A notable exception is Ethel Barrymore. I first contended with Miss Barrymore in 1940 when both of us were victimized by Vincent Sheean's *An International Incident.* Later that year, I was with her in *The Corn Is Green,* her most enduring hit. When I suggested that she submit to a studio sitting that her likeness might adorn ads for the Sheean play, she arched her eyebrows and eyed me so scathingly I was sure there was egg on my necktie. She had a silhouette that would serve, she said. And so it did. This profile had been fashioned from a Charlotte Fairchild photograph taken before World War I. It had been used in ads for all her plays for thirty years.

Miss Barrymore posed for hundreds of production stills on the stage and approved their use in ads for *The Corn Is Green.* But studio sittings were taboo. I never knew why. In 1940, as now, Miss Barrymore was one of the most striking women ever to mount a stage or cow a press agent.

A candid photograph of Tallulah Bankhead, as a temperamental actress in *Foolish Notion,* filled a page in *Life* in 1945. Outraged by its distortions, Miss Bankhead was all for invading Henry Luce's lair and dismembering him. Dissuaded from this sortie, she insisted on blistering *Life's* editors by mail. Her counter-attack charged them with malice aforethought. In the offensive picture, she looked more like the second witch in *Macbeth* than Sophie Wing, the mercurial actress she impersonated, she protested. Malice aforethought? They were also guilty of vandalism, barratry, sadism and contempt for the public weal.

Miss Bankhead has a low boiling point. With her I have coined communiqués in which, with fine impartiality, she has blasted Tennessee Williams, Elia Kazan, the editors of *Time,* and a balcony customer from East Orange, New Jersey, who complained he couldn't hear

a word she said in *Dear Charles*. In her riposte, she urged the
unfortunate to rush to his otolaryngologist without delay.

Rarely has there been so insouciant an actress as Florence Moore,
a roughhouse comedienne I encountered in the 1924-25 edition of
the *Greenwich Village Follies*. On viewing proofs of her studio pictures her eyes glazed and she faked a swoon. On recovering she
said, "Well, I guess he did the best he could with the material he
had." The late Constance Collier, who spent seventy-four of her
seventy-seven years in the theatre, was undismayed by pictorial
horrors. Her instructions to the retoucher when appearing in a
revival of *Hay Fever* were illuminating. On the proofs she penciled
these memos, "Tuck in chin," "De-wart," "Reinforce eyebrows,"
"Comb hair." Recently I asked a photographer to erase the mole
on Judith Anderson's chin. Sight of it might add to her anxieties as
she rehearsed *In the Summer House*. On looking at the retouched
proofs, Judith ordered the mole back. "Let's have no lily gilding,"
she said. "The mole is part of me." A rugged type, that Judith, and
the best Lady Macbeth I ever saw.

Jane Cowl, a capricious beauty whose offstage performances
matched her triumphs as Juliet, Cleopatra or Mélisande, often blew
a fuse on viewing a photograph which fell short of her desire. On
the eve of her opening in *The Merchant of Yonkers,* I jeweled the
lobby with life-size reproductions of Jane as the comedy's Mrs. Levi.
I was to rue it. On viewing them, Miss Cowl demanded their
removal. She was about to demand mine, too. She charged that the
photographer and I were in a conspiracy to ruin her. Few producers
care to cope with an outraged star before an opening. They'll go
to any length to appease her. Though irked by Miss Cowl's tantrum,
producer Shumlin told me to remove the offensive murals and burn
the negatives. When next we met, Jane embraced me. Crises
in the theatre evaporate as quickly as they erupt.

Most performers think one side of their face more fascinating
than the other. This presents problems when they're photographed
in profile. A star partial to the left half of her phiz is tortured when
photographed facing a lesser player. The caption beneath a reproduction of the two will list them left to right. To be identified first,

the star must expose her inferior side. I've cheered up many a prima donna with the news that in the prints positions can be reversed. Through this transposition, beauty and billing are served. When two stars, both infatuated with their sinister section, face each other one must be frustrated. Asked why they rarely appeared in the same movie, Lilli Palmer said both she and Rex Harrison had the same flattering side. Stalemate!

If actresses must have their hair washed before being photographed, some actors seek postponement because their hair is not available. Not available? Here's the evidence.

It is 1:30 P.M., Tuesday, January 2, 1956. I'm on the stage of the New Amsterdam Roof, an aerie where once paraded the sylphs of Ziegfeld's *Midnight Frolics*. But I'm not there to pay homage to the departed maestro. A historic moment impends. In half an hour, director Moss Hart will call the company to order and the first rehearsal of *My Fair Lady* will be under way.

With me is a photographer. In the half hour before the drill gets under way, he is to pose stars, authors, producer and director, collectively, individually and in combinations. These shots will aid historians who attempt to recapture *My Fair Lady's* first fling. I introduce myself to Rex Harrison, the musical's Henry Higgins. Will he pose with his co-star, Julie Andrews, with Alan Jay Lerner and Frederick Loewe, with Herman Levin and Moss Hart? Rex agrees, then adds a condition. He must be snapped with his hat on. Why? He didn't have his hairpiece with him. His hairpiece is the swatch he applies to the depilated fraction of his forehead.

I took Rex's proviso in stride. This wasn't my first concession to alopecia. I'd done as much for George Jessel in *Show Time* and for Maurice Evans, both of whom wore "rugs," trade term for artificial foliage, on the stage.

Producer Levin and I agreed that the newspaper ads in New Haven and Philadelphia, tryout sites before the New York opening, should carry pictures of the stars in character, Rex in white tie and tails, Julie in Cockney getup. But the costumes weren't ready. This hitch was quickly solved. Rex could wear his own evening clothes and costumer Helene Pons could improvise Julie's flower-girl garb. Moss Hart said both would be available for a sitting at noon Thursday.

Thursday morning I called Rex at the Pierre. "Don't forget to bring the hairpiece," I said. "Can't do it, old boy," he replied. "It's in my trunk." "Can't you get it out of the trunk?" I asked. "No," he replied, "my trunk's in customs." That's why the out-of-town ads showed Henry Higgins in a twelve-inch silk tile.

News photographers are the gypsies of journalism. Their co-workers patronize them. Given only seconds to execute assignments, pictures of their victims often are harsh and cruel. They scorn retouching and other professional rubbish. Aside from agility and mechanical skill, their assets are indifference to insult and danger. They're happiest when filming a hostile. Failing his co-operation, they trap him through stealth. Most of them are desperate men, half technician, half bandit. Their tribal customs are akin to those of smuggler and second-story worker. But their audacity is understandable. An editor may forgive a reporter who flubs an interview. He can't be blamed if his man wouldn't talk. But the photographer who comes back without a picture is damned. He's supposed to shoot anything he can see, even if he has to look through a transom.

I have seen more than one lensman maimed in line of duty. Consider the unfortunate who undertook to photograph Hedi Stenuf, star skater in *It Happens on Ice,* a carnival which I plugged for Sonja Henie in 1940. I had persuaded a newsphoto syndicate that action shots of Miss Stenuf in her spectacular jettes and entrechats would fascinate photo editors. Ted Deglin, Garden press agent, loaned me Iceland, one of its rinks, for the adventure.

Miss Stenuf was photogenic. In a jeweled tutu, she ravished the eye. Following a fifteen-minute warm-up, she did a series of stunning splits six feet above the ice. The photographer was fascinated. He'd only be content when he caught her at the apogee of this vault.

He had the necessary equipment. His small speed camera swiveled from a tripod. Three powerful lamps sprouted from adjustable stanchions. The lamps were hooked up to a remote outlet by cables. They were so synchronized that the three flash bulbs would explode simultaneously when my man pressed the plunger. Though his tools were adequate, the photographer was defeated by environment. The temperature was in the twenties. The ice was slippery and his shoes slick. He wore a seersucker suit. He had no overcoat. To compensate for his flimsy clothes, he had a pint of bourbon in his back pocket.

It took him a long time to properly space his lamps, to adjust their height and define the area on which they must focus. Like all his tribe, he fiddled interminably with his light meter. In trial flights Miss Stenuf eluded his lens. This necessitated realignment of his gear. After an hour of trial and error he started to ice over. Miss Stenuf was near exhaustion. Lest the management charge me with exhausting the star, I warned my man we'd adjourn in fifteen minutes, picture or no picture.

Five minutes later he croaked he was ready. Removing his necktie, he laid it on the ice to indicate the spot from which Miss Stenuf should take off. Half frozen, he took a final swig from his flask, grasped the plunger which would detonate the lamps, crouched for perspective, then signaled Miss Stenuf to take off. As she neared the crest of her arch, disaster overtook him. His feet flew out from under him and upset the tripod. Clutching for something that would break his fall, he seized the cable linking the lamps and brought all three down on him. As he lay in a welter of blood, bourbon, glass slivers, cable and contorted tubing, Miss Stenuf whipped up and showered him with shaved ice as she braked to a stop.

"Did you get it?" she asked. "Best jump I ever made."

If actors grouse about their pictures, they often explode on reading the captions under them. So brilliant were the costumes worn by Mary Martin, Yul Brynner and McKay Morris in *Lute Song,* musical variation of the Chinese classic *Pa-Pa-Ki,* that *Collier's* reproduced three of its scenes in color. On seeing them in the weekly McKay Morris screamed. In a bitter letter, he charged me with treachery. Rage had rendered him incoherent, he said.

McKay's lament was valid, but he was belaboring the wrong man. As Prince Nisou, Imperial Preceptor at the Chinese Court, he sported the most magnificent robe he had worn in his thirty-four years in the theatre. Schemed by Robert Edmond Jones, it ravaged the spectrum. Only in color could its radiance and luster be detailed.

In this finery, McKay appeared in three pictures in the layout—but in none was he identified. For all the reader knew, he might be an anonymous flunky for Tchao-Ou-Niang (Miss Martin) or Tsai Yung (Mr. Brynner). He closed with the guess that I'd be consumed in hell fire.

I tried to solace McKay. I told him he had my deepest sympathy, which, indeed, he had. But, I added, editors didn't seek my aid when writing captions. I didn't think *Collier's* would repeat the display or apologize for its lapse. However, I'd write the editors a letter. Perhaps they'd print it. I did and they didn't. I still top Judas in McKay's list of apostates.

Goal of every press agent is a picture spread in *Life*. These displays serve many purposes. They caress the egos of all who appear in them. Because of the weekly's circulation, they stimulate the box office. They authenticate the hit status of the play or musical cited since *Life's* editors rarely memorialize a work that isn't selling out or assured of a long run. Like all experts in thrall to Henry Luce, they feign omniscience. To maintain this illusion, they must exercise caution. Staff men still shudder when reminded that *Life* announced the election of Thomas E. Dewey in '48. Heads might roll if *Life,* out on Thursday, blazed with pictures of a show that closed the preceding Saturday.

I've been fencing with *Life's* editors since 1936, the year the magazine started. Though the stars viewed the proceedings with alarm, I persuaded Noel Coward and Gertrude Lawrence to submit to *Life's* cameras that the delights of *Tonight at 8:30* might be aired in an early issue. Daniel Longwell, one of *Life's* editors, went all out in his quest of candid shots of the pair. His trigger-happy crew shot them from the fly gallery, from the front row during performances, and from roosts in the wings. They shot them from the orchestra pit, from balcony boxes and while prone on the floor.

Though one of the most nonchalant actresses in the theatre, Miss Lawrence thought American know-how was getting out of hand when a Longwell agent, hidden behind a dressing-room screen, leaped out and bagged her in the buff. All hands balked when

Longwell insisted one of his troopers lie in the footlights trough and shoot Coward and Miss Lawrence as they romped in *Red Peppers* —one of the nine one-act plays which made up *Tonight at 8:30.* Though but twelve of the fourteen hundred pictures shot by *Life* appeared in the magazine, all of us rejoiced.

While the press agent, the actors and the management regard a *Life* layout as a certificate of merit, these displays often generate bitterness and frustration. The picture session follows an evening performance. Under Equity rules the operation must be concluded in four hours for a musical, in three hours for a play. Should the ordeal last longer, all players involved must be paid an eighth of a week's salary. A picture call is a bonanza for the stagehands. The union sheltering these mechanics insists that the entire crew be paid maximum wages for a minimum of three hours, even though some of them are home in bed or hoisting a few at Joe's Place. The sight of a photographer approaching a theatre causes stage-hands to whinny and paw the ground.

With furnishings stationary, and properties constant, a sequence of scenes in a one-set comedy could be photographed with the aid of an electrician to raise or dim the lights. It could be, but it isn't. The entire crew must be paid for three hours, though all sleep through the session.

The stagehand expense in shooting a musical may run to $600. The management pays this, even though it has no assurance that the pictures will appear in *Life*. *Life's* editors are many and they are mercurial. Pictures that intoxicate one nauseate another. These conflicts make for delays. The excitements of larger events may crowd out a pictorial bouquet. In a rare display of confidence, *Life* photographed Maurice Evans and Judith Anderson in *Macbeth* on an October night during its tryout in New Haven. The pictures appeared eighteen weeks later, the week the revival closed in New York.

Every witch and murderer in the tragedy, every actor from Fleance to Macduff, held me responsible. "When are the *Life* pictures coming out?" they chorused. Hadn't they stayed up until three in the morning to humor me? Gone without sleep and food? I didn't know when they would appear and neither did *Life's* editors. The late fall of '41 was strewn with crises. An entire edition of the magazine was devoted to one of these—Pearl Harbor.

I've gloated prematurely over more than one *Life* splurge. Some were discarded because of editorial caprice, others because the show was stricken before its art could be developed. An unpublished layout is the press agent's cross. Bludgeoned by circumstance, I offer no alibis to the outraged. Damned as a delinquent, there's no point to encouraging attacks on my veracity. The reasoning of my opponents is elemental. They wot little of editorial fevers. Didn't I prod them into the adventure with promises of fame and fortune? Didn't they co-operate to the hilt?

If I've been disillusioned by phantom spreads, I once hoaxed *Life* with a show that never went into rehearsal. The conspirators were screen writer Ken Englund and scene designer Stewart Chaney. Summoned to Englund's chamber in the Essex House on a hot night in '46, he and Chaney dilated on *He and She,* a revue with music by Vernon Duke and lyrics by Ogden Nash, which they were going to produce as soon as they could lay hands on $200,000. At the moment they were shy of their goal. This didn't disturb me. Hadn't The Theatre Guild been similarly embarrassed with *Oklahoma?*

Englund and Chaney told me the deficit would be solved within a week. They'd borrowed an impressive apartment from a friend. In it they would give an audition for potential backers. The joint would be crawling with wealthy idlers, they hoped. Englund, author of the sketches, was to preside. Vernon Duke would be at the piano. Equity was sending over four or five of its unemployed to read the dialogue and sing Nash's songs.

Their prospectus was conventional and so was their strategy. "What did you need me for?" I asked. "I wouldn't put a quarter in a musical show."

They needed a little publicity, they confessed. The investors they'd bagged were getting jumpy. So was Davy Wayne, who they hoped would play He. Since I was to press agent *He and She* throughout its dazzling run, perhaps I'd help them out. Had *Life* ever covered an audition for backers? I told them I thought it unlikely. Its editors try to avoid imponderables. "All the more reason they might do it," said Englund. "Why don't you feel them out?"

I called Tom Prideaux, head of *Life's* entertainment department. Tom was apathetic. Shows that opened were risky enough, he said. He didn't care to get entangled with a mirage. When I continued to harp on the note of the prospects, and the skill of Duke and Nash, Tom relented. "After all, it's summer," he said, "There's nothing going on in the theatre. Send me a list of the guests. If enough notables show up, I'll cover it."

Marlene Dietrich and Katharine Hepburn headed the list improvised by Chaney and Englund. It included the elite of stage, screen and café society. The producers weren't sure any of these illuminati would show up. Worse! They weren't sure any of them were in town.

When Englund rapped for order, he faced a lady bullfighter, a culture-crazed wrestler, fifty speculators of assorted sexes, King Peter of Yugoslavia, lately upset by Marshal Tito, and his Queen, and other riffraff. Englund had started his opening address when I noticed that the girl photographer from *Life* was having trouble. Seeking altitude for one of her lamps she overextended its standard. As I watched, the lamp started to totter. It fell like a pine in a Zane Grey novel, its bulb scoring a bull's eye on Peter's pate. Since the Luce periodicals rejoice when they catch the mighty in an awkward pose, I was sure *Life's* caption for this snafu would read, "King Konked."

Once the exile combed the splinters from his mane, the concert resumed. What's more, thanks to Ogden Nash's verse, *He and She* made *Life*. It never made anything else. Indeed, it never opened. Within six weeks, Englund and Chaney went over the hill. I wasted no time in regret. My loss on the reverie was $33.25—cab fares for visits with the plotters.

While articled to *Arsenic and Old Lace,* I connived with *Life* to have Boris Karloff haunt a house. I borrowed Jeanie Rosenfeld's home on the edge of Greenwich Village and rigged it with skeletons, spider webs, tambourines and ectoplasm.

To ensure a four-page spread in *Life,* I needed a mess of ghost fanciers and lens lushes. I offered prospects free liquor, a buffet supper, and association with other exhibitionists. Fred Allen scorned my bid. "The promise of an anonymous role in a group picture in *Life* doesn't appeal to me," he said. My old friend and employer, Ed Wynn, the man with the convulsive eyebrows, reluctantly agreed. "I'd only do this for you, Dick," he croaked. "It will be the first time I've left the house since Christmas."

George Karger, a sawed-off version of Hendrik Van Loon, was the cameraman. He shot hundreds of spooky pictures. Around two in the morning, George had an inspiration. "Who's that beautiful girl with Ed Wynn?" he asked. "Do you think she'd remove her dress and pose in her slip with Karloff and the skeleton?" Worming my way to the comedian, I told him of Karger's whim. Wynn grew apoplectic. "What do you think she is? A whore?" he yelled at the top of his lungs. "Why don't you get that dame Lindsay's trying to make?" At this Howard Lindsay and Russel Crouse, producers and authors of *Arsenic and Old Lace,* rushed up and tried to soothe him. Wynn denounced both. Wailing like a banshee, he stormed out, dragging his innocent behind him.

Later I read that Wynn was about to produce *Laugh, Town, Laugh,* a vaudeville show in which he would scuffle with a trick mule, a flamenco dancer, a ventriloquist and Smith and Dale. Shortly George Wood, Wynn's agent, called me. Wynn had told him he needed a press agent. "What about Dick Maney?" asked George. "The last time Dick and I met we had a misunderstanding," replied Wynn. The comedian wouldn't tell Wood the nature of our differences. Would I tell him? I did. He screamed. "See him at his hotel this afternoon. I'll square everything," said George.

When I entered Wynn's suite the young woman who had failed *Life* was with him. "Haven't you two met before?" asked our host. "Yes, indeed," we chorused. I was pleased that the great man had forgiven me. Wynn, W. C. Fields and Chaplin are the funniest men I've ever seen on stage or screen.

If a press agent purrs over a *Life* layout, he's transported by a *Life* cover. In my set, such treatment borders on canonization. When Julie Andrews, in Cockney flower-girl costume, graced *Life's* cover of March 25, 1956, I rejoiced. In my elation I forgot the confusions which attended her glorification, and the wringer she went through to achieve it.

My Fair Lady was in its third week of rehearsal when Prideaux told me Julie was under consideration for a *Life* cover. When could she be photographed in character? The costumes wouldn't be ready for another week, I told him. If he'd let me know which costume she was to wear, I'd urge Helene Pons to expedite it. The ballroom costume, he said. This seemed an odd choice. *Life's* covers were in color. Julie wore five costumes in *My Fair Lady*. All of them, save the ballroom gown, were splashed with color. It was sheer white. In it Julie would look like any other attractive young girl in evening dress. I suggested he consider the cockney flower-girl getup. In it Julie would be recognizable as Eliza Doolittle by everyone.

Seven months earlier, Cecil Beaton, who designed the clothes for *My Fair Lady* had snapped Julie in the loft of Miss Pons. Miss Pons had improvised a flower-girl costume. Beaton is the official photographer for the Court of St. James's. In a dingy room, on a sunless afternoon, with a camera no larger than a club sandwich, he caught her in thirty brilliant poses. I asked Prideaux to look at these. He agreed, but returned them that same afternoon. He still wanted Julie in the ballroom dress.

Working overtime, Miss Pons completed the ballroom gown and assembled shoes, hose, jewels and other accessories which complemented it on January 28. I alerted Prideaux. A delay ensued.

Although *Life* has fifteen or twenty cameramen on its staff, or subject to call, the man it tapped for Julie was in North Carolina. This delay posed problems. The show was to open in New Haven a week hence. The wardrobe trunks carrying the company's stage clothes would be shipped out Monday. On Prideaux's assurance that the lensman would show up Tuesday, I called the wardrobe mistress. She agreed to hold out the ballroom gown. One of her aides could bring it to New Haven Tuesday night when *My Fair Lady* would have its first dress rehearsal. The wardrobe mistress said she'd detail a dresser and a hair stylist to assist Julie at the studio.

Returned from North Carolina, *Life's* man posed Julie for three hours Tuesday. The Tuesday following the New Haven opening, Prideaux called again. He had just seen Julie's proofs. They weren't any good. Julie must pose again in New Haven. This request chilled me. Though the musical was a sensation, authors Alan Jay Lerner and Frederick Loewe and director Moss Hart were still pruning it. To ask for four hours of Julie's time might invite their wrath. Because of rehearsals, the stage wouldn't be available.

I called Phil Adler, *My Fair Lady's* manager. Phil came up with a solution. Because of the time needed to install its revolving stages and hang its scenes, the show wouldn't open in Philadelphia until Wednesday. Julie would be in New York on Monday, en route to Philadelphia. Why couldn't *Life* rephotograph her then? Why indeed? Adler said he'd have a wardrobe woman bring the costume to the studio, along with a dresser and hair stylist. I called Prideaux. He agreed. Monday afternoon Julie posed for another three hours, same costume, same photographer.

The second camera session in New York was as sour as the first. During the show's second week in Philadelphia, Prideaux rented a small ballroom in the Warwick Hotel. In this he installed photographer Leonard McCombe. To this makeshift we dispatched Julie—in the flower-girl costume. McCombe shot her fifty times. One of these shots made the cover.

Orson Welles waved me aside when I asked him to interrupt the drill of *Native Son* for three hours that *Life* might capsule the tragedy pictorially. "Which is more important," he asked, "getting a layout in *Life* or having the play open on time?" Orson's plea didn't upset me. Left to his own devices, he'd rehearse for months. But he had a sounder argument. Because of the financial status of the management, *Native Son* would not have the advantage of an out-of-town tryout. Audience reaction is vital to the director seeking pace and rhythm in the performance. Exposure to cash customers accents a play's delights and bares its flaws.

As I was about to depart, Orson came up with a compromise. "Have *Life's* photographer here tomorrow night at eight. I'll give him half an hour—no more." This was absurd. It would take a half hour for the photographer to set up his lamps and adjust his lenses. But I jumped at the offer. Welles was mercurial. He often flouted his own orders.

Life's photographer was Alfred Eisenstaedt. Welles became so fascinated by his technique he forgot about rehearsals. The half-hour call developed into an all-night carnival with Welles improvising special groupings and effects. Around midnight, Welles lured Eisenstaedt into the lobby. How would he like to leave *Life* and work for him? With *Native Son* behind him, he said, he hoped to revolutionize motion pictures. Eisenstaedt would head his camera crew. Together they'd explore new vistas. Welles is a man of lofty and awesome visions with words to match. Eisenstaedt resisted Orson's song.

A mural in my office at the Playhouse carries this inscription. "Poet and Peasants Saluted by Henry Luce." It embraces *Time* covers dedicated to Tallulah Bankhead, Barbara Bel Geddes, Carol Channing, T. S. Eliot, Julie Harris and Rex Harrison for their contribution to plays I've touted. *Time's* cover tributes are accompanied by four- or five-page assessments of the subject's life and works. Since *Time's* editors profess to give balanced judgments of those they crown, and since they're fascinated with both sides of the cameo, beneficiaries of their benisons alternately purr with joy and scream with rage.

Stage pictures taken by *Life, Time, Vogue, Harper's Bazaar,* and a few other magazines are exclusive. They are not available to the press agent for use elsewhere. Prior to the opening of his attraction, and throughout its run, he distributes hundreds of action pictures to drama editors, fashion editors, women's page editors and feature editors for syndicates and wire services. He'll also need character studies for lobby displays, for cartoonists and caricaturists who find them helpful, and for magazines partial to theatrical art but allergic to the expense of exclusive coverage.

New York's seven newspapers feature pictures of new plays and shows on the Saturday or Sunday prior to their opening. It's the press agent's job to provide them with a variety of art. Only the *Times* and the *Herald Tribune* demand exclusive pictures. Pictures must be in the hands of the editors not later than Tuesday. These pictures commonly are taken after the second out-of-town performance in New Haven, Wilmington, Boston or Philadelphia, four of the more popular initiation centers.

Unless his show has a star with veto power, the press agent fixes the date for the adventure after consultation with the director. If the opening performance reveals flaws, the picture call may be delayed to permit additional rehearsals. The director is responsible for the performance. He is likely to reject interruptions that tire his cast. Pictures are never taken after the first out-of-town performance. The actors are too exhausted or too discouraged.

Because of the time limit imposed by Equity and stagehands on a picture call, the press agent seeks an experienced photographer rather than an inspired one. The nominee should be tactful and conditioned to the moods and megrims of his opponents. He must know how to cajole them into compliance. To approximate the sixty or seventy negatives needed, press agent and cameraman must have the co-operation of players, stagehands and, above all, the stage manager. It's the job of the last named to have the players available when called.

The time allotted the exercise starts with the fall of the curtain. But operations can't start until the theatre is emptied. To raise the curtain prematurely would attract laggards and husbands crawling under seats for their wives' mittens. Press agent and photographer plot the pictures desired in advance. Each picture, and the players involved, is cued with a line of dialogue. A copy of the schedule is handed the stage manager. He juggles the sequence to minimize scene and costume changes. Complying with this strategy, the last scene is shot first; succeeding scenes reverse the order in which they're played.

No matter how carefully worked out, the schedule rarely is followed. Intangibles and imponderables intrude. It can be breached by a veteran character actress who has to be in bed by midnight— "Doctor's orders, you know!" It may be scrambled by author and producer, gentlemen I can't openly flout. It may be derailed by the arrival of coffee and sandwiches, brought in lest the management face charges of "undue hardship" and "willful neglect." The star may refuse to pose before the second-act fireplace with her stage lover.

She isn't mad at this Romeo, but she loathes the house robe she wears in the scene, though it's by Mainbocher and set the producer back $1,400. Promise of a new robe next week doesn't sway her. She'll wait until next week to be photographed. She may wait, but I can't. Time may be lost taking pictures of the juvenile who'll get his notice Saturday night—though he doesn't know it.

I understand, and condone, the sulking, stalling and quibbling which attend an out-of-town picture call. It comes at the worst time possible. The players are in a state of shock. They have but two performances under their belts. They're not yet familiar with the properties and furnishings. The script is being cut and doctored. They've been rehearsing day and night. They've lost a lot of sleep. Though the show was cheered by the Connecticut newspapers, though both audiences have been friendly, they're full of apprehension. New Haven isn't New York. What if the show doesn't get to New York?

Often the photographer is responsible for a traffic snarl. With sixty pictures scheduled, he uses up a half hour on the first shot. He fiddles with his lamps, his range finder and his light meter. He adjusts his lens, then readjusts it. He huddles with electricians. He may blow out a few fuses. He ebbs and flows between stage and auditorium. He seems to be scheming something for the Louvre, whereas I want something for the Newark *News*.

Trying, too, is the stage-struck photographer, eager to entertain the company rather than duplicate it. George Karger—he's the man who routed Ed Wynn—is a skilled magician. He's photographed a dozen plays for me. If I so much as turned my back, he'd whip out a deck of cards and panic the cast by pulling the ace of spades from the stage manager's ear.

Off to dawdling starts, photographers become beavers as time runs out. The snail who took thirty minutes for the first picture gets twenty in the last half hour.

One of the production stills of *The Male Animal* almost caused an international contretemps. In the second act, Elliott Nugent, playing an Ohio State professor, got plastered. Prior to the company's departure for Princeton, I'd made a deal with Somerset Importers, American agents for Haig and Haig. In return for two cases of their product each month, Nugent would flourish one of their pinch bottles throughout his carouse. At the picture call in Princeton, a pinch bottle wasn't available. We used a Ballantine bottle instead. When a picture of Nugent and the wrong fifth appeared in the Baltimore *Sun* the following week, the head of Somerset Importers, vacationing in Washington, blew his stack. He called Somerset's New York manager to tell him he'd been swindled. The Ballantine pictures must be replaced by Haig and Haig half-tones immediately or the deal was off. The head of Somerset Importers? Joseph P. Kennedy, then our Ambassador at the Court of St. James's.

With luck, a press agent may salvage fifty negatives from an out-of-town call. This would suffice for the run if the cast was constant. But it isn't. Players defect, even from a hit, for one reason or another. Some decamp on June 1, when run-of-the-play contracts expire. The flight of featured players to Hollywood may wipe out one third of my stock. This necessitates new pictures to honor the replacement.

When Tallulah Bankhead left *The Skin of Our Teeth,* to be replaced by Miriam Hopkins, the company had to submit to a second picture call. I briefed Miss Hopkins in advance. The quicker we started, the earlier we'd finish, I told her. Photographer Karger was familiar with the play. He had taken the original shots in Washington. If Miss Hopkins could be on stage when the curtain was raised, we'd be on our way home a little after midnight.

The house curtain was hoisted. Miss Hopkins was missing. Five minutes elapsed. Still no Miss Hopkins. The company was fuming. I sent the stage manager to fetch her. He returned to say she was closeted with John Gunther. They were discussing the fall of Bizerte. To interrupt them, he felt, might be unpatriotic. I had no such scruples. When I entered her dressing room, Miriam and Gunther were in Tobruk with Field Marshal Montgomery.

"The cast has been waiting on stage for fifteen minutes," I said. "If you don't intend to come down, I'll dismiss them." "Of course I'm coming down," she said. "Why didn't someone call me?"

Peering into the mirror she adjusted an eyebrow, retinted her lower lip, and fluffed her mane. The filibuster ended, she preceded me down the stairs to the first entrance. Gaily tripping onto the stage, she was greeted by the glares of Karger and her colleagues. The stagehands didn't glare. The longer Miriam loitered, the higher their pay.

Despite this grim start, things went smoothly until Miriam donned the red silk bathing suit she wore as a Bingo Parlor hostess on Atlantic City's boardwalk. To expedite matters, Karger was duplicating pictures he had taken of Miss Bankhead in this scene. Miriam demurred. She undertook to tutor Karger in technique. George ignored her. Slouched in the fourth row, Mr. Gunther suddenly volunteered a suggestion.

Though aware of his note, I felt constrained to mute the journalist. After all, I hadn't intruded when he was writing *Inside Latin America*. Only a loose translation of the ground rules permitted him to view the exercises, I said. If he cared to remain he must cease coaching from the sidelines. Scowling now became epidemic.

We adjourned at 1 A.M. without any more border incidents.

Touchy about their images, suspicious of reproductions of same, the players' anxiety over pictorial problems is trifling compared to their concern with a life-and-death matter: Billing.

14

Billing Without Cooing

T*HE Skin of Our Teeth* had been selling out for three weeks, even though Adolphe Menjou said he couldn't understand it, when producer Michael Myerberg decided we should have a poster reflecting the play's timeless quality. Mike wanted something in the style of Toulouse-Lautrec. The debauched cripple, yet to be immortalized by José Ferrer, was at his best in studies of circus and music-hall types, he said. Where was Don Freeman? He was the artist to do it.

The prospect of a fee caused Freeman to abandon whatever magazine he was trying to start. Within a week, Don and Mike showed me a rough sketch of the poster with which they hoped to honor Thornton Wilder and lengthen the lines at the Plymouth box office. I detected a flaw in the composition. The sketch showed Tallulah in a bathing suit, Fredric March in muffler and fur hat, romping over the tundra with a dinosaur.

"There's something missing," I said.

"What's missing?" asked Myerberg impatiently.

"Florence Eldridge is missing."

"Rot!" said Myerberg. "Florence can't squawk. Neither Tallulah nor Freddy is identified in the caricature. The required billing will immediately follow Don's art work:

234

TALLULAH	FREDRIC	FLORENCE
BANKHEAD	MARCH	ELDRIDGE

in

THE SKIN OF OUR TEETH

"Florence will bow to no dinosaur that's ever been excavated," I protested. "She'll regard her omission from the drawing as a personal insult and a breach of contract. What's more, if subpoenaed as a witness, I'll agree with her."

"Leave it to me," said Mike. "I'll take care of Florence."

"I'm glad to leave it with you," I said. "Don't try to leave it with me when Florence blows her top."

Three weeks later the finished poster glowed on my desk. It was a superb job. Even as I looked at it, a seventy-year-old member of the Billposters Union was plowing into ticket-agency windows with its duplicates.

At four o'clock, Myerberg called me. He croaked like Hamlet's father on the battlements at Elsinore. "Can you lay hands on Gus Meyers?' he asked. I could. Gus was the elderly billposter. "Tell him to pick up every card he put out before sunset."

This was no time to rub salt in my employer's wounds. I didn't need a transcript of the dialogue between him and Florence to confirm my earlier prophecy. In three weeks we had another poster, more Toulouse-Lautrecish than the first. Miss Eldridge looked very fetching as she, too, romped down Freeman's road.

Billing is the *ne plus ultra,* the be-all and end-all of the theatre's children. To achieve it they will sacrifice their young, slash their salaries, forage for food and sleep in the subway. To maintain or enhance it they'll stop at nothing short of murder. Billing is official recognition. It's the symbol of prestige and the confirmation of success in a profession in which the envious outnumber the meek, 100 to 1.

The ultimate in billing is stardom. The player reaches this dizzy height when his name is bannered above the title of play or musical in programs and advertisements, on posters, houseboards and theatre marquees. Stardom is to the player what the D.S.C. is to the top sergeant. To most of those voted this certificate of pre-eminence, it is a climax of years' work, of devotion to a trade strewn with booby traps. Its achievement compensates for prior despair and defeat, for squalid dressing rooms, evil hotels and wretched food, for the humiliations suffered in three-act disasters.

In recent years, the qualifications for stardom have been lowered and debased. A youthful unknown may win this pinnacle for a striking performance in a listless play. Such a device may revive a swooning box office. But all concerned have twinges of conscience.

Players short of star stature battle like saber-toothed tigers for featured billing. The names of those thus appeased appear beneath the title. Debate over priority rights in this category have led to settos unmatched since the Sioux scrambled Custer on the Little Big Horn. Actors are not alone in their insistence on recognition. Milliners have gained it, and so have modistes and backers. Programs crawl with bows to obscurities whose contribution to the work is trifling. But it doesn't cost anything to list them in the program, and it salves their egos. Such coddling may forestall a request for a wage hike.

All contracts between the producer (party of the first part) and author, actor, director, scene designer, costume designer, composer, lyric writer, choreographer, orchestrator, arranger, and lighting expert (parties of the second part) have a billing clause, fraught with explosives. Minimum requirements for many of these are riveted into the basic agreements between the employer and the guilds and unions which shelter them.

Some of the billing clauses in producer-actor pacts read like a codicil to the Magna Charta. They're a distillation of the actor's desire, the invention and insistence of his agent, and the confused semantics of opposing counsel. They're also a clue to the producer's capacity to absorb threat or resist folly.

The specimen which follows is a fraction of the treaty between producers Richard Aldrich and Richard Myers and actor Tod Hunter which I tried to decode as *A Girl Can Tell,* an error by F. Hugh Herbert, was about to be exposed in the fall of '53.

The manager does also agree that the Actor is to receive no less than second feature billing on the same line and in the same type and boldness as that of the Actor or Actress receiving first feature billing. However, in no event shall the size of the type be less than 50 per cent of the size of type used in the title of the play. The manager further agrees that in addition to the name of the Actor or Actress who receives first feature billing, the only other Actor or Actress whose name shall appear to the left or above that of the Actor, is that of Janet Blair, whose name will either be starred above or below the title, and Paul McGrath, who is playing the role of Mr. Benton, and who is to receive first feature billing. The Actor is to have the aforesaid billing in all forms of advertising and publicity released or authorized to be released by the manager, including but not limited to houseboards, billboards, programs, posters, magazines, periodicals, newspapers, etc., including ABC ads in the daily newspapers. [Hunter's agent must have dozed. What about skywriting? RM] If the manager elects not to feature any actor in the daily ABC ads, with the exception of Janet Blair, then he is not obligated to feature the Actor, but if any other Actor is featured, the Actor is to have billing as aforesaid described.

The bafflements in this and similar covenants can so addle a manager that, too late, he discovers he has signed conflicting agreements. I was faced with such an impasse when I tried to compose the first ad for *Swingin' the Dream,* a musical violation of Shakespeare's *A Midsummer Night's Dream* blessed with the services of Benny Goodman and Louis Armstrong. Producer Erik Charrell's agreement with Goodman provided that his name was to appear on a line by itself, above the title and above all other players. The bond with Satchmo provided that he was to have equal billing with any principal, and that no player's name might precede or flower above his.

The contracts negated each other. Charrell was stricken with producer's fever—excessive enthusiasm plus a faulty memory. It seemed *Swingin' the Dream* might make history—the only musical ever to open without an ad. After three weeks, a compromise was effected. The whims of both woodwind and trumpet player were honored in alternate ads and in alternate newspapers.

Consider the vertigo of Vinton Freedley. About to rehearse Ethel Merman and Jimmy Durante in *Red, Hot and Blue,* he broke into a cold sweat on discovering he had promised both Jimmy and Ethel star billing above the title. Trying to escape the noose he had fashioned, Freedley threw himself on the mercy of the stars. He threw himself in vain. Both were relentless. His delirium abated when an escape artist came up with this solution:

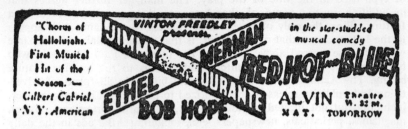

Since such typographical convulsions are taboo in the alphabetical newspaper listings, this display was anchored above the classified grouping throughout the run of the musical, an expensive solution.

Dwight Wiman was similarly mauled by Jane Cowl and Peggy Wood when he presented them in John van Druten's *Old Acquaintance*. Elated at bagging such divinities, he agreed to run their names on one line, same size and style of type for both. Subsequently he promised Miss Cowl sole star billing. Her name must precede the title, Miss Wood's follow it. Wiman wormed out of this trap by angling *Old Acquaintance* between the implacables, while keeping both on the same line. Because of its jigsaw construction, this ad too was denied alphabetical listing.

The illogic of actors scheming exclusive billing is touched with witchcraft. Though conditioned to their aberrations, I was numbed by the demand of Jackie Gleason, rushed into the cast of *Along Fifth Avenue* in Philadelphia following the death of Willie Howard. Nancy Walker was starred in this mishmash and eight or ten players, headed by Carol Bruce and Hank Ladd, were listed in the Sunday ads below the title. To please the newcomer, then known to few and rarely employed, producer Arthur Lesser gave him preferential billing: "and JACKIE GLEASON" would be centered below the other performers on a line by itself.

Gleason rejected this offer. He insisted "with JACKIE GLEASON" be sandwiched in between "Sketches by Nat Hiken and Charles Sherman" and "Scenery by Oliver Smith." I could only guess that he thought proximity to other actors would contaminate him. Seeking isolation among noncombatants, he seemed to be trying to avoid identification as a performer.

Consider the dementia of Dennis King. As the Henry Higgins of the touring *Pygmalion,* he protested ads which read:

GERTRUDE LAWRENCE

in PYGMALION

with DENNIS KING

That "with" implied inferiority, gave him caddy status, Dennis charged. On his insistence the offensive preposition was changed to "and," an alteration which set syntax back a thousand light years.

Until someone invents rubber type and elastic letters for electric signs, the concordats between producers and their players cannot be validated. It's not always possible for a printer to set the name of an actor in type 40 per cent the size of the name of the star, though he has at his elbow all the type fonts, faces and styles that have been fashioned since Johann Gutenberg composed the Mazarin Bible. Billing-crazed stage folk scorn approximations. Suspecting betrayal, they'll whip out calipers, spirit level and agate rule. On discovering a discrepancy, their screams, plus those of their agents, can be heard off Sandy Hook. When bilateral agreements cannot be solved with type, the names of the contestants are handlettered to scale.

But the letters on electric signs defy billing geometry. Their sheet-iron channels are inflexible, immune alike to prima donna's lament and tap dancer's moan. Most signs have three lines of letters, fifteen letters to a line. Their cozy structure precludes all but the name of the attraction and the star. Because these signs cannot cope with producers' promises, they're rapidly becoming as rare as aardvark in Central Park. Thanks to lobbyists for more and better billing, they're being replaced by metal boards. On these painters can enroll all the elite, even though the names of many of them can only be read by a man with 20/20 vision atop a stepladder.

The first theatrical posters were pictorial. They were designed and colored to catch the eye, to fascinate those who read on the run. The more striking caught something of the quality of the play or the excitements of the star. Text was sacrificed for art. Today they lack allure.

Specimens on view in Times Square are so littered with credits they're indistinguishable from *cartes-du-jour* or pages from the classified telephone directory.

When a producer puts his name on a poster, he touches off a chain explosion. If his name appears, so must that of the author. If the playwright is cited, the director must be acknowledged. Recognition of the director makes salutes to the designers of scenery and costumes obligatory. Enlargements and extensions of interlocking honors destroy the poster's pictorial worth. Only the play, its authors and its stars rate such kudos. The names of all the others wouldn't sell ten tickets if the carnival ran for ten years.

Dark Eyes had the most effective poster of all the attractions I've publicized. On it was the head of a provocative, sloe-eyed Russian temptress. The title glowed on her flaring shako. "Belasco Theatre" appeared in the lower left-hand corner.

The connoisseurs who congregate in Shubert Alley applauded me. The text was a model of brevity and a boon to art, they said. Only a hypnotist, they added, could have induced the comedy's brass to forgo representation. They were cheering the wrong man.

The simplicity and beauty of the card was due to the rancor of my employer. The original sketch named Jed Harris as producer. Eugenie Leontovich and Elena Miramova were listed both as its stars and its co-authors. Mr. Harris, as the director, drew a second mention. Viewing this rough, my master grew incoherent. He had developed a distaste for the authors before rehearsals started. During the drills, his distemper mounted into rage. As soon as he could speak, he ordered both Muscovites purged—as players and as authors. I reminded him that under the standard Authors' League contract, playwrights must be listed if the producer's name intrudes. His anger triumphed. Off the card went Eugenia and Helena, and off went Jed.

Some actors, authors and directors with billing rights are shocked when drama editors and reporters ignore their guarantees. It's idle for the press agent to point out that his prose is not sacrosanct, that newsmen did not sign the original treaty, hence cannot be penalized for violations. In the dark recesses of their minds festers the conviction that their rights are being breached through connivance.

I shrug off these infantile charges. Belly-aching about billing is implicit in the theatrical bill of rights. It's chronic and incurable and gets progressively worse. The gnomes who scheme dresses for TV's weather girls are noted as regularly as humidity and high and low pressure areas.

15

The Night of the Long Knives

BILLING and photographic gripes are forgotten in the anxieties which grip the contestant on the opening night in New York. This Armageddon climaxes fears and tensions that have simmered since the first rehearsal. However spectacular out-of-town business, however ecstatic the Boston and Philadelphia reviews, all know that success or failure rests on this performance, that eight weeks' effort may be scrambled in three hours. If the critics cheer they may bask in a two-year run. If they jeer, all may be vagrants by midnight Saturday—or sooner. The first night of *A Pin to See the Peep Show,* a melodrama I advocated in '53, was also its last.

Frightening as is this test for author, director and producer, who may writhe in private, to the actor it is a night of terror. He must mount the scaffold and face the mob. For he's to be judged by an audience unlike any he'll meet again. Only the press is neutral. The floor is jammed with partisans, hostiles and exhibitionists, most of whom behave deplorably. For comparable conduct they'd be bounced from a waterfront dive.

Who are the occupants of the torture chamber? Two thirds of them are professionals or semi-professionals, people who work in the theatre or batten on those who do. Champions of the accused include friends and relatives, agents and adjutants of the cast and the management, of the author and director, of the costumers, designers and choreographers. Well disposed, too, are investors in the enterprise flanked by their caddies and consorts. These sympathizers applaud indiscriminately. The entrance of a bit player triggers a demonstration by her aunts and uncles. The play's first words may be lost in the salvo given the décor by cronies of the scene designer. The ill-timed tributes of these claques irritate the critics. They demoralize the actors and destroy the play's rhythm. Most of these nuisances are well intentioned. Their testimonials, too long and too loud, symbolize their loyalty or mask their doubt. They're the victims of self-hypnosis or wishful thinking.

However vociferous, this corps is outnumbered by the carpers and men of ill will. These pessimists are attracted by the potential of disaster. The failure of others dissipates memories of their own blunders. This legion was exhilarated when Rodgers and Hammerstein abandoned Graham Greene's *The Heart of the Matter* in Boston and when they came a cropper with Steinbeck's *Burning Bright*. The rout of such invincibles as Dick and Oscar eased their sense of guilt and incompetence.

Among the vindictives are three or four producers who bypassed the work being tested. Its success will smear their judgment, its failure confirm it. In for the kill will be two or three directors, familiar with the script, seeking and finding flaws in the staging. Present, too, will be idle, therefore envious, actors trying to mask their contempt for their fellows. The opening attracts lighting, scenic and costume experts convinced the work will suffer needlessly through lack of their ministrations.

These skeptics sit on their hands. Occasionally they raise an eyebrow. Otherwise they mute their resentment. Low animal cunning warns them against vocal dissent. Questioned, they resort to fulsome praise. It would be folly to antagonize a potential associate or employer.

Each opening attracts its quota of show-offs and crackpots, native and alien. They're interested in neither play nor players. They've come to be seen and heard. These yahoos have their own code of misconduct. They arrive late and depart early. They use the aisles for a parade ground, the lobby for a gymnasium. They're the joy of autograph seekers and cretins who swarm the entrances for a glimpse of the infamous. During intermissions, they jostle through the crowd to perform on the sidewalk. A dozen repair to a nearby bar for a couple of snorts. They return to their seats ten minutes after the play resumes.

Who are these trapeze performers? Where do they come from?

Riffraff from café society, elated at this opportunity to air their vulgarities. Visiting screen witches, scanty in attire and talent. Frustrated gag men, full of studied ad libs. A platoon of epicenes engaged in tribal pirouettes. Slummers from the Social Register, awash with boredom and brandy. International tramps. Assorted sadists, sycophants and mental cases.

How does this trash get in? Why doesn't the management bar them?

Of the orchestra seats that remain, after the press agent has placated the press and allied media, sixty or more are pre-empted by the theatre operator. He can do this because his trusties man the box office. They order the tickets from the printer. The balance are at the disposal of the producer. If advance reports have been rosy, if the show has a top-drawer author or a star, he has ten bids for each ticket. On demand each applicant will submit an affidavit from his medium or his broker to support his claim to priority.

Weighing the credentials of these fanatics, the producer may come down with vapors. With few exceptions all want to sit in the third row on the aisle, seats assigned to the critics. Denied these pews, petitioners who wind up in P 14-16 scream that they've been betrayed, that their benefactor is an ingrate and a poltroon. Condemned to chairs along the foul line, they sulk like camel drivers. By their standards only aisle seats in the center section can match their eminence.

Periodically employers talk about policing opening nights. Hereafter, they swear, they'll handpick their audiences and stiff-arm objectionables and four-time offenders. However flinty their resolve, they're circumvented in the end. The creeps they would outlaw are crafty as rum runners. Rebuffed, they harry the theatre owner, influential newsmen and the play's angels. They may get seats through proxies. The producer can't control the detours of seats once he's issued them. Still frustrated, they may wave a fifty dollar bill under the nose of box-office man or ticket scalper. Thus suborned, one of these jinn may pass a miracle.

The disorder out front is communicated to the players and sharpens their concern. Even veteran stars have opening-night nerves. The immune would not flinch were hot darning needles jabbed under their fingernails. The more sensitive the player, the more susceptible he is to terror and doubt. His ears pound. His vision clouds. He's nagged by a dozen fears. What if he blows a line? What if he dries up? Will he remember the new second-act lines added by the author last night, or blurt out the discarded words? Will his opposite toss him the wrong cue? Will the door jam when he exits? Will his props function? Will his zipper foul? Will the lights go on when he flicks the switch?

Despite the shenanigans out front, and the anxiety backstage, invariably the actors rise to the challenge. I honor them for their courage and their gallantry under fire. Their behavior throughout this auto-da-fé would shame their tormentors, were they capable of shame.

For twenty-five years, Joseph Maloney was New York's most constant first nighter. Over that span he never missed one unless there were conflicts. His attendance dwarfed the records of such inveterates as Rita Katzenberg, Herbert Bayard Swope, Jules Glaenzer and Hope Hampton. Mr. Maloney was unique among first nighters. He sought anonymity. Mr. Maloney was a plainclothes detective, attached to the pickpocket squad. It was Maloney who recovered Lucius Beebe's jeweled gardenia at the opening of *Tonight at 8:30,* an event that ignited the international set, come to pay homage to Gertrude Lawrence and Noel Coward. Hanky-panky and chichi, bluster and bravado were the order of the evening.

Beebe wore the gardenia at the suggestion of Marcus, Fifth Avenue jeweler. If it was worn by so dauntless a dandy, Marcus felt his bauble might start a trend. Once Beebe agreed to sport this dingus, Marcus insured it for $15,000 and hired a private eye to tail him.

The eye was seated directly behind Beebe when the curtain rose. At the first intermission, Beebe, eye and newsgirl Inez Robb repaired to the Aviation Bar and Grill next to the theatre. When Beebe returned to the lobby, his gardenia was missing. So was the eye.

Discovering his loss, Beebe bore down on me crying, "Succor! Succor!" I summoned Maloney. He vetoed Beebe's proposal to seal the theatre and frisk the congregation. The town's blue bloods might resent prying hands, he said. He probed Beebe for clues. When did he miss the bijou? Did he have any enemies? Confused by the plot of *Red Peppers*—one of the Coward playlets—and three slugs of Armagnac, Beebe wasn't much help.

While Maloney and I were trying to calm the boulevardier, we were joined by the daughter of Geoffrey Parsons, chief editorial writer of the *Herald Tribune*. Learning the cause of Beebe's agitation, she said she'd seen a woman lift the trinket from the lapel of his dinner jacket in the bar. She thought the ornament was a fancy flower, hence hadn't warned him. Miss Parsons' reconstruction of the snatch refreshed Beebe's memory. The poacher had been on the arm of an acquaintance, a wealthy vagrant with a Roman numeral trailing his name. Consulting a floor plot in the box office which identified the occupant of every chair, I discovered the pair were in H 1-3.

An usher brought the playboy to the lobby, where Maloney gave him an ultimatum. Unless his wench gave up the gardenia, he'd call the wagon and take them both to the Forty-seventh Street station. Though feigning indignation, the playboy barged down the aisle, whispered with his partner, and came back with the trophy. It had been a jolly lark, he said. His companion had intended returning the gem to Beebe on her next visit to the trough. From Coward I learned differently. A tarnished member of the aristocracy, she was a notorious kleptomaniac. One night in London, she rifled Mr. C.'s dressing room while he was on stage.

To check on the details of the gardenia grab, I addressed Beebe in Virginia City, Nevada, where he now luxuriates. "I understand that the British Embassy, hearing of the affair, asked her family

to please take her home and that shortly thereafter she died of
booze in a nursing home," he replied.

In his note, Beebe reminded me of the fey strategy of one of
my comrades at the opening of *Mahogany Hall*. This carnal idyl
was the work of Charles Robinson and dwelt on the emotional conflicts of the madam of a Washington bordello who had fallen in love
with her piano player. It was fitting that Charles Washburn should
tout this drama. A few years earlier he had written *Come into My
Parlor*, a salute to the Everleigh Club, long one of Chicago's busiest
bagnios. To add zest to the première, Washburn invited the two
Everleigh sisters, now retired, and seated them next to critic Percy
Hammond. Percy, Charley and the errant sisters had all matured
and prospered in Cook County. Washburn's gesture reflected his
devotion to Chicago and its sons and daughters.

Efforts to abate first night confusions sometimes backfire. Norman
Bel Geddes was singed as he sought to ensure decorum at his revival
of *Hamlet*, with Raymond Massey as the moody Dane. That his
obeisance to the Bard might not be messed up by late comers,
Norman ruled that no one would be admitted after the rise of the
curtain. Nor could the tardy loiter in the lobby until the first intermission. Fearful that theatre attachés would not enforce this edict,
he engaged private detectives to patrol the entrance. The first
dawdler to be evicted was Mrs. Joshua Cosden. Mrs. Cosden was
Bel Geddes' angel. She'd put up all the money. The second victim
was Robert Garland, critic of the *World-Telegram*. The third scamp
to be ousted was an artist who had sketched Raymond Massey in
doublet and hose during the dress rehearsal. Inflamed by Jamaica
ginger, this intruder was in his underwear, a raincoat draped about
his neck, when he spilled from a taxicab with his tribute to Massey.
One of Norman's sleuths kicked the etcher for a field goal from a
difficult angle.

Bel Geddes' *Hamlet* was hexed from the start. Set on a superla-
tive cast, Norman dispatched Courtney Burr to London to engage
a Laertes, an Ophelia, a Claudius and other items in the *dramatis
personae*. Relaxing in a Piccadilly supper club, Burr was fascinated

by a female impersonator. After a three-hour study, he signed the
impostor to a six-week play-or-pay contract at a high fee, and
guaranteed him round-trip first-class passage from London. Inflamed
by one thing or another, Burr felt he'd bagged a bonanza. This coup
might climax his career in the theatre. Competitive bids of rival
vaudeville theatres would rocket the mime's New York wage to record
heights. The difference between the impersonator's salary and the
sums they'd get might run to $2,000 a week. Such were the propor-
tions of Burr's delirium.

Back in New York, Burr was quickly disillusioned. The top variety
theatres rejected his discovery. That their investment might not be
a total loss, Burr and Bel Geddes farmed the impostor to a grind
house on Washington Heights at a fourth of his assured wage.
After six weeks, they were faced with the obligation of sending
the bogus belle back to London. They had neither a ticket nor
the money to get one. Their dilemma was solved with the closing
of *Hamlet.* Fortunately they had return fares for all aliens in the
revival. As this group was about to sail, the actor who had played
Claudius was reported missing. Thanks to this circumstance, they
sent the impersonator home on the king's ticket.

About to dedicate *The Magnificent Yankee,* with Louis Calhern
as its Justice Oliver Wendell Holmes, Arthur Hopkins pondered
the advisability of barring delinquents. He compromised by refusing
to seat anyone during the first scene. Discussing the no-admission
gambit with me, Hopkins mulled its consequences. "What if someone in the theatre wants to get out after the curtain goes up?"
he asked. "If I restrain him, won't I be violating his civil rights?"

An unprogrammed episode almost scrambled the opening night of
Fifty Million Frenchmen. Genevieve Tobin, the musical's leading
lady, had a thin, reedy voice, barely audible over the trumpets,
strings and oboes. Midway through her first song, a white-tied tosspot,
eighth row center, cried out, "I can't hear a goddamned word!"
Before being disposed of by a posse of ushers, he twice repeated
his protest. In better voice than Miss Tobin, he was heard in the
last row of the second balcony.

Billy Rose staged an odd and unsolicited prologue to the opening of Laurence Olivier and Vivien Leigh in *Caesar and Cleopatra.* Early that afternoon he phoned me to ask if news photographers would cover the ceremonies. I assured him the Ziegfeld would be crawling with cameramen. This was the stars' first joint appearance in New York since their *Romeo and Juliet,* ten years earlier, and they would be greeted by the town's elite. Rarely did the *bon ton* have the opportunity to pay tribute to a classic and salute a knight and his lady at the same time. It would be the theatrical event of the season.

Rose's call roused my curiosity. There was more to it than touched my ear. I was not under his jurisdiction. True, he was the proprietor of the Ziegfeld, but I was employed by Gilbert Miller. Why did he question me about so routine a tactic? What was he up to?

I found out what he was up to at seven-thirty that night. The audience was seated. A hush of expectancy hung over the theatre. Then Rose came in with Joyce Matthews on his arm. All cameras were focused on them. They were the center of all eyes as they swept down the aisle. It was an entrance to tingle Duse or Bernhardt. For months the gossip columns had boiled with play-by-play reports of the romantic adventures of Billy and Joyce, of the difficulties they encountered in their efforts to mount the altar. This was their first public appearance. They'd picked a good night for it. Next morning the tabloids blazed with their pictures. In the captions they were hailed as successors to Héloïse and Abélard. The commotion they created obscured both Caesar and Cleopatra.

A deluge was coming down when the curtain fell on the first performance of *Antony and Cleopatra* the following night. The Ziegfeld lies beyond the periphery of New York's amusement area. Few taxicabs cruise the area after dark. So violent and prolonged was the downpour, half the audience sought refuge in Chinatown Charlie's next door. Top-hatted rowdies swarmed over the few cabs which drew up to the Ziegfeld. Contestants exchanged nasty words.

After paying my respects to Miss Leigh and Sir Laurence, I, too, retired to Chinatown Charlie's. The management was in a panic. The unexpected horde had drunk up its stock in ten minutes. Drenched employees were staggering in with new supplies from nearby taverns. Shortly I was seated with George Jean Nathan and actress Julie Haydon. Nothing to worry about as long as the Scotch held out, George and I agreed. It must stop raining sometime. It always had. Miss Haydon was more practical. She had no intention of being cooped up in Chinatown Charlie's all night. She asked George for a dime. Shortly she returned. A cab would be in front in ten minutes, she said. This news stunned us. How had she worked this miracle? Her coup was out of character. I always thought Julie the dreamy type! It was also a reflection on our resource and ingenuity.

It was very simple, Julie said. She called her midtown hotel and asked the manager to send a cab to the Ziegfeld. It arrived five minutes later. As it pulled up half of Chinatown Charlie's customers charged it, waving bills. The driver waved them aside. When order was restored, Julie and George walked to their carriage followed by me. Some of the Chinatown Charlie's captives were removed on litters, long after the rain had ceased.

The applause erupting at the end of a play often is synthetic. The "Bravos!" and cries of "Author! Author!" may be instigated by agents of the management, lurking in the rear of the auditorium, or by cronies of the accused. Through long experience, I can distinguish between feigned and genuine outbursts. False applause has a tinny sound. Its authors operate in jerky fashion. If their initial salvo doesn't gain support, the timid grow self-conscious and try to crawl back into the woodwork. The bitter-enders continue until the ushers shoo them out.

Though aware that many demonstrations are rigged, the professionals lay great stress on first-night curtain calls. Their number and volume rocket their hopes or confirm their despair. The critics don't see or hear these huzzas. They're racing for the street as the play's last words are spoken. To dally would be dangerous. Getting out of a crowded New York theatre is comparable to escaping from Alcatraz, so narrow are the aisles, so awkward the exits and so cramped the lobby.

If the audience competes with the reviewers in the dash to the exits, it's an evil omen. But if it remains fixed in its seats through ten or twelve curtain calls, I count the day won. *The Lark, Death of a Salesman* and other plays with great emotional impact leave even calloused first nighters limp. The final curtain reduces them to stunned silence. Seconds pass before the spell is broken. The ovation that follows rattles the rafters. As such moments the theatre becomes the most thrilling place in the world. Exalted by a common experience, carpers and cousins become one. There's no mistaking these tributes. They're from the heart. They never fail to stir me.

After the final curtain, professional first nighters charge backstage like hartebeests headed for the waterhole. They jam the stage door. They barge through curtained entrances behind the boxes. The daring scale the footlights. Friend and foe alike are caught up in the raid. They flood the stage and swarm the dressing rooms and clog the stairways. They knock over lamps, trip over cables and fall through trapdoors. They singe the scenery with their cigarettes and deface the furniture. The surge of these vandals is frightening. Ostensibly they've come to congratulate the star and the featured players, to pump the hand of the producer and the director. That many are unknown to their targets in no wise stays their advances. The truth is they're trying to convince themselves, and rival invaders, that they are among the anointed, that they belong.

The words of these hooligans are as offensive as their actions. They hose one and all with odious superlatives. Their gushes embrace, but are not confined to, "My dear, you were simply magnificent," "This was your greatest performance," "The show will run for years," "Wonderful," "Terrific," all laced with a spate of "darlings." Experienced players, conditioned to first-night drivel, listen to it with fixed smiles and masked nausea. They're aware that their serenaders drench plays and players—good, bad and indifferent—with the same gibberish at every opening.

On the afternoon of a New York first night, the theatre's elite break out in a rash of *noblesse oblige*. In token of their good will, or a reasonable facsimile thereof, they pepper the defendants with assurances of their confidence and devotion. Filed within a three-hour period, these messages keep Western Union messengers on the run. For the opening-night telegram is one of the theatre's oldest traditions.

It pre-dates the footlight and the paper drinking cup. The star will receive hundreds of these testimonials, some of them from people she knows. Featured players, producer, director and designer also are showered by their contemporaries. Some of these protestations are genuine, many are as phony as a three-dollar bill.

The authors of these effusions sweat and writhe in an effort to say something witty. They're aware that wires to the players will festoon their dressing-room walls as long as the play runs. If the exercise is a hit, they'll be read by hundreds of backstage visitors. Do they come up with an epigram, they may be cited for their invention in one of the columns. But there are few Sydney Smiths among them, and fewer Wildes. A mute walk-on in Maurice Evans' revival of *Henry IV, Part I,* was unnerved by this greeting: "Don't just stand there. Say something." "Better luck next time" gleamed with premeditated malice. Two hours before he opened with Gertrude Lawrence in *The King and I,* Yul Brynner received this graceful wire from Rex Harrison: "The king is dead! Long live the king!" Earlier Harrison had played the Brynner role in the screen's *Anna and the King of Siam.*

Not all first-night messages come from show people. Many outsiders barge into the contest. A wire is an inexpensive way to caress a heroine. It gives its author a sense of participation, of contact with the cloistered. The heroine is stimulated, too. She welcomes greetings from strangers. They symbolize both the range of her fame and the devotion of her subjects. There will also be dispatches from her doctor and her dentist, from her hairdresser and her handyman. There'll be compliments from her analyst and her astrologer and from the proprietors of "21," the Stork Club, Sardi's, Downey's and other taverns eager to retain or gain her custom.

Though flowers over the footlights are taboo—this practice loosed charges of conspiracy and stuffing the ballot box—our girl's dressing room will be strewn with wreaths and sprays and blossoms. After noting the donor, she'll send them to Bellevue or the Polyclinic.

Relatives dispersed and poachers routed, costumes and make-up removed, telegrams riffled and roses sniffed, she's off to an opening-night party or a supper with her intimates. At long last she can relax. The die has been cast, the inquest is over. Her performance is beyond recall. Relax, did I say? Can the accused relax while the jury is still out?

Opening-night parties are a risky business. Schemed as celebrations, they may turn into wakes. More than one proposed rout has been vetoed by the guests. Two hours will elapse before they know the verdict of the morning reviewers. Sensitive types prefer to sip their suspense in seclusion or with a few intimate friends. They aren't up to a public vigil.

If there is a party, the producer probably will be the host though he's down to his last dime. He tosses it in a water-over-the-dam gesture, with forgive-and-forget implications. He's aware that it may climax his folly or honor his vision. If they're still *en rapport,* the producer and author may co-sponsor one of these shindigs. I've survived a hundred first-night frolics.

The size, quality and site of these bees varies widely. Producer Kermit Bloomgarden and author Lillian Hellman commemorated the revival of *The Children's Hour* with a get-together in a bar-and-grill on Lexington Avenue. Invitations were restricted to the company and staff, their mates and escorts. Curious about their choice of a playground, I learned it was the haunt of Kim Hunter, one of the tragedy's doomed teachers. She was partial to its spaghetti.

Bloomgarden and Miss Hellman awaited judgment on *The Lark* in a private room at the Plaza. Their guests included close friends, star Julie Harris, Boris Karloff and most of the superb company. Miss Harris was a reluctant guest. She'd rather submit to the water drip than attend any party, anywhere. I joined the celebrants at twelve-thirty with a copy of Atkinson's eulogy. As the bearer of hot tidings, I was tolerated until I undertook to read Brooks' report. Miss Hellman said my delivery was faulty. It lacked fire and eloquence. In my mouth, the review lost its punch. There were extenuating circumstances, I pleaded. I was reading the ruling through the bus boy's glasses.

Man, boy and referee, I've toasted Lillian at first-night fracases for twenty years. Not all of them were festive. The gala thrown by

Ralph Ingersoll, then general manager of Time, Inc., following the
dedication of her *Days to Come* was ill-timed. As early as nine
o'clock, it was evident all was not well. Evil omens abounded. The
acting was erratic and the audience restless. Business in LaHiff's
Tavern next door started to pick up. There was only a spatter of
applause at the final curtain. On arrival at Ingersoll's Fifth Avenue
castle, the guests seemed in a state of shock. So did Miss Hellman.
Ingersoll was an expansive host. He plied the sufferers with potent
tonics, but they grew progressively moodier. Bulletins from Times
Square confirmed their fears. *Days to Come* was not long for this
world.

One of our ablest, not to say one of our more defiant, playwrights,
Miss Hellman doesn't capitulate readily. On learning of the dissents
in the early editions, she bristled, then launched into a vivid counter-
attack. Seeking corroboration, she turned to novelist Dashiell Hammett, deep in debate with novelist James T. Farrell. "Dash, didn't
you tell me last week that *Days to Come* was the best script you'd
ever read?" Disengaging himself from Farrell, Hammett rose to his
feet, reached for his cape, swirled it over his shoulder and replied:
"I did indeed. But I saw it tonight at the Vanderbilt and I've changed
my mind." With that, he squared his shoulders and stalked into
the night.

Though he could ill afford it, thanks to professional mishaps and
enthusiasm for the wrong horses, producer Herman Levin feted
three hundred on the St. Regis Roof following the opening of
Gentlemen Prefer Blondes. This gaudy gesture reflected his relief
on christening a carouse he'd almost had to abandon four months
earlier. (He couldn't raise the necessary $220,000.) *Blondes* vindi-
cated the St. Regis rout and Levin's tenacity with its ninety-three-
week run at the Ziegfeld. A year later, following the opening of
Bless You All, Levin celebrated with a party in the Crystal Room
at the Ritz Carlton. His playmates were the companies of *Bless You
All* and *Gentlemen Prefer Blondes* and such somebodies as Noel
Coward, Quentin Reynolds and Billy Rose. If Levin thought an
opening-night party essential to success he was quickly disillusioned.
After a ten-week coma, *Bless You All* passed away in its sleep.

I, too, was disillusioned. I invested $1,500 in this clambake after hearing one of the authors outline three of the revue's sketches. *Blondes* made half a million. *Bless You All* lost $300,000.

If midnight revels were a requisite of first nights, if *Blondes* rated a blowout at the St. Regis and *Bless You All* a revel at the Ritz, *My Fair Lady* rated a gala to shame the excesses of Belshazzar, Lucullus and Elsa Maxwell. But Levin ruled against a victory celebration. Victory had been certain since the opening in New Haven five weeks earlier. The New York opening could only reaffirm it. He had no doubters to coddle, no prima donnas to pamper, no critics to fear. In triumph he could afford to be modest.

The first night of *My Fair Lady* was spine tingling. Friend and foe, carpers and quibblers, relatives and agents, all were bowled over by its magic. The curtain calls rocked the Hellinger to its foundations. The texture and volume of the applause had added significance for Levin. It was in the Hellinger that his *Bless You All* laid such an elaborate egg.

After the performance, I accompanied Herman and Dawn McInerney, his bride-to-be, to Sardi's, oldest and best known of New York's theatrical roosts. On our entrance, Herman was given a standing ovation. Though dedicated to doubt and conditioned to disaster, theatre people are quick to hitch onto a sensation. A newsman present said he hadn't seen such spontaneous ecstasy since LeClerq's Corps rode down the Champs Elysées the day Paris was liberated. Herman had made hundreds of entrances to Sardi's. Never before had he created a stir. Now he was embraced by strangers and bussed by babes he didn't know. Around two in the morning, we fell in with authors Alan Lerner and Frederick Loewe, Rex Harrison and Moss Hart, holed up in a private room at "21." Conviviality was getting out of hand. An hour or two later, Miss McInerney, Levin and I broke bread or something with designer Oliver Smith and choreographer Hanya Holm at El Morocco, where Levin was reembraced and rebussed. This was my first visit to this spa. We had a gay time there—or so I was told on my recovery.

Each first night in which I'm implicated finds me in black tie and dinner jacket. This attire is obligatory for press agents and

company managers at all first nights. Such dress is supposed to give
a cachet to the proceedings. It serves as a vote of confidence and
a badge of loyalty and indicates to our employers that we're sensitive
to the historic significance of the occasion.

At these festivals, I sit in the last row on the aisle. It's been
charged that I occupy this remote chair that I may be the first
to escape if the audience gets ugly. This is a canard. A man who has
sat through the dedication of *Four Twelves Are 48, Mrs. Gibbons
Boys* and *Deadfall,* is not easily intimidated. In the last row, I'm
inconspicuous and accessible. After the curtain's rise, I may be summoned to admit a newsman who has lost his tickets or left them
in his other suit, or to repel an impostor with forged credentials.
Usually I sit alone, or with one of my associates. My wife, a woman
of taste and discrimination, is allergic to first nights. She prefers
dress rehearsals or first nights in New Haven, an hour's ride from
our Westport home.

At intervals I may slip into the lobby for a smoke or an informal
huddle with the producer and his manager. All these huddles start
with the same question, "How's it going?" Most producers and
authors are too tense to be confined to a seat. They pace the rear
of the auditorium or lurk on the balcony stairs. I can look upon a
first performance with considerable detachment. As a rule, I've seen
two or three performances out of town and have strong convictions
about its critical and box-office fate. If I think it's doomed, I mute my
suspicions. Pressed for my opinion by my superiors, I resort to evasive
answers. There's no point in throwing cold water on optimistic colleagues. Their apparent optimism may mask fears as grave as mine.

First man on the sidewalk at intermission, I casually circulate
among drama critics, editors and reporters, and keep my ears open.
Once the curtain's up, my producer's sure to ask, "What have you
heard?" Decoded, this means have I inklings of a critical trend.
But I listen in vain. Such clues as I have are secondhand. A ticket
broker says, "Coleman likes it." The wife of a backer whispers
that Atkinson is sitting directly in front of her, that he laughed
throughout the second scene. This evidence is sketchy and often
inaccurate. The drama men with whom I talk volunteer nothing

and I ask them nothing. To do so would violate my oath of office.

"Casually circulate," did I say? How absurd! No one circulates at a first-night intermission. Five hundred people wedged into a lobby no larger than a freight car reduce traffic to a snail's pace.

With the exception of Gilbert Miller, all my employers ask me to phone them résumés of the morning notices at the earliest moment. If I'm fortunate enough to reach Zolotow at the *Times,* I may have the gist of Atkinson's verdict by a quarter of twelve. By prearrangement I call Chapman on the *News* at midnight, at which hour he's finished with his report. He will read me his lead, or the paragraph in which he sums up for or against the defendant. Shortly thereafter, a friend on the city desk of the *Herald Tribune* briefs me on Kerr's conclusions. At the agreed hour and place, I capsule these for my benefactor. They enthuse, confuse or dismay him, according to their nature. I'll not see or hear from him again—unless we collide at a party— until late in the morning when we meet in his office to discuss tactics, if any, ads or flight for the border.

I cannot conclude this survey of first nights without citing the concern of Courtney Burr three hours before the christening of *A Case of Youth.* Uncommonly nonchalant, in view of the grisly character of the play he was about to launch, Burr called me for advice. He'd just finished reading a blistering essay by George Jean Nathan. In it Nathan jeered producers for their first-night conduct. Butt of his attack were the stoics who, in white tie and tails, brazen out the night from the fourth row on the aisle, no matter how evil their offering.

"There's no point in annoying George unnecessarily," said Courtney. "What do you suggest I wear tonight?"

Since I had suffered through a preview performance the night before, I could answer without hesitation: "Your track suit."

16

The First Ladies

IN the past twenty years at least nine actresses have been named "The First Lady of the Theatre" by pollsters, critics and other agitators. A cautious fellow, perhaps a craven, I list the laureled alphabetically: Judith Anderson, Tallulah Bankhead, Ethel Barrymore, Shirley Booth, Katharine Cornell, Lynn Fontanne, Helen Hayes, Gertrude Lawrence and Laurette Taylor. The donors of these diadems are either delirious or parochial. Their nominations are defensible only if they mean "The First Lady of the American Theatre." Any list of eligibles which ignores Britain's Sybil Thorndike, Peggy Ashcroft, Celia Johnson, Wendy Hiller, Margaret Leighton, Edith Evans and Vivien Leigh should be fumigated and its proponents given three days in the stocks.

There's another oddity about the empurpled nine. The seven now practicing are all over fifty. On their deaths Miss Lawrence was fifty-four, Miss Taylor over sixty. Qualifications for these phantom tributes should be redefined. For all I know to the contrary, thirty-two-year-old Julie Harris may be the best actress in our theatre.

I have strummed the lyre for all of the anointed save Lynn Fontanne and Laurette Taylor. (This will startle E. V. Durling, syndicated Hearst columnist, who recently informed his readers that I got my start with Miss Taylor, and that I ingratiated myself with the star by walking her mutt Michael throughout the run of *Peg o' My Heart*.) To all nine, I raise a glass. All served the theatre long and brilliantly. But the theatre is an ungrateful rip. It flouts its most eloquent and exciting spokesmen.

As I write this—late April of '57—Shirley Booth is the only one of the seven surviving first ladies employed in the theatre. She's entertaining Chicago in *The Desk Set*. Tallulah has had but one new play in twelve years, a shoddy adaptation of a Henry James novel that gave up the ghost after twelve performances last February. To circumvent the sheriff, shortly she'll take off for London for a night-club engagement. Denied a New York platform for three years, Judith Anderson mutters that next season she'll emulate Sarah Bernhardt and have a go at Hamlet. Ethel Barrymore hasn't graced a New York theatre in over ten years. She's reduced to occasional screen and television assignments, all unworthy of her talents.

Miss Fontanne? She's at Genosee Depot, Wisconsin, with husband Alfred Lunt, trying to forget *The Great Sebastians*. Betrayed by *The Dark Is Light Enough* two years ago, Miss Cornell recently submitted to a television appearance in a mutilated version of *There Shall Be No Night*, one-time vehicle for the Lunts. Except in brief revivals of *The Skin of Our Teeth* and *The Glass Menagerie*, Helen Hayes has not illuminated our stage in four years. She, too, has been obliged to swallow the bitter TV pill.

All these idle ladies have great box-office potency. The magic of their names has redeemed many a three-act mediocrity. Why doesn't the theatre make use of their exceptional gifts? None of them slum in TV's channels from choice. Unless on a cultural bender to prove their devotion to Shaw, Shakespeare or Ibsen, all shrink from revivals as they would from exposure to the black pox. Any one of them would jump at the chance to appear in a moderately good play. Only in the theatre are they content despite affidavits they may have made to the contrary.

The authors and the producers must share the guilt. On their heads must rest the shame. Do you find Stan Musial, Ted Williams and Mickey Mantle unemployed in mid-season?

I first was entranced by Gertrude Lawrence in 1924 on hearing her sing "Limehouse Blues" in *André Charlot's* Revue. Her performance moved Percy Hammond to write: "Miss Lawrence's conquest of last night's audience was quite the most definite thing of its kind I have ever seen. Every man in town is, or will be, in love with her." Twelve years later, John C. Wilson engaged me to chant the praises of Miss Lawrence and Noel Coward in *Tonight at 8:30,* collective title of nine of Mr. Coward's one-act plays shown in three rotating bills.

This miscellany provided Miss Lawrence with a challenging gamut. Variously she was a music-hall hoyden, a Victorian belle in hoop skirts, a Cockney slattern, a Mayfair witch, a married flirt and a light-fingered lady looting her hosts on the Côte d'Azur. In these playlets she danced and she sang, she nagged and she mugged. Successively she was tender and strident and heart-breaking. Coward told me she was the only woman in the English-speaking theatre capable of bravura performances in all nine roles. And he added, "She's the only actress I know who gives a grand performance at the first rehearsal."

The *Tonight at 8:30* series was a sellout from the start. The ticket brokers bought up all the seats on the lower floor for sixteen weeks, a practice now taboo. But the stars were indifferent to publicity. Long runs palled on Coward. Facing capacity audiences he became restive. "Nervous Gertie," as she identified herself during the token rehearsals—the company had recently finished a long run in London —insisted on getting back for the inauguration of Edward VIII. In proof of this, she told me she was having her jewelry dipped in gold. To minimize demands on their time, I became a depress agent.

Though Miss Lawrence's 10 per cent of the gross business ran to $2,500 a week, her fiscal position was perilous. More than once I created a diversion after a matinee that she might escape through the front of the house. This ruse was inspired by a process server at the stage door. Miss Lawrence had run up fancy arrears with a fashionable Fifth Avenue shop during her reign in *Private Lives* five years earlier. Despite her sumptuous weekly swag, she was always on the brink of bankruptcy. She was as prodigal with her purse as she was with her talents.

With the clamor for tickets at its peak, Miss Lawrence and Coward stunned the town by adjourning after fifteen weeks at the National. They also stunned me and producer John C. Wilson. In my eulogies to the pair, I had been partial to "mercurial." Little did I think they'd validate that adjective in such explosive fashion.

It would be eight years before I trafficked with Miss Lawrence again. In the meantime she had conquered in *Susan and God, Skylark* and *Lady in the Dark.* These demonstrations convinced me she was the most versatile of all the first ladies. It was in this interval, too, that she married Richard Aldrich.

In the summer of '44, I announced that Gilbert Miller would star Gertrude Lawrence in *Errand for Bernice,* a wartime fable by Jacques Deval, writing for the first time in English. "When will rehearsals start?" I asked Mr. Miller. He wasn't sure. Miss Lawrence, he said, was entertaining British troops on the Continent and he couldn't reach her. When he pressed Fanny Holtzman, Miss Lawrence's business manager, she grew evasive. Six weeks passed. Miller's efforts to wring a confession from Miss Holtzman were fruitless.

Not feeling up to further palavers, Miller suggested I beard Miss Holtzman. Had I met the lady? No. Miller briefed me rapidly. I'd be well advised to keep my wits about me, he warned. My quarry was a touch aggressive, and a touch garrulous. She was chummy with everyone in the Almanach de Gotha and had testimonials to prove it.

On my arrival at Miss Holtzman's chambers, she led me through her gallery of notables—even before I could explain my mission. Her walls crawled with photographs of the great and the gaudy. I peered at H. G. Wells, Lady Astor, Mrs. Wellington Koo, Justice Cardozo, King George of Greece and other eminences. On these her victims had scrawled assurances of their affection and devotion.

When I told Fanny what I was up to, she waxed conspiratorial. If I could be trusted with a secret, she'd give me the lowdown on Miss Lawrence's delay. She was solacing British troops in Holland.

When she told them she was about to leave for America, they threatened to mutiny.

"If insistence on Gertie's return is going to create a breach in Anglo-Saxon relations, perhaps it would be wise of Miller to call the whole thing off," I suggested. Miss Holtzman was against such impulsive action. "Call me in the morning," she said. "I'll know Gertrude's decision then."

Fanny was a woman of her word. Miss Lawrence would arrive in Baltimore by plane two days later. "Will you set up the press conference there?" she asked. I demurred. A discussion of the star's war activities arranged by a theatrical press agent might be misinterpreted, I said. My opponent was undismayed. "Never mind," she said airily, "I'll have Paul Patterson take care of it." Mr. Patterson was publisher of the Baltimore *Sun*. I received but one more call from Miss Holtzman, but it froze my blood. "Do you think Miss Lawrence should come ashore in battle dress?" I grow frightened thinking about Miss Holtzman. Miss Lawrence is something else again. She was as gay and gallant and glamorous a gal as ever trod a platform. Mercurial, too.

Errand for Bernice was buried in Cleveland without benefit of clergy. Deval, inventive and amusing in the French originals of *Her Cardboard Lover* and *Tovarich,* was inscrutable in his first tussle with the English language.

The suggestion that Gertrude Lawrence had a wider range than any of her sisters is sure to bring Tallulah's champions storming out of the barracks on the double. Their protests must be heard. The Alabama rebel has triumphed over every medium which has taunted her—save one.

Tallulah's Regina in *The Little Foxes* was a brilliant characterization of a malevolent woman, and her Sabina in *The Skin of Our Teeth* a glittering creation. Her performance in Alfred Hitchcock's *Lifeboat* was voted the best of the year by the New York screen critics. Radio was picking at the coverlets when Tallulah revived it as mistress of ceremonies for *The Big Show*. On her TV debut, the *Times's* Jack Gould hailed her as a female Durante. She convulsed the capacity audience assembled in the McFarlin Auditorium on the campus of Southern Methodist University in Dallas in her first appearance on the lecture platform. While stricken with shingles, she made a shambles of the floor show at the Sands Hotel, Las Vegas, in her night-club christening. Her autobiography topped the best-seller list for months.

Baited for years by Irving Berlin to ignite a musical show, Tallulah was ambushed in an abortive revival of the *Ziegfeld Follies* as recently as the spring of '56. Thanks to her box-office pull, this witless charade sold out in its two weeks in Boston. But its odor spread rapidly. It closed in Philadelphia so rapidly one wag said Tallulah took her final bow from the rear of a moving van. The debacle was none of her doing. She was shabbily betrayed by authors, composers and producer. How did she get involved in such an atrocity? Why? She needed the money.

Tallulah can be as good as she wants to be, but she's not among the dedicated. The theatre ceased to fascinate her once she achieved stardom in London at twenty-one. She sees no point in scaling Everest twice. The whole apparatus of the theatre bores her—dieting, hairdressing, costuming, photographs, train rides, room service, matinees and other demands of her trade. Challenged by a new medium, she can rise to spectacular heights. But she has no capacity for sustained effort.

She's haunted by the necessity of making enough money to meet her profligate expenditures. This need inspires her forays into fields she abhors.

Beyond that of other first ladies, Tallulah's name has impact on the consciousness of her countrymen. Proof? In January of '54, producers Aldrich and Myers presented *Dear Charles* for a week in Washington, with Lili Darvas in the leading role. It was flayed by the reviewers. So hostile was its reception and so evil its business, the comedy closed forthwith. A year later Tallulah invaded Washington in the same play. In view of the earlier catastrophe, this booking seemed suicidal. Why did Aldrich and Myers want to revisit the scene of the crime? In its first Washington week, *Dear Charles* played to a pitiful $2,700. With Tallulah at the helm, it played to $37,000. It was still a wretched comedy. Her name was the magnet which attracted the curious and the faithful.

A few of the sorority may act as well as Tallulah, but none can match her in personality. Offstage or on, she has a style and tang and bravura that set her apart. No one can watch her or listen to her unmoved. She excites, agitates or confuses everyone she meets. In some she lathers emotions of which they wot not. Fascinated or repelled, all exposed to Tallulah are shaken up.

Tallulah's flame is a fusion of promise and menace, of excitement and temptation. In her is a lethal concentration of the qualities which flower in *la femme fatale*. Her pantherlike walk, her mezzo-basso voice, her explosive laughter, her conversation, her scorn for convention, her tawny mane, her off-beat deportment when exhilarated by the grape—all these contribute to her legend. She's the only living woman identifiable to every peasant in the land by her given name. In a fit of exuberance I once wrote:

"Melliflous, liquid, Tallulah is a name to inflame the flank of a Pullman car, or to blow on a bugle. It's a name to rally the tribesmen in battle, to summon the faithful to prayer. Because of its phonetic potential it is a challenging name, one to inspire its owner to adventures above and beyond the call of duty."

Efforts to snare the essence of Tallulah's sorcery have beggared better vocabularies than mine. "Tallulah is one of those girls who could lure a Scotch elder into any indiscretion. Her lips are as scarlet as a Guardsman's coat," wrote Reginald Arkell thirty years ago. "Tallulah is like a Greek fragment—or, rather, an Egyptian head put on a Greek torso. Her eyes are like hieroglyphics. Like a cricket she chirps all night," is the testimonial of Viola Tree. Cecil Beaton went off the deep end in his paean to the fugitive from Huntsville, Alabama:

"Tallulah is a wicked archangel with her flowing ash-blonde hair and carven features," he wrote. "Her profile is perfectly Grecian, flow of line from forehead to nose like the head on a medallion. She is Medusa, very exotic, with a glorious skull, high pumice-stone cheekbones. Her cheeks are huge acid-pink peonies. Her eyes are built out with hot liquid paint to look like burnt matches, and her sullen, discontented rosebud of a mouth is painted the brightest scarlet, and is as shiny as Tiptree's strawberry jam." See what I mean?

I'm an authority on Tallulah. I've hymned all her plays, except *Clash by Night,* for the past twenty years. I publicized *Foolish Notion, The Eagle Has Two Heads* and *Private Lives* on her insistence. Both The Theatre Guild, sponsor of the first named, and John C. Wilson, producer of the last two, had able press agents. Normally they would have heralded these romps. But normalcy flies out the window when Tallulah swaggers through the door. Those seeking Miss Bankhead's services must meet Miss Bankhead's terms. I was one of her terms.

Tallulah's contract for *Foolish Notion* stipulated footlights, me and Peter Davis, in that order. Davis had been her company manager when she toured in *The Little Foxes.* She would have no other. The Guild could like it or lump it. Producers are not likely to haggle about press agents and company managers when trying to bag a star of Tallulah's scope. Since she finds acting an ordeal, and attendance at the theatre depressing, Tallulah surrounds herself with compatibles. The proximity of heretics who share her tastes, her thirsts and her prejudices mitigates her megrims. A knowledge of slams and finesses was obligatory for mimes seeking roles in her plays during her contract-bridge phase.

I first met Tallulah late in '38 when she signed to play Regina Giddens in *The Little Foxes.* We hit it off from the start. In that remote day I liked to stay up late, too. Tallulah didn't rise until late afternoon, hence made few demands on my daylight hours. Her integrity was unassailable. She'd endorse no product, however spectacular the fee. She stiff-armed hostesses of women's clubs, lawn parties and receptions, all hoping to hop up attendance through her presence at their rodeos, on the cuff. But she'd lavish her money and her talents on a cause in which she believed or on a fellow player in distress.

Following a performance, her dressing room was as jammed as the Bronx Express during the six-o'clock rush. Through it flowed priests and panhandlers, jockeys and judges, authors and outfielders

and sons and daughters of the Confederacy. I first met Theodore
Roosevelt, Jr., playwright George Kelly—uncle of Her Grace of
Monaco—Mel Ott of the Giants, and a blues singer out on bail in
her cell at the National. As often as not, ten or twelve of these
wayfarers would accompany her to her hotel suite to await the
dawn.

George Brown, head of the IATSE (the stagehands' union), invited
Tallulah's wrath shortly after the start of rehearsals. Brown, later
jailed for blackmailing the screen studios, was trying to take over
the entire amusement field. She denounced this dreamer in a broadcast teeming with invective and violent words. After jeering Brown
for his arrogance and delusions, she ended on this classic note:

> Upon what meat doth this our Caesar feed,
> That he is grown so great?

Tallulah's curse on Brown made all the newspapers. Anathema
from so silken a source was welcomed.

The Little Foxes provided Tallulah with her best play and her
finest role, but the engagement was full of fireworks. Though she
had great respect for the skills of author Lillian Hellman and
director-producer Herman Shumlin, Tallulah didn't see eye to eye
with them politically. Descended from a long line of Alabama legislators, Tallulah, when agitated, was prone to denounce anyone with
whom she disagreed as "a dirty Communist." Intermittently she thus
stigmatized me. Lillian and Shumlin leaned to the left. When Tallulah
announced that she would give a benefit performance for Finnish
relief, author and producer vetoed it. This led to mutual recriminations.

Relations between star and author and producer became so strained
that they communicated only through semaphores. When visibility
was poor, I served as liaison officer, carrying water on both shoulders.
It's a tribute to my ancestors that I came through this melee
unscathed.

Trying to arrange a truce, I introduced Tallulah to Bleeck's, a
block south of the National. She was charmed by the Mission's infor-

mality and the nonchalance of the newsmen. Distracted by its tonics, her turbulence ebbed—until the next afternoon.

Why didn't I press agent *Clash by Night?*

I was suspicious of this work before I read it. If the Clifford Odets play had merit, why was Billy Rose producing it? Night-club triumphs didn't qualify him to duel with the drama. On reading the play, my suspicions were confirmed. Tallulah was to be a Polish hussy, wasting away on Staten Island for love of Joseph Schildkraut. Joe was a motion-picture operator whose projection booth would become his tomb once husband Lee Cobb discovered Tallulah's dalliance.

I told Rose of my doubts. In part he agreed with me. He had an antidote, he said. He'd have two grand pianos in the pit.

Michael Mok, lately ace reporter and feature writer on the New York *Post,* was press agent for Rose's Diamond Horseshoe. To publicize *Clash by Night,* Mike had to join the press agents' union. This set Rose back $535 for dues and initiation fees. No sooner had Mike been certified than Tallulah told Rose I must be the press agent. This ultimatum shriveled Rose's spine. Apprehensive of one press agent, he was threatened with two. After casing the combatants I decided I'd sit the fracas out. No good could come from this collusion. Tallulah wouldn't condone Rose's economies, his threats and his delusions of omniscience. I had other reasons for ducking. I scented a fiasco, perhaps a civil war. Though I was conditioned to flops and intramural strife, my participation could only embarrass Mok, an old friend.

Rose applauded my decision. I would have added to his overhead. Mike presented no such problem. His wage at the Diamond Horseshoe exceeded the press-agent minimum for a stage play, but no union regulated his activities there. Rose reallocated his Horseshoe wage so that it covered both assignments. In the eight weeks that *Clash by Night* huffed and puffed, Mike worked for nothing, a new minimum. But he was to profit by the experience. For years he's been general press representative for Rodgers and Hammerstein, the most hit-happy men in the trade.

Tallulah had other aversions. Her contracts outlaw benefit performances, favorite device of charitable organizations seeking funds.

Cued by John Wilson, I soaked up a lot of daiquiris in "21" trying to persuade her that fifty sold-out benefits would provide a handsome box-office backlog for the revival of *Private Lives*. I could have spared myself the hangover. Her refusal was explosive. She'd rather play to fifty people in the first four rows than submit to the stoics who make up benefit audiences. "They never applaud," she argued. "You couldn't thaw them out with an acetylene torch." Benefit audiences are the scourge of actors, but only Tallulah rejects them categorically. She alone can inflict her conviction on the management.

Private Lives? It ran for seven months at the Plymouth.

"May I bring Bill with me?" said Tallulah, when I asked her to lunch at "21."

Bill was William Langford, a young actor who had toured with Tallulah in *Private Lives* the previous season and who would play the role created by Laurence Olivier when the Coward comedy was revived six weeks hence.

I arrived at "21" on the dot. Tallulah awaited me.

"Where's Bill?" I asked.

"I sent him into the men's room to brush his hair," she replied. "I want him to make a good impression."

Tallulah has still another allergy—understudies. She favors them for other players, but bristles when one is suggested for her. She argues that no understudy could approximate her performance. An alternate would be a swindle. Producer Myerberg hired a young woman to ape Tallulah in *The Skin of Our Teeth,* and rehearsed her furtively. This hopeful never had an opportunity to test Myerberg's vision. Although Tallulah's co-stars, Fredric March and Florence Eldridge, were replaced when ill, Tallulah played over two hundred consecutive performances in the Wilder fantasy though racked with ulcers. What would have happened had Tallulah been forced to recess? I shudder to think. It's my guess that the detonation would have leveled Manhattan Island from Macy's to Grant's Tomb.

Tallulah's hapless proxy, I'm told, later made quite a stir on the screen. There she's known as Lizbeth Scott. I'll say one thing for Lizbeth. She gave a great impersonation of Tallulah in the Plymouth lobby.

Grasping at straws to stimulate the fading *Foolish Notion,* I asked Tallulah to submit to a radio interview with Mary Margaret McBride. Her refusal was curt and eloquent. When business continued to ebb, I asked her again. Millions of housewives hung on Mary Margaret's every word, I said. It was reasonable that some of them might race to the Plymouth after the set-to. To humor me, Tallulah agreed. Dedicated to the diversion, Tallulah went all out. Uproarious in her responses, she climaxed the session by snatching the commercials from Mary Margaret's hand, reading the whole mess and ad libbing asides that startled the sponsors.

Bristling with vitality and bursting with words, Tallulah can be a trial to those with conventional appetites and codes of decorum. Restless, driven by demons she can't define, she's the victim of hundreds of fictions. I don't think she's been in five night clubs in the last five years, yet the gossip columnists constantly place her in obscure cellars and dives. That's one of the penalties of a legend. Over that same period, I don't think she has written five letters. What's more, she doesn't open letters she receives. Addressing her through the mail is as chancy as placing a note in a bottle and tossing it overboard. When communicative, she lays waste long distance.

Quick to help an afflicted friend, Tallulah's ministrations sometimes boomerang. Harken to the testimony of Charles Mooney.

In the summer of '54 Tallulah was touring the summer theatres in *Dear Charles,* prior to bringing this antique to New York. Co-producer Richard Aldrich operated the Cape Playhouse at Dennis, Mass. Mooney was his manager. To clear up confusing items in Tallulah's New York contract, Mooney drove one hundred miles to Matunuck, Rhode Island. At midnight everything was ironed out. Mooney, about to depart, remarked that he was exhausted. How was he going to stay awake during the drive back to Dennis?

"Rose! Bring me my pills!" barked Tallulah.

Rose Riley, long in Tallulah's service, rushed in with what she calls "Tallulah's suicide kit." Tallulah handed Mooney a fresh highball and two pellets. "Gulp them down," she ordered. "They'll stimulate you. You'll get back to Dennis bright as a button." On his departure, Mooney crossed to the parking lot and entered his heap.

He came to five hours later. The sun was shining in his eyes. The scene was familiar. He was still in Matunuck. Tallulah, angel of mercy, had given him sleeping pills. Mooney was still nodding when he reported to Aldrich six hours late.

Indifferent to eminence and unawed by king or commoner, Tallulah pipes down when Ethel Barrymore is presiding, though they've been friends for thirty years. In her long reign in the theatre, Miss Barrymore dominated every stage she trod, every room she entered. She's matchless in her ability to wither an opponent with a glance. Her voice, her eyes, her gestures indicate her scorn for, and suspicion of, her adversary. She doesn't encourage familiarity. I'd no more address her by her given name than I'd yodel in a cathedral.

After being mired in dim dramas for twelve years, Miss Barrymore hit the jackpot as the Welsh schoolmistress in *The Corn Is Green*. Old associates and acquaintances stormed her dressing room. She flouted them, and their tributes, too.

"Now that I'm in a hit, people I haven't seen or heard from in years are banging at my door," she told me bitterly. "They're crawling out from under the rocks, and worming their way out of the woodwork. What scum!"

Miss Barrymore neither forgives nor forgets, as George Kaufman can attest. As chairman of a theatrical committee that was organizing a Bundles for Britain benefit at Radio City Music Hall, George sought the services of every star in New York. To add zest and variety to the tribute, George asked the headliners to forsake their conventional specialties for off-beat demonstrations. He persuaded Lily Pons to come over from the Metropolitan to sing "Minnie, the Moocher." To cap this, he schemed an interlude in which Ethel Barrymore, Ethel Merman and Ethel Waters would startle the congregation with a song-and-dance specialty. He was going to bill it as "The Three Ethels."

George called Miss Barrymore in her dressing room and outlined his plot.

"On what night does the benefit fall?" she asked.

"The second Sunday in April," said George.

"So sorry," she replied. "On that night I'm going to have laryngitis." The laryngitis gambit touched off a gong in George's head. As his memory thawed, his blood froze. "On that night I'm going to have laryngitis," was a line he and Edna Ferber had written for Julie Cavendish in *The Royal Family* a dozen years earlier. *The Royal Family* was a gay and irreverent caricature of the Barrymore clan and their fits and fevers. The comedy was a great success but Miss Barrymore loathed it. Thus she rejoiced at the opportunity to clobber Kaufman with his own prose.

Ethel Barrymore had been a star since she opened in *Captain Jinks of the Horse Marines* on February 4, 1901. Mulling this statistic after the opening of *The Corn Is Green,* I felt a celebration of her forty-year reign was in order. If Miss Barrymore would co-operate, I could kick up quite a commotion. I nudged the National Broadcasting Company. It welcomed the opportunity to salute so great a lady. If Lionel and John would participate, they'd salute Miss Barrymore in a one-hour coast-to-coast program on the night of February 4, 1941.

I told Miss Barrymore of my design six weeks in advance. She vetoed it without hesitation. But I knew from experience that her "no" was not final. It was a delaying action. It gave her time to mull. Two weeks later I prodded her again. This time she consented. She thought Alexander Woollcott should preside, failing Woollcott, Arthur Hopkins.

Enthused over a nationwide tribute to the star, I was chilled when the William Morris office told me Lionel's appearance was doubtful. Moguls from Metro-Goldwyn-Mayer pictures, the cartel to which he was indentured, reported Lionel in bad health. A five-minute testimonial to his sister might prostrate him. "He wasn't too sick to bellow Scrooge all Christmas Day," said Miss Barrymore bitterly. She condemned Lionel too hastily. Louis B. Mayer, Metro's all-highest, was trying to muscle into the act. The price of Lionel's appearance was a bid to Mayer. Though outraged at this squeeze, we agreed. The Mayer maneuver was characteristic of Hollywood's delicacy and manners.

Arthur Hopkins said he'd be proud to preside. He had presented

all the Barrymores, singly and in lethal combinations. He had the
respect and affection of all three. Possibly he was the only person
alive of whom this could be said.

As originally planned, a three-way ad-lib conversation between
brothers and sister would highlight the hour. An NBC sage questioned
this. "Did it occur to any of you the program may be off the air in
short order if Ethel, Lionel and John start to exchange compliments
and recriminations?" he asked. It never had. Scripts were prepared,
submitted for their approval, then edited and sandpapered.

The radio tribute to Miss Barrymore went off flawlessly. She was
eulogized by Helen Hayes, Hopkins, Herman Shumlin and other
stage notables. Woollcott's panegyric was funneled in from the stage
of Ford's Theatre in Baltimore where he was playing in *The Man
Who Came to Dinner*. At Alex's invitation, the audience at Ford's
sat in on his salute. The banter between Ethel, John and Lionel
fascinated millions. Mayer, horning in from Hollywood, said his
failure to keep Miss Barrymore in Hollywood after she appeared in
Rasputin and the Empress with Lionel and John was the great regret
of his life. On hearing this, the star bristled. Turning to the musicians
banked behind her in the studio, Miss Barrymore announced in
clarion tones, "That's a damned lie."

Miss Barrymore's fortieth anniversary was given acres of space.
She was interviewed by every newspaper in New York and by
the syndicates and wire services. Rival press agents complimented
me on the volume and quality of the homage. But there was a fly
in my ointment. Coincidental with this barrage, business for *The
Corn Is Green* tapered off. It's because of contradictions like this
that press agents can't be trusted with straight-edged razors.

Miss Barrymore was a fellow fan. Her devotion to baseball
was stressed the Sunday afternoon she entertained the cast of *The
Corn Is Green* at her home in Mamaroneck. To her dismay, the
guests started to filter in during the eleventh inning of a scuffle between the Dodgers and the Cardinals. Deep in Red Barber's play-
by-play report, she asked me to divert them until the tie was broken.
Couldn't I do a few bird calls? Card tricks? She'd be distraught until

she knew the Dodgers' fate. Masking my own concern—I'm a Cardinal man—I stepped into the breach. Her smile on her entrance ten minutes later indicated evil, i.e., the Dodgers, had triumphed.

Miss Barrymore is an authentic sports enthusiast. Calling her on a Thanksgiving morning, I was told she couldn't come to the telephone. When I apologized for so early an intrusion, I was disillusioned by her son Sammy. His mother was listening to the Brown-Colgate football game. "I see the Bums blew two today" was her greeting when I entered her dressing room on a September night in '41. This meant the Dodgers had dropped a double-header to Chicago. Miss Barrymore is a great fight fan. She risked sunstroke at the ringside in Toledo the afternoon Dempsey poleaxed Jess Willard. The game room of her Mamaroneck home had one of the finest collections of fight pictures in the country.

It was Miss Barrymore who capsuled Thomas E. Dewey with the observation: "How can anyone vote for a little man who looks like the bridegroom on a wedding cake?" though the remark was credited to Alice Longworth. A lifelong Republican, she joined Tallulah in rooting for Harry Truman when all but the diehards conceded in 1948. It pleased me when she endorsed Adlai Stevenson four years later.

Miss Barrymore seethed when Broadway was used as a synonym for New York. She thought Broadway cheap and noisy and vulgar. Her only visit to Bleeck's followed a radio broadcast in which she played a scene from *The Corn Is Green* with Emlyn Williams. Miss Barrymore spoke from a studio on Broadway, Williams from BBC in London. Bleeck's customers came to order as soon as she entered and remained in order throughout her stay.

I was surprised when she agreed to appear with me on *Information Please,* even more surprised when she agreed to play the piano. On the afternoon of the adventure, I called to reassure her about time and place. "Why did I ever let you trick me into this?" she said. "I wish I was dead." Her alarms were groundless. She delighted Clifton Fadiman, John Kieran and F. P. Adams with her responses. Tallulah, another knowing gal, shied away from this inquisition. So did Maurice

Evans. Trying to break down Evans' resistance, I assured him some of Fadiman's questions would involve quotes from Shakespeare. "That's what I'm afraid of," said Maurice.

I last saw Miss Barrymore at the opening of *The Cocktail Party*. She was in New York between screen assignments. She attended the T. S. Eliot riddle with an old friend, Herbert Bayard Swope. After the performance, I paid my respects. The play had thrilled her. "All our playwrights should be forced to see *The Cocktail Party*," she said. "Then they should go home and burn their typewriters."

Now flirting with eighty, still a classic beauty, Ethel Barrymore is one of the theatrical personalities of our century. Aloof and sardonic, defiant in defeat and victory, Miss Barrymore is a challenging and exciting lady. Association with her was stimulating. She kept me on my toes.

Ham is the theatre's word for excesses of conduct. It describes scenery chewers. It identifies those who distort and inflate their roles to smother competition. An actress thus afflicted makes a production out of peeling an orange or opening a window. Ham characterizes those with delusions of self-importance. Ham is a fluid word. It covers both genial show-offs and offensive exhibitionists.

A little ham is an asset to the actor. It contributes to his color and charm. But an all-out ham can be as obnoxious as a drunk on a roller-coaster. Ham is not peculiar to actors. All the theatre's workers are infected. The ham in the actor is more apparent because he has better opportunities to display it.

Paradoxically, this discourse on egomania serves to introduce Helen Hayes, who has less ham to the inch, less ostentation to the ounce, than anyone on the rolls of the Actors' Equity Association. Helen runs no fevers. She screams no protests. She fakes no ulcers. She has yet to menace the management with laryngitis. She does not demand an escort of native beaters when entering a restaurant or boarding a train. I first met Helen in '27 when she was the tragic heroine of *Coquette*. Sixteen years later, I was touting *Harriet* in which she impersonated the author of *Uncle Tom's Cabin*. In between I served *Mr. Gilhooley* and *Ladies and Gentlemen*, both unworthy of her. Thanks to her performances, *Harriet* and *Coquette* were enduring hits, though mediocre plays. Helen radiates courage, honesty and credibility. She can validate the most fatuous line through the authority with which she delivers it. In manuscript her final speech in *Harriet* was mawkish. Spoken by Helen, it sounded like the Gettysburg address.

Helen is slight, short and soft spoken and modest in dress. Offstage she could pass as an alert schoolmistress. She lacks the stature of Katharine Cornell and Ethel Barrymore and the personality of Tallulah. But once Helen steps on stage she is transformed. Her voice becomes vibrant and musical. She gives off a glow. Ben Hecht snared her essence when he wrote that Helen and Laurette Taylor were the two actresses capable of making an audience cry merely by standing still and smiling at it. As squat Victoria or as six-foot Mary Stuart, Helen Hayes was every inch a queen.

Shortly after the opening of *The Front Page,* Whitney Bolton agreed to interview authors Hecht and MacArthur and actor Lee Tracy, simultaneously. Bleeck's was the agreed locale. It was difficult to corral Hecht, MacArthur and Tracy at one time because of their habits. After three postponements, the trio swore they'd show up Tuesday. At eleven that morning, MacArthur popped into my office. "I can't make it," he said. "Something vital has come up. I can't tell you what it is."

When I denounced him for his treachery, Charlie swore me to secrecy. "Helen and I are getting married this afternoon." The union of the star of *Coquette* and the co-author of *The Front Page* had great space potentials, I pointed out. The story was sure to leak. Why didn't he let me sound the tocsin? "It won't leak unless you sell us out," said Charlie. "Helen wants complete privacy." With that I subsided, with this warning, "Don't tell me the time, place or the name of the clergyman. I don't want to take the rap when it does leak."

Helen and Charlie were made one before one of the greatest clutters of cameramen ever to bulge a judge's chambers. Charlie had sworn the wrong man to secrecy. It's my guess that he was betrayed by the judge who presided. Since it was unlikely he would have such an opportunity again, the crazed magistrate alerted all the city desks and photo-assignment editors on Manhattan Island. When news of the nuptials hit Chicago, newswoman Carol Frink, Charlie's former wife, screamed that he was the all-American bigamist. In retrospect I'm not sure that the judge blew the whistle. It could have been MacArthur, a man with an impish and perverse sense of humor.

Helen stunned me when she endorsed Dewey in the 1944 Presidential campaign. How could so sound a woman make so daffy a decision? I wired her in Boston expressing my grief and that of the theatre. She replied immediately: "I know. I should keep my mouth shut." She told me later that Dewey had convinced her he could end the war and stop the draft.

Throughout the run of *Harriet,* Helen drove to the theatre each day from the farm she and Charlie operated across the Hudson. I couldn't picture Charlie as a tiller of the soil. My suspicions were shared by Nunnally Johnson. Learning from a mutual friend that Charlie was a major in the Chemical Corps, Nunnally blurted, "My God! Aren't they afraid he'll drink it all up?"

To validate her role of farmerette, Helen shared her eggs with the players in *Harriet* and showered them with the fruits of her garden. The operation was unsound, she confessed. "I've figured out that our milk cost $8 a quart," she told me.

Seeking escape or security, stars are forever buying country homes in which they rarely live, thanks to the gypsy nature of their profession. This longing presents a paradox. They can only enjoy their retreats when idle, but if idle they can't afford them. While in *The Skin of Our Teeth,* Tallulah picked up an eighteen-acre estate at Bedford Village, thirty miles from New York, for a paltry $25,000. She swore Windows was her heart's desire. At last she had a roof over her head. Here she'd take root, she said. Here she'd die. Shortly she was disillusioned. A new well and a swimming pool set her back $35,000. Flower gardens, arbors and other knickknacks in keeping with her whims boosted her investment to $100,000. Three summers in a row she toured the strawhat theatres. When playing in New York, she holed up in a suite at the Elysee. Windows was a dream house—for her butler, cook and gardener. Two years ago she chucked the whole business for a town house in New York's East Sixties. She isn't there much, either.

Shirley Booth was Mrs. Loschavio, an Italian woman on a wayward ferryboat, when I met her in *Excursion*. It had been twelve years since she and Humphrey Bogart faced the New York critics in *Hell's Bells*. When our paths crossed again—*Come Back, Little Sheba*—Shirley, too, had turned farmer and bewildered me with talk about Guernseys, Poland Chinas and Leghorns. Shirley and her husband had surrendered to Bucks County, Pennsylvania, favored haunt of such grangers as Oscar Hammerstein and Robert Whitehead.

The New York critics voted Shirley's Lola Delaney in *Come Back, Little Sheba* the best performance of the year by an actress. Twelve months later, they cited her Aunt Cissy in *A Tree Grows in Brooklyn* as the season's best musical-comedy performance. Lola was heartbreaking, Cissy hilarious. The twin awards testified to her range and variety. No other actress has grabbed both. The two roles also won her a bushel of the medals, scrolls and trophies annually voted by clubs and societies in the throes of cultural cramps. She deserved them all. She grabbed an Oscar for her re-creation of Lola in her first screen assignment. Almost as versatile as Lawrence, almost as hamless as Hayes, Shirley rates prizes as a person.

In one scene in *A Tree Grows in Brooklyn,* a baby's cry had to be simulated from the wings. This business took place while Shirley was enjoying a ten-minute respite in her dressing room. But each night she interrupted it to ape the squawler. Why? Because no one could do it so well. It never occurred to her that a star was above so thankless an assignment.

Dropping in to see her one August night during the run of *A Tree Grows in Brooklyn,* I found her sweltering.

"Has the air-conditioner broken down?" I asked.

"No, it's working," she replied.

"Then why don't you turn it on? Do you want to suffocate?"

The air-conditioner gave her dog the sniffles. Sniffles might lead to pneumonia. Then why didn't she leave the dog at home? "He'd be lonely. That's why," she said. "My dogs miss me. One of them chewed up two volumes of John Dos Passos in my absence."

"Two volumes? I didn't know Dos Passos came in sets," I said.

Shirley explained. While idling in the late twenties, another player loaned Shirley *Manhattan Transfer*. The first night she read fifty pages. She skipped out early the next morning on the tip that Archie Selwyn was casting a new comedy. On her return, Towser had consumed *Manhattan Transfer* through page 256. Shirley knew that she must replace the book, an expense she could ill afford. To get it she'd have to forgo the subway and lunch at Liggett's counter. Armed with a new copy, Shirley felt she should finish the story. Another phone call. Another fruitless search for a job. No dog to ignore a coincidence, Towser went through *Manhattan Transfer* once more, cover to cover. Shirley has never read a line of Dos Passos since. Indeed, she only read half of *Manhattan Transfer*.

Shirley is no glamour girl. She might be your middle-aged maiden aunt. She'd provoke few whistles walking past the drugstore. Her idea of a wild time is a midnight snack at Sardi's. I can best describe Shirley's status by echoing Ethel Merman's estimate of Mary Martin. "All she's got is talent!" As the tragic heroine of *Sheba,* as the gambler's moll in *Three Men on a Horse,* as the luckless Ruth in *My Sister Eileen,* Shirley has shredded my emotions.

I wish I could say as much for Katharine Cornell. Many critics rate Miss Cornell our finest actress. She has been a star for thirty years. As Candida, Juliet, St. Joan and Elizabeth Moulton-Barrett, she's been cheered from San Diego to Boston, from Seattle to New Orleans. Yet Miss Cornell chills me in the theatre. Handsome, statuesque, well spoken and well tailored, Miss Cornell to me is all form and technique. Her performances lack warmth, humor and humanity.

My only association with Miss Cornell was in *Herod and Marianne,* one of her rare failures. The stagehands called this fragment of Judean history *Heroin and Marijuana.* You'll not catch Miss Cornell doing cartwheels on the mall, or badgering the Shuberts in print. She's as aloof and cloistered as Maude Adams.

There's evidence that Miss Cornell is a better judge of acting than I am. I press agented eight plays for her husband, Guthrie McClintic, over a five-year span. Some of these opened in Buffalo, Miss

Cornell's birthplace. There she attended the opening of *The Morning Star* in 1942. This import had such British players as Gladys Cooper, Jill Esmond, Cecil Humphreys and Wendy Barrie. A young actor named Gregory Peck undertook the role author Emlyn Williams had played in the London original. Miss Cornell enthused about Peck's performance. She was sure he'd go far in the theatre and motion pictures. I thought Peck awkward and miscast, out of his element amid those clipped English accents. I last saw Mr. Peck in *Roman Holiday* with Audrey Hepburn. He has improved. Now, at least, he looks like an actor.

The bones of actresses who have feigned Lady Macbeth pile higher than the remains of actors done in by Hamlet. The sleep-walking scene has a fatal fascination for ladies who should know better. The Scotch Jezebel has challenged Peg Wolffington, Mrs. Siddons, Fanny Kemble, Charlotte Cushman, Ellen Terry and Mrs. Pat Campbell. Thanks to Max Beerbohm, I can report that when *Macbeth* was first acted for King James in 1606, Hal Berridge, who was to impersonate Mrs. Macbeth, "fell sudden sicke of a pleurisie, wherefor Master Shakespeare himself did enacte in his stead." Max mined this bit out of Aubrey, English antiquarian.

Are you impressed by this show of research? I employ it to introduce Judith Anderson, the most eloquent and frightening Lady Macbeth ever I laid eyes on. (How many Lady Macbeths have I seen? Let's avoid statistics.) Judith and Laurence Olivier created quite a stir when they plotted Duncan's death at the Old Vic in '37. Four years later, she dwarfed Maurice Evans in his production of the tragedy in New York. Cheering this gave me a cultural glow. With the exception of the Irving-Terry revival in London in '88, the Anderson-Evans duplication ran longer than any *Macbeth* anywhere.

Judith is superb as a passion-racked sorceress in poetic tragedy. Give her a Medea, a Clytemnestra or a Lady Macbeth to sink her teeth into and she'll give you a performance of searing grandeur and black iniquity. She also scares the pants off you. Judith seems six cubits tall at the peak of a blank-verse tirade. Her eminence lends itself to cubits, rather than feet, since she's usually impersonating a legendary fury. Her Mrs. Danvers in *Rebecca* was the essence of evil. Unfortunately, for Judith, many think tragedy the dirtiest word in the dictionary. They associate it with empty seats and short runs. There's point to their aversion. Tragedies, classic or contemporary, rarely pay off. They're box-office poison. To thus identify a play is to solicit the kiss of death. Tragedy isn't the only word that terrorizes producers. They're suspicious of all categorical labels save "comedy" and "musical comedy." They shrink from "satire" and "farce" and "melodrama" as they would from the Loch Ness monster or the abominable snowman.

Not all their fears stem from thoughts of failure. "Satire" might lay them open to charges of counterfeiting. They recall George Kaufman's quip, "Satire is something that closes on Saturday night in Wilmington." By their confused standards, "farce" and "melodrama" are symbols of the cheap and second rate. Befuddled, they take refuge behind "a new play," an evasive slogan which minimizes the potential of guilt.

Press agents linked to tragedies thread a perilous path. However grim may be the proceedings, our overseers warn us to avoid mention of its doom-and-disaster items lest the public panic and bolt into the timber. Stress the play's comic phases, they cry. This presents problems to the wretch saddled with *Hamlet* or *Macbeth* or their modern derivatives. I bow to the man who can sell *Titus Andronicus* in terms of *Hellzapoppin.*

But to get back to Judith. Our first meeting was not auspicious. Desperation must have caused her to play Valerie Latour, ex-German spy, in *The Drums Begin.* I'm sure she knew it was doomed even as she started to rehearse. Indeed, I think I can prove it. *Drums* ceased to roll after eleven performances, but Judith had a four-week play-or-pay contract.

Twenty years after this catastrophe, *In the Summer House* supported us at the Playhouse. Jane Bowles's Freudian fable confused the clods and touched off considerable controversy. Judith's delivery of the ten-minute monologue which opened the play startled the faithful accustomed to seeing her in flowing robes and snorting fire.

After seeing the first performance in Hartford, I told Judith she should play the role for nothing. She delivered the opening tirade from a fifteen-foot balcony, an eminence which enabled her to face the audience and look down upon her associates. Her roost was a star's dream of heaven, I told her. She would be the envy of every actress who had upstaged a leading man.

I hope Judith comes to grips with Hamlet. She wouldn't be the first actress to take on the Dane. Charlotte Cushman undertook Hamlet, as did Sarah Bernhardt. So did Eva Le Gallienne, and there are codgers up on Cape Cod who saw her do it. I want to be in the audience when Judith first sights her father's wraith on the battlements. It should be quite an evening.

I think the actresses cited in this chapter privately would agree that Laurette Taylor was the best of our generation. Miss Taylor's death would cancel out dissents of those who might hesitate to crown a competitor. Miss Taylor led a tortured life following the death of her playwright husband, Hartley Manners. She was the despair of producers and authors eager for her services. Despite her lapses, despite her infrequent appearances in her last twenty years, at her best she had a magic unmatched by her peers. For the Irish girl who for years trod a *via dolorosa,* it was poetic justice that her greatest performance should be her last. Rarely has an actress been showered with such superlatives as greeted her performance in *The Glass Menagerie.*

I never met Laurette Taylor, but, like everyone else in the theatre, I was aware of her great gifts and grieved over the manner in which she dissipated them. All who knew her, all who worshiped her from afar, should read her tragic, heart-breaking story brilliantly told by her daughter, Marguerite Courtney, in *Laurette.* It's the best book about an actress I've ever read.

I have encountered a lot of gay and stimulating actresses, and my life has been gayer and richer because of them. Some of them have been shy and aloof, some rowdy and reckless. All are a little tetched. All have raw courage, otherwise they could not have endured. They have survived cold-water flats, six-flight walk-ups, drugstore lunches, the snubs of office boys, the barbs of critics, months of idleness, thoughts of suicide, the drudgery of stock, first-night horrors, family jeers, stagefright, hunger and black despair. Is it to be wondered that they are so jealous of their billing, that they fight with tooth and claw to maintain the rating they've won at such a bitter price?

I have twitted them, I have scoffed at their fevers and pooh-poohed their alarms. I've been annoyed by their suspicions, by their pets and peeves. But I salute them all. They have my respect and admiration. Only a clod would carp about the peccadilloes of such radiant ladies. Their occasional tantrums and revolts add to their glow. My life would be dull if they all conformed. If they have talent, I'm all for the rebels, for the convention flouters. They make the theatre exciting. And they make better copy. But the pretensions of the untalented and the inexperienced bore me. Temperament ill becomes an ingénue who hasn't starved in stock.

I've been thrilled by a lot of actresses who never achieved first-lady status. Though it's been over thirty years since I saw Mary Morris in *Desire Under the Elms,* her Abbie Putnam still is vivid in my mind. So, too, is Ethel Waters' Hagar in *Mamba's Daughters,* Eloise Stream's Pearl in *Broadway,* Haidee Wright's Fanny Cavandish in *The Royal Family,* Josephine Hull's Abby Brewster in *Arsenic and Old Lace* and Sara Allgood's Juno in *Juno and the Paycock.*

I've been torn by the heart-breaking dipsomaniacs of Patricia Collinge in *The Little Foxes* and Peggy Ashcroft in *Edward, My Son.* Maxine Sullivan's swing variation of "Loch Lomond" will linger in my mind after I've forgotten a half-dozen Ophelias. I can still see seventy-year-old Jessie DeMotte rehearsing astride a horse at three in the morning in the Hippodrome. I was moved by the Gaelic ballads of Ella Logan, crooned in an all-night bottle club just before dawn. To continue this alcoholic survey, my first drink of vodka was poured by Eugenie Leontovich while I was trying to solve her accent in *Twentieth Century.*

As a theatrical press agent, I have rewards beyond my wages and agreeable hours—the fun and excitement provided by the people whom I praise. Not every salesman is entertained while he works. Consider the Fuller brush man! Reflect on the press agent for the Teamsters' Union! Ponder the plight of the publicist assigned to gild the Chicago Cubs. They're all denied the song and dance and drama implicit in my chores.

Twice I've exulted on seeing an unknown redeem a shabby play with a radiant performance. Without Audrey Hepburn, *Gigi* wouldn't have lasted two weeks. Doomed, too, was *For Love or Money,* had it not been for June Lockhart. Neither June or Audrey had ever appeared in a play prior to these salvage operations. Their dramatic experience was confined to bit roles on the screen. Their grace and charm and youthful vivacity masked the flaws in both plays. Together Audrey and June almost destroyed the bricks-without-straw wheeze.

On their stage debuts both were snarled in screen contracts. June was a chattel of Eagle Lion, Audrey was a Paramount apprentice. Producer Bernard Straus, a novice, had borrowed June from Eagle Lion. Though tied to that company by an option-cluttered contract, her assignments had been trifling. But Eagle Lion pricked up its ears when June glittered in *For Love or Money.* It had harbored a find without knowing it, an old screen custom. As June's fame rocketed, so did Eagle Lion's clamor for her return. Citing a fine-type proviso in its contract with Straus, Eagle Lion snatched her from the play at the peak of its run. June went back to Eagle Lion, and oblivion. This was a dog-in-the-manger maneuver. It had no role for her and no prospects of a role. She remained idle for the rest of her sentence. Eagle Lion joined June in oblivion three years later.

Though hobbled by Paramount, Audrey fared better than June. When Paramount plucked her from *Gigi,* it spirited her off to Italy to make *Roman Holiday* with Gregory Peck. What's more, the picture was made. So was Audrey!

Though I capitalized on the youth and beauty of Audrey and June, I was oblivious to the potentials of Shelley Winters and Lena Horne when these unknowns inhabited *The Night Before Christmas* and *Dance with Your Gods.* Miss Winters' play passed away after nine performances, Miss Horne's after twenty-two.

I had never heard of Edith Piaf when Ben Marden and Clifford Fischer summoned me to herald her New York engagement in 1947. Virgil Thompson, then music critic of the *Herald Tribune,* briefed me on the Parisian street singer. "The best of her kind. Another Yvette Guilbert," he said. She had been the idol of the GI's in Paris after the liberation. Alone in front of a curtain, wearing a

simple black frock, this waif enthralled New York with her songs of
love among the lowly. To a Francophile like me, Piaf seemed the
embodiment of France, Marianne herself. In her husky vibrant voice,
I heard the drums at Marengo, snatches of the "Marseillaise" and
muffled bugle calls. The French language does things to my spine.
On hearing a train announcement in the Gare de l'Est in Paris, I
wanted to enlist in the Foreign Legion.

Two nights before she was to open, Piaf told Clifford Fischer
she must sing one song in English. The lingual fireworks that followed
made me regret my casual approach to Racine and Daudet. When
the exchange burned out, Fischer, in English, elaborated on the
treachery of Maurice Chevalier. Chevalier, he swore, had told Piaf
she must sing one song in English. Without it she would fail.
Fischer grew apoplectic all over again. Chevalier wanted her to sing
in English to ensure her failure, he said.

All this confused me. My research indicated Chevalier had discovered Piaf. I mentioned this to Fischer. This was a mistake. He
grew incoherent. The veins stood out on his head like treads on
a tire. To put an end to suspense, La Môme, as she was known to
her worshipers, stuck to her Parisian routines. I've since heard her
sing in English. Fischer was right. But I suspect that he may have
slandered Chevalier. I publicized the man in the straw hat on his
last visit to our shores. He sang half his songs in English. That was
a mistake, too.

But enough of heroines. Let's get on to the heroes. There are
fewer of them, they're less photogenic and most of them are aware
of their handicaps.

17

From Walter Huston to Rex Harrison

LONG on first ladies, our theatre is singularly short on first
gentlemen. No native actor has been credited with pre-eminence since
the distant day of John Barrymore and George M. Cohan. There
are no masculine equivalents for Bankhead, Cornell or Hayes. Lunt?
He's indistinguishable from Lynn Fontanne. Orson Welles? AWOL!
Paul Muni? His Clarence Darrow in *Inherit the Wind* was his first
stage role in New York in ten years. Fredric March? A split-
allegiance case, shuttling between stage and screen. Maurice Evans?
Begat in Britain! José Ferrer? Giving aid and comfort to the enemy,
i.e., the screen.

Each spring for the past nineteen years, *Variety* has polled the
New York drama critics to determine "the best of the season" in some
fifteen categories. Here are the actors cited over that span for "the
best performance in a play":

1938-39 Robert Morley in *Oscar Wilde*
1939-40 Alfred Lunt in *There Shall Be No Night* and Barry Fitzgerald
         in *Juno and the Paycock*
1940-41 Paul Lukas in *Watch on the Rhine*
1941-42 Burgess Meredith in *Candida*
1942-43 Alfred Lunt in *The Pirate*
1943-44 Elliott Nugent in *The Voice of the Turtle*

1944-45   Frank Fay in *Harvey*
1945-46   Laurence Olivier in *Old Vic Repertory*
1946-47   Dudley Digges in *The Iceman Cometh* and Fredric March in
          Years Ago
1947-48   Paul Kelly in *Command Decision*
1948-49   Lee Cobb in *Death of a Salesman*
1949-50   Alec Guinness in *The Cocktail Party*
1950-51   Claude Raines in *Darkness at Noon*
1951-52   José Ferrer in *The Shrike*
1952-53   Victor Moore in *On Borrowed Time* (revival)
1953-54   Lloyd Nolan in *Caine Mutiny Court Martial*
1954-55   Paul Muni in *Inherit the Wind*
1955-56   Michael Redgrave in *Tiger at the Gates*
1956-57   Fredric March in *Long Day's Journey Into Night*

Of the nineteen players laureled, only two were cited twice, Lunt and March. Morley, Guinness, Olivier and Redgrave were visitors from England. Eight—Lukas, Nugent, Kelly, Cobb, Raines, Nolan, Muni and Fitzgerald—were fugitives from Hollywood's cameras. Rarely are they bathed by foot and border lights. Frank Fay and Victor Moore were song-and-dance men. Of the five that remain, Dublin's Dudley Digges is dead, as is Paul Kelly. Aside from short spins at the City Center, Ferrer hasn't played in New York since brevetted for his performance in *The Shrike*.

Lunt, March and Meredith are the residue. Only Lunt and Meredith are constant in their devotions. Even these loyalists are buffeted about. In the 1956-57 season Buzz found shelter in a revival of *Major Barbara,* while Lunt scoured the country with Lynn Fontanne in *The Great Sebastians*. I'm sure both assignments were south of their heart's desire.

What's the moral of this evil arithmetic? The theatre is without gratitude. If it's false to its maids, it's downright ornery in its treatment of its males. Those eight fugitives from the screen all started in the theatre. In it they achieved their first success. They didn't desert the theatre. It deserted them. Their apparent defections are born of a desire to survive.

And that, my friends, is why our stage actors have no king, nor a pretender to the throne. There's no lack of regal timber in their ranks. What's lacking is the opportunity to reign. It would be awkward to inaugurate an idle actor.

Of the nineteen knighted in *Variety,* my vote goes to Barry Fitz-gerald for his Captain Jack Boyle in *Juno and the Paycock.* Alec Guinness' Unidentified Guest in *The Cocktail Party* is runner-up. Show money goes to Robert Morley for his impersonation of Oscar Wilde. Since I was a one-man claque for each of these, my judg-ment will be challenged. In the role of critic I present a paradox that would have daunted G. K. Chesterton. But press agentry is no profession for timid souls. Like Ajax, its practitioners must defy the lightning. The performances of Fitzgerald, Guinness and Morley were distinguished by their eloquence and humor and variety. All had great style. I'm partial to style. That's why I prefer Guinness to Olivier; that's why I rate George Sisler over Lou Gehrig.

Walter Huston and Rex Harrison bracket my thirty-two years in the New York theatre. I hymned Walter for his Ephraim Cabot in *Desire Under the Elms* in '25. Now I serenade Rex for his Henry Higgins in *My Fair Lady.* Few are fortunate enough to have their activities embraced by so skilled a pair. Mulling their merits, I find Huston and Harrison are paragons of courage. Huston had been thirty-five years in the theatre when he sang for the first time in *Knickerbocker Holiday.* Remember "The September Song"? Harrison had been acting for thirty-two years before he got his lyric start in *My Fair Lady.* This coincidence negates the wheeze that you can't teach an old dog new tricks.

In the interval between Walter and Rex I've flattered hundreds of actors of all ages, sizes and races. C. Aubrey Smith, yet to be knighted, was seventy-eight when I served him in *Spring Again.* The Belgian acrobat for whom I searched on Pier 56 was twelve. This imp, imported for the *Greenwich Village Follies,* vanished while his sire was going through customs. We found him in the steerage searching for his box of animal crackers. Elapsed time: three hours. For touting the tots in *Seventeen* and *A Tree Grows in Brooklyn,* I won the glares of their mothers.

I bragged about the altitude of a seven-foot giant in *Jumbo,* and the brevity of Andrew Ratousheff, three-foot shrimp in *The Skin of Our Teeth.* I've sounded off for a Spanish ventriloquist (Señor Wences), a Chinese magician (Long Tack Sam), the pride of Puerto

Rico (José Ferrer) and Dublin's Arthur Sinclair. In proof of my racial range I can cite adventures with France's Maurice Chevalier, Holland's Philip Dorn, Mexico's Romney Brent, Harlem's Canada Lee and Joseph Spurin-Calleia, the hyphenated Maltese. From Vienna came Oscar Homolka, whom I condoled in *Gray Farm,* and Helmut Dantine, who perished with Tallulah in *The Eagle Has Two Heads*.

I've clashed the cymbals for a distinguished corps from London's West End. In addition to those named earlier—Guinness, Morley, Olivier, Aubrey Smith—it includes Noel Coward, Emlyn Williams, Edmund Gwenn, Cedric Hardwicke, John Williams, Wilfrid Hyde White, Leo Genn and Robert Flemyng. Though I may be jugged for treason for saying so, this group cannot be matched in the ranks of the Actors Equity Association. English actors are better trained than ours. They have more respect for the language. They have more polish and style.

Of all the actors I've applauded, Emlyn Williams had the most desolate start—a pit boy in a Welsh coal mine. Paul Roebling, the Dauphin in *The Lark,* was luckier. On reaching his majority, he picked up two or three of the Roebling millions. Wealth isn't Paul's only peculiarity. He shuns interviews. I blanched when he told me he couldn't be photographed without the approval of his agent. I have a feeling Paul's delusions will be his undoing. Dauphins are not cast every day.

In successive Septembers Fred Finklehoffe and Paul Small produced *Show Time, Laugh Time* and *Star Time*. Finklehoffe was co-author of *Brother Rat*. He had schemed screen scenarios. He was married to Ella Logan. Small was a reformed acrobat, turned actor's agent. Because of his excessive tonnage, he'd once doubled for Paul Whiteman on the screen. Though big-time vaudeville had been pronounced dead with the closing of the Palace in 1932, Small and Finklehoffe thought it had been buried alive. With *Show Time, Laugh Time* and *Star Time* they hoped to revive it. They almost did.

Show Time was the best variety show I ever saw. Like its successors, it was long on talent and short on scenery. With George Jessel, Jack Haley, Ella Logan and the dancing De Marcos heading the bill, it was cheered by the critics and its thirty-week run at the

Broadhurst set a new record for vaudeville. I remember *Show Time* and *Laugh Time* best for two jokes. In the midst of Haley's monologue, a statuesque blonde whispered in his ear. Seemingly stunned, he came to the edge of the apron and whispered to the audience:

"Things look pretty black. She just told me Jessel's about to enlist."

Here Haley paused, looked into the wings on either side of the stage as if fearful of being overheard, then confided to the audience: "If Jessel's going to enlist, the Japs must be in the lobby."

Frank Fay, Bert Wheeler and Ethel Waters headlined *Laugh Time.* Wheeler's monologue was interrupted by another curvaceous stooge:

"Why aren't you in the army?" she demanded.

"I'm a father," bristled Bert.

"Before Pearl Harbor?" she challenged.

"Before Pearl White," he replied. (Who is Pearl White? Heroine of *The Perils of Pauline,* silent screen serial which fascinated America in 1915-16.)

The three *Time* shows were as informal as an Elks' picnic. The comedians pranked and ad-libbed outrageously. Jessel and Small played gin rummy in George's dressing room each night from eight-thirty to the final curtain. When a cue summoned George to the stage, he stuck his cards in his pocket and resumed play within seconds of his exit. Since Jessel was on and off repeatedly, play was sporadic. But Small was patient. Enforced recesses gave him more time to study his hand. But the interruptions vitiated Jessel's game. After a twelve-minute monologue and feigned telephone conversations with his mother, he found it difficult to remember Small's discards and pickups.

Haley, whose cell adjoined Jessel's, had a theory about this marathon gin game.

"Small thinks George is getting too much dough," he told me. "The gin game enables him to adjust his wage without altering his contract."

Constant exposure to Frank Fay fretted Bert Wheeler. Seeking surcease he'd dodge to Sardi's bar across the street. After a couple of bourbons, Fay seemed more tolerable. Though a megalomaniac with a genius for creating hostility, Fay was one of the most gifted

performers ever to tread a variety stage. Suave and sardonic, with a
superb sense of timing, Frank was an incomparable master of ceremonies. After a quarter of a century in vaudeville and musical comedy,
Fay routed the skeptics and conquered the critics with his characterization of dipsomaniac Elwood P. Dowd in *Harvey*.

Small was married to Estelle Taylor, former screen star and wife
of Jack Dempsey. Shortly after the opening of *Laugh Time,* a friend
questioned Estelle about Small's shrunken silhouette. "How did he
lose all that weight?" she asked. "Taking bows in the lobby," Estelle
replied.

Small and Finklehoffe assembled and tried out their shows in San
Francisco before bringing them to New York. On the eve of the
Star Time, I was summoned to their office, the curb in front
of the Majestic. "We're in a fix," they chorused. "The baggage car
carrying our scenery has gone astray. What should we do?"

"Don't worry about the décor," I said. "Dig up a cyclorama and
a back drop. I'll inform the critics of our misfortune. It may work
to our advantage."

Once the reviewers were seated, an usher handed them an
announcement which read:

THE FLY IN OUR OINTMENT!

Our scenery, in case anyone cares, was last heard of somewhere between
Las Vegas, New Mexico, and La Porte, Indiana. En route from San
Francisco, we fear it has met with foul play.

Want to hear more about our scenery? Well, you're going to. It was
and is, for all we know, a fusion of the best features of the Taj Mahal,
the late Joseph Urban, the Grand Canyon and Early Loew's State. At a
later date we may give it a special showing to satisfy nonbelievers.

In our extremity, we have whipped up such velour and lumber as was
available at the nearest salvage piles. If it's a little on the ersatz side
we know, in your vast tolerance, you'll understand. The show, as some
dope once illogically remarked, must go on.

— PAUL SMALL and FRED FINKLEHOFFE

In the next day's reviews this apologia got as much applause as
Lou Holtz, Benny Fields and the De Marcos.

The Small and Finklehoffe carouses and *Laugh, Town, Laugh,* a
commotion which embraced Ed Wynn, a flamenco dancer, a trick
mule and Smith and Dale, these are my variety adventures. I

mourn the passing of vaudeville along with every theatre-goer over fifty. For years it was the amusement manna of the masses. Vaudeville theatres littered the land from the Rio Grande to the Saskatchewan, their stages supported trained seals and cinnamon bears, tap dancers, burnt-cork comics and barbershop quartets; jugglers, acrobats and magicians; female impersonators, monologists and harmonica players; xylophonists, dog and pony acts and unicyclists.

Assured forty weeks' booking and a fee well beyond their conventional wage, such immortals as Sarah Bernhardt, Emma Calvé, Lily Langtry and Mrs. Pat Campbell vied with marmosets and mindreaders in our music halls. Sir Harry Lauder made four farewell tours of America. Keith's, Washington, provided relaxation for Woodrow Wilson throughout his stay in the White House.

The two-a-day was strangled by talking pictures. Overnight thousands of performers—bipeds, quadrupeds and winged vertebrates—were dispossessed. Some found shelter in stage shows, some in motion-picture cathedrals, some in night-club cellars. Many were reduced to eating their own young. In variety's heyday (1915-25), it boasted four thousand theatres. They've all gone the way of the mammoth.

The annihilation of vaudeville had repercussions in the theatre. It sealed an incubator in which were hatched Groucho Marx, Fred Allen, Jimmy Durante, W. C. Fields, Willie Howard, Will Rogers, Eddie Cantor, Al Jolson, Jack Benny, Joe Cook, Bert Williams, Ed Wynn and Charlie Chaplin. The first victim of vaudeville's passing was the musical revue. Gone are the Ziegfeld *Follies,* the *Scandals,* the *Vanities,* the *Greenwich Village Follies,* the *Music Box Revue,* the *Little Show,* the *Passing Show* and other annuals which flourished in the twenties and early thirties. These revues were lavishly dressed vaudeville shows festooned with girls, a musical score and song-and-dance flurries.

The headliners for these recurrent larks were recruited from vaudeville. A good many brought their material with them. This eased the concern over skits and blackouts. If skit or blackout laid an egg in the New Haven tryout, it was excised, pronto! A funny vaudeville act could be tossed into the proceedings without rehearsal. There was no anxiety about it clicking. It had convulsed audiences for years.

The screen, radio and, latterly, TV absorbed vaudeville's titans. The wages the Marxes, Bennys and Durantes command in radio and television put them beyond the reach of stage producers. Their comedians snatched by the enemy, the perennials perished of malnutrition. Today a producer who undertakes a revue qualifies for the loony bin. Recent specimens have been witless and expensive, and crashing bores. In the last dozen years there have been only two successful revues—*Call Me Mister* and *Lend an Ear*. Both operated on a low budget. No actor in them got over $500 a week.

The last revues for which I've blushed—*Bless You All* and *The Ziegfeld Follies*—lost $690,000. Had each run two more weeks, they would have lost $750,000.

But enough of this meandering! Before I went off on that vaudeville bender I was lamenting the wealthy groundling who high-hatted interviewers and photographers while impersonating the Dauphin.

Sir Laurence Olivier had a more understandable allergy. When I announced that he would star with Vivien Leigh in alternating performances of *Caesar and Cleopatra* and *Antony and Cleopatra,* hucksters charged at me waving sheaves of currency. Sir Laurence only had to testify to the miraculous properties of their lotions, ales and deodorants to pick up fifty or sixty grand.

During rehearsals I told Larry of the riches that awaited him. (Larry? That's the way I addressed him. Wasn't I one of the survivors of his *Romeo and Juliet* fiasco?) In cool but scornful words, he told me to bid the varlets begone. "A pox on their importunities!" he cried, or words to that effect. I applauded his disdain. Knighthood would be under a cloud if so conspicuous a peer affirmed the magic of a mouthwash.

Ten days after the opening of what the newspapers called "the Cleodramas," Olivier called me. Could I come to his dressing room that night? His voice was pregnant with misgiving. Something evil must be afoot if he couldn't discuss it over the telephone. Something evil was afoot. He had endorsed a cake, for nothing. After dismissing visitors and asking his dresser to step into the hall, Larry detailed his lapse.

Thrilled by proximity to a knight and his lady, a baker, three blocks north of the theatre, had whipped up a cake and sent it to the pair by messenger. "It was an excellent cake," said Larry. "Viv and I devoured it to the last crumb." The spell of the confection still on him, Larry dictated a letter of thanks. After signing it, he added this postscript: "It would have been even better with more banana in the filling."

Blown up to heroic size, his letter now blazed in the bakery window. How was he going to get it out? The crestfallen Caesar perked up when I reminded him that a letter is the property of the author. Only with his consent could the pastryman flaunt Sir Laurence's folly. When I told the baker of Olivier's embarrassment, he was devastated. He'd remove the offensive placard forthwith, he swore. "Would they like another cake?" he asked.

A handsome screen star in my charge wasn't so finicky. Throughout the run of a so-so comedy he badgered me about the failure of the Calvert whisky people to tap him for their Men of Distinction gallery. In my hero's lexicon only an Academy Oscar was preferable to a MOD decoration. Producer Vinton Freedley and columnist Danton Walker had been decorated by Calvert, he complained. Why not him? Why not, indeed, I echoed.

Tommy Mitchell, best known as Scarlett O'Hara's father in *Gone with the Wind*, is one of the saltiest actors in the theatre. I first collided with him when press agenting *Cloudy with Showers*, a comedy he plotted with Floyd Dell and in which he played the leading role. After performances we'd adjourn to Frankie and Johnny's, a roost half a block south of the theatre, to settle cosmic problems and cheer from afar the forays of the Sinn Fein.

Articulate and full of words—Latin words, bitter words and words of Alexander Pope—Tommy was more than a salty actor. He was a skilled author and director. He had a low boiling point. Tommy was born too late. As a rabble-rouser he would have matched Danton or Marat. He belonged on a barricade with a brick in his hand. His barroom philippics stunned customers into silence. When inflamed his comment on the weather had the fire and thunder of

the "Curse of Rome" speech in Bulwer-Lytton's *Richelieu*. He's
a rare companion.

Cloudy with Showers had been closed for a year before I heard
from Tommy again. Betty answered the phone. "Who is calling?"
she asked. "Mr. Frohman," was the reply. "Speed without delay
to the Morosco," said Tommy. "Matters of great moment impend."
In a hutch atop the theatre I found Tommy and Louis Weitzenkorn,
one-time Sunday editor of the New York *World* and author of *Five
Star Final.*

"Louis and I are about to produce *Forty-Nine Dogs in a Meathouse*," said Tommy. "We want you to publicize it." Though suspicious of a pastoral with such a title, I agreed. When would the play
go in rehearsal? When could I have a script? Tommy ignored these
trivia. "Before we go into details, let's seal our association with
a drink," he said. Fifteen hours later, Betty called the Missing Persons
Bureau. Her husband had been mislaid, she said.

It was ten years before Mr. Frohman called me again. "Come post
haste to the Savoy Plaza," he cried. "Your hour has struck! All is
forgiven! I await you with open arms!"

He'd luxuriated too long among the lotus eaters, said my friend.
He was fed up with the fleshpots. A murrain on Hollywood! The
theatre was his first and only love. Contrite and humble, he was
returning to it.

He handed me *I Am I*. Tommy was the author. He would star in
it as soon as he could open an office, book a theatre, and assemble
a cast. My pledge to serve him set off a salvo of toasts. The next
afternoon, the Lost and Found Office of the New York, New Haven
and Hartford denied I'd left a manuscript on the midnight to
Westport. I knew I had. I sketched some of the plot. "There's a
corpse under a sheet in the living room, stage center, when the
curtain rises on the second act," I said.

"What was the name of the play?" asked the L. and F. man.

"*I Am I*," I replied.

"Who do you think you're kidding?" said my opponent. "I haven't
time for practical jokes."

Forty-Nine Dogs in a Meathouse and *I Am I*? After those duels with Mitchell I never heard of either again. I'm not sure *Forty-Nine Dogs* existed. I never saw the script. All I remember about *I Am I* is that stiff in the parlor. I discovered him just as the train pulled into Stamford.

I'm not the only press agent who's been engaged to herald a mirage. Two hundred productions are listed in pre-season prospectuses. Three-quarters of them will never find a stage. These hoaxes are not announced in malice, nor with intent to deceive. Often their sponsors can't raise the moolah. Some are the fruit of wishful thinking. Some are symptoms of desperation. A declaration of intent may rouse investors, thus relieve the shoestringer of the onus of soliciting in the streets.

Of all the stars I've bugled, Maurice Evans is the canniest businessman. He knows more about wage scales, costs of materials, box-office trends and budgets than any other player in our theatre. He's the only actor-manager currently functioning. He amassed a fortune in successive productions of *Dial M for Murder, Teahouse of the August Moon* and *No Time for Sergeants.*

Dial M for Murder had recovered its production cost at the end of its third week in New York. By managerial standards this was a fiscal miracle. Even with standee business, few plays get out of the red in less than three months. Sellout musicals are fortunate to regain their cost in six. Thanks to Maurice's concern with the overhead, *Dial M* showed a profit for its tryout engagements in Hartford and Washington, a coup which stunned his contemporaries. Cool and contained and inconspicuous, Evans plots a production with the precision of an engineer and with an awesome respect for minimum expense. In a business in which estimated costs are a mockery, in which rehearsal bills in New Haven may exceed the receipts, Evans is a model of frugality. He rates a monument in Central Park for still another triumph: He made Shakespeare pay, a feat unmatched in our century.

While I was having cocktails with Evans during a rehearsal break of his four-hour *Hamlet,* Larry Hart, then Gilbert to Dick Rodgers' Sullivan, came to our table. Hart was an ardent classicist. We talked of Hamlets of other days—Irving, Beerbohm Tree, Booth, Barrymore and Alec Guinness, about to undertake the Dane in London in modern dress. Mention of another notable Hamlet caused the impish Hart to cry out, "I couldn't tell which one was Ophelia."

During World War II, Evans was in charge of Army Entertainment in the Central Pacific Area. On his return, he told me of an open-air performance of *Hamlet* for an audience of Marines. Nothing untoward developed, he said, until he delivered, "Thus conscience does make cowards of us all, and thus the native hue of resolution is sicklied o'er with the pale cast of thought." Before he could continue, a Gyrene piped up, "You can say that again, brother!"

The war with the Japs was a minor issue, Evans said. "The real war in the Pacific, waged with relentless fury, is between the press offices of the Army, Navy and Marine Corps."

Evans towers above his peers in his ability to fuse art and commerce successfully. Steeled by their agents, many stars can be tough in negotiating wages and terms of employment. But in speculations outside the theatre they are kin to the crapshooter rather than to Andrew Carnegie. Ruled by emotions and prey to superstition, they're hunch players. U. S. Steel common is not for them when Continental Chowchow is available at $2 a share.

Consider Ed Wynn, the man with the acrobatic eyebrows and the nervous giggle. While press attaché for his *Boys and Girls Together,* I was summoned to Ed's Park Avenue hideaway to discuss ads, posters and other box-office stimuli. The agenda was scuttled before I could remove my coat. Ransacking his desk, Wynn handed me a canceled check for $260,000, made out to the Collector of Internal Revenue. He had mislaid another for $250,000, made out to the same payee.

"A nice round sum," I said. "I didn't know you were making that kind of dough."

"Bear with me," said Ed. The tale he unfolded iced my marrow. "Remember *The Laugh Parade?*" he asked. I did indeed. I succeeded Robert Sisk as its press agent in '32. Ed produced this hilarious hit and starred in it. "Remember *The Fire Chief?*" I saw Wynn's first performance in this radio show on the Amsterdam Roof. Between revue and radio show, said Wynn, he was netting $12,000 a week. Since he was a mathematical noodlehead, Wynn gave one of his relatives power of attorney. His kinsman, a self-confessed financial wizard, filed Wynn's tax returns and invested his loot in "blue chip" stocks.

Ed's experiment in nepotism was catastrophic. His relative's reports to the tax people were inadequate. Omissions lead to penalties and adjustments—a half a million dollars' worth. To compound his folly, Wynn bought a radio station. Before he could disentangle himself from this beacon, he sloughed off another fortune. The blue-chip stocks paled. In view of these calamities, perhaps the problems of *Boys and Girls Together* were petty, Ed suggested. I agreed.

Ed had other anxieties. One of them was his son, Keenan. Ed thought Keenan was hexed. In his first stage adventure, Keenan appeared in two roles. To mask his deception, he used an alias for the lesser one. The impostor drew the praise of the reviewers, while Keenan was ignored. Ed thought his heir should be exorcised. Astride a motorcycle, Keenan was a greater scourge than Genghis Khan. When he told his father that he wanted to go into the theatre, Ed replied, "What will you do in the theatre? Ride your motorcycle up and down the aisles?"

Flouting parental aid, Keenan persisted. In '39 he could be seen in *One for the Money* with two other hopefuls, Alfred Drake and Gene Kelly. I was promoting this revue.

"How's Ed?" I asked Keenan one night.

"He isn't talking to me."

"Why?"

"You'll never believe it, but it's gospel," he replied.

"Guess who was in the audience this afternoon?" Keenan had greeted Ed on returning home after a matinee.

"Who?" asked Ed, flourishing his eyebrows.

"Frieda."

Frieda was Wynn's second wife.

"How do you know?" his father asked.

"I saw her in the fourth row during my second-act number."

"What did you do?" asked Ed, eyebrows in convulsions.

"What did I do? I went on with the number. What should I have done?"

"You should have walked off the stage," thundered his father.

Erratic in his financial and marital speculations, Ed also defied craft conventions as actor-manager. When the straight man in *Boys and Girls Together* was stricken, the idle Keenan was summoned to replace him. Eager to impress his sire, Keenan pounced on the stage manager.

"Give me a script," he said. "We'll run through my lines and cues and business."

"I know all your lines and business," said the stage manager. "I'll give them to you orally."

"I'd rather do it from a script," insisted Keenan.

"I can't let you have a script," his opponent stammered.

Keenan bristled. "Why not?" he yelled.

"Because there isn't any," was the reply.

Boys and Girls Together didn't need a script. Wynn was on stage all night in a succession of monologues. When mute, he got knotted up with acrobats and jugglers. When Jane Pickens burst into song, he accompanied her on a three-wheeled piano, the easier to pursue her. Most comedians are arrogant. They reek superiority. They pout when the audience doesn't respond. Other players are the butt of their barbs. Wynn reversed this formula. He was apologetic. He professed awe of the audience. He was childishly eager to please. Though the star of the proceedings, he assigned himself the meanest tasks.

About to introduce his show girls, Ed paid tribute to their beauty, discussed their origins and ambitions, and dwelt on the expense incurred in trapping them. Then he mounted a thirty-foot stair, got down on his hands and knees, and rolled a red carpet down to the footlights that his houri might have a fashionable entrance. At the rim of the apron, now flat on his stomach, he raised his head, whinnied his satisfaction, and said, "You won't catch Katharine Cornell doing this."

There's another reason why I rank Wynn, Chaplin and W. C.

Fields as the great clowns of our time. Ed's never committed a vulgar act nor uttered an off-color line in his fifty years in the theatre. It's pleasant to report that he's adding to his laurels as a dramatic actor in television. Keenan's doing all right, too.

No list of prodigals is complete without Orson Welles. Orson agrees with Francis Bacon that "money is like muck, no good except it be spread." Elsewhere I've dwelt on Orson's crash when he tried to telescope four of Shakespeare's plays in *The Five Kings*. As press agent for *Native Son,* I was impressed by his contempt for costs and budgets and his indifference to overtime and other expensive penalties. In gratitude to Canada Lee for his superb performance, the management presented the Negro star with a new car. Four gold stars blazed on its front door—a duplication of the symbol employed by *News* critic Burns Mantle to indicate exceptional merit. Canada didn't have the car long. When payment installments lagged, the finance company took it away.

Five years later, Welles came a cropper again with *Around the World,* a musical extravaganza fashioned from Jules Verne's *The Tour of the World in Eighty Days.* Job's ordeals were trifling compared to the shocks and mishaps that bedeviled Welles from the start. He had written the musical's book. Michael Todd, the ersatz Ziegfeld, was to produce it. Reading the fine type in his contract, Orson came upon a clause which stated Todd was to have artistic supervision of the musical. Revolted by this effrontery, Orson bolted.

Divorced from Todd, Welles decided to put the musical on alone. The first requisite was $200,000, an underestimate of the sum necessary to set this gargantua in motion. Devoted to art, Orson approached this sordid chore casually. Required to put up bonds covering two weeks' salaries for actors, stagehands and musicians, and pay out advances to designers, arrangers and orchestrators, Welles raised the money through guest appearances on radio networks programs. His fees for these trifles ranged from $5,000 to $10,000. (I first met Welles on a radio show. When his Mercury Theatre of the Air put on a condensation of *Twentieth Century,* I received fifty fish for a guest appearance and some eerie banter with Elissa Landi.)

Rashly Orson put *Around the World* in rehearsal while still

$100,000 shy of his goal. In desperation, he sold the screen rights (this is called a pre-production deal in the trade) to Alexander Korda, British film magnate, for $100,000. But he couldn't use this alien coin until he had raised the complete sum for which *Around the World* was capitalized.

Orson described his next coup as "mortgaging my blood." He got large advances from Jack Cohn of Columbia Pictures for agreeing to star in feature films at a later date. These sums and such wampum as he could snatch from the unwary were shoveled into the show.

In addition to writing and producing *Around the World,* Welles was directing it. With an eye on the record of Hercules, he took on another assignment in New Haven. Irked by the performance of the actor playing Dick Fix, Welles played the part for a performance that the wayward mime might have a better notion of its potential. The actor took the next train back to New York after seeing Welles's demonstration. He said he could never approximate Welles's rich and racy impersonation. Welles was Fix for the duration.

Invading New Haven, Boston and Philadelphia, prior to New York, *Around the World* experienced heavy losses. The stages in these cities couldn't accommodate all of his scenery and properties— he had a three-carload surplus of lumber, wire and canvas.

It required fifty-five stagehands to maneuver the thirty-six scenes in Welles's supercolossal. The travelogue embraced a Hindu suttee with elephants and burning ghat, a Japanese circus featuring a slide for life and a yardful of ducks, a train racing over a collapsing bridge at Medicine Bow, a salute to Britannia involving a platoon of Marines and a life-sized eagle snatching up the hero, and Welles's magic act. In this last, Welles caused doves to materialize in an empty net, skewered a dancing girl with his rapier and produced aces of spades from unlikely ears. He rehearsed this act after hours in Al and Jack's bar across the street.

Welles elected the evening of Decoration Day for the New York opening. (Holiday nights traditionally are the worst in the theatre year.) The Shuberts had promised Welles an air-conditioned theatre. Instead they gave him the Adelphi, in hot weather an approximation of a Methodist hell. *Les frères* Shubert had to go to a lot of trouble to negate their pledge. To provide Welles with this inferno they had to dispossess Ray Bolger and *Three to Get Ready* and move them to the chilled St. James.

Despite these evil omens, Wolcott Gibbs and John Chapman cheered *Around the World* as a spectacular roughhouse. One critic said it had everything but the kitchen sink. Welles remedied this oversight immediately. On the second night, he made his entrance with a kitchen sink. With the show open, Welles sought new outlets for his creative urge. Since it required thirty-six musicians to interpret Cole Porter's tunes, Welles felt he should provide them with further employment. Overnight he whipped up a cantata version of *King Lear,* which he hoped to show on Tuesday, Thursday and Saturday afternoons. This project was vetoed by six unions.

There was no Friday-night performance of *Around the World* since Welles had a radio show that night at ten. Irked by this conflict, Orson conceived a solution. Instead of doing the radio program at the CBS studio, he'd do it on the stage of the Adelphi. He'd recess *Around the World* at 9:55, then resume at 10:35. His audience would see two shows for the price of one. This proposal went the way of the cantata variation of *Lear,* and for identical reasons. The prodigal had another radio show on Sunday afternoon—*Orson Welles's Almanack.* On the Sabbath following the opening of *Around the World,* he invoked a vodoo curse on the critics who had found his musical slated.

Aside from these multiple activities Welles was writing *If I Die* for Columbia Pictures, and scheming two films for Korda. Badgered and beggared, Welles's ordeal reached a climax each Saturday afternoon, when he had to pay off actors, stagehands, musicians and staff. A $5,000 bite on his butler-dresser enabled him to hurdle one weekend. Toots Shor stood for a $5,000 tap for another. Throughout the run Welles drew no salary. But his sacrifices and magic were to no avail. When *Wellesapoppin',* as it was facetiously called, adjourned its losses were roughly estimated at $400,000. Estimates on Welles's adventures are always rough.

The curtain is now lowered to denote the lapse of ten years.

Welles is back in New York after eight years of voluntary exile in Europe. In that interval he has played Macbeth with a Scotch accent, toured Western Germany in his own version of *Dr. Faustus,* starred in Paris in one of his own works, *The Unthinking Lobster,* made *The Third Man* film in Vienna (remember the zither music?), and aroused the London reviewers with *Moby Dick.* He adapted the Melville classic, directed it, schemed the scenery and impersonated the ivory-legged Captain Ahab.

Shortly Martin Gabel and Henry Margolis, for whom I had touted *Reclining Figure* and would tout *Hidden River,* confessed they had financed Welles's pursuit of the white whale. What's more, they'd seen it and liked it. More startling intelligence followed. They had ransomed Orson and shortly would present him in alternating performances in *King Lear* and *Volpone.* This repertory fluctuated daily after the prodigal's return. One day it included *Twelfth Night* in modern dress, another the aforecited *Moby Dick.*

Gabel suggested I call on the great man in his quarters at the Volney. I was the bearer of good tidings. Ed Murrow wanted to interview Orson on his *Person to Person* TV show. The chat with Murrow would provide him with an opportunity to discuss his repertory before millions of fairly discriminating folk. Orson liked Murrow. But he'd rather do the interview after he'd opened, he said. His amendment wasn't sound. *Person to Person* was heard every Friday night from 10 to 10:30, at which hour Welles would be bellowing at Cordelia or circumventing Mosca.

Stimulated by my talk with Welles, I left after three hours and four Scotches. I said I'd call him the next day about *Person to Person.* "Don't call me," said Orson. "I'm allergic to telephones. Can't talk over them." "How will I communicate with you, sire?" I asked. "Skywrite over the Volney?" "Address me through the mail," he said. "You'll get a prompt reply."

I returned to my office and wrote Orson a letter. When could he appear on the Murrow show? Two days later he replied: "I guess I didn't make my TV situation clear to you. The fact is I cannot consider doing anything. Not even Ed Murrow's show. Not until after our opening in New York."

At a council of war in Sardi's, I reminded him again that, once his rotating plays opened, he couldn't appear on the Murrow show unless he canceled a performance. He arched his eyebrows and roared with laughter. Three pictures fell off Sardi's rear wall. "Another thing, Orson. This telephone allergy! What if a *crise* arises? Matters of great moment might be dissipated while the postman loitered."

"There's point to your protest," said Orson. "Once a *crise* arises, dilly-dallying is out of order. Call me only if it's a matter of life and death. I'll arrange a code with the Volney switchboard. When you call, don't ask for me. Ask for Suite 662. I'll instruct the operator to put such a call through to me."

Crises are a dime a dozen when allied with Orson. One popped up the next afternoon. I called the Volney. "Give me Suite 662," I told the operator.

"Mr. Welles isn't taking any calls," she replied.

I continued to heckle him about Murrow through the mail. Tipped off he was lunching with Margolis in the Oak Room at the Plaza, I trapped him during the salad course. Orson had a new set of objections. "Murrow interviews subjects in their homes," he said. "I haven't got a home."

"Murrow will interview you in a subway kiosk if you'll name a Friday night," I countered.

"I can't name a Friday night," said Orson. "Mrs. Welles is about to have a baby. She might have it on a Friday night. Would Murrow interview me in the hospital?"

"How about the Volney?" I replied.

"My suite at the Volney isn't big enough for Mrs. Welles, the baby and me."

"What baby?" I asked. "Murrow only wants to talk to you."

I enlisted the aid of Henry Margolis. He has his finger in a lot of hotels. He assured me he'd get a suite for Welles at the Sulgrave, if I could pin him to a date.

Welles couldn't be pinned. After Mrs. Welles's daughter was born, I tried again to crash Orson's blockade. I didn't get beyond a secretary. Fed up, I called John Aaron, co-producer of the Murrow show at CBS, and told him we'd better forget the whole thing. He agreed. I apologized for my mercurial patron, and his procrastination. Aaron understood. The year before, Welles, without a dime, had turned down a $2,000,000 offer from CBS for a series of spectaculars.

This was the second time within two months that Aaron had been fouled up through the nonfeasance of one of my clients. Early in September, following three or four telephone calls to Paris, I persuaded Maurice Chevalier to submit to a Murrow interview on the eve of his engagement at the Lyceum. His chat with Murrow would stimulate the box-office sale tremendously. This coup was strangled by Chevalier's TV agent. To quote *Variety:* "Don Sharpe, radio-TV packager, axed the Murrow shot (1) on the allegation 'NBC' wouldn't like it, because (2) Chevalier is set for a NBC video spectacular, and (3) Murrow is CBS, hence opposition." The weekly then added: "Richard Maney, press-agent for Gilbert Miller's presentation of Chevalier, couldn't see it that way and told off Sharpe in his characteristic brand of flats-and-sharps language."

A half hour after conceding defeat to Aaron, I had a call from Orson's secretary.

"Mr. Welles will be glad to appear on Murrow's show on Friday night," she said.

"Where?" I asked. She didn't know.

"Let me talk to Orson," I said.

"He isn't talking any calls," she replied.

I hung up and called Aaron immediately. Since I had conceded defeat, he might have bagged another guest.

"Forget that call of half an hour ago," I said. "I have it on the unsupported word of Orson's secretary that he'll confront Murrow on Friday night, November 25."

Aaron laughed ghoulishly. "Fine," he said. "When can he have lunch with Murrow? And where will the interview take place? We must case the joint to determine the necessary equipment."

I told John I was withdrawing from the tournament. I gave him the phone number of Welles's secretary. Marie Torre, radio-television editor of the *Herald Tribune,* commenting on the Welles-Murrow hide-and-seek, wrote two days later: "All that the 'Person to Person' people have to do today is to find out if Welles has an apartment, and if he has one where it is, and begin setting up for the Friday telecast. They expect to learn, too, whether Mrs. Welles will be on the show now that she's no longer pregnant. 'From a time standpoint,' said Mr. Aaron, 'it's not unusual for us to begin working on a subject's home on Monday for a Friday telecast. What is unusual is to have a subject who doesn't know where he lives.' "

The interview came off in a suite at the Sulgrave. Orson was eloquent and impressive and majestic. He introduced his wife, Paola Mori, and whipped out a picture of twelve-day-old Beatrice Judith Welles, asleep in the next room.

Three days before Welles's dialogue with Murrow, New York's Mayor Robert Wagner greeted Orson at City Hall and announced to newsmen that shortly Mr. Welles would appear at the City Center for six weeks in alternating performances of *King Lear* and *Volpone*. The news stories carried another significant line: "Henry Margolis and Martin Gabel, who are responsible for Mr. Welles' return to this country, consented to postpone their Broadway plans for him 'as a friendly gesture to the City Center.' "

A friendly gesture? To me it sounded more like a sigh of relief. Though Gabel and Margolis had tremendous respect for Welles and his talents, they couldn't harness him to any definite plan. His visions extended beyond their periphery and their purse. They fluctuated wildly from day to day. Indeed, they started to fluctuate shortly after Mayor Wagner's announcement.

His voice tense with excitement, Margolis called me one night as I was about to take off for Connecticut.

"Is there time to get an announcement in tomorrow's papers?" he asked.

"Ample time," I said. "What's the story?"

Henry was calling me from Toots Shor's, where he'd spent the afternoon with Welles and Jackie Gleason. Everything had been very festive. The two titans were *en rapport*. In proof of their mutual esteem, they were to co-star in *Volpone*. That was the story.

"Co-star for whom?" I asked. "You and Martin? Or the City Center?" Henry said they hadn't discussed that.

I told Henry I wouldn't be a party to such a hoax. The marquee was yet to be built which could support both their names. "The story is a cinch," I said, "but who will write the retraction?" Henry said he'd call me later with more details. I didn't hear from him. Gleason's press agent didn't wait for details. The story flared on next day's drama pages. And the Welles-Gleason collusion ended with the closing of Shor's that night. It was never heard of again.

What happened at the City Center? Welles played *King Lear* for three weeks. He played it in a wheel chair. He had insisted on a raked stage. Rehearsing on this treacherous terrain, he had fallen and broken his ankle two nights before the opening. On opening night, he sprained his other ankle. The City Center faithful couldn't condone a chair-locked Lear. As customary in Welles's ventures, the City Center's budget was riddled. *Volpone?* It never went into rehearsal.

Welles is one of the most gifted men I've encountered in the theatre. He breeds excitement and confusion. I suspect that the stage is too puny an arena for his inspirations. Costs and restrictions on time and space cramp his style. Profits are repugnant to him. To function at his peak he needs the support of the Ford Foundation.

If Welles is charged with confidence, his Hollywood brothers are ravaged by doubt. Sought for stage roles in New York, they're paralyzed by fear of failure. All of them would give an arm for a New York triumph, but few can steel themselves to the gamble. When Robert Morley fled *Edward, My Son* at the peak of its run, Gilbert Miller persuaded urbane George Sanders to take his role. Miller felt that Sanders' screen note would compensate for Morley's exceptional performance. On the eve of rehearsals, Sanders succumbed to funk. Convinced he couldn't match Morley's characterization, he begged off.

Boris Karloff, long the screen's leading ogre, came down with the willies after rehearsing for a week in *Arsenic and Old Lace.* Anguished at the prospect of facing a live audience, he pleaded for his release that he might return to the cameras. Producers Lindsay and Crouse reassured him in a pep talk that would have done credit to

Knute Rockne and solaced him with a piece of the play. He rewarded them with a top-drawer performance. During the Christmas tryout week in Baltimore, I talked him into playing Santa Claus for the city orphans, a contradiction that made all the wire services.

With *Arsenic and Old Lace* a New York sellout, Lindsay and Crouse bagged Eric Von Stroheim, another screen menace to head the Chicago company. As in the case of the original, this duplication opened in Baltimore. At the end of the first act on the opening night, von Stroheim announced that he was taking the next train back to California. After thirty years' success on the screen, he said, he didn't propose to submit to such abuse in his first stage role. "What abuse?" we all asked. "I was hissed all through the first act," he raged. "Why didn't someone put a stop to it?"

In the nick of time a stagehand named the culprit. The hisses came from a leaky off-stage radiator. This monster muffled, von Stroheim went on to Chicago, head high.

Actors are sensitive folk. Slurs on their skill leave open wounds. Consider the strange case of James Barton, for years the Jeeter Lester of *Tobacco Road.*

Barton was Hickey, drunkard turned evangelist, and Dudley Digges was Harry Hope, proprietor of a scabby waterfront saloon, in *The Iceman Cometh,* first new Eugene O'Neill play in a dozen years. At the première Barton's performance was ragged. His lapses threw the proceedings out of focus. Pondering its tour of subscription cities, Lawrence Langner and Terry Helburn, Theatre Guild directors, thought the play would profit if Digges and Barton exchanged roles. This switch called for diplomacy. It could only be made with Barton's approval since he had a run-of-the-play contract.

After a two-hour discussion in a restaurant near the theatre, Barton agreed to the shift. About to affirm it with his signature, Jim's hand was stayed by a gratuitous jibe.

"Now that it's all over, Jim, you must confess you fouled things up on opening night," said Langner.

Barton was enraged. He said he'd see the Guild and all its executives in hell before he'd switch roles. Having assured Digges he'd be the touring Hickey, the Guild was obliged to get a new Harry Hope and pay both him and Barton. Burned because they had to pay Barton while he loafed on Long Island, the Guild bigwigs were prostrated on learning they had to raise his salary for the tour he would not make. The raise was obligatory under the terms of his contract. Barton may be the only actor alive to get a pay boost while idling.

Every acrobat wants to play Hamlet. That's one of the theatre's oldest axioms. Though I've never polled the contortionists, I can testify that Lou Holtz feels he'd be at home at Elsinore. Mr. Holtz, Palace Theatre hero and a veteran of three of George White's *Scandals,* made this hair-raising disclosure in Fanny Brice's suite in the George V, Paris, in the summer of '32. Warmed by Fanny's vintage stuff, Holtz swore Hamlet was his mutton. In proof of his conviction, Lou ripped off a soliloquy. To placate the deranged dialectician, Fanny played Guildenstern to my Rozencrantz. The Gallic bellhop, summoned to replenish the ice, was fascinated by his performance.

It's possible Holtz became deluded after observing conflicts between role and interpreter which recur each season. Off-beat casting has jeopardized more than one play I've handled. Seeking an actor to play the fanatic young Frenchman who shot down Admiral Darlan in Irwin Shaw's *The Assassin,* producers Carly Wharton and Martin Gabel were gulled into signing Frank Sundstrom. Sundstrom was a young Swede imported by David Selznick, screen mahatma. Certain he had a male Garbo on his hands, Selznick signed the Swede to a long-term contract. He was soon disillusioned. Sundstrom lost by a knockout in his first setto with the English tongue. In adversity, Selznick sought refuge in the French slogan, *Sauve qui peut.* In a demonstration worthy of Franz Mesmer, he convinced Wharton and Gabel that his import would make a great French hothead. In his haste to unload his prodigy, Selznick forgot to tag him *caveat emptor.* Only in pantomime did Sundstrom live up to David's boasts.

Consider the conduct of George Abbott and Philip Dunning when confronted with Oscar Jaffe, lunatic producer in *Twentieth Century.* Conceived as a composite of Morris Gest, David Belasco and Jed Harris, Jaffe was of Jewish accent and mien. To animate this megalomaniac they chose Moffat Johnson, whose burred Scotch accent stirred memories of Harry Lauder. Lacking a Ben Hubbard for *Another Part of the Forest,* Lillian Hellman and producer Bloomgarden imported Leo Genn. Hubbard was indigenous to Snowden, Alabama. Genn's speech reflected his Cambridge University training.

But the theatre's casting contradictions are trifling compared to the somersaults of the screen. *Oklahoma!* was filmed in Arizona. The Sooner State didn't meet the scenic demands of the movie men.

The theatre teems with paradox. Blunders often cue their authors into triumphs. In proof of this I cite Edward Choate. Choate, a fugitive from the Shubert office, slaved for a year to produce Paul Vincent Carroll's *Kindred.* I grieved when the critics brushed it off as unworthy of the author of *The White Steed* and *Shadow and Substance.* Among the casualties was Barry Fitzgerald.

The funeral rites were interrupted by the late Robert Edmond Jones, superb scene designer and confidant of Eugene O'Neill. Jones urged Choate to revive Sean O'Casey's *Juno and the Paycock.* Fitzgerald was available for his original role of Captain Jack Boyle. So was Sara Allgood, greatest of the Abbey Theatre's Junos. Betrayed by one Irishman, Choate reasoned he might be redeemed by another. His revival of *Juno and the Paycock* opened nine days after *Kindred* closed, a feat unmatched in the theatre for speed of execution.

The critics who had chided *Kindred,* cheered *Juno and the Paycock.* Well they might cheer it. I have never seen finer acting than Allgood's and Fitzgerald's in the scenes they played together. The impromptu revival ran for thirteen weeks, the longest run enjoyed by the great Irish slum play in its New York history. (Here I'd like to intrude a bitter reflection. Many authorities rate O'Casey as the finest dramatist since Shakespeare and *Juno* and *The Plough and the Stars* two of the best plays in English. Yet O'Casey's royalties from all his plays since *The Shadow of a Gunman* in 1922 probably do not add up to the sum realized by George Axelrod from *The Seven Year Itch.* What price glory?)

I'd be derelict did I not cite Marlon Brando. There are two or three schools of thought about this zouave. One holds he's an invention of the Psychiatrists Guild. Another brands him a calculated eccentric. A third argues he's a distillation of all the graduates of the Actors' Studio. All agree that he has given memorable performances on stage and screen.

I first encountered this fakir when John C. Wilson engaged him to shoot Tallulah Bankhead in *The Eagle Has Two Heads*. In this Cocteau charade Miss Bankhead was Queen of a Graustarkian country. On the curtain's rise she was mourning her mate, victim of an assassin's bullet fifteen years earlier. Into her chamber burst Stanislas (that's Brando), a loutish revolutionary hell-bent on doing her in. In a thirty-minute monologue, the Queen undertook to dissuade the hothead. Come to slay, Stanislas remained to love. But the Queen brushed off his advances. Crazed by her taunts, Stanislas shot the Queen, then drained a lethal cup.

The conduct of Mr. Brando on our arrival in Wilmington, where the conundrum was trying out, was off-beat. The company manager invited Brando to share his cab to the Du Pont Hotel. Marlon declined. He needed a cab to himself. He was going to ride about for an hour, practicing on his African drums.

Throughout the rehearsals, Wilson had interpreted Marlon's trance-like conduct as a manifestation of genius. He hesitated to correct him lest he upset his mood. That night Wilson's mood was addled while watching Brando during Tallulah's soliloquy.

He squirmed. He picked his nose. He adjusted his fly. He leered at the audience. He cased the furniture. He fixed his gaze on an offstage property man instead of his opponent. But these didos were nothing compared to his surprise finish. On cue he plugged the Queen and watched her pitch headlong to the stairway. Then, in defiance of Cocteau, Wilson and Equity's Board of Governors, he refused to die. Instead he staggered about the stage, seeking a likely spot for his final throe.

The audience was in convulsions. Spread-eagled on the stairway, head down, Miss Bankhead was having a few convulsions of her own. Why wouldn't this misbegotten clown cash in his chips? Marlon had been mooning about for a full minute on the apron when suddenly he collapsed as if spiked by an invisible ray. The curtain came down with the audience in hysterics. If Tallulah could have gotten her hands on a gun, the coroner would have had a customer then and there.

Marlon was succeeded by Helmut Dantine, a newcomer from Vienna. Observing the amenities, and Cocteau's stage directions, Dantine died on cue. Would that *The Eagle Has Two Heads* had been as punctual.

A visit to Washington was more enjoyable. With the cast of *Watch on the Rhine,* Lillian Hellman and Herman Shumlin, I had supper in the White House on a Sunday night in '42. The supper followed a performance of the play for President Roosevelt's Birthday Fund for Infantile Paralysis. The President saw the performance from a balcony box. The audience crawled with diplomats, politicos and Secret Service agents. Andrew Kelly, dramatic editor of the Washington *Times-Herald,* was in charge. He deputed me to certify members of the company to Secret Service men at the White House entrance. I could have outlawed an actor with a shake of the head.

Shortly before the end of the performance I was approached by Jacob Wilk, one of Warner Brothers' panjandrums. Mr. Wilk wanted to know about his tickets to the White House supper. I told him there were no Wilk tickets. He was not on the guest list. He'd better get on it, he said. Hadn't Warner Brothers bought the screen rights to the play? If he and producer Hal Wallis didn't crash the supper, he would consider my conduct an unfriendly act.

I explained the White House was the presidential residence. We were invited guests. We'd be outraging protocol if we tried to smuggle in so much as one Warner. Wilk retreated, muttering vengeance. Later he routed Marvin McIntyre, the President's secretary, out of bed to appeal the decision. He didn't get into the White House.

One of the actors was mildly ribbed by the President. On shaking his hand Roosevelt said, "Your name is familiar. Isn't it possible I know some of your family?" The actor was John Davis Lodge, grandson of Henry Cabot Lodge, the Tory who scuttled the League of Nations. John Davis, believe it or not, became Governor of Connecticut, and now is our Ambassador to Spain.

But enough of actors! Away with them! Weightier folk impend: The playwrights. Denied their words, all of us might have to go to work. What a frightening thought!

18

Author! Author! Author!

DEAD or alive, the playwright is the theatre's only indispensable. When he idles or defaults it becomes a disaster zone. The playwright is indispensable because he is the theatre's only creator. Actors, directors, designers and technicians may enhance or corrupt his words, but his words they must have. Without them they're helpless. But if playwrights make the theatre possible, they're also responsible for its ebb and decay. There is always a dearth of good plays, but New York is glutted with actors and directors eager to tackle anything in three acts. Manned with gifted performers and staged by an intelligent director, a good play rarely fails. Contrariwise, skilled players and directors have redeemed many a mediocrity. What does this prove? It proves that there are more able actors and directors than there are able authors. That's the crux of the theatre's plight.

I use the phrase "dead or alive" advisedly. The two most popular and successful playwrights of the 1956-57 season were Eugene O'Neill and Bernard Shaw. Though both Celts are in their graves, their works towered over the output of all who survived them. Shaw was represented by *My Fair Lady,* derived from *Pygmalion, The Apple Cart* and *Major Barbara*; O'Neill by *Long Day's Journey into*

Night, A Moon for the Misbegotten and *New Girl in Town,* extracted from *Anna Christie.* This salute to the departed enables me to intrude on the décor. You'll recall, I hope, that O'Neill's *Desire Under the Elms* was my first success in New York as *My Fair Lady* is my last, a pleasant, if boastful, way to bracket my activities.

Few of the authors whose plays I have puffed were fledgling Shaws and O'Neills. The desire to write a play has gripped almost every adult familiar with the alphabet. Thousands give way to the impulse. Piled one atop another, the unproduced plays typed in a given year would reach to the observation tower of the Empire State Building. To the eager but inept, playwriting may be a form of therapy, a secret vice or the vengeance of a man denied an audience. There is no law against playwriting. Indeed it should be encouraged, perhaps subsidized. But the legislators are remiss in their failure to provide penalties for the production of bilge whose dialogue and design would nauseate a goatherd.

Not all dramatists are to the manner born. Not all are chummy with the Greek unities. Policemen write plays and so do newspaper publishers (Joseph Medill Patterson), school teachers (Paul Vincent Carroll and J. B. Priestley) and lawyers (Elmer Rice and John van Druten). The Walter Livingston Faust who wrote *This Rock,* a diversion I plugged for Eddie Dowling, was a vice-president of Standard Oil of New Jersey. The Gustav Eckstein who composed *Christmas Eve,* a five-night sorrow I mourned with Guthrie McClintic, was a zoologist at the University of Cincinnati. The Paul K. Paley who chilled both me and the critics with *Right Next to Broadway* operated in New York's garment center.

But professional origin or prior condition of servitude in no way indicates the potential of a playwright. O'Neill was a sailor. Lillian Hellman a press agent and Sean O'Casey a day laborer. Benn Levy represented Eton and Slough in the House of Commons when I publicized his *Clutterbuck. Arsenic and Old Lace,* which provided me with three years' employment, was by Joseph Kesselring, a music teacher from Bethel, Kansas. Patsy Ruth Miller, silent screen star, wrote the book for *Music in My Heart,* an operetta about the romance of Tschaikovsky and Désirée Artot, a French singer, which beggared its backers in '47. I don't know where Patsy did her research. Authorities in such matters assure me that Peter Ilich had no heterosexual inclinations.

I may twit a producer or a prima donna but I'm prudent in my traffic with playwrights. That's because I have more respect for writers than I have for their interpreters or salesmen. As a class authors are more literate and amusing, more civilized and better informed than actors, managers or press agents, hence are more desirable companions. They function in seclusion. Few of them are publicity crazed. Few are blessed with the bravado of a Hemingway or a Saroyan. A liberal and articulate crew, most of them lean to the left, a stance I recommend to leaners.

Since I'm partial to newspapermen, I prefer the company of authors with newspaper backgrounds. They have more humor and less respect for the anointed. They're not awed by pomp or circumstance. Association with such braves as James Thurber, Ben Hecht, Charles Mac-Arthur, Vincent Sheean, Russel Crouse, Gene Fowler, Thomas Mitchell, all escaped from the city desk, stimulated me.

Speaking of stimulation reminds me of Konstantin Simonov, Moscow journalist and Russia's wealthiest and most prolific playwright. I met Konstantin at Bleeck's in the fall of '46. Ira Wolfert and I were working on our third Scotch highball when we were joined by Joe Barnes, foreign editor of the *Herald Tribune*; Barnes introduced us to his companion, Simonov. Simonov and Ilya Ehrenburg, journalistic hatchetmen for the Kremlin, and General Galaktionov, a warrior with literary delusions, were here as guests of the American Society of Newspaper Editors. Wilbur Forrest, equerry of Ogden Reid, publisher of the *Herald Tribune,* was the president of ASNE. The editors had feted the visitors in Washington. Now the trio was touring the country and the editors were going all out to entertain and enlighten them.

When Simonov came to New York, Forrest tapped Barnes to divert him. His choice was inevitable. Barnes had been the *Herald Tribune's* Moscow correspondent before the war. He spoke Russian fluently. He had made a brilliant translation of Simonov's *Days and Nights,* a novel based on the siege of Stalingrad. He had accompanied Wendell Willkie in his flight to Russia in 1941.

After Ira and I toasted the tourist, Barnes told us Simonov wanted to explore New York's night life. Joe said he wasn't qualified for such an excursion, since he confined his drinking to Bleeck's.

"I could do with a little help," he said. "You boys get around more than I do. Here's your chance to improve Russo-American relationship."

Though Wolfert and I did most of our drinking in Bleeck's, too, we volunteered. In turn we visited "21," the Stork Club and Café Society Uptown. Simonov was a chain-cigar smoker and an indiscriminate drinker. He sloshed down Scotch, bourbon, rye and gin with impartiality. Simonov showered us with words, none of which Ira or I understood. We deafened Konstantin in retaliation. This put a burden on Barnes. He had to translate the trialogue. Midway in our stay in the Stork Club Joe's larynx caved in.

Our interpreter a casualty, the volume and pitch of the conversation doubled. Monologists are indifferent listeners under any circumstances. Tipsy soliloquists scorn the words of rivals, English, Russian or Choctaw. As the babble at Café Society reached a crescendo, Barnes went over the hill. Dappled dawn was rising as I weaved from the forum. Ira had dozed off. But Konstantin, on his seventh cigar and experimenting with anisette, was still fulminating.

Wolfert, war correspondent who had weathered Utah Beach and Guadalcanal, called me that afternoon.

"Where did everybody go?" he said.

I never saw Simonov again. On his return to Moscow he batted out *The Russian Question,* a play with an American newspaper publisher for its villain. Stalin pinned another medal on his chest. A year after our good-will soiree, I plucked my zither for Simonov's *The Whole World Over.* I didn't pluck it long. In Cleveland, where the play was to open on March 15, I received a frantic call from producer Paul Moss. We'd been done in by the diplomats, he swore. The Big Four Foreign Ministers had just convened in Moscow and Molotov was getting out of hand. Hostility toward Russia was mounting by the minute. I'd best mute the Russian origin of *The Whole World Over*. And while I was at it, I might as well smother Simonov. "There's no use courting trouble," he ended. "We might be charged with giving aid and comfort to the enemy."

Forthwith I de-Slaved all my copy and fumigated the ads. Though *The Whole World Over* was about the conflicts of love and the housing shortage in postwar Moscow and crawled with Dmitris, Sergeis, Nadyas and Feodors, thereafter I identified it as "a romantic comedy of postwar Europe." But we couldn't de-Slav the program or the plot. Simonov's characters couldn't be masked or rechristened. My evasions were transparent. The cat was out of the bag as soon as the *Plain Dealer's* Bill McDermott inspected the work.

Though Konstantin is Russia's most successful playwright, his real talent lies in another field. He is the most artful of the dodgers. He has survived a dozen purges and Stalin, too! And he still has all his rubles.

Empty the desk of any newspaperman and you're sure to find an unfinished play, buried under cleaning tissues, bottle openers, and old copies of the *Manchester Guardian*. Newsmen are furtive and sporadic playwrights. Since they can't afford a six-month leave to hew out another *Front Page,* they do their tinkering between assignments and after hours. Craft loyalty often cancels out hope of royalties and security. Since they're the last of the romantics, newsmen are suspicious of their fellows who hack in Hollywood or sell out to the hucksters.

I had a pleasant week in Atlantic City in the summer of '27 as I alerted the shore to *Man's Estate,* a play by Beatrice Blackmar and Bruce Gould. Miss Blackmar was a feature writer on the old New York *World.* Mr. Gould was on the New York *Post* and doubled as critic for the *Wall Street News.* Beatrice and Bruce were husband and wife and *Man's Estate* was their first effort. They were ecstatic when Jed Harris told them he would produce it. Though the tryout was three months off, Beatrice and Bruce started to worry me about their hotel rooms at the Ritz and their first-night seats in New York. With the start of rehearsals they were confronted with greater crises. Harris had drastic notions about rewriting, replotting and recasting and he voiced them in high-voltage words. When *Man's Estate* opened the authors were in a state of shock. Both paled when Jed told them the play was short of his standards and that he wasn't bringing it to New York.

Crushed by this verdict, they were revived by The Theatre Guild. But the Guild's production of *Man's Estate* ten months later confirmed Harris' suspicions. It folded after six weeks. Still outraged, Miss Blackmar and Mr. Gould retaliated by writing another play, *The Terrible Turk*. The villain was a thinly-disguised theatre manager in the throes of paranoia. *The Terrible Turk* never found a platform but it rid the authors of the rancor which threatened to consume them. *Man's Estate* and *The Terrible Turk* behind them, Miss Blackmar and Mr. Gould went on to more profitable adventures. Since 1935 they've edited the *Ladies' Home Journal,* the most successful magazine in its field.

Newsmen floored in their first bout with the drama rarely demand a rematch. Purged of the compulsion to write a play, they recuperate rapidly and resume their trade. On enlisting with Jed Harris' commandos, one of my first assignments was *Spread Eagle,* a bitter play about our chauvinists in Mexico. *Spread Eagle* was by George S. Brooks, an upstate newspaperman, and Walter Lister, city editor of the New York *Telegram.* Cheered by most of the reviewers, *Spread Eagle* folded after ten weeks at the Martin Beck. Though stimulated by their venture, neither tried again. These past ten years Lister has been managing editor of the Philadelphia *Bulletin.* When last I heard of Brooks, he was Mayor of Croton, New York.

By-line pieces by authors of new plays are standard features in the drama section of the *Times* and the *Herald Tribune* the Sunday prior to the opening. Rightly, the editors reason that the author is best qualified to comment on the intent and content of his work, the ordeals experienced in its composition and the frustrations suffered in getting it cast and produced.

Though flattered by the opportunity to pontificate on the same page with Atkinson and Kerr, most authors shun these assignments. Awaiting sentence, the accused would prefer to remain mute.

The prospect of saying something that might irritate his judges paralyzes him. Why connive at his own destruction? Why add to his risk, already frightening? Because of these conflicts and alarms, pre-opening pieces by playwrights are flat, stale and unprofitable.

Negotiations between editor and author funnel through the press agent. He must assure the first while placating the second. In my time I've badgered dozens of playwrights about these compositions. I've heckled them by telephone and telegram in New Haven and Philadelphia, in Boston and Washington and other tryout towns. The flaw in my procedure is its timing. A man trying to rewrite the second-act love scene and coin a new curtain line is in no mood to bat out a thousand words for a drama editor. More than one has said he wished I was frying in hell. In the end I'm usually able to cajole or worry them into compliance. The distemper of an author is more endurable than the frown of the *Times*.

I rejoice in authors who spit out their convictions, no matter whom they ruffle, who bat their opponents bowlegged when interviewed. Sidney Kingsley, Pulitzer Prize winner at twenty-seven, is such a brave. I was his propagandist when he wrote and mounted *Lunatics and Lovers,* a raffish salute to adultery in a mid-town fleabag. Despite its carnal content, Kingsley spoke of it in lofty terms. He mined the title from *A Midsummer Night's Dream.* In discussing it with me, he spoke of Eros and touched on Nietzsche and his notions of morality as set down in *Thus Spake Zarathustra.*

The *Times* wanted to know why the author of such socially significant plays as *Men in White, Dead End* and *The Patriots* lapsed into low jinks. Farce was a dramatic form that had flowered with Molière, wrote Kingsley. With *Lunatics and Lovers* he hoped to restore some of its pristine glory. Anticipating doubts that might be raised by his sudden switch to comedy, Kingsley didn't pussyfoot. He recalled the grammar-school teacher who scrawled "a future Mark Twain" across one of his compositions.

In linking himself with Molière and Twain, Kingsley arched a lot of eyebrows. But his profanities served a purpose. They loosed discussion and controversy. Discussion and controversy are the essence of publicity. They sell tickets. Such devices are grist to my mill. Though *Lunatics and Lovers* was short of *Le Médecin Malgré Lui,* it kept me employed for almost a year and netted Kingsley and his allies $125,000.

I have said that I'm partial to authors who make good copy. Ben Hecht is my beau ideal. Ben is a rebel and a scoffer. He delights in a donnybrook. Incorrigible in victory, in defeat he goes berserk. The mocking essays he and Gene Fowler wrote to preface the opening of *The Great Magoo* were funnier than the play. So were the stage directions. The authors said that the play was a valentine to a flagpole sitter and his Coney Island doxy, "something like Romeo and Juliet!" In his opening address in the *Times,* Ben said that Fowler, whom he identified as "a New England apache," thought it was about the Unknown Soldier. When the reviewers blackjacked their fable, Hecht was outraged. In tirades boiling with invective, he denounced them as poltroons and worse.

Hecht's prose is vivid and biting under any circumstances. His hoots and jeers when angered are models of vituperation. When Billy Rose voiced a dissent during the rehearsals of *The Great Magoo,* Hecht denounced him as "an evil little Igorot" and ordered him from the theatre.

Ben belabored Rose again three years later when the producer suggested there were too many words in *Jumbo.* He was still steaming three or four years later when Sam Goldwyn offered $100,000 for the screen rights to this lyric circus. Ben's cut of this swag would have been $30,000. But he brushed the offer aside. The story of *Jumbo* was in the public domain, he told Goldwyn. It was based on a one-ring romance Rose had seen in Budapest or Bucharest. Sam could screen his own variation.

But Ben is mercurial. Of late years he's been Rose's staunchest champion. He waxed lyrical over the erstwhile "Igorot" in his autobiography. Hear ye! Hear ye!:

The outside layers of Billy Rose, the showman, are made of neon lights and the best Bessemer steel. Within exists a man of deep modesty and astonishing sensitivity. Before any evidence of talent Billy is as wistful as a June bride. Genius holds him spellbound. The secret of his keen showmanship is that he himself is full of applause for every human performance of merit.

So help me, Hannah, that's what Ben wrote in *A Child of the Century*.

Some eight months after the burial of *Ladies and Gentlemen,* a hybrid he and Charlie MacArthur had wrenched from the Hungarian for Helen Hayes, Ben phoned me.

"Meet me in Bleeck's in half an hour," he said. "It's urgent."

Over a highball Ben told me his problem. He was just back from Hollywood, where he had written, directed and produced *Angels Over Broadway* for Columbia Pictures.

"Douglas Fairbanks, Jr., and Rita Hayworth are in it and it's pretty good," he said. "But I've just had a call from Lee Garmes, my cameraman. In the three days since I left they've butchered the film. Come with me to the Columbia offices. I'm going to deliver an ultimatum. If these swine don't capitulate, I'll have a couple of hours' work for you. Your fee will be $500."

In the elevator that bore us to Columbia's headquarters, Ben briefed me further: "They know I'm coming. Let me do all the talking."

Facing Jack Cohn, head of the cartel, Nate Spingold, Columbia pooh-bah, and one of their legal beagles, Ben refused to sit down. Indicating me with a wave of the hand, he said: "This is Richard Maney. He is a press agent, widely and favorably known in the amusement world. I have told him that your West Coast mercenaries have mutilated *Angels Over Broadway.* Unless it is restored immediately to the form I approved last Tuesday, Mr. Maney will wire every movie editor and critic in the land of your infamy tonight. He'll brand you as vandals. He'll detail your treachery. He'll blast your pretentions and spotlight your ignorance."

"Come, come, Ben. Be reasonable." chorused Spingold and Cohn. "You wouldn't do that. Let's talk it over. We'll . . ."

Signaling me to precede him, Ben stalked to the door, then turned to deliver his valedictory: "You have two hours to think it over and confer with your hatchetmen in California. Mr. Maney and I are going to '21' for refreshments. You can reach me there. If I do not hear from you by four o'clock I'm turning Maney loose."

Ben and I had been in "21" about forty minutes when one of the Kriendlers approached. There was a telephone call for Ben. He came back from the booth, his face wreathed in a triumphant leer. "You're out five hundred clams," he said. "They've thrown in the sponge."

Hecht doesn't confine his attacks to critics and producers and the screen's swamis. During the war he denounced Great Britain's treatment of the Jews in Palestine so violently that his works were outlawed throughout the realm.

I last shared a barricade with Ben when he wrote and directed *Lily of the Valley* for Gilbert Miller. The critics pounced on it with little animal noises.

On reading their reports, I leaned back and awaited the explosion. I didn't have long to wait. Ben called me at noon.

"I've just dashed off a sonnet," he said. "I want a copy for each of the cast. Alert your printer. I'll send it over with a messenger."

I didn't ask him about his text. I knew without asking. In fourteen lines, following the Elizabethan rather than the Petrarchan rhyme scheme, Ben belted the reviewers from hell to breakfast. In his third quatrain he toasted the players for their co-operation and gallantry under fire. His final couplet was a lament. Victimized by clods, they must share a common martyrdom.

Done with iambic pentameter, Ben lathered his typewriter with an open letter to the drama editors. In this he identified his tormentors as

so many descendants of Will of the Mill, open-mouthed and empty-skulled. . . . I saw them this morning as a group of aesthetically exhausted old men with literary nerve centers worn out from too much slapdash service in the theatre. I saw them as a fungus-egoed coterie of fretful and wearied scribblers. . . . That these persnickety and groping gentlemen of the aisles full of some prep school mumbo-jumbo about playwriting and literature—that these perpetual amateurs of letters and blank cartridge-shooting ogres can make or break so valiant a play as the *Lily* is one of the chief reasons for the theatre's present-day littleness.

But Ben has mellowed. In his memoirs he confesses that those he once dubbed "parasites and fatheaded sophomores" are "men of courage, the most literate of journalists and the custodians of the Theatre's ideals." His somersault saddens me. His dirk out, his hair on fire, and lusting for vengeance, Ben stimulated and inspired me throughout the six fracases in which we conspired. My job crackled with excitement and suspense when Ben was around. Humdrum assignments took on the guise of guerrilla warfare.

Gene Fowler, Hecht's co-defendant in *The Great Magoo,* and Charlie MacArthur, his confederate in *The Front Page, Twentieth Century, Jumbo* and *Ladies and Gentlemen,* were raffish and derisive types, seething with sedition. A night on the town with Hecht, Fowler and MacArthur was fraught with peril. Only once did I see them routed. With flier Al Williams, the trio dropped in on a dress rehearsal of *Twentieth Century.* Their festive entrance irked director George Abbott, a chilly teetotaler with little taste for shenanigans. Deeming their intrusion out of order, George ordered the roisterers to depart. Depart they did. Next day they thawed George with apologies.

When exhilarated, Fowler was a menacing figure. At once he suggested a freebooter rampaging the Spanish main, Robespierre haranguing the Assembly, and a smuggler trying to worm the Kohinoor through customs. Following gymnastics at various fountains, Fowler accompanied me home to dinner one night during rehearsals of *The Great Magoo.* Meeting my wife for the first time he roared, "Are you a career woman?" Only when Betty reassured him of her innocence would he be seated. At sight of Fowler, my stepson, Jock, fled to his room and barricaded the door. Betty's attempts to get him to come to dinner were fruitless. "I'm afraid of that man," he insisted. "He's got a knife on him."

My ability to wheedle authors into writing pieces for the papers has led to the charge that I bully my betters into doing my work. I choose to ignore this canard. Fortunate is the press agent with an author who will tattoo his typewriter on cue. Doubly blessed is the press agent with co-authors. Hecht and Fowler were such a godsend and so were James Thurber and Elliott Nugent, the Ohio State alumni who coined *The Male Animal.*

Herman Shumlin's production of the Thurber-Nugent comedy further discredited the bromide that drinking never pays. One of the rewards was the opportunity to wassail with Thurber. I had been a Thurber fan long before I met him, thanks to his hilarious *New*

Yorker essays and his caricatures of frustrated men and defiant women. A common concern for baseball and Scotch, jeering and gaming, cemented our friendship.

While caterwauling with Jim one night, he confessed he had written a play with Elliott Nugent. It had been tried out that summer in California, he said, and had won the acclaim of oracles on Malibu Beach.

"It's a sure hit," boasted Thurber. "We're putting it in rehearsal as soon as we can get a producer."

Amused by Jim's optimism, I sought to disillusion him.

"There's no such animal as a sure hit," I said. "Not one play in six makes a nickel."

His judgment challenged, Thurber exploded. "I'll bet you fifty fish that it runs thirty weeks," he said.

To needle my opponent—Thurber's scorn when aroused is beautiful—I replied, "I'll bet you fifty fish it never opens."

After two or three rounds of taunts, I asked Thurber what producer he hoped to honor. He named a gentleman who had narrowly escaped lynching in his previous try. I jumped at the opportunity to parade my wisdom and experience.

"You're mad as an adagio dancer," I sneered. "Blank's imprint on a play is insurance of disaster. Why handicap yourself with a clown?"

"All right, Effendi! Who do you suggest?" snarled Jim.

"Herman Shumlin," I replied impetuously. "He'll give you double service as producer and director."

I named Herman out of respect and loyalty, though suspicious of his flair for comedy. He had done a superb job with *The Little Foxes,* the Lillian Hellman play I was crying. When Henry, the bartender, turned the lights out, it was agreed that I'd arrange a meeting of Thurber and Shumlin for noon that day. Shumlin called me at five. He was fascinated by *The Male Animal.* It would open under his management in New York in January after tryouts in Princeton and Baltimore. I rejoiced. I hadn't acquired my hangover in vain.

Superficially an uproarious comedy about campus conflicts of mind and muscle, underneath *The Male Animal* was an eloquent plea for academic freedom. It more than justified Thurber's barroom boasts. Irked by skepticism, he had bet me it would run thirty weeks. It prospered for thirty weeks and three days.

As press agents without portfolio, Thurber and Nugent were spectacular. Instead of the conventional weekend pictorial displays prior to the opening, the drama sections crawled with Thurber's cartoons. Editors vied for his prose. Well they might. He was a better writer than anyone on their staffs. His wit and irreverence sparkled in interviews. Fascinated by his skill and industry, I persuaded Thurber to illustrate the ads and design the window cards and three-sheet posters.

"I was elated when Shumlin agreed to produce and stage the play," said Thurber later. "It would be a lot of fun having Maney working for me. But I was living in an opium world. No sooner had the play opened in Princeton than I was working for him—day and night."

Some three thousand words ago I wrote that with few exceptions playwrights hesitate to stick out their necks on the eve of their trial, that because of this their pre-opening observations on the drama pages commonly are flat and evasive. James Thurber is a brilliant exception. In proof of this I submit his address to the readers of the *New York Times* on Sunday morning, January 7, 1940, with the opening of *The Male Animal* sixty hours away. Mr. Thurber:

Science has not yet discovered why a man who has a good stomach, a great many things to do, and enough to live on, should suddenly decide to write a play. Science has zipped the atom open in a dozen places, it can read the scrawlings on the Rosetta stone as glibly as a literary critic explains Hart Crane, but it doesn't know anything about playwrights. It is only fair to say that neither do I.

"Well, why did you write a play, Mr. T.?" (There will be voices coming into this at intervals.)

All I can say is that the idea came to me one day in October, 1938, while I was standing on top of a garage. Whether the idea was there and I walked into it, or whether I unconsciously took the idea there, I do not know; no one knows. Sometimes I think I had the basic idea eight years ago; sometimes I say it was ten. And then, at other times, I think it came to me on top of this garage. The play, as it happens, has nothing to do with garages. This is one of the soundest things about it.

It doesn't even have anything to do with typewriters, alhough at one time that's all there was in it. You see, there was this pretty wife who could fix her husband's typewriter when it began to act that funny way. You sort of began with that: the husband all tied up in a typewriter ribbon, like the Corticelli kitten.

("You'll have to cut that out—nobody knows what the Corticelli kitten is."

"Well, let's just say 'tied up in a typewriter ribbon.' "

"That isn't funny."

"Cuts out four words, and we're long now."

"Let's cut out the whole typewriter scene. We aren't going anywhere with it.")

It is very hard for a man who has never had anywhere to go to begin going somewhere. That is, it is very hard for a man who has always just sort of started to write pieces and begun to make scrawls on paper, wondering what they were going to turn into, to encounter what is known as the three-act play. The three-act play has sharp, concrete edges, rigid spacings, a complete dependence on time, and more than eleven hundred rules, all basic. "You can't run a first act fifty minutes"; "You can't have people just sitting and talking"; "You can't play comedy in a dim light"; "You can't keep people in the theatre after 11:07 o'clock"; "Anybody can write a first act"; "If you have trouble with your third act, there is something the matter with your first act"; "Vision is lost in revision"; "Where there is no revision, the playwrights perish."

These rules you learn from doormen, ushers, actors' cousins, stage-hands, property men, and the little old woman in the shawl who wanders into rehearsal under the impression that she is in Schrafft's or Lord & Taylor's.

The little old woman in the shawl bends over you, heavy with suggestions, as you sit in the dark auditorium listening to actors repeat lines which, after you have heard them one hundred and eighty-six times, seem to have no bearing whatsoever on the English language. They all sound like this: "If you had not semestered the spoons, we could have silvered this up." "If *I* had not semestered the spoons! The decided ash is all I have to resolve, personally!" The little old lady at this point whispers: "He should say 'Snows are the wear of Lester's Lear.' " You dismiss this at first, proudly and petulantly, but after you get back to your hotel you realize she is right, so you put the line in.

For a writer in his middle years, who has learned to write slowly and not too often, who sometimes puts a piece by for a year or two because he doesn't have the slightest idea what to say on page 3, and has no desire to say it even if he could think of it, it is not the easiest thing in the world to have someone whirl around and say, "Give me a new line for Joe right here." "Hm?" says the middle-aged writer. "You don't mean today, do you?" "I mean right now!"

In this familiar theatrical crisis a curious psychological thing happens to me. The only lines I can think of are lines from other plays: "Please God, make me a good actor, good-bye, Mr. Chips! Hey, Flagg, wait for baby! Aren't we all? The rest is silence. It only seems like never." It is needless to say that these lines do not get you anywhere; but, as I said before, I never was really going anywhere.

There was this pretty girl fixing the typewriter, and because it was early on a lovely October day, and I felt cheerful, I wired Elliott Nugent as follows: "You and I are going to write a play together." His reply was prompt and to the point: "No we're not." So I went out to Hollywood and showed him the typewriter scene, and he sighed and sat down, and began cutting it out. The collaboration was on. The little old woman said good-bye to her niece, put on her shawl, and started out, headed for the same place we were.

After you have worked on nothing but dialogue for five months, you wonder if you can ever learn to write straight English prose again, the kind that comes in paragraphs and looks so nice. At first you are scared to try it, but finally you realize you have to, so you sit down, and, for practice, just to get back into the swing of the thing, you try to set down Lincoln's Gettysburg Address. And what comes out is this:

Four score and seven years ago, our fathers brought forth . . .
Your fathers! Always *your* fathers!
I said ours.
You meant yours!
. . . on this continent, a new nation, conceived in liberty . . .
I know! I know! And delegated to the proposition . . .
Not delegated! Dedicated!
. . . that all men are created equal.
ELLEN (bitterly)
All men are created equal! That sounds fine coming from you!
Enter JOE
"What's the matter with that tall, thin man at the typewriter, mamma?"
"Hush, child, he's going crazy."

To me Thurber's keynote is a model of its kind. It has gaiety and humor. Its style and tone faithfully reflect the quality of *The Male Animal*. Veiled in apparent nonsense are great fundamental truths about the theatre and the anxieties and confusions which bedevil its writers.

As Tommy Turner, meek professor beset by domestic and academic woes, author Nugent was *The Male Animal's* star. His second-act comment on the ferocity of penguins, leopards and swans defending their females is the funniest drunk scene I've ever heard in a theatre. Fearful I'd be charged with discrimination, I found assignments for

Elliott between performances. He, too, whipped up comic pieces for the papers.

As a survivor of dozens of shindigs with Thurber in Bleeck's and, more recently, in Tim Costello's Third Avenue retreat, I support Elliott's contention that there are at least a half-dozen James Thurbers, all formidable. I also support those who rate him America's top humorist, not to say one of our best writers.

It's significant that *The Male Animal* was more successful on its revival in 1952 than when first produced twelve years earlier. In 1940 attacks on academic freedom were rare, now they're epidemic.

My luck with collaborators fluctuated. Eager to gild Howard Lindsay and Russel Crouse, masked aides of Joseph Kesselring in fashioning *Arsenic and Old Lace,* I heckled Lincoln Barnett, staff writer for *Life.* (Barnett's the man who explains Einstein and other esoterica to Mr. Luce's clientele.) The pair, I argued, were excellent material for a Closeup. As literary partners they vied with Addison and Steele, Gilbert and Sullivan and Harrigan and Hart. Together they had schemed *Life with Father,* a box-office bonanza, and three or four musicals.

Barnett said he'd prod his editors. He did. They decided to forgo Lindsay and Crouse, instead do a Closeup of me. What's more, they were asking Crouse to do it. This paradox disturbed me momentarily. When I told the authors how my overtures had boomeranged, they dismissed it with a shrug. For $1,500 Crouse eulogized me in twenty-five hundred words. His research was simple. As an employee I was available. So was Wolcott Gibbs's profile of me in *The New Yorker* three years earlier.

Crouse's enthusiasm for me was ephemeral. Midway through the run of *State of the Union* I was sacked by unanimous vote of Lindsay, Crouse and Leland Hayward, convened in Hollywood. Why? They said they wanted an exclusive press agent. I still don't know why I was cashiered.

As a press agent I've rubbed against a lot of eloquent writers. Though I read *The Bridge of San Luis Rey,* Pulitzer Prize novel, in 1928, I didn't meet Thornton Wilder until I agitated for his *Merchant of Yonkers* ten years later. Lunching with him at the suggestion of producer Herman Shumlin, I was impressed by his culture and modesty and awed by his knowledge of the theatre.

It all started innocently enough when I asked about Johann Nestroy, to whom he was indebted for *The Merchant of Yonkers.* Thornton cleared Johann up in a hurry. Nestroy, he said, was of a school of Viennese dramatists, specializing in farce, who had flourished in the first half of the nineteenth century. He cited eight or ten others of this tribe, none of whom I had ever heard of.

"Farce," he said, "has always flourished in ages of refinement and great cultural activity." I was in no position to contest or affirm this observation. My knowledge of farce and its history was microscopic. The only farces I could remember were *Baby Mine* and *Excuse Me,* which I had seen at the Moore in Seattle.

Pursuing the affinity of farce and refinement, he touched on Aristotle, Terence (a Roman dramatist, I learned later, who had flourished 150 years before Christ), Goldoni, also unknown to me, Molière, Beaumarchais, Shakespeare and Richard Brinsley Sheridan. He also cited Bergson and Freud and their theories about laughter. Thornton's airy analysis of farce left me appalled by my own ignorance.

Though it was directed by Max Reinhardt, at mention of whose name European actors prostrated themselves in the dust, and had Jane Cowl in the leading role, *The Merchant of Yonkers* expired after five weeks. Revived in 1956 as *The Matchmaker,* with Ruth Gordon in the Cowl role, and Tyrone Guthrie as its director, it sold out for months. Why this startling discrepancy? As played by Cowl and directed by Reinhardt, *The Merchant of Yonkers* was a roguish lark. Guthrie and Miss Gordon reduced it to bawdy slapstick. Plays are like omelets. Using identical ingredients one chef turns out a dish light as lark's down, another a concoction tough as rawhide. I don't propose to pursue this parallel further. The domestic omelet is our national shame.

Four years after Thornton briefed me on Nestroy, I was raising a din over *The Skin of Our Teeth,* his jocose tribute to man. Mine wasn't the only din. Its champions hailed it as a comic masterpiece. Motion-picture actors and other dolts denounced it as gibberish.

They'd have no truck with a play that had a talking dinosaur, a Western Union messenger, the inventor of the wheel and an actress mooning over "Rain" tangled up in one scene. This medley of cheers and jeers was music to my ears. Furtively I prodded both camps to further excesses.

Producer Myerberg grew apprehensive when fifteen peasants walked out on the play the night it opened in New Haven. "We must do something to forestall these lugs," he told me on the phone. "I think a synopsis of the plot in the program might do the trick." His suggestion was sound, I said. Who was going to write it? "You are," he blurted. I demurred. "Wilder should write it," I said. "He's the only man qualified." But Wilder wasn't available. He hadn't seen a rehearsal. Since June he'd been with the U.S. Air Corps Intelligence. He wouldn't see the play until the opening night in New York.

Though eager to please Mike, I worried about the assignment. Wilder might resent my interpretation. Had he thought a preface necessary he would have written it. Myerberg pooh-poohed me. "Don't worry, I'll take the rap," he said. "Send me the copy tonight."

Still awed by Wilder, I wrote and tore up half a dozen synopses. What I sent Mike that night follows:

PROGRAM NOTE:

"The Skin of Our Teeth" is a comedy about George Antrobus, his wife and two children, and their general utility maid, Lily Sabina, all of Excelsior, New Jersey. George Antrobus is John Doe or George Spelvin or you—the average American at grips with destiny, sometimes sour, sometimes sweet.

The Antrobuses have survived fire, flood, pestilence, the seven-year locusts, the ice age, the black pox and the double feature, a dozen wars and as many depressions. They have run many a gamut, are as durable as radiators, and look upon the future with a disarming optimism. Alternately bewitched, befuddled and becalmed, they are the stuff of which heroes are made—heroes and buffoons. They are true offspring of Adam and Eve, victims of all the ills that flesh is heir to. They have survived a thousand calamities by the skin of their teeth, and Mr. Wilder's play is a tribute to their indestructibility.

Faced by Wilder on the opening night in New York, I awaited his rebuke. "I've just read your program note," he said. "It's fine." His words were the equivalent of a decoration on the battlefield. This was praise from Sir Hubert.

Wreathed in controversy, *The Skin of Our Teeth* was an immediate hit. Ability to debate its ambiguities became a social must. Wilder's triumph placated all his champions save one: Alexander Woollcott.

On the eve of the opening Brooks Atkinson left for China. His chair on the *Times* was filled by Lewis Nichols. In his review Nichols wrote: " 'The Skin of Our Teeth' is the best play the Forties have seen in many months." Along with excerpts from other critics, I used Nichols' summation in the ads and emblazoned it over the entrance to the Plymouth.

On the evening these encomiums were displayed, Woollcott dropped into the theatre with Helen Hayes. I greeted them on the curb. On seeing Nichols' cautious endorsement, Alec raged. "Are you responsible for putting that up?" he cried. When I admitted my guilt he denounced me before the hundreds who spilled out during intermission. " 'The best play in many months!' Are you proud of that wretched tribute? You and Myerberg should both be horsewhipped. With the finest play ever written by an American on your hands, you behave as if you were fostering a revival of *East Lynne*. Shame! Shame!"

In vain I tried to appease him. I, too, regretted Nichols' tepid enthusiasm. But the omission of the verdict of the town's most influential newspaper would be awkward. The unknowing would misinterpret it. But Alec was beyond appeasement. Grabbing Miss Hayes, he stormed off, snorting fire and brimstone.

From whatever cloud he plucked his harp Alec must have exulted when *The Skin of Our Teeth* was revived and sent to Paris by ANTA, along with *Medea, Oklahoma!,* the New York City Ballet and the Philadelphia Orchestra in a cultural Salute to France in the spring of '55. But he wouldn't have exulted long. In the roles originated by Tallulah Bankhead and Fredric March, Mary Martin and George Abbott were lamentable. Their performances were flat and monotonous, unrelieved by humor or style. Mary, a delight in musicals, was fifty fathoms beyond her depth as the capricious Sabina. As Antrobus, benefactor of Homer and Moses and sire of Cain, George was as stoic and inscrutable as a Dalai Lama. Though one of the most versatile men in our theatre, George must have been deranged when he accepted the role. It had been twenty years since he impersonated John Brown, Harpers Ferry martyr. As his press agent I had witnessed his gruesome demonstration. What compulsion moved him to compound the felony?

The Maney Award for heroic conduct under fire goes to F. Hugh Herbert. As the thrall of Aldrich and Myers, I had sounded off for Herbert's *The Moon Is Blue* throughout its three-year run. His next entry was *A Girl Can Tell,* a rewrite of one of his forgotten screen works. The critics slapped it silly. Convened with Herbert, Aldrich and Myers the day after the massacre, I reported that though I'd combed the reviews I couldn't find a quote with which to banner the daily ads.

A lull followed this gloomy statement. "Must we have a critical quote?" Aldrich asked. "Indeed not! We're paying for the ads. We can say anything we want to say," I replied. "What's your suggestion for a hot quote from any source?" asked Myers.

Inspiration came to me like a thief in the night. Thanks to its spectacular run at Henry Miller's and its popularity on the screen, *The Moon Is Blue* was a symbol of sex and excitement. Agreed? "Then here's our slogan," I said. "Funnier than *The Moon Is Blue.*" "Who are we to credit with this libel?" stammered Herbert. "The man best qualified to voice it. You!" Herbert winced. Shaking his head like a man trying to get water out of his ears, he said, *"A Girl Can Tell* is my baby. Pin the guilt on me. And may the Lord forgive me!"

F. Hugh's whopper didn't save *A Girl Can Tell* but his derring-do was the talk of Sardi's, Downey's and other theatrical gymnasiums for weeks.

The late Philip Barry rated a citation, too, for his insouciance in defeat. Addressing me the morning his *Foolish Notion* had been condemned, he said, "Your display ad should be no problem. All you need say is 'Solid Press.' "

Not all authors are as co-operative as Herbert. Here on some arcane adventure late in the year-long run of *The Cocktail Party,* T. S. Eliot stiff-armed me. Peppered with requests for interviews with the great exile, I could only say that he preferred to remain incommunicado. Even knowledge of his isolation was second hand. I wormed it from Robert Giroux of Harcourt, Brace & Company, his American publishers. When I told Giroux that *Life's* editors wished to photograph Eliot greeting the company, when and if he visited Henry Miller's Theatre, he was shocked at my impudence. His reaction couldn't have been worse had I asked the Nobel Prize winner to pose in the nude in Macy's window. Eliot's reluctance to meet newsmen still baffles me. Most of the New York critics had hailed *The Cocktail Party* as a masterpiece and its success here enriched him to the tune of $100,000.

The playwright I've serenaded most frequently? William Shakespeare! I'm a wiser if no better man through exposure to *Richard III, The Merry Wives of Windsor, Hamlet, Romeo and Juliet, Henry IV, Part I, Macbeth, Richard II* (with Richard Whorf as the "bunchbacked toad"), *Twelfth Night, Antony and Cleopatra* and *Much Ado About Nothing.* The revival of *Twelfth Night* for which I pleaded in '49 initiated the ubiquitous Roger Stevens, our most prolific producer. And I'll always cherish Maurice Evans' full-length *Hamlet.* Two of its critics provided me with the most spectacular quotes ever to headline a display ad:

THE FINEST ACTOR OF OUR DAY
—John Mason Brown, *Post*
in
THE GREATEST PLAY EVER WRITTEN
—Brooks Atkinson, *Times*

Though I didn't protest at the time, I think Mr. Brown may have been intemperate. But I'd be an ingrate to quibble with Brown. Bland, witty and perceptive, a cavalier with a wide range of interests, he is my notion of a civilized citizen. The theatre lost some of its gaiety and gloss when he fled it for the lecture platforms and the microphones.

Aside from the Bard, Lillian Hellman has been my most constant patron among the playwrights. It's been my good fortune to publicize all her plays. I was thrilled by *The Children's Hour* in '34 and twenty-one years later tingled to her adaptation of *The Lark. The Little Foxes* is one of the great American plays. Her *Watch on the Rhine* was our theatre's first articulate blast at the Fascist menace. Lillian's dialogue is taut and pungent and free of seaweed. Her plots are tough and graphic. They reflect the temper and trouble of our time. Charged with fierce convictions, she never toys with a trifling theme. Her play is her forum. By any standards she's been one of our top playwrights over the last quarter century.

Lillian is a rugged opponent in rehearsal, controversy or poker. She never dissembles. She can be blunt and bitter. She asks no concessions to her sex. Her temperature rises when she's identified as "one of our leading women playwrights." Better than most she should understand the problems of my craft. She invaded the theatre as the press agent for *Bunk of 1926*. Her first and only husband, Arthur Kober, was a press agent until he succumbed to Hollywood. Lillian should understand my problems but on at least one occasion she added to them. Early in the run of *Autumn Garden,* her variation on *The Cherry Orchard,* producer Bloomgarden started to spray me with publicity suggestions. These were so grandiose and revolutionary, and so unfeasible that I smelled a mouse. Shortly I discovered Kermit was voicing the cues of Miss Hellman. She in turn was being briefed by Ben Sonnenberg. I was startled that this yogi should meddle with anything so trifling as the theatre. Commonly only industrial giants benefited from his hallucinations. To filch the caption of a *New Yorker* cartoon, I thought his conduct was "unethical and lousy."

A perfectionist, Lillian expects perfection from her colleagues. When she doesn't get it, ructions may ensue. She's unrelenting in her quest for vengeance. Her feud with Tallulah Bankhead hasn't been matched in ferocity since the Hatfields and McCoys crimsoned Kentucky.

Though none of her sisters had Lillian's power and punch, all, save one, co-operated when I cried for help. Betty Smith, who wrote *A Tree Grows in Brooklyn,* Sally Benson, who did the song-and-dance version of Tarkington's *Seventeen,* and Anita Loos, who wrote *Gentlemen Prefer Blondes,* were undismayed by my requests.

Undismayed, too, was Elizabeth Ginty, until I mentioned David Belasco. Miss Ginty had been Belasco's personal secretary for thirty years. Belasco was the theatre's leading sorcerer for most of his professional life. Affecting a clerical collar, a white mane and raven dress, his activities as director, playwright and producer had a voodoo quality.

In her long service with Belasco, Miss Ginty secretly worshiped outlaw Jesse James. Seven years after Belasco's death she brought *Missouri Legend,* her first play, to Guthrie McClintic. Its theme was Jesse's last eight days. As McClintic's agent, I called on Miss Ginty on the eve of rehearsals. Her East Side apartment was bursting with souvenirs of Belasco. When I mentioned his name, Miss Ginty burst into tears. On departing I witlessly mentioned the mystic again. Another flood of tears. That's why there were no interviews with Miss Ginty.

That notable exception I cited? Agatha Christie. The world's most successful author of crime fiction, Miss Christie scorns photographers, newspapermen, critics and press agents. She's seemingly indifferent to the homage of her readers and to the thousands of New Yorkers stunned by the explosive surprises in *Witness for the Prosecution.*

My London spies report that nothing short of a regal writ can get her to view her own plays. Buried under royalties from her three-act villainies, when in need of relaxation Miss Christie grabs a spade and with her husband starts digging for artifacts on the Euphrates or other fabled stream.

Whatever I may blurt to the contrary, I do not quarrel with an author's concern for privacy. Like T. S. Eliot, Miss Christie is content to let her work speak for itself. A nice contrast, don't you think: T. S. Eliot and Agatha Christie. *The Waste Land* and *The Spider's Web.*

Our domestic playwrights are not so indifferent to the clamor of

the congregation. Hosannaed for the miracle that was *Oklahoma!,*
Oscar Hammerstein acknowledged the cheers with an ironic ad in
Variety, bible of show people. It read:

HOLIDAY GREETINGS
Oscar Hammerstein II
author of
Sunny River
(6 weeks at St. James Theatre, New York)
Very Warm for May
(7 weeks, Alvin Theatre, New York)
Three Sisters
(6 weeks, Drury Lane, London)
Ball at the Savoy
(5 weeks, Drury Lane, London)
Free for All
(3 weeks, Manhattan Theatre, New York)
I'VE DONE IT BEFORE AND I CAN DO IT AGAIN

I salute all playwrights, major and minor, immortals and hacks.
I honor Shakespeare and Shaw and Sartre, Coward and Chekhov,
Cocteau and Chodorov and the hundred others who have amused and
informed me. All have contributed to my comfort and security.
Thanks to authors of a biographical bent, I'm better acquainted
with Admiral Darlan and Justice Holmes, with Julius Caesar and
Stephen Foster, with John Brown and the Comtesse Du Barry, with
Daniel Webster and Oscar Wilde. In what other profession could
I have practiced to such profit?

19

Private Life of a Press Agent

A FEW chapters ago I was chanting an anthem to Helen Hayes, Gertrude Lawrence, Tallulah Bankhead and other madonnas of the marquees. My survey of these sorceresses was cautious, perhaps craven. With an opportunity to laurel my favorite I hid behind the arras. Belatedly I make amends. I raise a glass to my First Lady— Betty.

Betty was born Elizabeth Breuil in Germantown, Pennsylvania. She has Spanish, French, English and Scotch blood running through her veins. Runs seems a tepid verb to describe the action of the fluid which sustains her. Spurts is more accurate. Her gaiety, her beauty and physical grace, the skill with which she could execute a cartwheel or a casserole, captivated me, occasionally startled me. They still do. She had the airy, saucy manner of screen star Mabel Normand. Not until we were one did Betty reveal that once she had impersonated Emmeline, slave of Simon Legree, in a stock production of *Uncle Tom's Cabin.* She had also feigned a model in *Potash and Perlmutter,* same stock company. What spurred her to these adventures? Ambition? No! Hunger!

We were married on a June morning in '31 at New York's City Hall, city clerk Michael Cruize presiding. The rites over, we repaired to the Hunt Club, a speakeasy in West Forty-fifth Street, to receive such scofflaws as were about at noon.

Though Betty's mother endorsed our union, her father thought she was insane. Francis Breuil had circled the world in a square rigger before he was twenty. He had prospected for gold in Alaska. He had been incarcerated in Morro Castle during the Spanish-American War. He had been superintendent of a silver mine in Macorito, Mexico. His gun collection was one of the finest in the country. It included the pistols of Captain William Bligh of *Bounty* fame. To such an adventurer press agentry was a paltry profession.

There were other circumstances which indicated Betty might be unbalanced. As we flew to Atlantic City for a weekend honeymoon, my sole source of income was *Crazy Quilt,* Billy Rose's bid for Ziegfeld's mantle. My rainy-day surplus had evaporated when I was upended by Public Service of New Jersey, American Founders, Andes Copper and other gilt-edged delusions eighteen months earlier. Though our economic position was perilous, Betty and I didn't give it a thought. Hadn't Herbert Hoover told us prosperity was just around the corner? With friends and acquaintances skidding toward the pit, we felt we were sitting pretty.

We were sitting pretty. From the estate of her late grandmother, Betty had salvaged furniture, etchings and silver, two oil paintings, miniatures of her alien ancestors, and an ice-cream freezer. With these we set up housekeeping in a one-flight walk-up off Central Park West, rent $90 a month. Within a year we had saved $2,500, thanks to my service with six flops, a revival of Noel Coward's *Hay Fever* and Ed Wynn's *Laugh Parade.* The six failures ran a total of eighteen weeks. One, *The Warrior's Husband,* boasted the lovely Katharine Hepburn; another, *The Fatal Alibi,* the unlovely Charles Laughton.

Since it was unlikely we'd be so flush again, we decided on a holiday in Europe. This excursion had a theatrical tinge. On our first night in London, John Cohen, motion-picture critic of the New York *Sun,* regaled us with a report of his interview with George Bernard Shaw. Five highballs later he confessed he hadn't seen

Shaw. But he had seen Robert Sherwood and Sherwood had spent two hours with Shaw. We were accompanied to Epsom Downs by John Byram, drama editor of the *New York Times,* and his Marian. The Derby was won by April the Fifth, owned and trained by actor-manager Tom Walls. With the Byrams we lunched with Gilbert Miller at Quagliano's. With them we saw Noel Coward's *Cavalcade,* Evelyn Laye in *Helen!, Musical Chairs* and Priestley's *Dangerous Corner.*

We tingled on seeing Amelia Earhart, who had flown the Atlantic solo, in the Cheshire Cheese. To retain our franchise in the tourists' guild we visited the Tower, the Abbey, Madame Tussaud's and St. Paul's Cathedral. We bellyached about the lack of ice and the inability of the Park Lane kitchen to produce four-minute eggs. When we apologized for sending eggs back a second time, the room waiter reassured us: "Many Americans send them back five and six times."

In our three weeks at L'Hôtel des Deux-Mondes on the Avenue de l'Opéra in Paris ($2.60 a day with breakfast) we ganged up with American newspapermen and made merry. It was easy to make merry in Paris in June of '32. The franc was pegged at four cents. Champagne cocktails retailed at twenty cents. You could scour the Bois in a taxi for a dollar.

Our first ride up the Champs-Elysées was spine-tingling. It recalled a line in Sinclair Lewis's *Dodsworth*: "There was Paris, gray with history." I was thrilled by a short crooked street named for Rouget de Lisle, and by others named for Lafayette, Foch, Voltaire, Kléber, Hugo, Rivoli and Sebastopol. It was awesome to stand before Notre Dame and reflect on the beauty of a cathedral standing three centuries before Columbus popped up in the Bahamas.

By day Betty and I cased the Comédie-Française, the Conciergerie, the Madeleine, the Panthéon, the Tuileries, the Sorbonne and the American Express Company. Out of dogged sense of duty we caromed through the corridors of the Louvre, to make token inspections of the Mona Lisa and the Venus de Milo. We absorbed Malmaison, Versailles's Hall of Mirrors and the Petit Trianon in an afternoon. Overwhelmed by culture and history, at night we relaxed at Brick-top's, Joe Zelli's, Fred Payne's, the Ritz Bar, the Casino de Paris, the Dôme, the Folies-Bergère and other havens popular with our countrymen.

Out to Chantilly to see Strip the Willow win the Prix du Jockey Club, we were deafened by "Broadway Sam" Roth, stentor of the New York ticket scalpers. He had been waylaid in the Hotel Scribe and looted of a lot of francs, he roared. "It looks like a François Villon job," I said. "Ask the Scribe's house detective if Villon's been hanging around." Sam said he would.

Our after-dark companions were Bill Boehnel, motion-picture critc of the *World Telegram,* the *Sun's* Cohen, Ben Washer, a press agent who had spent a year at the Sorbonne, and Jack Kirkland, St. Louis newspaperman. Kirkland had been a fellow passenger on the *Lafayette,* and had shared our trampolin in London. He said he was headed for the South of France to write a play from an Erskine Caldwell novel. We dismissed this threat with a shrug. After four drinks all idle newspapermen were off to the South of France to write a play or novel.

We could have saved ourselves a shrug. Kirkland took off for the Mediterranean. On his return to New York he had the script of *Tobacco Road* under his arm. This fable of the depraved Lesters ran for eight years and enabled Kirkland to luxuriate in a fashion foreign to his past.

It wasn't the Arc de Triomphe, a trip to Les Halles or the grandeur of Notre Dame that gave Americans in Paris their greatest thrill in June of '32—it was meeting other Americans. Our fellows, freed from the bondage of the Prohibition Act, scuttled from bistro to bistro like schools of salmon. Conditioned to bathtub gin and other ersatz stimulants, we ran amok when exposed to authentic tonics. Betty and I had sniffed our first martini on the *Lafayette* suspiciously. Made of London gin and Italian vermouth, its aroma was alien to our noses. Our reaction was not unlike that of prospectors to eggs after five years in the Klondike. Used to the storage variety, on their return to Seattle they complained fresh eggs didn't have any kick. After the third martini our suspicions evaporated in a golden haze.

Our after-dinner forays precluded devotions in the theatre. Lingual

difficulties were another deterrent. With Fanny Brice we saw one act
of *Mademoiselle,* a Jacques Deval riddle. "I can't understand a
goddamned word," our hostess whispered hoarsely, ten minutes after
the curtain's rise. To me, a dedicated Francophile, Paris was more
dramatic than anything its theatres had to offer. The gaiety and beauty
of the city intoxicated me. Ten years later I would weep over a
drawing in *The New Yorker.* The scene was the Café de la Paix,
its sidewalk tables crowded with German officers, necks cropped,
ramrod straight. A single word sufficed for the caption:

"PRINTEMPS"

After Paris, Berlin was a desolate city. Its people were gripped by
despair. Though it would be six months before Herr Hitler was
named Chancellor, the Germans behaved like the doomed. A dis-
mayingly competent and industrious tribe, the Teuton lacks style and
grace. He has little capacity for fun. His hand is as heavy as his
food. If there's a synonym in his language for insouciance it should
be stricken from the dictionary.

Holed up in the Bristol, in the shadow of the Brandenburg Gate,
Betty and I lamented our folly in fleeting Paris. The Unter den
Linden was littered with beggars and bicycles. In Paris we had been
enchanted by Jeannes and Jacques swarming through the Bois du
Boulogne. Such pleasures were denied the Germans. The Tiergarten
bristled with *verbotens.*

Gloom ruled at Potsdam, on the *Autobahns* and on the Kurfürs-
tendamm. Even the Bristol's bartender was in the dumps. He faced
the customers only when threatened. The headwaiter was a gay type.
Bullets had whistled by his head in the Carpathians and at Verdun,
he said, and he had no desire to take an encore. He was most morose
when detailing life in the Bristol during the inflationary twenties. An
order of penguin, masquerading as duck, sold for a million marks.

The newsmen with whom we pranked in Paris by-passed Berlin.
Lacking collaborators, Betty and I sought surcease at the Winter
Garden, a music hall where one could gnaw on knockwurst, guzzle
beer and eye acrobats simultaneously; at the Femina, a night club
with grisly attempts at convivality; and at a Bavarian beerhall on

the Friedrichstrasse. All depressing. We visited El Dorado, touted
by a tourist whom we met at Potsdam. The hostess at our table was
the best-looking girl I had seen in Berlin—trim ankles and almond
eyes, with a hairdo reminiscent of Betty Compton in *Fifty Million
Frenchmen.* I was about to undertake a polka with this Lorelei when
Betty's maniacal laughter stayed me. Since I'm no Vernon Castle, I
interpreted her snickers as a slur on my dexterity. Defiantly I embraced Brünnehilde and was about to take off when Betty blurted out
the reason for her hysterics. My hostess was a he. Too late I learned
that the El Dorado was the favorite lair of all the deviates between the
Havel and the Spree. My aplomb splintered, I paid the check and
stalked out. The bogus belle pursued me to the door, spitting Prussian
reproaches because I hadn't tipped it.

Most of my embarrassments abroad were due to lingual lapses.
When I asked for the check at Weber's in the Rue Royale, the waiter
brought me a cigar. I phoned for the valet in the Bristol and the hall
porter popped in with a two-foot vase. Life would have been simpler
had I known that *épinard* is French for spinach. I loathe spinach.
How was I to know that Omelette Florentine and Eggs Madeleine
would be garnished with this evil herb?

Franc notes were another problem. Flimsy in texture, they tended
to disintegrate under rough handling. It was awkward to return from
a night in *les rues et les places* and find my surplus reduced to
confetti. Fortunately the concierge at Les Deux Mondes was skilled in
patching fractional notes.

Berlin, under the chancellorship of Fritz von Papen, had little entertainment. The Haus Vaterland dedicated five floors to Coney Island
sideshows. Aside from *Maedchen in Uniform,* an excellent film, we
enjoyed most the penguins and the polar bears at the zoo.

I am not a good traveler. Comfort and curiosity are incompatible.
I fret and pine without New York newspapers. Train and plane
trips bore me. I refuse to participate in organized tours. I remember
the Park Lane, the Hôtel des Deux Mondes and the Bristol for an
identical reason: the milk was tepid and sour. My insistence on iced
tea at Le Bon Accueil caused a commotion. French *logique* couldn't
cope with such a contradiction. I have no talent for sightseeing.

I don't enthuse over parades, monuments or museums. Once I'd paid my respects to Bonaparte, Ney and Davout, I felt I'd canceled my debt to the past.

My distaste for touring dates from the years I spent in advance of the *Greenwich Village Follies*. Since then I associate travel with bad food and bleak hotel rooms, with cold coffee and warm grapefruit. Though hotel food is invariably dull, it's inspired compared to the messes served on trains. Ham and eggs is the only safe bet in a dining car. More complicated dishes are botched. What America needs is a Cooking Academy. Only the British excel us in the ability to ruin food.

Back in New York in mid-July, for six weeks, I was one of the country's twelve million unemployed. Though our bank balance was under a thousand dollars, Betty and I faced the future with idiot complacency. Our optimism was characteristic of theatre people. Unemployment is no novelty to them. Though our economy was going to hell in a handcar, most of us were unaware of the national plight. The theatre is conditioned to catastrophe. Despite mounting threats of doom, 174 stage productions opened in New York between Labor Day of '32 and June 1 of '33. Over that same interval in 1956-57, with national assets at a new high, there were but 62.

This paralyzing contradiction is further proof that statistics are illusory. Numerically impressive, the 1932-33 season was a box-office bust. There weren't enough customers to go around. The theatre's descending production spiral dates from 1927-28, a season that boasted 264 plays, musicals and revivals. Not since 1937-38 have as many as a hundred presentations reached New York in one season.

By stage standards I thrived throughout the depression. I profited from piecework. In the three terms ending June 1, '35—a span covering the blackest years of the blight—I huffed and puffed for twenty-four shows. Only three of these made a dime. Eight of them played less than two weeks in New York. Yet in that interval my wages ran to $55,000. Sharing Billy Rose's penthouse office, I had no professional overhead. I had neither secretary nor assistant. It wasn't until press agents became members of an A. F. of L. local in 1938 that aides became obligatory. Under union regulations, a press agent must engage an associate when he has a second attraction. If he undertakes a third, he must hike his man's wage. A fourth client demands a second associate. A fifth tilts his fee. Six attractions —the legal limit—and a third associate is automatic.

Rarely, and then only briefly, have I had to contend with such a clutter. Press agents' offices aren't equipped for quartets. What with files, typewriters, mimeograph machine and other trade apparatus, it's difficult to find room for more than two confederates. When obliged to engage a third, I sought a gnome of the dimensions of Eddie Arcaro. Bulkier types couldn't be wedged in behind the water cooler.

Our union is formally known as the Association of Theatrical Press Agents and Managers. "Managers" embraces both company and theatre pilots. The press agent's wages and other conditions of employment are established in a pact between the union and the membership of the League of New York Theatres. The last-named group is made up of producers and theatre owners and operators. Minimum wage for a press agent in New York is $220 a week. He goes on the payroll three weeks prior to the week in which his attraction opens. The associate, necessitated by a second show, gets a minimum of $145. Does his principal take on a third drama or musical, his fee is at least $197.50. For my services to plays, shows and whatnots since I took up arms for *Desire Under the Elms* I've been paid something like $750,000. This sum is exclusive of fees to associates.

In the past twenty years I've had an army of auxiliaries. Many of them now are my competitors with associates of their own. Frank Goodman, John Latham Toohey, Arthur Cantor, Abner Klipstein, Reuben Rabinovitz and Sol Jacobson, all graduates from my galley, last season collectively tootled for *Auntie Mame, New Girl in Town, Damn Yankees, Long Day's Journey into Night, No Time for Sergeants, Middle of the Night, Most Happy Fella* and *Bells Are Ringing.* Henry Sember, another escapeé, is the press agent for the New York Telephone Company. Another, Ted Goldsmith, exaggerated the delights of *Fanny* on tour. A racy and impudent crew, my ex-adjutants. When *Time* termed me "the mercurial super press agent," four of my equerries, identifying themselves as "present and former members of The China Boy Association," presented me with a framed enlargement of the testimonial. To it they added my portrait, congratulations and a single printed question: "Why not try getting the clients' names in the papers occasionally?"

While wrestling with *Frivolities* I occupied a cell in the Longacre Theatre. On being inducted by Jones and Green, I had an aerie atop the Forty-eighth Street Theatre. In my four years with Jed Harris, successively I was stationed in the Selwyn Theatre, the Sardi Building and a rookery over the Morosco. Loew's State Theatre Building was my base while praising *Fifty Million Frenchmen* and *Top Speed*. I shared a compartment with the telephone operator in my stay with Billy Rose. The hallowed Empire, where once the Frohmans reigned, was my sanctum for fifteen years. Since June of '53 I've functioned in The Playhouse, fifty feet east of the Forty-eighth Street Theatre, my shelter in '25.

My orbit is limited. It's confined to the Forties. I had a larger arena in Chinook. Though my domain is cramped, it's ample for my activities. New York's twenty-eight legitimate theatres are in an area ten blocks long and two wide. New York's rialto is bounded on the north by Fifty-first Street (the Mark Hellinger), on the south by Forty-first Street (National). Sixth Avenue is its easterly limit, Eighth Avenue its western flank. Rarely is it necessary for me to leave this quarter. Messengers carry releases and photographs to the newspapers and other media. The amusement advertising agencies come to my office for copy and bring me proofs for approval. Interviews, story assignments and pictorial layouts are set up on the telephone. Prose essays are submitted by post.

I haven't sortied south of Fortieth Street in ten years. Not since *Gentlemen Prefer Blondes* jammed the Ziegfeld have I ventured as far north as Fifty-fourth Street. (Then an amusement outpost, the Ziegfeld has been usurped by television.) It wasn't always thus. In the early twenties press agents prowled the newspapers in packs every Tuesday afternoon. Our route ranged from Columbus Circle to Park Row. Laden with portfolios of prose and photographs, successively we spread our wares before the drama editors and other prospects of the *American, Tribune, Times,* morning and evening *World, Herald, Globe, Mail, Post, Journal, News, Sun, Telegram* and *Mirror.* Why Tuesday? Wednesday was the deadline for the Sunday drama pages.

Though this practice maintains in Boston, Philadelphia, Chicago and other centers, it's taboo in Manhattan. Few editors could long survive palaver with fifty press agents every Tuesday. Fifty press agents? Ah, yes! Seventy theatres were operating in the twenties. Remember? This stampede cluttered up traffic, overtaxed the elevators and led to departmental confusion. Our targets likened these invasions to the descent of the seven-year locusts.

Being an affable crew, the drama editors humored most of the contestants. It was simpler to accept a five-hundred-word tribute to an ingénue than to debate its merit or timeliness. Avoiding definite commitments, the editors salved petitioners with "I'll get it in if I have room." Once the author had departed, he could resort to a pocket veto. Questioned later on the fate of the monograph, he could say it moldered in the overset. This device preserved the *entente cordiale.*

Despite overproduction, a lot of press-agent copy was printed in that remote day. The fourteen newspapers—now there are but seven —devoted a lot of space to the theatre. Competition from radio and screen was slight. Television was a myth out of Jules Verne. The standards of drama editors ranged from loose to negligible. An industrious press agent, capable of a succession of declarative sentences, could place all the copy he could write.

Starting with the mid-thirties, the press agent's prospects steadily ebbed. The *Herald,* both *Worlds,* the *Globe* and the *Mail* folded or merged with competitors. Later the *American* and the *Sun* gave up the ghost. The amusement sections of the survivors were drastically reduced. Talking pictures and radio challenged the theatre for space. Editors became more discriminating. Press-agent copy was subjected to fierce scrutiny. Theatre casualties matched those of newspapers. West Forty-second Street, once crowded with playhouses, surrendered to the screen. In quick succession the Selwyn, Times Square, Apollo, Republic, Eltinge, Lyric, New Amsterdam, Liberty, and Wallach's gave up the ghost. Once a glittering thoroughfare, Forty-second Street is now a shabby alley.

As theatres and papers dwindled, so did press agents. With the number of dailies halved and the amusement sections restricted, for the most part, to the prose of staff members, there was no longer a reason for our Tuesday forays. Our decision to forgo them had the ecstatic support of our quarry. Allergic to subways and travel, I welcomed the armistice. I haven't visited an editor, except by appointment, in twenty years.

To compensate for reduced amusement sections, for embargoes on blurbs and fewer papers, press agents sought new outlets. Happily these were available. As newspapers declined, columns multiplied. Today's papers are littered with these pillars—cooking columns, fashion columns, gossip columns and political columns; sports columns, "think" columns, drama columns and society columns; music columns, book columns, radio and television columns; financial columns, bosom columns and Hollywood columns; Washington columns, astrology columns and columns for the lovelorn, the delinquent and the unhealthy; for bridge players, surf fishermen and the camera crazed. Most of these are syndicated. In varying degrees all invite the press agent. Composing five or six columns a week puts a strain on the conductor. He welcomes cues from constant readers. Press agents are constant readers. Obviously it's more difficult to smuggle an adagio dancer into a financial column than into one rigged for music. Correspondingly it's more satisfying.

Radio and television program managers jump at the opportunity to interview stage players, to employ them as judges, as quiz contestants, as shills and fronts for charity drives. Such publicity is self-defeating. With few exceptions radio and television interviews with stage people are banal and boring. Excerpts from plays, no matter how exciting in the theatre, seem vague and witless out of context. There is little evidence that such adventures stimulate the box office. Indeed, I think the reverse is true.

Despite my suspicions of electronic scuffles, I often aid and abet them. Faced with so-so notices for the work on which he has risked all, a producer doesn't quibble over publicity potentials. He grasps at any straw. I'm of the "familiarity breeds contempt" school. Exposed to millions in badly written, badly lit television escapades, an actress loses allure. After seeing her for nothing in a TV fiasco, a peasant isn't likely to shell out $4.60 to see her in the theatre.

Before I wandered off into the tribal customs of press agents, I had touched on my domestic status. With the chair's consent, I will resume.

After four years in that West Seventy-fifth Street walk-up, Betty and I luxuriated in an elevator apartment house at Ninety-sixth and Central Park West. This was a token of my continuous employment. Our flat was shadowed by two churches. Three blocks away was a riding academy. In a jiffy Betty was in jodhpurs, tearing through Central Park like one of Desaix's cavalry at Marengo. Proximity to that stable brought out the hussar in my wife, latent since she'd taken fences as a child in Pennsylvania.

Lithe and active, Betty found New York confining. A skilled horsewoman and swimmer, she found Central Park and indoor pools short of her desire. To appease her, I rented a cottage on Old Mill Beach, Westport, Connecticut, one of the rockiest strands between Baffin Bay and Tierra del Fuego, for the summers of '40 and '41. While I commuted, Betty cased the countryside. Frequently she cited the advantages of rural life. She said she detected in me symptoms of Thoreau. When I scotched this slander, she made another pitch. If we lived in Connecticut, she said, I wouldn't have to pay state income tax in New York. If we lived in Connecticut and I didn't pay the New York State income tax, I might get two years in Dannemora, I replied.

But Betty is not easily balked once she makes up my mind. Four months before Pearl Harbor I became one of the landed gentry. Our five-acre estate had a railed-in pasture, two stables and a saltbox house. The major mews had an attic apartment, hayloft and nine box stalls, each of them larger than the living room in the saltbox. Our bower was framed by Norwegian spruce, magnolia and Japanese cherry trees, weeping willows, privet hedges, mole runs and crab grass. The night air was heavy with the scent of blossoms and saddle soap.

Mrs. Maney negotiated the purchase of this eden with Morton L. "Cappy" Smith, star of a hundred horseshows. When the final papers were signed before a swarm of attorneys, bank officials and notaries, she gave a sigh of relief. "At last Crackerjack has a home," she murmured. Her murmur startled me. "Who," I asked, "is Crackerjack?" He was an aged nag she had purchased furtively a year earlier. Confined in that Ninety-eighth Street riding academy, said my wife, he'd developed claustrophobia. A few romps in an open field and he would be as frisky as Pegasus or Rosinante.

Dismayed by eight empty box stalls, Betty solved this void in record time. While I alerted New York to Edmund Gwenn in *The Wookey,* she conspired with a weatherbeaten groom she'd encountered while guiding Crackerjack through the sumac. Shortly groom and wife were installed in the flat above the barn. With them came ten horses. Betty's pact with them provided that they could operate a riding academy for children in return for coddling Crackerjack, stoking the furnace, mowing the lawn and trimming the hedges.

When Crackerjack succumbed to ringbone, Betty bought Cooey, a handsome Irish hunter. Cooey's prior owner said he was the last horse to leave Ireland after the start of World War II. His record indicated Cooey was eight. Peering into Cooey's mouth our hostler swore he'd never see ten again. Scanning Cooey's papers through a magnifying glass, Betty suspected the date of his birth had been altered. Aroused by this chicane, she demanded confirmation. Though deep in campaigns for *The Skin of Our Teeth, Show Time* and three short-run dramas, I addressed a letter of inquiry to the London Jockey Club. The secretary of that body replied promptly. In a formal note, freighted with sympathy, he said Cooey was twelve. We'd been had.

Eight or twelve, Cooey was a delight to both of us. Astride this noble gray, Betty was in her element. Joyously they took fences and hedges. They scoured the pines, the woods, the fields and the paths that flanked the Merritt Parkway. Currying Cooey's coat, preparing his food or oiling his gear, Betty was in paradise.

The Allied invasion of North Africa brought Cooey a companion. Just returned from a mission to Washington in behalf of Helen Hayes and *Harriet,* I dropped into Bleeck's of a midnight early in '43. At the bar I encountered Tex O'Reilly, ace reporter for the *Herald Tribune.* He said he'd been tapped for overseas duty with General Leclerc's Free French forces in the Sahara.

"How would Betty like another horse?" Tex asked me two hours later.

"She'd be delighted," I said. "What horse? And where is he?"

"Dark Boy," said Tex. "Whitey Reid gave him to me a year ago. He's a thoroughbred jumper. I may be away a year. I'd like to find a good home for him."

"Why don't you leave him on your farm?" I asked.

"Gladys—Mrs. O'Reilly—is afraid of him," he said. "So am I. He's bucked me off four times. He's Betty's if she'll take him."

"She'll take him. I'll call her now and break the good news," I said.

Henry, the bartender, interrupted. "You must be out of your mind," he said. "It's three o'clock. A call at this hour is a confession of guilt." Tex nodded agreement.

"I can call her about a horse at five in the morning," I replied.

Betty and Tex chatted for half an hour. "She's sending a van for Dark Boy the day after tomorrow," he said on rejoining me.

Under Betty's hand Dark Boy was gentle as a lamb. Why had he tossed Tex? My friend had tried to conquer him with a Western saddle, a barbarity Dark Boy couldn't abide.

My nightly visits to theatres precluded daily commuting. From Monday through Thursday I holed up at the Astor in the heart of Times Square, a practice I still follow when hitched to more than one attraction. The Astor was, and is, the best hotel on New York's West Side. It's a convenient base. From it I can walk to any theatre in five minutes. (Inflationary note: The room for which I paid $3 in '41 is now $8.40.)

While I toiled in New York, Betty practiced husbandry on an erratic and secret scale. Devoted to animals, she couldn't turn her back on a displaced quadruped. At various times our barns sheltered an assortment of stray horses, two goats and eight cocker spaniels. One Saturday afternoon I discovered thirty turkeys in our smaller barn. That explained why the electric-light bill had jumped so spectacularly the preceding month. The brooder which hastened their birth had been hitched to a light socket for weeks. This flock was the fruit of Betty's collusion with the successor to the riding master.

On another Saturday morning I was roused by a call from the city desk of the New York *Post*. "A dame has just been pinched for riding her horse into an Amsterdam Avenue saloon," said the caller. "She says she's your secretary." "She's an imposter," I protested. "I haven't got a secretary. What's her name?" Betty solved this riddle. The tipsy cowgirl was an alumna of the Ninety-eighth Street riding academy. They'd cantered together in the Park many a morning. Since news is scarce and papers are thin on Saturdays, this rowdy and I made page 1 of all the afternoon dailies.

In my role of country squire I was confronted with crises unlike any I'd faced in New York or on tour. Though superficial judges likened our saltbox to the hut of Hansel and Gretel, it was a nest of booby traps. Visitors presented themselves at the kitchen door, since there was no entrance on the side facing the road. The front entrance, concealed by shrubbery, faced the residence of Nathan Perlman, a judge in General Sessions. Later we discovered that our plot and that of Judge Perlman once had been one. Our cottage was built for the coachman of the nabobs who preceded Judge Perlman.

To placate Washington bureaucrats, who warned of a coal shortage, we removed the furnace and converted to oil. Then came the rains. Following an hour's downpour, there was two feet of water in our cellar. A plumber plucked out the oil burner in the nick of time. He told us to waterproof the cellar walls. We did. With the next storm the cellar filled in record time. We summoned a cellar expert. He removed the oil burner. When the flood receded, he chipped through the cellar floor and installed a sump pump. To accommodate its discharge he dug a shallow trench in our roadway. Following the next thunder clap, both pump and burner were awash. Undismayed, our man ripped another hole in the floor and installed a second pump. Our back yard was strewn with chunks of concrete.

It rained again and both pumps went under. The expert retired, but not before handing me a bill for $350. To my check for his disservices, I pinned this observation:

"A novice in the country, I wasn't aware that anyone familiar with the rudiments of drainage must know that pumps were unnecessary since the outlet across the highway is two feet lower than the cellar floor. You'll agree, I hope, that water, unimpeded, runs down hill."

Enter now a carpenter, a one-time resident of our natatorium. He'd dry us out in a jiffy, he swore. This vandal dug a trench six feet deep from the ditch which fed the culvert under the highway to our cellar floor. In it he laid lengths of three-inch pipe. His underground surveys convinced him that the ditch was blocked by the roots of our weeping willow. The willow must come down, he said.

The willow uprooted, trench filled in and debris trucked off, the dredger faced Betty triumphantly. "Your troubles are over," he smirked. "An Oriental rug would be safe on the cellar floor."

Only a trout would have been safe in the cellar. Following an hour's downpour three days later a pontoon was rigged across our roadway that Betty might reach the barn. The trench became a quagmire. The torrent lapped the kitchen floor. The cocker spaniel had his first swim. The coward in me came out. The fifth floor of the Astor was well above flood level.

While mulling flight to the hills, Betty was visited by Westport's superintendent of roads, Anthony Manere. Mr. Manere was our salvation. After soundings and surveys, he recommended a steam shovel. The arrival of this monster attracted a dozen natives, fascinated by the potential of disaster. After three scoops near the kitchen door, a geyser erupted. On Manere's order the highway was closed. A conduit was laid from the pit across the road and into the wood. In it went eighteen-inch water pipe. Prior tunnels and pipes had dammed instead of releasing the water. At the peak of this operation our yard suggested the preliminaries to Boulder Dam. The end of our house, explained Manere, was over an old box ditch which drained the slopes above it. When it rained this ditch became a hidden river.

"I could have told you that dry ditch was there," said a neighbor, fifty years a resident. Indeed she could have. But the Nutmeggers are a tight-lipped tribe. They only confess when tortured.

The carnival of sappers, plumbers, engineers, plasterers and painters had raged intermittently for three months when Manere rerouted the concealed canal. The fees of these clowns ravaged our budget. The sum of their bills came to a third of the house's cost. For native mechanics there is no closed season on commuters. We're their year-round prey, subject to looting on call. For years I kept two souvenirs of our struggle with the waters: twin sump pumps. They were symbols of the incompetence of the horde which prowled our cellar, ruined our lawn and violated our trees.

When hay went to $60 a ton we sold our home on Sturgis Highway to Mrs. Joshua Barney, famed horsewoman. Dark Boy had been stricken with asthma and Cooey was the victim of periostitis. Their deaths desolated us. Charging and cavorting across the field at dusk in a succession of bucks and vaults they were a dramatic pair.

Since September of 1945 Betty and I have rejoiced in our home on Wolfpit Road. Our two and a half acres are a riot of greenery in summer. Yew hedges flank the entrance. Lofty elms screen us on the south. Maples, fire and pine trees mask Wolfpit Road. Our lawn, moleless because of the activity of the tomcat, is sheltered by virburnum, mock orange, laurel, rhododendron, weigela, bridal wreath and pampas grass. Pachysandra blankets shady spots and the ground beneath the hedges. Our rear yard, with rock garden, slopes into a ravine. There honeysuckle twines the rose bush and carpets the walks.

Our home lacks a cellar, an omission we endure with tranquillity. Our co-tenants are Tiddy-Bee and Piper, miniature schnauzers, and Pi Jo, a basenji. Pi Jo is a paragon of grace and nonchalance and has a taste for literature. He's partial to fiction, frequently consumes a novel in one sitting. Basenjis can't bark. Three barkers in the family is enough.

A lot of eyebrows went up when friends and acquaintances learned I had a home in the country. I wasn't the commuter type, they scoffed. It was unlikely I could adjust myself to the perils of rural life after fifteen years in the Forties. Bleeck's and a saltbox were irreconcilable. Failure of electric power due to thunder and sleet storms was a comonplace in Fairfield County, said these skeptics. The first time I was denied water, heat, light and night games at Ebbets Field and Yankee Stadium, I'd flee Connecticut, they insisted.

Au fond, I replied, glad of an opportunity to air a French phrase, I was a son of the soil. I came from a long line of Irish peasants. Hadn't I ridden the range in Montana? Listened to the lament of the coyotes? Palavered with the Crees and the Crows? The New Haven local held no terrors for a man who had scaled the Cascades and the Rockies in a boxcar, with a kitchen range for a couch.

Whatever my qualms about commuting, they quickly evaporated. Except in line of duty I never spend a night in New York. From June to September, when the theatre's at its ebb, I catch the 9:15 in Westport and the 5:25 in Grand Central. Betty is my chauffeur, since I can't drive a car. My weekends are holidays. I ignore phone calls. I seldom venture out of doors lest I be tricked into some violent physical activity.

What do I do in the country? Loaf! Sporadically I read. Our house is cluttered with fifteen hundred books ranging from Spalding's *Baseball Guide for 1908* to Proust's *Remembrance of Things Past* in four volumes. Recently I've been reading the Memoirs of Madame Junot. Once I get this odyssey behind me I may tackle Proust. Where can I get a copy of *A Page of the First Empire?*

20

A Toast to the Fabulous Invalid

*F*RIVOLITIES, you may remember, was my first New York assignment. I had issued perhaps three or four nervous bulletins about this revue when the theatre was racked with civil war. My initiation didn't cause this catastrophe. Indignant because the producers ignored their demands for improved working conditions, the actors in eleven of New York's twelve stage attractions went on strike. On August 7, 1919, Broadway became a desert.

Six years earlier the players had organized as the Actors Equity Association. Equity's bids for recognition as bargaining agent for its members were ignored by the managers. Incensed by these brush-offs, Equity affiliated with the American Federation of Labor in July of 1919. This alliance ensured the support of stagehands and musicians. Shortly it presented the Producing Managers Association with a bill of grievances. It asked for an eight-performance week, a time limit on free rehearsals, and full pay for the week before Christmas and for Holy Week. Up until then, actors often rehearsed six to fifteen weeks and drew half pay in the two leanest weeks in the year.

Modest as were these demands, the managers spurned them. They swore they'd board up their theatres, even put them to the

torch, before they'd traffic with an actors' union. The managers
were confident of victory. Actors were a feckless lot, they sneered.
They were an emotional and envious tribe. They had no talent for
sustained indignation or concerted action. Two weeks of idleness
would bring them to their knees. To intimidate the mimes they
raised a war fund through assessment of members and established
stiff penalties for cravens who might seek a separate peace.

The strikers gave a series of benefits to raise funds for their
needy and hungry. Such headliners as Ethel Barrymore, Al Jolson,
Ed Wynn, Marie Dressler and Raymond Hitchcock participated,
and seventeen-year-old Tallulah Bankhead sold programs. Wealthy
stage-struck laymen were summoned to the colors. Firebrands urged
the actors to do or die at frantic mass meetings. To dramatize their
plight, the actors paraded through Times Square. Broadway boiled
with threats of suits and counter-suits. Exchanges between the an-
tagonists set a new high in invective. Friendships of a lifetime were
shattered. Though street fighting was sporadic, name calling was
epidemic.

Attempts of dissenting companies to continue collapsed when
the stagehands respected Equity's picket lines. *Happy Days,* spectacle
at the four-thousand-seat Hippodrome, suspended when its three
hundred stagehands took a walk. Only one attraction stayed open:
Owen Davis's melodrama *At 9:45.* Boasting a single setting, it could
operate without stagehands.

George M. Cohan, the most popular figure in the theatre, was
caught in the middle of the strife. Cohan was both actor and manager.
When he cast his lot with the producers, the entire Friars Club,
which he served as Abbott, marched to his office to beg him to recon-
sider. Instead, he financed and helped to organize the Actors' Fidelity
League—contemptuously called the Fidos—to negate Equity.

The strike lasted thirty days and ended in victory for the actors.
In retrospect their triumph was modest. It wasn't until 1924 that
managers were obliged to put up a pre-rehearsal bond covering two
weeks' salary for the cast. This compulsion ended defaults of shoestring operators. Frequently these shysters lammed after a three-act

fiasco. The wage bond also dissipated the actor's nightmare, stranded without funds far from his base. No Equity member has hitchhiked home from Denver or Des Moines in over thirty years. Not until 1935 did Equity win a token wage for its members during rehearsals.

Despite its bitter start, the 1919-20 season was rich and rewarding. Fred and Adele Astaire were dancing in *Apple Blossoms* at the Globe. John and Lionel Barrymore were available in *The Jest,* Sister Ethel in *Déclassée,* and Uncle John Drew in *The Cat-Bird.* Fanny Brice and W. C. Fields were clowning in Ziegfeld's *Midnight Frolic* atop the New Amsterdam. Alfred Lunt was playing the title role in Booth Tarkington's *Clarence,* expertly aided by nineteen-year-old Helen Hayes.

In the year of my induction Eugene O'Neill's *Beyond the Horizon* won the Pulitzer Prize. (O'Neill would win the award a fourth time in 1957 with *Long Day's Journey into Night.*) Frank McGlynn was at the Cort in Drinkwater's *Abraham Lincoln* and Jack Donahue, a dancing immortal, glittered in *Angel Face.* Jim Barton graced *The Passing Show,* Ina Claire *The Gold Diggers,* and Jane Cowl *Smilin' Thru.*

If the season was rich and rewarding, I was insensitive to its glories. I was too confused by the challenges and complexities of *Frivolities* to note the merit of its rivals. In that season the critics cheered or choked 140 productions. The clinker with which I fumbled may have been the frowziest of the lot. My ministrations didn't help it any. As a potter I was unworthy of my clay.

Our theatre has changed radically since that distant day. (Only the note of O'Neill remains constant.) Its life has been menaced by the magic lantern, the phonograph and silent movies; by *thé dansants,* radio and talking films; by scrabble, night baseball, harness racing and other noises and nuisances too offensive to recite here. At the peak of each of these crazes Cassandras started to chant the theatre's threnody. Their dirges were premature. The theatre has survived a hundred sinking spells and crawled out of as many comas.

More than once there was evidence to support the prophets of doom. When Al Jolson sang "Blue Skies" and "My Mammy" in

The Jazz Singer, the theatre started to turn blue. Even its partisans despaired when the public became channel-conscious. I summed up the predicament in a guest column for John Crosby:

The keening of the grave-diggers reached a crescendo when television antennae started to flower on every roof in New Jersey. This contraption would do the theatre in in short order, said trend detectors. There was some talk of a mercy killing, that the agony of the afflicted not be prolonged unduly. Many theatre people shared these ghoulish sentiments. How could the theatre compete with entertainment which could be viewed from the living-room couch? What cove would pay $9.20 for two orchestra chairs, buck crosstown traffic and be spiked by tardy arrivals, when he could see Milton Berle for nothing and slouch into the kitchen for a snifter if he already owned a Buick?

The alarms of my fellows were groundless. Instead of weaning people away from the theatre, television is driving them back to it. Nauseated by quiz shows, wrestling matches, Charlie Chan, private eyes, two-gun pastorals and off-key thrushes, the disillusioned are rushing back to the theatre in the hope of regaining their sanity. Outraged by the gibberish of TV's shills, their nerves jangled by jingles, the strays are repenting.

Television's potential for amusement and instruction is tremendous. It cries out for adventurers, explorers and men of imagination. But it cries in vain. Its sponsor-cursed operators are dedicated to the tried and shopworn and to the saw that imitation is the sincerest form of flattery.

Television has a marked suicide complex. Not since Cro-Magnon man embellished his cave with polychrome murals has a communicative medium gone to such lengths to alienate its audience. Beggared for material, television increasingly seeks stage and screen plays and musicals for reproduction. The vandalism it practices on the specimens it gets would revolt a Jibardo headhunter.

The running time of a three-act play is approximately two hours, exclusive of intermissions. TV's corruptions are squeezed into fifty minutes on one-hour programs. The differential is consumed by commercials, credits and station breaks. Excising seventy minutes from the original, deplorable practice under any circumstances, calls for surgery to dismay anyone but a *Reader's Digest* editor. Instead the dramas are subjected to wanton butchery, with acting to match. To spectators familiar with the original, these condensations are appalling. Those unfamiliar with the original can only guess that they hoaxed the critics who praised them. Adulterations and defilements of musical comedies and screen plays are equally revolting. Attempts to prune them to conform to TV's straitjacket are as painful as those of a man with 12-A feet trying to walk in 8-A shoes.

Both stage and screen err in condoning these outrages. To many videots the theatre is as alien as the betel nut. Disillusioned by TV's mutilations, it's unlikely they'll care to know it better.

The theatre has enough trouble without submitting to outside seductions. Only in New York does it prosper. Its season is bracketed by Labor Day and Memorial Day. Over that span Boston, Philadelphia, Washington and New Haven may see as many as twenty-five attractions, half of them during their pre-Broadway engagements. Only Chicago, San Francisco and Los Angeles of the nation's other major cities see as many as ten plays and musicals in that interval.

The road I ranged with the *Greenwich Village Follies* is moribund. Then eighty or ninety original companies or their duplications prowled the land. Cleveland, Cincinnati, Baltimore, Buffalo, St. Louis, Newark, Pittsburgh and Indianapolis had two or more legitimate theatres, each assured thirty weeks' booking. Today Buffalo and Newark are without a theatre. The others are reduced to one, intermittently occupied. Companies profited from fifteen-week tours of the South. Today the South is a theatrical wilderness. Hedonists of Houston, New Orleans, Richmond, Atlanta and Birmingham are fortunate if they see two New York productions in a year.

As pilot for the *Greenwich Village Follies* I visited Saginaw, Kalamazoo, Grand Rapids, Flint, Ann Arbor and Battle Creek in Michigan each season. En route to the Pacific I paused at Butte, Helena, Great Falls and Billings in my native Montana. All are now one with the dodo. When the pictures started to talk, the road tottered. Moribund, did I say? What quibbling! The road is as dead as a doornail.

The decline of the road stimulated New York box offices. Starved for plays at home, visitors to our island feasted. When I got my commission with *Frivolities* only *Lightnin'* had played as many as seven hundred consecutive performances in New York's history. Since then fifty-two have proved as enduring. Year-long runs, then a phenomenon, now are commonplace.

Of the shows that venture beyond the Hudson, song-and-dance carnivals and comedies fare best. Serious plays have rough sledding unless headed by dazzling stars. The outlanders seek escape in the theatre. They shrink from plays that jab their minds. Conditioned to radio, screen and television pap, slaves to conformity, they panic when confronted with ideas at odds with the creed of Warren Harding.

It's frequently charged that the theatre's plight is due to the excessive price of tickets. Stuff and rubbish! Orchestra seats for *Broadway,* 1927's top dramatic hit, were $4.40; orchestra seats for *No Time for Sergeants,* current long-run drama, are $4.60. Musicals in 1927— *Rio Rita, Countess Maritza, Criss Cross*—asked $5.50 for front pews as opposed to the $8.05 demanded by *My Fair Lady.* Exclusive of taxes, the bite for *Broadway* and *Sergeants* is identical, with current musicals 40 per cent higher than their forerunners. But over that same span production costs have risen spectacularly. In '27 a one-set play could be mounted for as little as $10,000. Today its duplication would cost $45,000.

In '27 Schwab & Mandel produced *Good News,* musical-comedy hit, for $85,000. It recovered half its cost in six weeks in Philadelphia. Four weeks in Manhattan and it was out of the red. *My Fair Lady* cost $405,000. Playing to standees at every performance it required thirty weeks to get square.

In '27 the minimum wage for chorus girls was $30. Now it's $100. Thirty years ago actors rehearsed six weeks in a musical without salary. Today all get $65 a week from the day of the first drill.

Contributors to *Good News* received 7 per cent of the box-office gross in royalties. The creators of *My Fair Lady* get 14 per cent for comparable services. In '27 the producer received 50 per cent of the motion-picture sale. Today he must be content with forty. Salaries of players, stagehands and musicians have spiraled to conform with increased living costs. In 1927 the daily *Times* sold for two cents, the Sunday edition for ten. Today the daily *Times* is five cents, the Sabbath issue twenty-five. In the *Good News* era, the amusement advertising rate in the daily *Times* was $1 an agate line, on Sunday $1.10. *My Fair Lady* pays $2.09 and $2.57 for the identical lines.

In view of this evidence the prices for theatre tickets are absurdly low. To compensate for increased production costs and salaries in the last three decades, *My Fair Lady* should be getting $12.50 for orchestra chairs, *No Time for Sergeants* $10—exclusive of taxes. Ironically enough, the cheaper the ticket, the more difficult it is to sell. Even with sellouts the second-balcony chairs are the last to go.

Since the dawn of the century Broadway has been the synonym for New York's amusement area. Until the mid-thirties the analogy was justified. The Knickerbocker, the Casino, the Criterion, the Empire, the Globe, the George M. Cohan, the Central, the Gaiety, the Astor, the Broadway, the Manhattan, and the Winter Garden faced "The Great White Way." Today the identification is moot. The Winter Garden is the only theatre abutting Broadway. On my first entrance, twenty of New York's seventy theatres sprawled south of Forty-third Street. Only the National remains. What happened to the rest? Many were razed to accommodate skyscrapers; the others were usurped by screen, radio and television vandals.

Have another statistic? No new theatre has opened in New York since the Ethel Barrymore and the Adelphi were christened in December of 1928. Those that stand are a touch antiquated. Many could stand sandblasting and new carpet on the balcony stairs.

Today's theatre twists and writhes in an economic trap, the victim of excessive production and operating costs. Plays and musicals must sell out or perish. There is no margin for error. Gone are the days when plays could enjoy long and profitable runs, though greeted by capacity audiences only on Saturday nights and holiday matinees. An example? Brock Pemberton's production of *Janie* ran a year and a half (1942-43). In its biggest week the box-office take was $12,000. Both attraction and theatre prospered. Today *Janie* would be booted out at the end of its second week, thanks to a $14,000 stop clause.

Do these melancholy speculations indicate the theatre is doomed?

That it's headed for the museum? That at long last it will be over-whelmed by its mechanical rivals? Of course not. It has survived a hundred crises, and will survive a hundred more. The theatre is both the cliffhanger and the phoenix of the arts. Its swoons are decep-tive. No gadget wired for sound, sight or ptomaine will ever subdue it. It may quake, it may shrivel, it may cry out in pain, but it will never die so long as there are people of taste and discrimination and intelligence, so long as there are people whose standards of entertainment and excitement and magic reject the please-everyone-offend-no-one formula of the electronic intruders.

The theatre is the last free institution in the amusement world. It brooks no blacklists. It scorns taboos and censorships. Perform-ance is the only requisite of employment in it. It doesn't blanch at ideas. It has many faults. Cowardice is not one of them. As much cannot be said for its competitors. All of them have a low intimidation point.

As spokesman for the often maligned actors, Equity ruled in 1948 that "no player shall be required to perform in any theatre in Wash-ington, D. C., where discrimination is practiced against any actor or patron of the theatre because of his race, color or creed." And no player did. For four years Washington, citadel of democracy, was without a theatrical attraction. Then the National, the capital's only legitimate playhouse, capitulated. For this action the actors deserve the gratitude and applause of the civilized world.

I have fared handsomely at the hands of the theatre. It has provided me with fun and excitement and association with thousands of daffy and delightful people. No other people live so dangerously. No others are so gallant in adversity. No others respond so quickly to cries of the hurt and the hungry. True, many of them are a little tetched but, then, so am I. Despite their crotchets and fevers and lunacies they have my affection and respect. They are the salt of the earth.

INDEX

363

Wood, Peggy, 238
Woods, A. H., 142
Woollcott, Alexander, 123,
127, 144, 175, 179, 180,
193, 214, 272, 331
Woolley, Monty, 140, 163
Worm, A. Toxen, 63, 64, 214-
215
Wright, Haidee, 282
Wynn, Ed, 226, 290, 291,
296-299, 338, 356

Wynn, Keenan, 297-299

Yeats, 145
Young, Roland, 84, 92, 178
Yr Obedient Husband, 14
Yurka, Blanche, 120

Zeckendorf, William, 90
Ziegfeld, Florenz, 6, 51, 57,
58, 62, 67, 73, 118, 219,
299, 338

Ziegfeld *Follies*, 146, 263,
291, 292
Ziegfeld Theatre, 169, 199,
249, 250, 254, 345
Zimmerman, Matty, 161
Zola, Emile, 107
Zolotow, Maurice, 196
Zolotow, Sam, 12, 193-194,
257
Zorina, Vera, 181
Zuleika Dobson, 122